BRITISH BATTALIONS IN FRANCE AND BELGIUM
1914

By the same author:

Collecting Metal Shoulder Titles
(Leo Cooper, 1980)

British Battalions on the Somme, 1916
(Leo Cooper, 1994)

British Battalions at Gallipoli
(Leo Cooper, 1996)

BRITISH BATTALIONS IN FRANCE AND BELGIUM 1914

by

Ray Westlake

LEO COOPER
LONDON

First published in 1997 by
LEO COOPER
an imprint of
Pen & Sword Books Ltd
47 Church Street, Barnsley, South Yorkshire S70 2AS

Copyright © Ray Westlake, 1997

A CIP catalogue record for this book is available
from the British Library

ISBN 0 85052 577 2

Typeset by Phoenix Typesetting
Ilkley, West Yorkshire

Printed by
Redwood Books Ltd,
Trowbridge, Wilts.

FOR
JAMES WESTLAKE

Introduction

Both *British Battalions on the Somme, 1916* (Pen and Sword, 1994) and *British Regiments at Gallipoli* (Pen and Sword, 1996) have achieved all that they set out to do. On the historical side it is now agreed by a large number of grateful historians, researchers, museum curators, librarians etc that for the first time they are able to establish quickly and conveniently what part each unit played in these important campaigns. It was also intended to provide family historians with a means of tracing the war service of their relatives. This again has been accomplished – reports from delighted battle-field visitors telling of how some old soldier`s footsteps have been well and truly followed, now being received almost on a daily basis.

British Battalions in France and Belgium, 1914 sets out with the same objectives in mind. As with the two previous volumes, no attempt has been made to produce a history of the 1914 campaigns. What has been provided, however, is a unique account of the 143 infantry battalions of the British Army that served in France and Belgium from August to the end of December, 1914. Detailed records of movements, both in and out of battle areas and on a day-by-day basis, being covered in the same meticulous style as before. Special attention has also been made to names of ships and officers that embarked, or were subsequently killed.

Normally, locations given are those where the majority of the battalion bivouacked or billeted. Often small parties (or individual companies) moved away for temporary attachment to other formations, or on work detail, and this has been mentioned where known. Normally a front (or firing) line would be occupied by part of the battalion, a portion being further back holding support and reserve trenches or resting up in a village close by. During the early days of the Retreat from Mons many battalions became split. Detachments ranging from small parties to whole companies making their own way independently until the main body of their unit was located.

Each regiment appears in the book according to its order of precedence. Battalions are then located by their numerical seniority. Regimental titles are those appearing in *The Army List* for 1914. Battle honours awarded for service during 1914, and subsequently shared by all battalions of the regiment, are listed below each regimental heading.

Sources of Information

The main source of information for this book has been the war diaries and unit histories of the regiments concerned. The latter amounting to some 250 volumes, making a list impractical. War diaries are held at the Public Record Office under WO95 classification. References drawn from published memoirs, letters, diaries, etc, have been acknowledged in the text. My own records (RAY WESTLAKE UNIT ARCHIVES) have been put to good use – the 6,000-plus files formed over the last twenty-five years providing in many cases hitherto unpublished information. The following works have been essential:

History of The Great War – Order of Battle of Divisions Part 1 – The Regular British Divisions. Major F. Becke. HMSO, 1935.

History of The Great War – Military Operations France and Belgium, 1914. Brigadier-General Sir James E. Edmonds, CB, CMG, RE. Macmillan and Co. Ltd, 1922 and 1925.

British Regiment 1914-18. Brigadier E.A. James. Samson Books, 1978.

The V.C. and the D.S.O. Sir O`Moore Creagh, VC and Miss E.M. Humphries. Standard Art Book Co., Ltd, 1924.

Monthly Army Lists. Various issues for 1914, War Office.

Officers Died in the Great War 1914-1919. J.B. Hayward & Son, 1988.

The Bond of Sacrifice. The Anglo-African Publishing Contractors, 1915.

The Cross of Sacrifice Volume 1. S.D. & D.B. Jarvis. Roberts, 1993.

List of British Officers Taken Prisoner in the Various Theatres of War Between August, 1914 and November, 1918. Cox & Co., 1919.

Battle Honours Awarded for the Great War – Complete List. HMSO, 1925.

Acknowledgements

The help given by the following individuals and organizations has made this book possible – Argyll and Sutherland Highlanders Museum, Bedfordshire County Record Office, Border Regiment Museum, Terry Carter, Lieutenant-Colonel P. Crocker, Geoffrey Crump, Colonel C.D. Darroch, Devon and Dorset Regiment Museum, Peter Donnelly, Duke of Wellington's Regiment Museum, Stuart Eastwood, Green Howards Museum, Imperial War Museum (Dept. of Printed Books), Simon Jervis, Jim Kellerher, King's Own Royal Regiment Museum, Richard Leake, Major R.P. Mason, Ernie Platt, Public Record Office, Royal Fusiliers Museum, Lieutenant-Colonel D.R. Roberts, Royal Hampshire Regiment Museum, Royal Scots Museum, Royal Warwickshire Regiment Museum, Royal Welch Fusiliers Museum, Lieutenant-Colonel A.W. Scott Elliot, Peter T. Scott, Alan and Margaret Stansfield, Graham Stewart, Suffolk Regiment Museum, Sussex Combined Services Museum, Mary Wilkinson, John Woodroff.

The following maps are all reproduced,
with the kind permission of the cartographer,
from
A MILITARY ATLAS OF THE FIRST WORLD WAR

by Arthur Banks
(Leo Cooper, 1997)

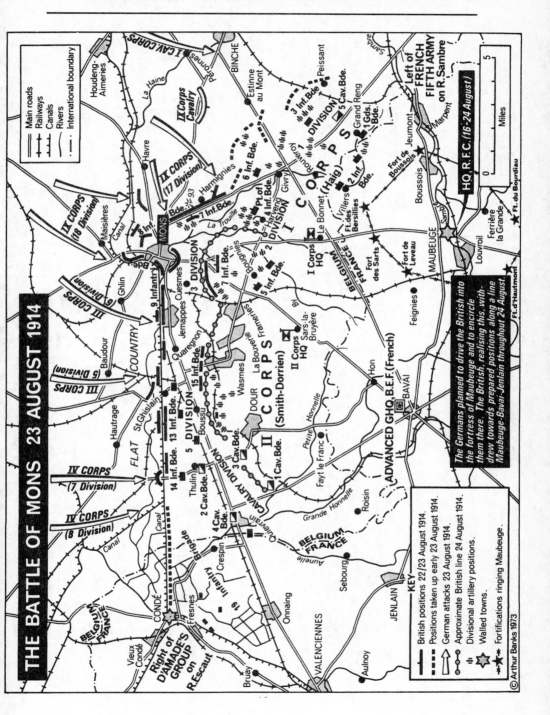

THE BATTLE OF MONS 23 AUGUST 1914

The Germans planned to drive the British into the fortress of Maubeuge and to encircle them there. The British, realising this, withdrew towards prepared positions along a line Maubeuge-Bavai-Jenlain throughout 24 August.

KEY

- ┤┤┤ British positions 22/23 August 1914.
- ▬▬ Positions taken up early 23 August 1914.
- ⇨ German attacks 23 August 1914.
- ○○○ Approximate British line 24 August 1914.
- ⊞ Divisional artillery positions.
- ✦ Walled towns.
- ★ Fortifications ringing Maubeuge.

© Arthur Banks 1973

THE ALLIED RETIREMENT 23 AUGUST–6 SEPTEMBER 1914

This map shows the day by day withdrawal of the Allied Armies of the Left, following the German successes at Mons, Charleroi, Dinant, etc.. Dawn positions have been selected in order to illustrate the amount of territory relinquished each day. Corps I and II of the B.E.F. parted on 25 August, were reunited during the day of 1 September. Corps III was formed during the daytime of 31 August, and comprised 4 Division and 19 Infantry Brigade. Taking 23 August as the commencement of the retirement to the Marne battlefield, both German and Allied armies have been broken down into corps strengths on that day.

Note: the rapidity of the German advance caused their lines of communication to become over-extended and supplies began to fail.

Main German Advance

GERMAN THIRD ARMY

GERMAN SECOND ARMY

GERMAN FIRST ARMY

GUARD RES.

GUARD

BELGIUM

FRANCE

BRUSSELS

Wavre

Hal

Namur

Dinant

Mettet

Philippeville

Beaumont

Chimay

Rocroi

Fumay

Les A

Sedan

Charleroi

Binche

Thuin

Mons

Maubeuge

Avesnes

Hirson

Vervins

Montcornet

Oudenarde

Courtrai

Renaix

Ath

Tournai

Conde

Valenciennes (Scheldt)

Cambrai (Scheldt)

Le Cateau

Bohain

Le Catelet

St. Quentin

Guise

Oise

Ypres

Lille

Lens

Douai

Arras

Bapaume

Albert

Péronne

Nesle

Estrées

Croza

Somme

Béthune

Amiens

Moreuil

Scarpe

Schelde

Canal

Sambre

Helpe

Maubeuge held out until 8 September.

Miles
0   5   10   15

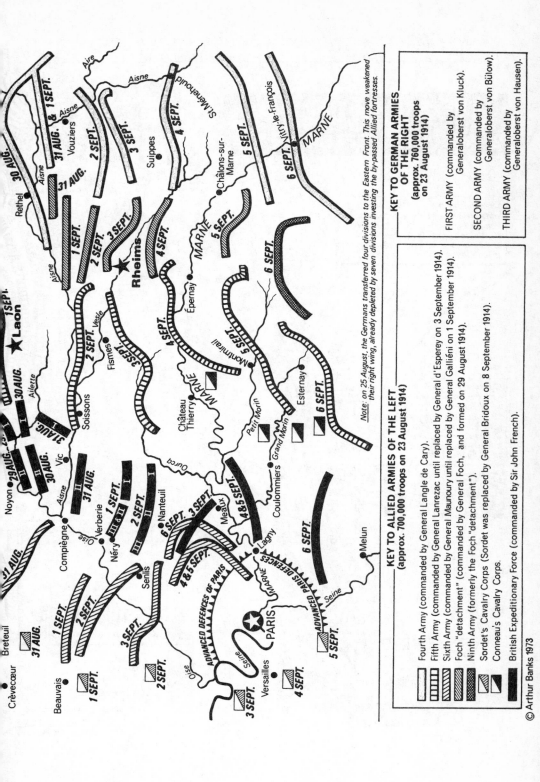

KEY TO GERMAN ARMIES
OF THE RIGHT
(approx. 760,000 troops
on 23 August 1914)

FIRST ARMY (commanded by
Generaloberst von Kluck).

SECOND ARMY (commanded by
Generaloberst von Bülow).

THIRD ARMY (commanded by
Generaloberst von Hausen).

Note: on 25 August, the Germans transferred four divisions to the Eastern Front. This move weakened
their right wing, already depleted by seven divisions investing the by-passed Allied fortresses.

KEY TO ALLIED ARMIES OF THE LEFT
(approx. 700,000 troops on 23 August 1914)

Fourth Army (commanded by General Langle de Cary).

Fifth Army (commanded by General Lanrezac until replaced by General d'Esperey on 3 September 1914).

Sixth Army (commanded by General Maunoury until replaced by General Galliéni on 1 September 1914).

Foch "detachment" (commanded by General Foch, and formed on 29 August 1914).

Ninth Army (formerly the Foch "detachment").

Sordet's Cavalry Corps (Sordet was replaced by General Bridoux on 8 September 1914).

Conneau's Cavalry Corps.

British Expeditionary Force (commanded by Sir John French).

© Arthur Banks 1973

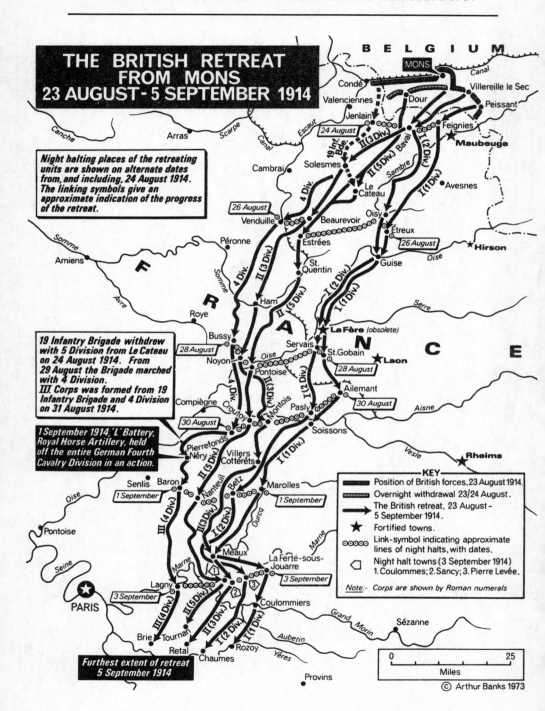

THE BRITISH RETREAT FROM MONS 23 AUGUST - 5 SEPTEMBER 1914

Night halting places of the retreating units are shown on alternate dates from, and including, 24 August 1914. The linking symbols give an approximate indication of the progress of the retreat.

19 Infantry Brigade withdrew with 5 Division from Le Cateau on 24 August 1914. From 29 August the Brigade marched with 4 Division. III Corps was formed from 19 Infantry Brigade and 4 Division on 31 August 1914.

1 September 1914, 'L' Battery, Royal Horse Artillery, held off the entire German Fourth Cavalry Division in an action.

Furthest extent of retreat 5 September 1914

KEY

- Position of British forces, 23 August 1914.
- Overnight withdrawal 23/24 August.
- The British retreat, 23 August – 5 September 1914.
- ★ Fortified towns.
- ◌◌◌◌◌ Link-symbol indicating approximate lines of night halts, with dates.
- ◁ Night halt towns (3 September 1914) 1. Coulommes; 2. Sancy; 3. Pierre Levée.

Note:- Corps are shown by Roman numerals

0 — 25 Miles

© Arthur Banks 1973

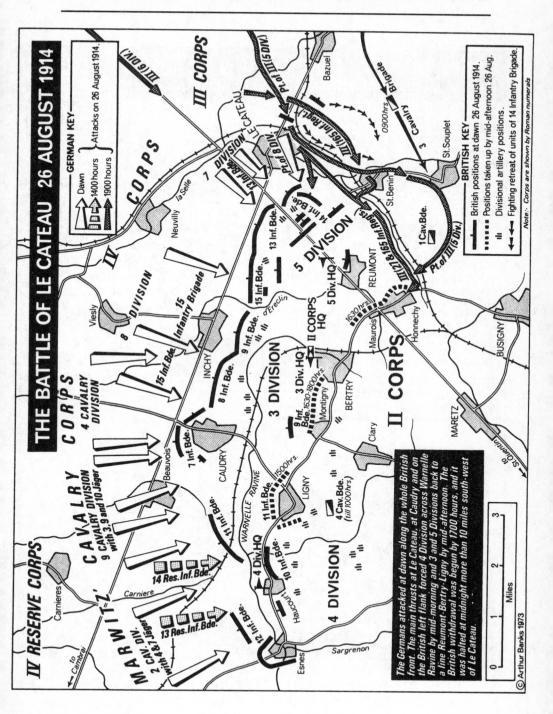

THE BATTLE OF LE CATEAU 26 AUGUST 1914

GERMAN KEY

Attacks on 26 August 1914.

Dawn
1400 hours
1900 hours

BRITISH KEY

British positions at dawn 26 August 1914.
Positions taken up by mid-afternoon 26 Aug.
Divisional artillery positions.
Fighting retreat of units of 14 Infantry Brigade.

Note:- Corps are shown by Roman numerals

The Germans attacked at dawn along the whole British front. The main thrusts at Le Cateau, at Caudry and on the British left flank forced 4 Division across Warnelle Ravine by mid-morning and 3 and 5 Divisions back to a line Reumont-Bertry-Ligny by mid-afternoon. The British withdrawal was begun by 1700 hours, and it was halted at midnight more than 10 miles south-west of Le Cateau.

Miles

0 1 2 3

© Arthur Banks 1973

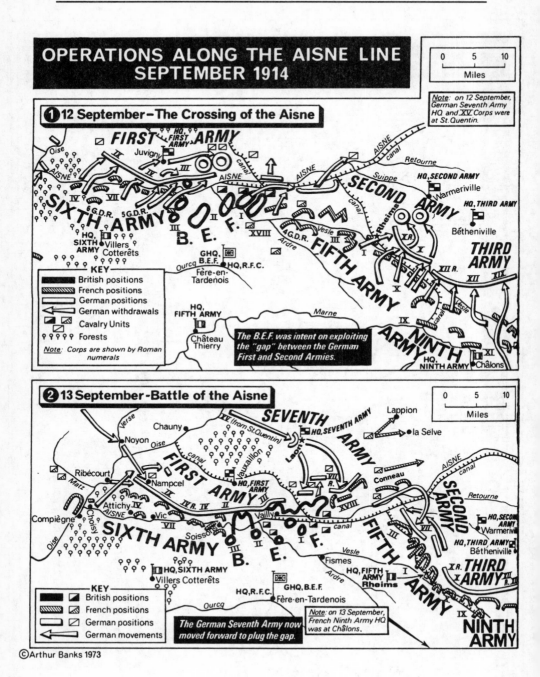

OPERATIONS ALONG THE AISNE LINE
SEPTEMBER 1914

❶ 12 September – The Crossing of the Aisne

Note: on 12 September, German Seventh Army HQ and XV Corps were at St. Quentin.

KEY
British positions
French positions
German positions
German withdrawals
Cavalry Units
Forests
Note: Corps are shown by Roman numerals

The B.E.F. was intent on exploiting the "gap" between the German First and Second Armies.

❷ 13 September – Battle of the Aisne

KEY
British positions
French positions
German positions
German movements

The German Seventh Army now moved forward to plug the gap.

Note: on 13 September, French Ninth Army HQ was at Châlons.

©Arthur Banks 1973

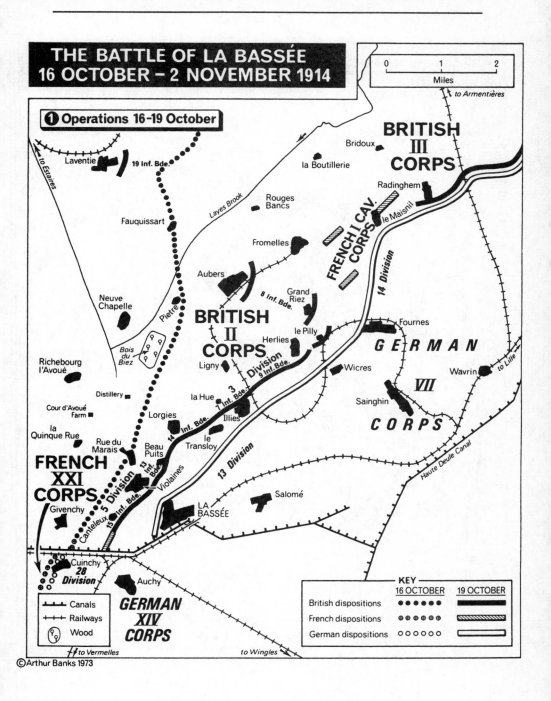

**THE BATTLE OF LA BASSÉE
16 OCTOBER – 2 NOVEMBER 1914**

0   1   2
Miles

to Armentières

①Operations 16-19 October

**BRITISH
III
CORPS**

Bridoux

la Boutillerie

Laventie

19 Inf. Bde.

Radinghem

le Maisnil

to Estaires

Rouges
Bancs

Fauquissart

Layes Brook

Fromelles

FRENCH I CAV.
CORPS

14 Division

Aubers

Pietre

Neuve
Chapelle

8 Inf. Bde.

Grand
Riez

**BRITISH
II
CORPS**

le Pilly

Fournes

G E R M A N

to Lille

Bois
du
Biez

Herlies

Richebourg
l'Avoué

Ligny

3
Division

9 Inf. Bde.

Wicres

Wavrin

Distillery

la Hue

3
Inf. Bde.

VII

Cour d'Avoué
Farm

Lorgies

Illies

Sainghin

la
Quinque Rue

14
Inf. Bde.

le
Transloy

C O R P S

Rue du
Marais

Beau
Puits

13
Inf. Bde.

13 Division

Haute Deule Canal

**FRENCH
XXI
CORPS**

5 Division

Violaines

15 Inf. Bde.

Canteleux

Givenchy

**LA
BASSÉE**

Salomé

Cuinchy

**28
Division**

Auchy

**GERMAN
XIV
CORPS**

KEY

16 OCTOBER   19 OCTOBER

British dispositions

French dispositions

German dispositions

Canals

Railways

Wood

to Vermelles

to Wingles

©Arthur Banks 1973

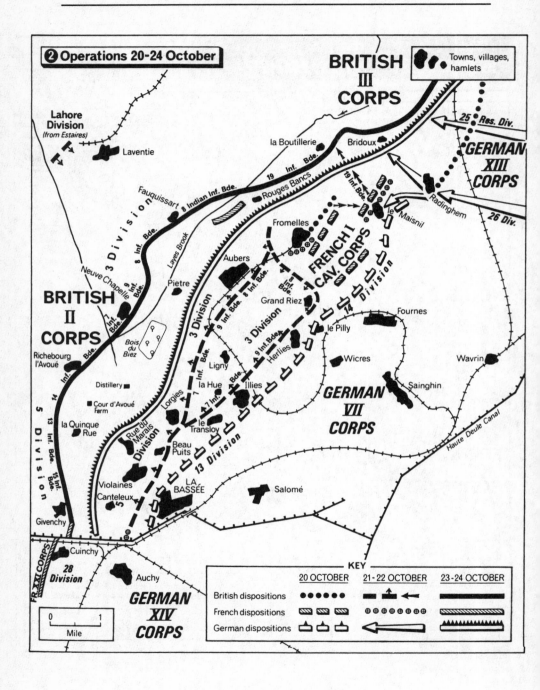

② Operations 20-24 October

BRITISH III CORPS

Towns, villages, hamlets

25 Res. Div.

GERMAN XIII CORPS

26 Div.

Lahore Division *(from Estaires)*

Laventie

la Boutillerie

Bridoux

Radinghem

le Maisnil

19 Inf. Bde.

Rouges Bancs

Fauquissart

8 Indian Inf. Bde.

19 Inf. Bde.

3 Division

8 Inf. Bde.

Layes Brook

Fromelles

FRENCH I CAV. CORPS

Neuve Chapelle

9 Inf. Bde.

Pietre

Aubers

Grand Riez

14 Division

BRITISH II CORPS

7 Inf. Bde.

3 Division

9 Inf. Bde. 8 Inf. Bde.

3 Division

le Pilly

Fournes

Richebourg l'Avoué

Bois du Biez

9 Inf. Bde.

Herlies

Wicres

Wavrin

Inf. Bde.

Distillery

Ligny

la Hue

Illies

Sainghin

Cour d'Avoué Farm

7 Inf. Bde.

Lorgies

GERMAN VII CORPS

5 Division

la Quinque Rue

7 Inf.

le Transloy

Rue du Marais Division

Beau Puits

13 Division

13 Inf. Bde.

Violaines

Canteleux

5

LA BASSÉE

Salomé

Haute Deule Canal

15 Inf. Bde.

Givenchy

Cuinchy

28 Division

Auchy

FR. XXI CORPS

GERMAN XIV CORPS

KEY

	20 OCTOBER	21 - 22 OCTOBER	23 - 24 OCTOBER
British dispositions	●●●●●●	▬▬ ↑ ←	▬▬▬▬
French dispositions	▨▨▨	⊕⊕⊕⊕⊕⊕	▨▨▨▨
German dispositions	⌂⌂⌂	◄═══	▲▲▲▲▲

0   1
Mile

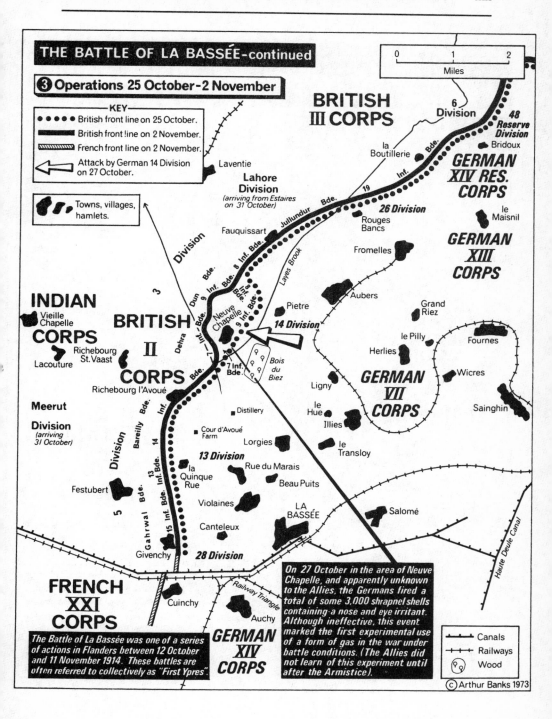

THE BATTLE OF LA BASSÉE-continued

❸ Operations 25 October-2 November

—KEY—
- • • • • British front line on 25 October.
- ▬▬▬ British front !ine on 2 November.
- ᔓᔓᔓ French front line on 2 November.
- ⟵ Attack by German 14 Division on 27 October.

🪨🪨🪨 Towns, villages, hamlets.

0   1   2
Miles

BRITISH III CORPS

6 Division

48 Reserve Division

Bridoux

GERMAN XIV RES. CORPS

la Boutillerie

Inf.

Bde.

19

26 Division

le Maisnil

Rouges Bancs

GERMAN XIII CORPS

Fromelles

Aubers

Grand Riez

le Pilly

Fournes

Herlies

Wicres

GERMAN VII CORPS

Sainghin

Laventie

Lahore Division
(arriving from Estaires on 31 October)

Jullundur Bde.

Fauquissart

Layes Brook

Pietre

Neuve Chapelle

14 Division

8 Inf. Bde.

9 Inf. Bde.

Dun Bde.

Division

3

INDIAN

Vieille Chapelle

CORPS

Richebourg St.Vaast

Lacouture

Dehra Bde.

Inf.

BRITISH II CORPS

7 Inf. Bde.

Bois du Biez

Ligny

le Hue

Illies

le Transloy

Meerut Division
(arriving 31 October)

Richebourg l'Avoué

Bde.

Inf.

Bareilly Bde.

14

Distillery

Cour d'Avoué Farm

Lorgies

Division

13

Bde.

Inf.

Bde.

13 Division

la Quinque Rue

Rue du Marais

Beau Puits

Festubert

5

Gahrwal Bde.

15 Inf. Bde.

Violaines

Canteleux

LA BASSÉE

Salomé

Givenchy

28 Division

Haute Deule Canal

FRENCH XXI CORPS

Cuinchy

Railway Triangle

Auchy

GERMAN XIV CORPS

The Battle of La Bassée was one of a series of actions in Flanders between 12 October and 11 November 1914. These battles are often referred to collectively as "First Ypres".

On 27 October in the area of Neuve Chapelle, and apparently unknown to the Allies, the Germans fired a total of some 3,000 shrapnel shells containing a nose and eye irritant. Although ineffective, this event marked the first experimental use of a form of gas in the war under battle conditions. (The Allies did not learn of this experiment until after the Armistice).

━━━ Canals
┼┼┼ Railways
🌳 Wood

© Arthur Banks 1973

THE BRITISH ADVANCE AT
ARMENTIÈRES – YPRES
16-18 OCTOBER 1914

These operations were part of the series of battles in Flanders, October - November 1914, known as "First Ypres".

KEY
- Towns and villages
- Canals
- Railways
- Woods

B.E.F.
(Sir John French)

GERMAN FOURTH ARMY
(Duke Albrecht of Württemberg)

DE MITRY

XXIII RES. CORPS

XXVI RES. CORPS

XXVII RES. CORPS

ROULERS

Oostnieuwkerke

Westroosebeke

Poelcappelle

Langemarck

½ 89 Terr. Div.

1 Cav. Div.

½ 87 Terr. Div.

3 Cav. Div.

6 Div.

BRITISH IV CORPS

Boesinghe

½ 87 Terr. Div.

Zonnebeke

Passchendaele

Moorslede

Waterdamhoek

Becelaere

Terhand

Kezelberg

19 Inf. Bde.

Vlamertinghe

YPRES

7 Div.

Menin Road

Hooge

Gheluvelt

HILL 60

Zanvoorde

Kruiseeke

Koelberg

Gheluwe

MENIN

Lys

COURTRAI

BRITISH CAVALRY CORPS

Hollebeke

Tenbrielen

HALLUIN

Locre

Kemmel

Wytschaete

Houthem

XIII CORPS

WERVICQ

BELGIUM
FRANCE

Drainoutre

2 Cav. Div.

Messines

Douve

Lys

COMINES

GERMAN SIXTH ARMY
(Crown Prince Rupprecht of Bavaria)

Wulverghem

1 Cav. Div.

St.Yves

Warneton

Deulemont

BAILLEUL

Neuve Eglise

Ploegsteert

4 Div.

Frélinghien

Deule (canalised)

Nieppe

Houplines

XIX CORPS

Steenwerck

Erquinghem

Funquereaux

Verlinghem

I, II, IV CAVALRY CORPS

BRITISH III CORPS

6 Div.

Lys

ARMENTIÈRES

Perenchies

Wez

Macquart

Premesques

Lomme

FRANCE
BELGIUM

Sailly sur la Lys

Bac St. Maur

Bois Grenier

Estaires

Rouge de Bout

Fleurbaix

Brook

Radinghem

Ennetières

Capinghem

Englos

Citadel

LILLE

Laventie

CONNEAU

Layes

le Maisnil

VII CORPS

Haubourdin

3 Div.

Fromelles

Aubers

Neuve Chapelle

Fournes

Wavrin

Haute Deule Canal

BRITISH II CORPS

KEY
- British positions 16 October.
- British advances 17 October.
- British positions 18 October.
- French advances 17 October.
- French positions 18 October.
- Belgian positions 18 October.
- German positions 18 October.
- German advances 18 October.

© Arthur Banks 1973

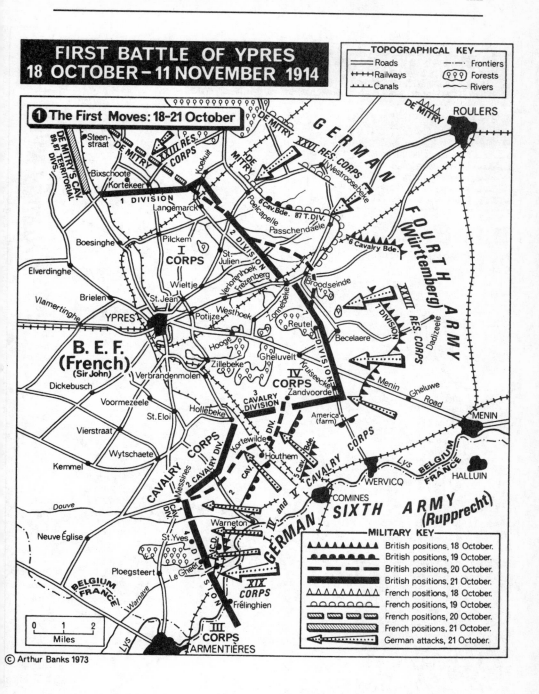

FIRST BATTLE OF YPRES
18 OCTOBER – 11 NOVEMBER 1914

TOPOGRAPHICAL KEY
- Roads
- Railways
- Canals
- Frontiers
- Forests
- Rivers

① The First Moves: 18–21 October

DE MITRY — ROULERS

DE MITRY'S CAV. 89,87 TERRITORIAL DIVS.

Steenstraat

GERMAN

DE MITRY — XXIII RES. CORPS

XXVI RES. CORPS

Westroosebeke

FOURTH ARMY (Württemberg)

Bixschoote
Kortekeer
Koekuit

1 DIVISION
Langemarck

6 Cav. Bde. 87 T. DIV.
Poelcapelle
Passchendaele
6 Cavalry Bde.

Boesinghe
Pilckem
2 DIVISION
St. Julien

I CORPS
Verlorenhoek
Frezenberg
Broodseinde

XXVII RES. CORPS
1 DIVISION
Dadizeele

Elverdinghe
Wieltje

Brielen
St. Jean
Westhoek
Zonnebeke
Reutel
Becelaere

Vlamertinghe
YPRES
Potijze

**B.E.F.
(French)**
(Sir John)

Hooge
Gheluvelt
Menin Road
Gheluwe

Dickebusch
Verbrandenmolen
Zillebeke
Kruiseecke
Zandvoorde

IV CORPS

MENIN

Voormezeele
St. Eloi
Hollebeke
3 CAVALRY DIVISION

America (farm)

CAVALRY CORPS
LYS
BELGIUM FRANCE

Vierstraat
Kortewilde DIV.
HALLUIN

Wytschaete
2 CAVALRY DIV.
Houthem
5 Cav. Bde.

Kemmel
Messines
2 CAV.
IV and V CAVALRY CORPS
WERVICQ

Douve
COMINES
**SIXTH ARMY
(Rupprecht)**

Neuve Église
Warneton
GERMAN

MILITARY KEY
- British positions, 18 October.
- British positions, 19 October.
- British positions, 20 October.
- British positions, 21 October.
- French positions, 18 October.
- French positions, 19 October.
- French positions, 20 October.
- French positions, 21 October.
- German attacks, 21 October.

Ploegsteert
St. Yves
Le Gheer

BELGIUM FRANCE
Warnave
XIX CORPS
Frélinghien

0 1 2
Miles

LYS

III CORPS
ARMENTIÈRES

© Arthur Banks 1973

**THE BATTLE OF ARMENTIÈRES
19 OCTOBER – 2 NOVEMBER 1914**

KEY
- British positions 19-20 October.
- British positions 21-22 October.
- British front line on 2 November.
- French positions (Conneau) on 19 October.
- French positions 22-24 October, with dates.
- German attacks 19-20 October.
- German attacks 21 October.
- German attacks 22-29 October, with dates.

B. E. F.
(Sir John French)

BELGIUM
FRANCE

le Bizet

to Bailleul

Nieppe

Pont de
Nieppe

ARMENTIÈRES

Lys

Erquinghem

Chapelle
d'Armentières

**BRITISH
III
CORPS**
(Pulteney)

Bac St. Maur

Sailly sur
la Lys

Fleurbaix

6 Division

Bois Grenier

Estaires

Lys

**Lahore
Division**
23 Oct.

Croix Maréchal

Touquet

16 Inf. Bde.

19 Inf. Bde.
19 Oct.

Rouge de Bout

la Boutillerie

Bde.

16

Bridoux

22-24 Oct.

Laventie

**BRITISH
II
CORPS**

to Aire

**Lahore
Division**
24 Oct.

Inf.

19

Bde.

**48
Res. Div.**

29 Oct.

Bacquart

**GERMAN
XIV RES. CORPS**
(Loden)

le Maisnil

3 Division
Fauquissart

Jullundur

(Smith-Dorrien)

8 Inf. Bde.

Rouges
Bancs

23-24 Oct.

20 Oct.

**19 Inf.
Bde.**

*The main area of operations during
this period was more to the north
where the Germans were attacking
in great strength near Ypres.
However, at this time, important
actions took place at Armentières
and La Bassée, influencing moves
and dispositions in the Ypres area.
This map is intended to illustrate
operations to the west of the "open
town" of Lille, virtually undefended.*

© Arthur Banks 1973

Fromelles

19 Inf. Bde.

22-23 Oct.

23 Oct.

Bas Flandre

Neuve Chapelle

Aubers

Pietre

8 Inf. Bde.
19 Oct.

Grand
Riez

8 Inf. Bde.

**14
Division**
27 Oct.

to Fournes

le Pilly

Fournes

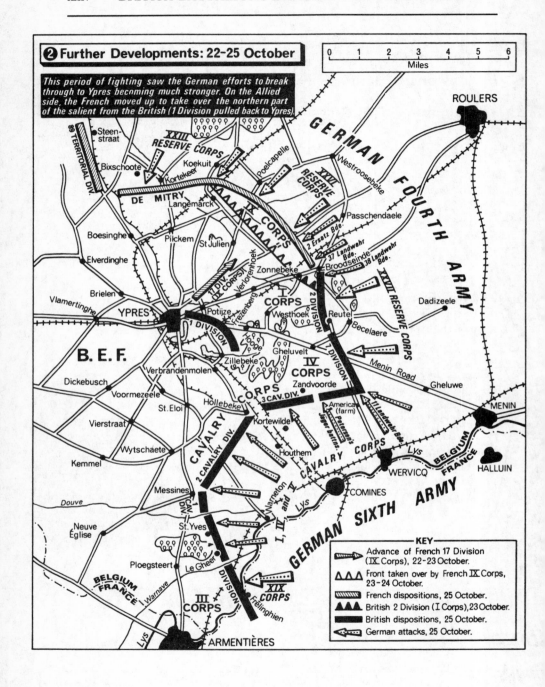

❷ Further Developments: 22–25 October

0 1 2 3 4 5 6
Miles

This period of fighting saw the German efforts to break through to Ypres becoming much stronger. On the Allied side, the French moved up to take over the northern part of the salient from the British (1 Division pulled back to Ypres).

ROULERS

89 TERRITORIAL DIV.

Steenstraat

XXIII RESERVE CORPS

Bixschoote

Koekuit

Kortekeer

DE MITRY

Langèmarck

Poelcapelle

Westroosebeke

XXVI RESERVE CORPS

GERMAN FOURTH ARMY

Boesinghe

Pilckem

St Julien

IX CORPS

Passchendaele

2 Ersatz Bde.

Elverdinghe

Verlorenhoek

Zonnebeke

37 Landwehr Bde.

Broodseinde

38 Landwehr Bde.

XXVII RESERVE CORPS

Brielen

I DIV. IX CORPS

Dadizeele

Vlamertinghe

YPRES

Potijze

Frezenberg

I CORPS

Westhoek

2 DIVISION

Reutel

Becelaere

B.E.F.

1 DIVISION

Hooge

Gheluvelt

IV CORPS

3 DIVISION

Menin Road

Gheluwe

Dickebusch

Verbrandenmolen

Zillebeke

Voormezeele

CAVALRY CORPS

Zandvoorde

American (farm)

Petersen's Jäger battn.

11 Landwehr Bde.

MENIN

St. Eloi

Hollebeke

3 CAV. DIV.

Kortewilde

Vierstraat

2 CAVALRY DIV.

Houthem

CAVALRY CORPS

Lys

WERVICQ

BELGIUM FRANCE

HALLUIN

Wytschaete

Kemmel

Messines

Narreton

Lys

COMINES

GERMAN SIXTH ARMY

Douve

Neuve Église

4 DIV.

St. Yves

I, II, and IV

Ploegsteert

Le Gheer

Frélinghien

BELGIUM FRANCE

Warnave

XIX CORPS

III CORPS

Lys

ARMENTIÈRES

KEY

Advance of French 17 Division (IX Corps), 22–23 October.

Front taken over by French IX Corps, 23–24 October.

French dispositions, 25 October.

British 2 Division (I Corps), 23 October.

British dispositions, 25 October.

German attacks, 25 October.

GRENADIER GUARDS

"Mons" "Retreat from Mons" "Marne,1914" "Aisne,1914" "Ypres, 1914" "Langemarck, 1914" "Gheluvelt" "Nonne Bosschen"

1ST BATTALION

AUGUST
Warley.

SEPTEMBER
Joined 20th Brigade, 7th Division at Lyndhurst.

OCTOBER
To Southampton (4th) and embarked SS *Armenian* and SS *Turcoman*. In his history of the Grenadier Guards, The Rt. Hon. Sir Frederick Ponsonby records that the former vessel was "fairly comfortable" while the latter was "just a cattle-boat." Sailed (5th). Officers – Lieutenant-Colonel M. Earle, DSO (Commanding Officer), Major H. St. L. Stucley (Second in Command), Captain G.E.C. Rasch (Adjutant), Lieutenants Lord Claud N. Hamilton (Machine Gun Officer), G.E. Hope (Signals Officer), J. Teece (Quartermaster), J.G. Butt (RAMC, Medical Officer), Second-Lieutenant H.W.R. Mackenzie (Transport Officer); King's Company: Major Hon. A.O.W.C. Weld-Forester, MVO, Captain Hon. L.P. Cary, Lieutenants W.S. Pilcher, H.L. Aubrey-Fletcher, MVO, J.H. Powell, Second-Lieutenant R.O.R. Kenyon-Slaney; No.2 Company: Captains Hon. C.M.B. Ponsonby, MVO, G.C.G. Moss, Lieutenant T.E.R. Symons, Second-Lieutenants R.S. Lambert, M.A.A. Darby; No.3 Company: Captains Lord Richard Wellesley, G. Rennie, Lieutenants Hon. A.G.S. Douglas-Pennant, P. Van Neck, L.G. Ames; No.4 Company: Major L.R.V. Colby, Captain R.E.K. Leatham, Lieutenant E. Antrobus, Second-Lieutenants S. Walter, N.A.H. Somerset, Sir G. Duckworth-King, Bart. Landed Zeebrugge (7th) and entrained for Bruges. Arrived and marched to billets at St. André. To Leffinghe (8th). Entrained at Ostend for Ghent (9th). The Battalion billeted near a dye-works from which the Belgian authorities issued large rolls of velvet in lieu of blankets. Moved forward to Destelbergen (10th) and took up outposts on edge of town. Withdrew to Somergem (11th). To Thielt (12th), Roulers (13th), Ypres (14th). Two companies set up outposts on Menin and Messines roads. Parties of Uhlans sighted, the first of the enemy

to be seen by the Battalion. To Zandvoorde (16th) and dug defensive positions on outskirts of village facing east. Sir Frederick Ponsonby records that this position had a good field of fire and a stream some 200 yards in front of the Battalion's line. Moved forward (17th) to Kruiseecke. Began attack (19th) but soon ordered to withdraw on line running Kruiseecke to Ypres-Menin road crossroads. Germans attacked during afternoon (20th) coming to within 200 yards of line before being forced back. Another attack (21st) repulsed. British artillery recorded as falling short and causing many casualties. Second-Lieutenants Walter and Somerset killed (23rd). During a counter-attack (24th) No.4 Company had to pass through a tobacco-drying ground which contained wire entanglements. The men's packs being caught up, the German machine guns enfiladed the party killing Major Colby, Lieutenant Antrobus and 100 men. During a night attack (25th) the enemy were heard to shout "Don't shoot! we are the South Staffords." There had been 2 companies of 1st South Staffordshire sent up as reinforcements that day and the Germans must have known this. Fortunately, German helmets were noticed and the Grenadiers opened fire. Some 60 shells per minute were noted (26th) as landing on small sections of the Battalion's line. Many men were buried alive and had to be dug out from under as much as 3 foot of earth. Many were suffocated. Lieutenant Van Neck killed. Later ordered to retire to billets on the outskirts of Ypres. During the retirement the King's Company, which had become isolated, marched in perfect order through Kruiseecke which was by that time occupied by the enemy. The Battalion's machine guns are on record as having been in action throughout the previous 7 days and using some 56,000 rounds of ammunition. Moved to bivouacs at Sanctuary Wood (27th). Casualties since moving to Kruiseecke sector – 310. Moved forward to hold line on Menin Road (Kruiseecke crossroads) (28th). Came under heavy fire from British artillery falling short during early morning (29th). Enemy attacked later and pushed Battalion back to support line. Major Stucley, Captains Lord Wellesley and Rennie killed, Major Weld-Forester and Lieutenant Douglas-Pennant mortally wounded. Lieutenant-Colonel Earle was severely wounded and subsequently taken prisoner. The Medical Officer, Lieutenant Butt was shot through the head while attending to his wounds. Later fell back to wood then counter-attacked. Some ground gained near the brickworks, then took up line in ditch on south side of Menin road. Relieved then during night marched to billets at Hooge. Roll called – 4 officers, 100 men. During (30th) a number of men came in bringing strength up to 250. Later moved forward to Brigade Reserve positions at Herenthage Château. Advanced to forward trenches (31st) and held off several attacks throughout day. Relieved and to Château. Strength now 5 officers, 200 men.

NOVEMBER

In wood south of Herenthage (1st). Moved to line Klein Zillebeke area (2nd). Relieved (5th) and to Locre. Marched via Bailleul to Meteren (6th), via Bailleul, Steenwerck and Sailly-sur-la-Lys to Bac St. Maur (14th). Began tours in trenches Fleurbaix sector.

DECEMBER

Trenches Fleurbaix sector.

2ND BATTALION

AUGUST

Wellington Barracks, London. Part of 4th (Guards) Brigade, 2nd Division. Entrained at Nine Elms for Southampton (12th) and sailed *Cawdor Castle* for France. Officers – Lieutenant-Colonel N.A.L. Corry, DSO (Commanding Officer), Brevet-Lieutenant- Colonel Lord Loch, MVO, DSO, (Second in Command), Majors Lord B.C. Gordon- Lennox, G.C. Hamilton, Captains E.M. Colston, MVO, D.C.L. Stephen, E.G.H. Powell, E.J.L. Pike, A.B.R.R. Gosselin, C. Symes-Thompson, Lieutenants I. MacDougall (Adjutant), Hon. W.A. Cecil (Machine Gun Officer), Hon. F.E. Needham, C.F.A. Walker, A.K. Mackenzie, R.W.G. Welby, F.W. Des Voeux, R. Wolridge-Gordon, H.H. Prince Alexander of Battenberg, GCVO, Hon. J.N. Manners, M.G. Stocks, F.W.J.M. Miller, Second-Lieutenants G.C. Fitz H. Harcourt-Vernon, G.G.B. Nugent, J.R. Pickersgill- Cunliffe, R.H.M. Vereker, A.K.S. Cunningham, G.E. Cecil, Hon. Lieutenant J.H. Skidmore (Quartermaster). Landed Havre (13th) and to rest camp. Entrained 2 am (15th) and travelled via Rouen, Amiens, Arras, Cambrai and Busigny to Flavigny. Marched to Grougis (16th), Oisy (20th), Maroilles (21st), La Longueville (22nd). Continued march (23rd) crossing old battlefield of Malplaquet and via Blaregnies and Genly bivouacked on outskirts of Mons. Later marched to Quevy le Petit and from there advanced through Harveng to high ground near Spiennes. Took up positions in support of 2nd Royal Irish Rifles. In his war history of the Regiment, Lieutenant-Colonel The Right Hon. Sir Frederick Ponsonby records that the Battalion took up positions on the reverse slope of the hill above a railway line. Bullets and shells whistling all around, a railwayman was noted walking along the line with complete disregard of what was going on around him and carrying out his normal duties. Retired towards Harveng 1 am (24th) but later ordered back to former positions. Arrived, then once again sent back to Harveng. Continued retreat to Quevy le Grand and dug in under heavy shell fire. Later withdrew and bivouacked at Malgarni near

La Longueville. Continued retreat (25th) marching via Pont sur Sambre, Leval and Noyelles to Landrecies. Took up defensive positions – Nos 2 and 3 Companies at level-crossing, No.1 Company further back in side roads, No. 4 Company at bridge crossing the Sambre. Enemy attacked after dark. Sir Frederick Ponsonby records Germans calling out "don't shoot, we are the French." Also strong attacks held off by stubborn resistance, German guns firing at point-blank range and case shot being fired down the road. Second-Lieutenant Vereker killed. Enemy retreated after midnight. Withdrew to Etreux (26th), Mont d' Origny (27th), Deuillet (28th). To Soissons (30th) and took up positions on ridge near Pasly. To Soucy (31st) and ordered to form rearguard. Dug in on high ground above village. No. 4 Company detached to position on ridge leading to Montgobert on right.

SEPTEMBER
Retired to Villers-Cotterêts (1st) and took up positions on main road running east and west through Rond de la Reine. Enemy engaged – Lieutenants Manners, Cecil, MacDougall killed, 161 other casualties. Withdrew to Boursonne and covered retreat of 6th Brigade. Later fell back to Thury then to La Villeneuve. Continued retreat 2 am (2nd) marching via Antilly, Betz, Puisieux and Barzy to Meaux. Crossed the Marne at Trilport (3rd) then via Montceaux to Pierre Levée. To Les Laquais (4th) then at dusk to Le Bertrand via Maisoncelles and Rouilly le Fay. To Fontenay via La Celle and Malmaison Farm (5th). To reserve positions at Le Mée (6th) then to Touquin. Marched via Paradis, Mauperthuis, St. Simeon and Voigny to Rebais (7th). Sir Frederick Ponsonby notes that in every village there were signs of the German retreat and much looting and vandalism. Engaged enemy at La Trétoire (8th). Captain Stephen killed, 40 other casualties. Advanced north of Boitron and bivouacked near Les Peauliers. To Pavant (9th), crossed the Marne at Charly and bivouacked on side of hill near Villers-sur-Marne. To Hautenvesnes via Domptin, Coupru, Marigny and Neuilly (10th), Oulchy via Priez, Sommellans, Latilly, La Croix and Breny (11th), Courcelles via Beugneux, Arey, Cuiry-Housse, Lesges, Lime and Braine (12th). To St. Mard (13th). Crossed the Aisne (14th) then to Soupir. Enemy engaged near La Cour de Soupir Farm. Sir Frederick Ponsonby records how a detachment under Second-Lieutenant Pickersgill-Cunliffe ran into the enemy and were taken prisoner. When the remainder of the advance guard came forward the Germans abandoned their prisoners, but not before their commanding officer shot dead Lieutenant Pickersgill-Cunliffe who was lying wounded on the ground. Lieutenant Des Voeux also killed. 300-400 prisoners taken. Dug defensive trenches and held under heavy bombardment and counter-attacks (15th). Captain Cecil and

Lieutenant Welby killed (16th). Relieved and to billets at Soupir (17th). Returned to front line trenches (18th). An average of 15 shells per minute counted during 6 hour bombardment. Relieved by 1st Irish Guards (21st) and to Soupir. To Chavonne (22nd) and took over front line trenches from 1st Cavalry Brigade.

OCTOBER
Relieved by French Territorials (12th). March via St. Mard and Vauxcéré to billets at Perles (13th). Entrained at Fismes for Hazebrouck (14th). To Boeschepe (17th), St. Jean (20th), positions near Hanebeek Brook (21st). Advanced and dug in about 400 yards east of the Zonnebeke-Langemarck road. Enemy attempted an attack in which Sir Frederick Ponsonby records – they called out "don't fire, we are the Coldstream." He notes the exactitude of the Germans who were careful to use the correct term "Coldstream" as opposed to the more likely term from someone outside of the Regiment "Coldstreams." Lieutenant Miller killed (23rd). Relieved and to Eksternest (24th). Moved forward to Polygon Wood (25th). Took part in attack on the Reutel Spur 3 pm. Withdrew to line and held against several counter-attacks. To Nonne Bosschen Wood (27th). Advanced to northern edge of Polygon Wood (28th). Later moved forward in support of attack. To Racecourse Wood (29th). Took up positions on right of the Klein Zillebeke-Zandvoorde Road (30th). Came under heavy shell fire (31st). Enemy attacked during afternoon – driven back by No.1 Company. Relieved by French troops during night and to positions behind Zwarteleen.

NOVEMBER
Moved forward to Bodmin Copse (1st). Attack driven off (2nd). Sir Frederick Ponsonby records that the enemy came forward beating drums and blowing horns. He also mentions a message instigated by the Germans and passed down the line – "Don't fire, the Northamptons are going to charge." Heavy casualties from shell fire among No.1 Company. Sir Frederick Ponsonby notes that this was almost wiped out. He also records the gallantry of Sergeant G.H. Thomas (later awarded DCM., killed 24th December, 1914) who was buried alive twice and had 3 rifles broken in his hands before leading the survivors of his platoon (3 men) back to Brown Road. Enemy attacked (10th) – Major Lord Gordon-Lennox and Lieutenant Stocks killed. Later withdrew to Corps Reserve at Bellewaarde Farm. Ordered forward to support attack south west of Polygon Wood (11th). Heavy casualties during march. Later assembled near Nonne Bosschen Wood and to Hooge Château. To positions on Menin Road (12th), Sanctuary Wood (13th), front line Brown Road sector (15th).

Enemy attacked (17th) – Captain Symes-Thompson killed. Relieved by 3rd Coldstream (19th) and to St. Jean. To Ouderdom (21st) then via Westoutre, Mont Noir and La Manche to billets at Meteren.

DECEMBER

To Béthune (22nd), Essarts area (23rd). In evening took over line at Rue de Cailloux. Trenches noted as up to waist-deep in mud and water. Part of enemy's line just 25 yards away. Enemy attack repulsed (24th).Relieved by 3rd Coldstream (25th) and to Le Touret. To front line (27th). Relieved by 3rd Coldstream (29th) and to Le Touret. To front line (31st).

COLDSTREAM GUARDS

"Mons" "Retreat from Mons" "Marne, 1914"
"Aisne, 1914" "Ypres, 1914"
"Langemarck, 1914" "Gheluvelt" "Nonne Bosschen"
"Givenchy, 1914"

1ST BATTALION

AUGUST

Blenheim Barracks, Aldershot. Part of 1st (Guards) Brigade, 1st Division. To Southampton and embarked SS *Dunvegan Castle* (13th). Officers – Lieutenant-Colonel J. Ponsonby, DSO (Commanding Officer), Major Hon. L. Hamilton, MVO (Second in Command), Lieutenants G.A. Campbell (Adjutant), F.W. Gore-Langton (Transport Officer), G.K.F. Smith (Machine Gun Officer), J. Boyd (Quartermaster); No.1 Company: Captains G.H. Brown, G.J. Edwards, Lieutenant J.B.S. Bourne-May, Second-Lieutenants Hon. G.F. Freeman-Thomas, Hon. M.H.D. Browne; No.2 Company: Major C.J.C. Grant, Captain W. St. A. Warde-Aldam, Lieutenants J.C. Sommers Cocks, D.M.B. Hall, Second-Lieutenants M.B. Beckwith-Smith, G.R. Lane; No.3 Company: Captains J.E. Gibbs, W.A. Fuller- Maitland, Lieutenants F.R. Pollock, T.L.C. Curtis, Second-Lieutenants A.E. Hardy, F.C.R. Britten; No.4 Company: Captains E.G. Christie-Miller, G.M. Paget, Lieutenants E.D.H. Tollemache, J.C. Wynne Finch, Second-Lieutenants Hon. G.P.M.N. Sturt, C.E. Tufnell. Arrived Havre (14th) and to rest camp. Entrained for Le Nouvion (15th). To Boué (17th), Cartignies (21st), via Maubeuge to Vieux-Reng (22nd), Rouveroy (23rd). Withdrew to positions near Bersillies (24th), Dompierre (25th), just south of Maroilles then Fesmy (26th). Took up defensive line at bridge crossing the Sambe Canal near Oisy (27th) then withdrew via Etreux and Guise to Jonqueuse. Continued retreat via Mont d'Origny, Danizy and La Fère to St. Gobain (28th), Allemant (30th). Bivouaced 2 miles south of Soissons (31st).

SEPTEMBER

To La Ferté-Milon (1st), Chambry (2nd). Crossed the Marne at Germigny (3rd) then on to Coulommiers. To Nesles (5th). Began advance to the Aisne (6th). Came under shell and rifle fire near Voinsles and fell back to Rozoy. Moved forward again about 5 pm and bivouacked near Voinsles. Casualties – 7 officers wounded, 5 other ranks killed, 33 wounded. Second-Lieutenant

Sturt was among the wounded and died of his injuries on 11th November, 1918. To Le Temple (7th). Advanced via Jouy (8th) then came under shell fire near Bellot. Casualties – 4 killed, 12 wounded. Later moved through village then via Sablonnières and Hondevilliers to bivouacs about 3 miles from the Marne. Crossed the river at Nogent (9th) then advanced to La Nouette Farm. To Latilly (10th), Bruyères (11th), via Fère en Tardenois and Loupeigne to Bazoches (12th), via Vauxcére, Bourg and Moulins to bivouacs in woods near Vendresse (13th). Took part in attack towards the Chemin des Dames above Troyon (14th). Withdrew into reserve near Vendresse during night. Second-Lieutenant Freeman-Thomas killed, 388 other casualties. Relieved 1st Queen's in firing line east of Troyon (18th). Relieve by 1st West Yorkshire after dark (19th) and to Oeuilly. Casualties – Captain Fuller-Maitland killed, Lieutenant Campbell mortally wounded, 19 other casualties. Moved forward to support line at Verneuil (21st) and then to trenches astride the Oise-Aisne Canal (24th). Relieve (26th) and to Oeuilly. Casualties – 20. Relieved 1st Queens in firing line near Troyon (27th).

OCTOBER
Relieved by French troops (16th) and via Bourg and Longueval to Blanzy. Casualties since 29th September – 100. To Fismes (17th) and entrained for Hazebrouck. To Poperinghe (20th), via Elverdinghe to positions around Pilkem (21st). Nos 1 and 2 Companies in support of 3rd Brigade's recapture of Koekuit. Took part in fighting around the Kortekeer Inn – Lieutenant Pollock killed (23rd). To Zillebeke (24th). Casualties – 31 killed, 93 wounded, 73 missing. Moved via Veldhoek and Gheluvelt (26th) and took part in attack towards Poezelhoek. Advance held up about 400 yards from village. Lieutenant C.J. Murray killed. Relieved 2nd Yorkshire after midnight in trenches around Nieuwe Kruiseecke. Enemy attacked in large numbers (29th). Lieutenant-Colonel Sir John Ross- of-Bladensburg in his war history of the Regiment notes how 1st Coldstream were low in numbers and their line finally overwhelmed. Survivors in deep and narrow trenches were unable to use their bayonets. At the end of the day's fighting just 1 officer (Quartermaster Boyd) and 60 other ranks remained. Casualties – Major Hamilton, Captain Brown, , Lieutenants Campbell, Smith, Hon. C. Douglas-Pennant, Second-Lieutenants Hon. V.D. Boscawen, C.W. Williams-Wynn killed. Rest of officers either wounded or taken prisoner. Other ranks – 180 killed, wounded or missing. Survivors pulled back to support positions.

NOVEMBER
Draft of 80 men under Captains Christie-Miller and H.R.A. Adeane arrived (1st). Moved forward to trenches in front of Veldhoek around the Menin road. Enemy attacked during morning (2nd) and entered Battalion's line. Captain Adeane killed, Captain Christie-Miller taken prisoner. Casualties among other ranks Approximately 100. Battalion withdrew from line and attached to 4th (Guards) Brigade at Polygon Wood. Moved to Divisional Reserve positions near Hooge (17th). Relieve (20th) and marched during night via Ypres to Meteren. Colonel Ponsonby rejoined (22nd). Battalion strength now 3 officers, 122 other ranks. Rejoined 1st (Guards) Brigade at Pradelles (23rd). Total casualties since arriving in France – 13 officers, 309 other ranks killed or died of wounds, 24 officers, 654 other ranks wounded, 4 officers, 184 other ranks taken prisoner.

DECEMBER
Marched via Strazeele to Béthune (20th). moved forward along the La Bassée road (21st) then via Pont Fixe took part in attack on enemy trenches at Rue d' Ouvert. Objective taken during morning (22nd). Relieved later by 1st Black Watch and via Pont Fixe to billets on south side of canal. Casualties – Captain G. Stewart, Second-Lieutenants B.D. Tollemache, L.F.R. Coleridge killed, Second-Lieutenant E.A. Beauchamp mortally wounded, 10 other ranks killed, 128 wounded, 57 missing. Relieve 1st Black Watch in firing line (25th). Relieved by 1st Black Watch (28th) and to Béthune. To Beuvry (31st).

2ND BATTALION

AUGUST
Victoria Barracks, Windsor. Part of 4th (Guards) Brigade, 2nd Division. Arrived Southampton (12th) and embarked SS *Olympia* and SS *Novara*. Sailed for France. Arrived Havre (13th) and to rest camp. Officers – Lieutenant-Colonel C.E. Pereira (Commanding Officer), Major R.A. Markham (Second in Command), Captains S. Wright (Quartermaster and Transport Officer), M. Sinclair (RAMC, Medical Officer), Lieutenants A.G.C. Dawnay (Adjutant), W.T. Towers-Clark (Machine Gun Officer), Second-Lieutenant S.G.F. Taylor (Scout Officer); No.1 Company: Captains F. Hardy, E.B.G. Gregge-Hopwood, Lieutenants N.W.H. Legge-Bourke, H.C. Loyd, Second- Lieutenants A.H.M. Ramsay, C.J.W. Darwin; No.2 Company: Captains G.B.S. Follett, MVO, J.S. Egerton, Lieutenants G.L. Gordon, L.G.C. Lord Petre, Second-Lieutenants W.G.

Shaw-Stewart, Hon. R.G. Winn; No.3 Company: Captains H.M. Pryce-Jones, Sir W.B. Barttelot, Bart; Lieutenants A. Leigh-Bennett, R.L.C. Bewicke-Copley, Second-Lieutenants H.E.de Trafford, R.W.M. Lockwood; No.4 Company: Major P.A. Macgregor, DSO, Captain J.H.J. Phillips, Lieutenants R.C. Graves-Sawle, H.W. Verelst; Second-Lieutenant C. Viscount Marsham. Travelled by train to Vaux-Andigny (15th). Marched to Vadencourt (16th), via Etreux and Oisy to Fesmy (20th), via La Groise, Landrecies and Maroilles to Noyelles (21st), via Pont sur Sambre and Hargnies to La Longueville (22nd). Moved forward to Hyon (23rd) then to Harveng. Moved back to Malgarni (24th) and Landrecies (25th). In support throughout night during enemy attacks. Covered retreat astride the Etreux road south of Landrecies (26th). Later fell back to Etreux. Marched via Vadencourt to Mont d` Origny (27th), via La Fère to Deuillet (28th), to Pasly (30th), via Pernant to high ground near Soucy (31st).

SEPTEMBER
Took part in fighting in the Villers-Cotterêts Forest (1st). Later withdrew to Thury. To Betz then Villeroy (2nd). Crossed the Marne at Trilport (3rd) and then to Pierre-Levée. To La Grande Loge Farm (4th) and dug in. Later to La Celle. To Fontenay (5th). Moved forward to positions around Nesles (6th) then to Touquin. Advanced via Mauperthuis and Chailly to St. Siméon (7th) and bivouacked on high ground north of river. Marched via Rebais and La Trétoire (8th). Crossed the Petit Morin and cleared enemy from Boitron. Later to positions around Petit Villiers. Engaged enemy. German casualties estimated at around 300 and some 100 prisoners taken. Battalion casualties- 3 killed, 9 wounded. Moved via Charly-sur-Marne to Villiers-sur-Marne (9th). To Cainticourt (10th), Oulchy-le- Château (11th), Courcelles (12th). Moved forward to high ground above St. Mard (13th). Later advanced towards the Aisne, coming under fire at Cys-la-Commune. Enemy forced back and river crossed. Later ordered to withdraw to Cys. Casualties – 1 killed, 22 wounded. No.1 Company remained guarding bridge at Chavonne. Took part in the fighting at La Cour de Soupir Farm (14th). Casualties – Second-Lieutenant Lockwood and 2 other ranks killed, 2 officers, 61 other ranks wounded. Dug in and positions held – 2 companies in front line, 2 resting at Soupir. Took over line near Chavonne (18th). Private F.W. Dobson gained the Victoria Cross for rescuing a wounded man from in front of German trenches (28th).

OCTOBER

Relieved by French troops (13th) and marched via St. Mard to Perles. To Fismes (14th) and entrained for Hazebrouck. Arrived (15th). Marched via Steenvoorde to Boeschepe (17th). Moved via Reninghelst and Vlamertinghe to Ypres (20th). Later moved forward to Wieltje sector then bivouacked north-west of Zonnebeke. Took part in attack on enemy positions on the Zonnebeke-Langemarck road (21st). Objective taken by 11.30 a.m. Casualties – 8 killed, 24 wounded, 1 missing. Gains held and consolidated. Casualties (23rd) – 6 killed, 10 wounded, 2 missing. Major Markham mortally wounded. Relieved during night and to Zillebeke. Moved to reserve positions east of Hooge (24th), Polygon Wood (25th). Took part in attack through wood (26th). Held positions in Polygon Wood. Lieutenant Legge-Bourke killed by sniper (28th).

NOVEMBER

Lieutenant Graves-Sawle killed by sniper (2nd). Relieved during night (16th) by French troops. Casualties since 26th October – 2 officers, 61 other ranks killed, 4 officers, 151 other ranks wounded, 1 missing. Marched to billets at Zillebeke but later sent to reserve positions near Klein Zillebeke. Relieved 1/1st Hertfordshire in firing line (19th). Relieved and marched via Ypres to billets at Meteren. Lieutenant-Colonel Sir John Ross-of-Bladensburg in his war history of the Regiment provides the following details regarding 2nd Battalion casualties since leaving England: 4 officers and 112 other ranks killed or died of wounds; 9 officers, 304 other ranks wounded, 15 taken prisoner. Only 9 of the original officers that embarked for France had not become casualties.

DECEMBER

Marched via Merris, Merville and Locon to Béthune (22nd). Moved to Le Touret (23rd) and took over firing line.

3RD BATTALION

AUGUST

Chelsea Barracks, London. Part of 4th (Guards) Brigade, 2nd Division. To Southampton (12th) and embarked SS *Cawdor Castle* for France. Arrived Havre (13th) and to rest camp. Officers – Lieutenant-Colonel G.P.T. Feilding, DSO (Commanding Officer), Major T.G. Matheson (Second in Command), Lieutenants J.U.F.C. Alexander (Adjutant), D.C.Bingham (Machine Gun Officer), F.T. Prichard (Quartermaster), J. Huggan (RAMC, Medical Officer), Second-Lieutenant H.A. Cubitt (Transport

Officer), No.1 Company: Captains E. Longueville, R. Whitbread, Lieutenants Hon. R.O.D. Keppel, G.R.F. Rowley, Second-Lieutenant A. Trotter; No.2 Company: Captains C.P. Heywood, J.H. Brocklehurst, Lieutenants N.A. Daniell, R.C. Viscount Hawarden, Hon. A. Windsor-Clive, Second-Lieutenant W.de Winton; No. 3 Company: Captains Hon. C.H.S. Monck, G.E. Vaughan, Lieutenants P.L. Wyndham, A.W.D. Bentinck, Second-Lieutenants C.S. Jackson, C.M. Cottrell-Dormer; No.4 Company: Captains A.G. Tritton, S.J. Burton, Lieutenants J.N. Horlick, G. Lambton, V.M.G. Gordon-Ives, Second-Lieutenant Sir R.J. Corbet, Bart. Entrained (14th) and travelled via Rouen, Amiens, Arras, Cambrai and Busigny to Wassigny. Arrived (15th) then to billets at Etreux. To Grougis (16th). Marched via Etreux and Oisy to Fesmy (20th), via La Groise and Landrecies to Maroilles (21st), via Pont sur Sambre and Hargnies to La Longueville (22nd). To Harveng (23rd) and dug defensive positions. Moved back to Malgarni (24th) and Landrecies (25th). In his war history of the Coldstream Guards, Lieutenant-Colonel Sir John Ross-of-Bladensburg, KCB, KCVO records how No.2 Company situated on the Le Quesnoy road, fired on advancing enemy patrols and drove them back. Later, No.3 Company in the same position was informed that retreating French troops were expected. Around dusk, a column was seen moving up the road. The men were singing French songs and when challenged an officer replied that they were friends. However, although the men at the front were wearing French or Belgian uniforms, it was noticed that those at the back were German. Captain Monck immediately gave the order to open fire, but quickly the enemy rushed the Coldstream piquet line. The attackers killed 1 man and retreated with one of the Battalion's machine guns. This, however, was soon recovered and the enemy driven off. Further attempts during night by enemy to enter Landrecies beaten off. Lance-Corporal G.H. Wyatt gained the Victoria Cross. Relieved by 1st Irish Guards during morning (26th) and withdrew to Etreux. Casualties – Lieutenants Viscount Hawarden, Windsor-Clive and 10 other ranks killed, 3 officers, 105 other ranks wounded, 7 missing. Enemy aircraft brought down by fire from No.3 Company. Marched via Grougis to Mont d'Origny (27th), via La Fère to Bertaucourt (28th), to Pasly (30th), via Pernant to Soucy (31st).

SEPTEMBER

Took part in fighting in the Villers Cotterêts Forest (1st). Later to Betz. Casualties – Lieutenant Lambton and 8 other ranks killed, 29 wounded, 8 missing. To Esbly (2nd). Crossed the Marne at Meaux (3rd) then to Pierre-Levée. Dug in at La Grande Loge Farm (4th). Later to La Celle. To

Fontenay (5th). Moved forward (6th) and dug in at Château de la Fortelle. Second-Lieutenant de Winton killed by shell. Moved later to Touquin. Advanced (7th) via Mauperthuis and Chailly to St. Siméon. Moved (8th) via Rebais and La Trétoire then crossed the Petit Morin. Advanced via Boitron to positions around Petit Villiers. Engaged enemy. Casualties – 8 killed, 45 wounded, 6 missing. Marched (9th) via Charly-sur-Marne to Villiers. To Cainticourt (10th), Oulchy-le-Château (11th), Courcelles (12th), St. Mard (13th). Took part in the fighting at La Cour de Soupir Farm (14th). Casualties – Captain C.W. Banbury, Lieutenants Bingham, Wyndham, Gordon-Ives and 21 other ranks killed; 2 officers, 151 other ranks wounded. Dug in and consolidated position. Farm heavily shelled (16th). Medical Officer, Lieutenant Huggan killed while evacuating wounded from burning building. Total casualties – 6 killed, 39 wounded, 12 missing. Relieved later and to Soupir. Relieved 1st Irish Guards in front line (19th).

OCTOBER
Relieved by 1st Irish Guards (3rd), Relieved 1st Irish Guards in firing line (6th). Relieved by French troops (12th) and marched via Chavonne and St. Mard to Perles. To Fismes (13th) and entrained for Hazebrouck. Arrived (14th). Marched via Steenworde to Boeschepe (17th), via Reninghelsy and Vlamertinghe to Ypres (20th). Moved later to reserve positions at St. Jean then to St. Julien. Took part in attack on Zonnebeke (21st). Casualties – Captain Monck, Lieutenant H.D. Wallis, new Medical Officer Lieutenant D. Rintoul and 13 other ranks killed; 60 wounded, 28 missing. Line held under heavy fire. Relieved during night (23rd) and to Zillebeke. To reserve positions east of Hooge (24th), Polygon Wood (25th). In support of 1st Irish Guards during attack through wood (26th). Relieved 1st Irish Guards in firing line (27th).

NOVEMBER
Relieved by French troops during night (16th). Casualties since 26th October – 25 killed, 141 wounded. Marched to billets at Zillebeke but later sent to reserve positions near Klein Zillebeke. Relieved 1st Irish Guards in firing line (18th), 2nd Grenadiers in front line – Brown Road sector (19th). Captain R.L. Dawson and 3 other ranks killed (20th), 10 wounded. Relieved and marched via Ypres to Meteren. Sir John Ross-of-Bladensburg gives Battalion's total casualties since leaving England as – 11 officers and 182 other ranks killed or died of wounds; 21 officers, 560 other ranks wounded; 1 officer, 11 other ranks taken prisoner. Just 4 of the original officers had not become casualties.

DECEMBER
Marched via Merris, Merville and Locon to Béthune (22nd). To Le Touret
(23rd) then into reserve billets at Rue de l' Epinette. Relieved 2nd
Grenadiers in front line – Rue de Cailloux (25th) and (29th).

Scots Guards

"Retreat from Mons" "Marne, 1914" "Aisne, 1914"
"Ypres, 1914" "Langemarck, 1914" "Gheluvelt"
"Nonne Bosschen" "Givenchy, 1914"

1ST BATTALION

AUGUST

Aldershot. Part of 1st (Guards) Brigade, 1st Division. Entrained at Farnborough for Southampton (13th). Embarked SS *Dunvegan Castle* and sailed for France. Arrive Havre (14th) then to camp at Harfleur. Officers – Lieutenant-Colonel H.C. Lowther, CB,CVO,CMG,DSO (Commanding Officer), Majors J.T. Carpenter-Garnier (Second in Command), B.G. Van De Weyer, Captains A.A.L. Stephen, DSO (Adjutant), R.G. Stracey, W.J. Wickham, C.E. de la Pasture, C.F.P. Hamilton, Sir V.A.F. Mackenzie, Bart, MVO, R.F. Balfour, J.D.P. Astley-Corbett, Lieutenants B.G. Jolliffe, C.F.F. Campbell, H.C.E. Ross, G.F. de Teissier, C.J. Balfour, Sir I. Colquhoun, Bart, R.N. Gipps, H.R. Inigo-Jones, D. Kinlay (Quartermaster), Second-Lieutenants R.A. Compton-Thornhill, W.B.W. Lawson, Sir G.N. Ogilvy, Bart, G.V.F. Monckton, A.G. Menzies, E.D. Mackenzie, J. Stirling-Stuart, W.G. Houldsworth. Entrained at Havre for Nouvion (15th). Moved to Boué (17th), Cartignies (21st), Grand Reng (22nd). Moved forward to the Rouveroy-Erquelinnes road (24th). Moved back later to positions west of Villers-Sire- Nicole, then at 5 pm. to La Longueville. To Taisnieres (25th), Rejet-de-Beaulien (26th), via Etreux to Jonqueuse (27th), St. Gobain (28th), via Terny to Allemant (30th), Vauxbuin (31st).

SEPTEMBER

Marched via Villers Cotterêts to La Ferté-Milon (1st). Digging in later at Marolles. To Chambry (2nd), Jouarre (3rd), Coulommiers (4th), Nesles (5th). Began advance to the Aisne (6th), marching first to Le Plessis. To Le Frenois (7th). Crossed the Grande Morin at Jouy (8th) then to Sablonnières. Machine guns engaged enemy near Bellot during march. Crossed the Marne at Nogent (9th) then via Charly-sur-Marne to La Marette. Marched via Le Thiolet, Torcy and Courchamps to Latilly (10th), Bruyères (11th), Bazoches (12th). Advanced under shell fire via Oeuilly, Pargnan and Paissy – Second- Lieutenant Houldsworth mortally wounded, 3 other ranks killed, 2 officers and 11 other ranks wounded. Moved forward through Moulins, Cerny-en-Laonnais to Chamouille (14th). Came into action just west of

Vendresse, advancing under heavy fire to positions near Chivy. Leading company withdrew later and joined rest of Battalion on the Vendresse Ridge. Casualties – Major Carpenter-Garnier mortally wounded, Lieutenant Inigo-Jones, Second-Lieutenant Compton-Thornhill and 16 other ranks killed, 2 officers, 86 other ranks wounded, 12 missing. Relieved (20th) and to Oeuilly. Relieved 1st King's Liverpool in trenches at Moussy (21st). Relieved (23rd) and to Verneuil. To bivouacs on the Vendresse road (24th). Three men killed by shell (25th). Moved back during night to Oeuilly. Took over trenches on the Vendresse Ridge (27th).

OCTOBER

Relieved (16th) and to Blanzy. Casualties since 13th September – 4 officers, 37 other ranks killed, 5 officer, 137 other ranks wounded, 12 missing. To Fismes (17th) and entrained for Hazebrouck. Marched to Poperinghe (20th). Advanced via Elverdinghe, Boesinghe and Langemarck (21st) and in action throughout day around Koekuit and Bixschoote. Second-Lieutenant Lawson killed by sniper (22nd). "C" Company in support of attack by 2nd Brigade (23rd). Relieved from trenches at Bixschoote by French troops (24th) and to Zillebeke. Casualties – 1 officer, 5 other ranks killed, 1 officer, 25 other ranks wounded, 5 missing. Moved forward via Hooge (26th) and took up positions in front line near Gheluvelt. Took part in attack on Poezelhoek, advancing to within 200 yards of enemy's trenches then digging in. Captain Hamilton killed, 2 officers wounded, approximately 130 other casualties. Later took over trenches from 2nd Bedfordshire on the Zandvoorde- Gheluvelt road near Zandvoorde Château. Captain Balfour killed (28th). Enemy attacked (29th). *The Scots Guards in the Great War* records that the enemy came on in large numbers, but came to a standstill within 200 yards of the Battalion's trenches after encountering the Guardsmens' "accurate fire." The Germans broke through on the right during the afternoon – "RF" Company, half of "B" and part of "C" were surrounded and "practically destroyed." Enemy came within 100 yards of "C" Company's line but "devastating fire" drove them back. Casualties – Captains Stephen and de la Pasture, Lieutenants Ogilvy, Hon G.E.H. Macdonald and Campbell killed or mortally wounded, approximately 240 other casualties. Enemy attacked again (31st) and Battalion involved in heavy fighting around Gheluvelt. Captain Wickham killed. Ordered to fall back and dig in between Gheluvelt and Veldhoek.

NOVEMBER

Positions held under continuous bombardment and attacks. Lieutenants Gipps and F.A. Monckton killed (7th), Lieutenant A.W. Douglas-Dick killed, Lieutenant B. Winthrop-Smith and Second-Lieutenant Stirling-Stuart mortally wounded, 20 other ranks killed, 30 wounded (8th). The regimental history records that the Prussian Guard attacked through Veldhoek (11th) capturing front trenches of 1st Brigade. Battalion at this time was holding a farm near Gheluvelt Wood and after heavy fighting was overwhelmed. Total casualties since entering into the Battle of Ypres are given as 9 officers, 105 other ranks killed, 7 officers, 151 other ranks wounded, 7 officers, 430 other ranks missing. Survivors – Captain Stracey and 69 men, moved back to Hooge (12th) then via Vlamertinghe to Westoutre (16th). To Borre (17th).

DECEMBER
Battalion, having received several drafts, moved to Béthune (20th). Moved forward along the La Bassée road (21st) and crossed La Bassée Canal at Cuinchy. Moved forward from positions west of Givenchy 4.15 pm and took part in attack to regain lost trenches near Rue d`Ouvert. Lieutenant H.G.E. Hill-Trevor and 2 other ranks killed, 23 wounded. Relieved by 1st Royal Berkshire (22nd) and moved back to south side of canal via Cuinchy. Three companies moved forward again during night. Relieved (28th) and to Béthune. To Annequin (31st).

2ND BATTALION

AUGUST
Tower of London.

SEPTEMBER
To Lyndhurst and joined 20th Brigade, 7th Division.

OCTOBER
To Southampton (4th) and embarked SS *Lake Michigan* and SS *Cestrian*. Sailed (5th). Officers – Lieutenant-Colonel R.G.I. Bolton (Commanding Officer), Majors Viscount Dalrymple (Second in Command), Hon. H.J. Fraser, MVO, Lord E.C. Gordon-Lennox, MVO, Captains T.H. Rivers-Bulkeley, CMG, MVO, Hon. J.S. Coke, C.V. Fox, Hon. D.A. Kinnaird, H.L. Kemble, MVO, G.C.B. Paynter, Lieutenants Sir F.L.F. FitzWygram, Bart., H.K. Hamilton-Wedderburn, G.H. Loder, E.C.T. Warner, Lord Cochrane, Lord G.R. Grosvenor, E.B. Trafford, H. Taylor, The Earl of Dalhousie, D.R. Drummond, W.H. Holbech, A.R. Ore, R.Steuart-Menzies, Hon. J. St. V.B. Saumarez, R.H.F. Gladwin, T. Ross (Quartermaster), Second-Lieutenants W.H. Wynne-Finch, Lord Garlies,

C. Cottrell- Dormer, Viscount Clive, R.C.M. Gibbs. Docked at Dover due to warning of German submarines in area. Sailed 7.30 pm. (6th). Arrived Zeebrugge (7th) and entrained for Bruges. Moved into billets at Varsenaeres, 2 companies providing guards on Ostend and Thourout roads. To Steene (8th). Entrained at Ostend for Ghent (9th) and during afternoon took up positions on Ghent-Antwerp road. Withdrew via Ghent to Somergem (11th). To Thielt (12th), Roulers (13th), Ypres (14th). Set up outposts near Zillebeke. Moved back to Verbranden Molen in Brigade Reserve (15th). Advanced towards Gheluvelt during night (17th). Two companies went forward to Kruiseecke and dug in. Remaining companies moved up (18th). Withdrew to Divisional Reserve at Reutl (19th). Company Sergeant Major Wilson accidently shot by sentry. Moved forward towards Kruiseecke under heavy shell fire (20th). Later withdrew to Zandvoorde. In action around Hollebeke Château (21st). Relieved during night and to Veldhoek. "F" and "LF" Companies in support at Polygon Wood (22nd). Captain Rivers-Bulkeley killed. "RF" and "G" Companies moved forward to Kruiseecke during afternoon. "F" Company heavily shelled (24th) – most of company buried alive or taken prisoner. Captain Kinnaird killed. Heavy casualties during night at Kruiseecke (25th) – companies surrounded. Major Fraser and Lieutenant Gladwin killed. Later retired to Hooge. Strength – 12 officers, 460 other ranks. Moved forward to Gheluvelt along Menin road during night (27th). Second-Lieutenant Gibbs killed by shell. Moved to Veldhoek during morning (29th). In action later at Gheluvelt – 31 killed, 104 wounded. Withdrew later to positions on Gheluvelt-Zandvoorde road. To Klein Zillebeke area (31st).

NOVEMBER
Lieutenant Drummond killed by shell-fire (3rd). Relieved (5th) and marched via Locre to Meteren. Drafts arrived. Moved to Sailly (14th) and relieved 2nd Royal Welsh Fusiliers in trenches at La Cordonerie Farm near Fromelles.

DECEMBER
Began attack near Rouges Bancs (18th), "F" and "LF" Companies moving forward with right on Sailly-Fromelles road, "G" Company in support. Heavy cross-fire from machine guns – 4 officers killed and approximately 180 other casualties. Private J. Mackenzie gained Victoria Cross – "For conspicuous bravery near Rouges Bancs on 19th December, 1914, in rescuing a severely wounded man from in front of the German trenches under a very heavy fire, and after a stretcher-bearer party had been compelled to abandon the attempt. Private Mackenzie was subsequently

killed on that day whilst in the performance of a similar act of gallant conduct" (*London Gazette,* 18th February, 1915). Withdrew to Sailly. Returned to front line (23rd).

IRISH GUARDS

"Mons" "Retreat from Mons" "Marne, 1914" "Aisne, 1914" "Ypres, 1914" "Langemarck, 1914" "Gheluvelt" "Nonne Bosschen"

1ST BATTALION

AUGUST

Wellington Barracks, London. Part of 4th (Guards) Brigade, 2nd Division. Entrained at Nine Elms Station (12th). Arrived Southampton and embarked SS *Novara*. Sailed for France. Officers – Lieutenant-Colonel Hon. G.H. Morris (Commanding Officer), Major H.F. Crichton (Second in Command), Captain Lord Desmond FitzGerald (Adjutant), Lieutenants E.J.F. Gough (Transport Officer), E.B. Greer (Machine Gun Officer), H. Hickie (Quartermaster), H.J.S. Shields (RAMC, Medical Officer), Hon. Aubrey Herbery, MP (Interpreter); No.1 Company: Captains Hon. A.E. Mulholland, Lord John Hamilton, Lieutenants Hon. H.R. Alexander, C.A.S. Walker, Second-Lieutenants N.L. Woodroffe, J. Livingstone-Learmonth; No.2 Company: Major H.A. Herbert-Stepney, Captain J.N. Guthrie, Lieutenants E.J.F. Gough, J.S.N. FitzGerald, W.E. Hope, Second-Lieutenant O. Hughes-Onslow; No.3 Company: Captain Hon. T.E. Vesey, Lieutenants Hon. Hugh Gough, Lord Guernsey, Second-Lieutenant Viscount Castlerosse; No.4 Company: Captains C.A. Tisdall, A. A. Perceval, Lieutenants W.C.N. Reynolds, R.Blacker-Douglass, Lord Robert Innes-Ker, Second-Lieutenant J.T.P. Roberts. Arrived Havre 6 am (13th) and marched to No.2 Rest Camp at Sanvic. Captain H.H. Berners joined. Entrained (14th) and arrived Wassigny during night (15th). Marched to Vadencourt (16th). Began advance (20th) marching via Etreux, Fesmy, Maroilles, Pont sur Sambre, Hargnies and arriving La Longueville (22nd). Moved 3 am (23rd), marching via Riez de l'Erelle, Blaregnies and Quevy le Petit to Harveng. Advanced to positions around Harmignes in support of 2nd Royal Irish Rifles. Battalion's first casualties – 5 men wounded from shelling. Covered retreat of forward troops from Mons area (24th) then at 2 am retired to Quevy le Petit. Entrenched defensive line between the Genly-Quevy le Petit road and Mons-Bettignies road. Held line during retreat of 2nd Division then retired via Blaregnies, Bavai and La Longueville to Malgarni. Continued retreat to Landrecies (25th). Relieved 3rd Coldstream in defensive positions north-west of Landrecies on the Mormal road during afternoon (26th). Later withdrew to Etreux. Enemy aircraft brought down by men of 3rd Coldstream after dropping bomb on Battalion`s position. Marched via Tupigny, Vandencourt and Noyales to Mont d`Origny. Moved via Châtillon, Berthenicourt and Moy to Vendeuil (28th). Covered withdrawal of 4th (Guards) Brigade at La Fère road cross-roads west of village then continued to Bertaucourt. Marched via Deuiuet, Servais, Folembray, Coucy-le- Château, Terny to Pasly (30th), Soucy (31st).

SEPTEMBER

Moved into the Villers-Cotterêts Forest (1st) and engaged advancing enemy. Rudyard Kipling in his war history of the Irish Guards, records that the fighting in the woods was "blind." The enemy coming on from all sides. He also notes how Lieutenant-Colonel Morris rode along the Battalion`s front "controlling, cheering and chaffing his men." Fell back in afternoon to position about 1 mile north of Pisseleux. Lieutenant-Colonel Morris, Major Crichton and Captain Tisdall had been killed. Two other officers were wounded, and 4 wounded and taken prisoner. Moved later to Betz. To Esbly (2nd), via Meaux to Pierre-Levée area (3rd). Dug in near Grand Lodge Farm on the Pierre-Levée-Giremoutiers road (4th). Relieved during evening and to Le Bertrand. To Fontenay (5th). Began advance to the Aisne, marching via Rozoy to Touquin (6th). Went forward via St. Siméon (7th) and bivouacked about 2 miles from Rebais. Advanced through Rebais (8th), crossing the Petit Morin and into Boitron. Engaged enemy in woods then to Ferme le cas Rouge. Crossed the Marne at Charly (9th) and advanced via Trenel, Villiers-sur-Marne, Cointicourt, Oulchy-le-Château and Courcelles to St. Mard. Crossed the Aisne at Pont d`Arcy (14th) and then to Soupir. Took part in attack on Cour de Soupir Farm. Captains Berners, Lord Guernsey and Lord Arthur Hay killed. Dug in around Soupir (15th) and held line under shell and sniper fire. Relieved by 3rd Coldstream (19th) and to billets at Soupir. Relieved 2nd Grenadier Guards in front line (21st). Relieved by 3rd Coldstream (23rd). Carried out further tours in front line, being relieved each time by 3rd Coldstream and resting at Soupir.

OCTOBER

Moved from Soupir Farm trenches (3rd) and relieved 3rd Coldstream in line east of Vailly. Rudyard Kipling recalls the deaths of 2 members of the Battalion. During the morning (5th), Private Michael O`Shaughnessy was killed by a sniper, the Guardsman having arrived with a draft only hours before. On the same day, Lieutenant G. Brooke was mortally wounded by a shell. Finding their officer, several of his men insisted on carrying him back to Vailly, making the RAMC stretcher-bearers walk behind. The men said goodbye and returning to their trenches wept as they left. Lieutenant

Brooke's last words to his men are recorded. He told them they were to "play the game" and not revenge his death on the Hun. Relieved by 3rd Coldstream (6th) and to Soupir. Lieutenant Brooke's body brought back to the Battalion and buried in Soupir cemetery. Relieved by French troops (13th) and to Perles. To Fismes (14th) and entrained for Hazebrouck. To Boeschepe (17th) and marched (20th) via Reninghelst and Vlamertinghe to Ypres. Later took over billets at St. Jean. Moved forward to Zonnebeke (21st) in support of 22nd Brigade. Relieved by French troops (23rd) and to Zillebeke. Moved forward (24th) to reinforce 20th Brigade at Hooge. Later moved to support positions at Polygon Wood. Advanced through Polygon Wood (25th). War Diary records Battalion fighting its way to within 200 yards north of Reutel and then coming under fire from enemy positions on a ridge. Casualties – 4 killed, 23 wounded. Attacked about 5.30 am (26th) but again forced to retire. Casualties – 9 other ranks killed, 42 wounded. Medical Officer Lieutenant Shields killed while attending wounded. Relieved by 3rd Coldstream during evening (27th) and to bivouacs on western side of Polygon Wood. Moved to Klein Zillebeke (30th) and dug in for night. War Diary records being under shell fire from 7 am to 11 pm. Lieutenant L.S. Coke killed. Rudyard Kipling records high casualties, especially among No.3 Company. Men were blown to pieces with no trace.

NOVEMBER
Heavily shelled again (1st) – No.3 Company position blown in with severe loss. Lieutenant G.M. Maitland killed. Enemy attacked during afternoon and drove survivors of No.3 Company back. Rest of Battalion retired and held enemy on edge of Zillebeke Wood. Casualties – Lieutenant K.R. Mathieson and 44 other ranks killed, Captain Mulholland mortally wounded, 4 officers, 205 other ranks wounded, 1 officer, 88 other ranks missing. Enemy broke through French line on right (6th) and took some ground. Counter-attack with 1st Life Guards regained most of lost trenches. Captain E.C.S. King-Harman, Lieutenants Hope and Woodroffe killed. Later fell back behind support lines. To front line (7th) and provided support fire during attack by 22nd Brigade. Major Herbert-Stepney killed. Relieved by 1st South Wales Borderers (9th) and marched via Zillebeke to bivouacs south of the Ypres-Zonnebeke road. Casualties for first week in November – 6 officers, 64 other ranks killed, 7 officers, 339 other ranks wounded, 3 officers, 194 other ranks missing. To Bellewaarde Lake (11th) and took part in fighting around Château Hooge. Moved to woods on the Gheluvelt road (12th) and dug-in just west of Veldhoek. Relieved by 2nd Royal Sussex (14th) then took over trenches from 1st South Wales Borderers at Klein Zillebeke same night . Several enemy attacks repulsed (17th).

Relieved by 3rd Coldstream (18th) and to billets at Potijze. To Meteren (21st).

DECEMBER

War Diary notes the issue of "American" pattern boots and records fears that the new footwear "may not stand the wear of the old Ammunition-Boot." Moved to Béthune (22nd). Relieved Indian troops in trenches near Le Touret (24th). Indian battalions included the 9th Gurkhas who, Rudyard Kipling points out, were much shorter than the average Guardsman. This, he records, necessitated numerous adjustments to fire steps and depth of trenches. The author also recalls the Christmas Truce as ". . . reaching the Battalion in severely modified form" – 2 officers and 6 men wounded (25th), 4 men wounded (26th). Also, on Boxing Day, British shells falling short killed 1 man and wounded 6. Captain Gough killed by stray bullet (30th).

THE ROYAL SCOTS (LOTHIAN REGIMENT)

"Mons" "Le Cateau" "Retreat from Mons"
"Marne,1914" "Aisne,1914" "La Bassée,1914"

1ST BATTALION

AUGUST
Allahabad, India.

OCTOBER
To Bombay (12th) and embarked HMT *Aragon* and *Neuralia*.

NOVEMBER
Arrived Plymouth (17th). Disembarked (20th) and to Mourne Hill Camp, Winchester. Joined 81st Brigade, 27th Division.

DECEMBER
Marched to Southampton (19th) and embarked SS *City of Dunkirk* for France. Commanding Officer – Lieutenant-Colonel D.A. Callender. Strength – 27 officers, 1,010 other ranks. Arrived Havre (20th) and to camp at Ste. Adresse. Entrained for Aire-sur-la- Lys (22nd) and from there to billets in French Army barracks at Château Moine. Commenced work digging line of defensive trenches.

2ND BATTALION

AUGUST
Plymouth. Part of 8th Brigade, 3rd Division. Lieutenant-Colonel H. McMicking, DSO in command. Moved by train to Southampton (13th) and embarked SS *Mombasa*. Arrived Boulogne and to rest camp at St. Martin. By train to Landrecies (15th) then to billets at Taisnières. To Dourlers (20th), via Maubeuge to Goegnies Chaussée (21st), Petit Spiennes (22nd). Dug defensive positions on Mons-Harmignies road and on right at Hill 93 near junction of Spiennes-St. Symphorien road. Enemy engaged and driven back during afternoon (23rd). War Diary records an attack in force – especially in front of "A" Company. Another attack between 7 and 8 pm also repulsed. Germans with lanterns seen searching for wounded after dark. Battalion's first casualties – Major G.S. Tweedie and 1 man wounded, 4 missing. Began withdrawal. Marched via Spiennes

to Nouvelles (24th) then to Bommeteau. Took up positions north of village. Relieved at 3 pm. and then to Bavai. Breakfasted in orchard at Amfroipret (25th) then marched via Le Quesnoy and Solesmes to Béthencourt. Here it began to rain and regimental historian Major John Ewing, MC records that French civilians came out and offered umbrellas to the men. Continued retreat via Caudry to Audencourt (26th). Dug defensive line east of village. Machine guns engaged enemy just to the north about 9 am. Village heavily bombarded. Transport, Pipes and Drums destroyed. Fell back to Elincourt during afternoon. Captain A.D. Shafto killed, 2 other officers wounded, 7 missing. Commanding Officer wounded and taken prisoner. Losses among other ranks high. "D" Company recorded as comprising just 17 men under Lieutenant M. Henderson. Marched via Vermand to Ham (27th). To Genvry (28th). Passed through Noyon (29th) and then through night via Autreches and Vic-sur-Aisne to Courtieux. Arrived Vaumoise (31st).

SEPTEMBER
Passed General Sir H.L.Smith-Dorrien (GOC. II Corps) at Lévignen (1st), who, Major Ewing records commented "There is not much wrong with that lot." Arrived at Villers St. Genest then ordered back 3 miles to outpost line on Betz-Fresnoy road. Withdrew about 2.30 am (2nd) and marched to billets at Monthyon. To Vaucourtois (3rd). Crossed the Grand Morin during evening (4th) and via Crécy Forest reached Châtres (5th). Later moved on to Retal where first reinforcements arrived under Captain A.M.C. Hewat. Began advance (6th), marching via La Houssaye, Crevecoeur and Crécy Forest to Courtoisoupe. To Chauffry (7th). Continued advance (8th). Came under shrapnel fire just west of Orly. Germans holding line in rear of canal. Advanced down hill and engaged enemy. Several prisoners taken. Captain Hewat killed, 20 other casualties. Left Orly (9th) and to Citry. Crossed the Marne during evening and to Crouttes. Marched via Vinly to Chezy (10th), Oulchy-la-Ville (11th), Braisne (12th). Came under shell fire at Chassemy (13th). Enemy had destroyed road and railway bridges across the Aisne. Battalion crosses via a narrow plank and moved into Vailly. Moved forward (14th). Fired on from close range then came under attack. Ground held but lack of ammunition forced withdrawal to ridge above Vailly. Line strengthened and held (15th). Captain C.L. Price killed and some 24 other casualties during heavy shelling (16th). Shelling continued. Patrols engaged small parties of Germans (22nd) and (23rd). Relieved by 1st Lincolnshire (25th) and to Courcelles. Inspection by General Smith-Dorrien (29th). War Diary records that he complimented the men on their turn out and spoke to several that he had served with in South Africa.

OCTOBER

Marched via Braine, Cuiry-Housse and Beugneux to Oulchy-le-Château (1st), via Rozet- St. Albin and Chouy to Trolesnes (2nd), via Marolles, Autheuil and Vaumoise to Crépy-en- Valois (3rd), via Duvy, Rully and Roberval to Moru (4th). War Diary records more men that usual fell out – probably owing to the cobbled roads. To Longueil Ste. Marie (5th) and entrained for Abbeville. Arrived during afternoon (6th) and marched to billets at Le Titre. Battalion paraded before Brigadier-General B.J.C. Doran (Commander 8th Brigade) (7th). War Diary records that he made reference to the "unnecessary" cases of falling out while on the march and to a certain amount of drunkenness. Marched through night (8th) to Raye. To Hesdin (9th) and on (10th) moved by motor lorries to Pernes. Marched via Auchel and Lozinghem during morning (11th), crossed La Bassée Canal during afternoon and then to Le Cornet-Malo. War Diary records that French Cavalry holding advanced positions nearby withdrew upon the Battalion's arrival. Moved to Les Lobes during morning (12th) and in afternoon advanced on Croix Barbée and Pont de Hem. Some casualties from German gun positioned in firing line. Enemy noted withdrawing through wood beyond canal. Crossed canal without opposition and took up positions on Fosse-Vieille Chapelle road. Casualties – about 70 including Lieutenant A.N. Trotter killed. Moved off 7 am (13th) – "A" and "C" Companies leading. "C" Company reached cross roads beyond Croix Barbée but isolated were forced to retire. War Diary records withdrawal to small village about 1 miles from Croix Barbée road.Casualties included Second-Lieutenants W.G. Hewitt and D.A. Kerr killed and 6 other officers wounded. Position held during (14th) with some 20 casualties. Major Ewing notes that the Battalion's position was dangerously exposed and that recent losses among experienced officers left it with just subalterns. War Diary records the death of Major-General H.I.W. Hamilton (Commanding 3rd Division) killed while walking along a road leading to the enemy's line. Captain G. Thorpe (Argyll and Sutherland Highlanders) took over temporary command (15th). Moved forward 2.15 pm. – attack held up by heavy machine gun fire from row of cottages some 500 yards west of Rouge Croix 5.15 pm. "A" and "B" Companies pushed forward during night and took positions on Pont du Hem – Neuve Chapelle road. Moved into reserve (16th) and to Aubers (17th). Lieutenant-Colonel H.B. Dyson took over command. To La Plouich (19th). Took up positions about 200 yards in front of Fauquissart- Neuve Chapelle road to cover withdrawal (22nd). German attack during night (24th/25th) repulsed. Second-Lieutenant R.C. Cowan killed (25th). War Diary records heavy rain and many rifles put out of action due to mud. Relieved by 2nd Suffolk (27th) and to reserve trenches near Rue de Bacquerot. Later to positions near Neuve Chapelle in preparation for attack. Attack cancelled and withdrew to billets at Rouge Croix. Moved forward (28th) and took part in attack on Neuve Chapelle. War Diary notes advance made difficult by machine gun and rifle fire from left front. Lieutenant R.M. Snead-Cox killed. Later ordered to retire and fell back to Pont Logy. Relieved by 6th Jats (30th) and to Baquerot Farm. Move at midnight (31st) and relieved 4th Middlesex in trenches at Baquerot.

NOVEMBER

War Diary (2nd) suggests that the Germans evidently understood the signalling system, as "misses" were indicated from their line after each shot fired by the Battalion's snipers. Also a strong attack on the 2nd Suffolk (3rd) which was repulsed. Relieved by 1st East Surrey (6th) and to Rue de Paradis. Arrived 4.15 am (7th), the relief taking considerable time due to enemy shelling and attack. Later marched to La Couture. Arrived 9 am, then ordered to Croix Barbée in support of 19th Indian Brigade. Relieved and to La Couture (8th). Later in afternoon returned to Croix Barbée and to La Couture (9th). In support of 19th Indian Brigade (10th-11th), returning to La Couture 5.30 am. Village came under heavy shell fire during afternoon then moved to billets at Richebourg St. Vasst in Corps Reserve. To La Couture (12th) and in afternoon relieved 1st Seaforth Highlanders in trenches facing Neuve Chapelle. Relieved by 1st Worcestershire (14th) and during night to La Couture. Moved 7.45 am (15th) to Bailleul. War Diary records march being 12 miles and through snow, sleet, rain and a driving wind. To Neuve Eglise (16th), the sight of a town (Bailleul) having been "appreciated" noted the War Diary, and then relieved 2nd Middlesex in line at Messines. Came under high explosive shrapnel fire while entering trenches – 2 killed and half of machine gun team wounded. Position noted as water filled and with no communication. There was shelling and sniping from both flanks all day. The men had to go without rations (17th) as supplies could not be brought forward. Relieved during night (18th) and to Neuve Eglise in Brigade Reserve. Relieved 2nd Suffolk in trenches in east of Wulverghem (21st). Reserve company billeted in village but moved to Neuve Eglise during day due to heavy shelling. War Diary (23rd) records death of one man asphyxiated by charcoal fumes from the braziers. Men of 1/1st Honourable Artillery Company attached for instruction in trenches. Suspected spy sent to Brigade Headquarters (26th), hands of clock on Wulverghem Church, War Diary records, were being used to signal to the enemy. Shell killed 4 and wounded 5 in trench (27th). Relieved by 1st Queen's Own Royal West Kent and to Neuve Eglise. Later marched to Westoutre. Casualties while in Messines sector – 9 killed, 58 wounded.

Inspected by Major-General J.A.L. Haldane (new GOC 3rd Division) (30th) then to Locre.

DECEMBER

Inspected by General Smith-Dorrien (1st) who informed the men that the campaign would end next June when the Germans had run short of ammunition. The General, War Diary records, was struck by the number of men in the Battalion that had done over 20 years service. He reminded them of their regimental history and the fact that the Regiment had served around Ypres as far back as 1650. Visited by HM King and HRH Prince of Wales (3rd). Later marched to Kemmel and took over front line trenches. War Diary records (5th) that trenches were very sodden and part of "D" Company were knee deep in water. The situation became worse when a field drain burst (6th) and flooded the remainder of "D" Company. Men now waist deep in water. Relieved 5 pm and via Kemmel and La Clytte marched to billets at Westoutre. Casualties since moving into line – 6 killed, 6 wounded. Relieved 1/10th King's Liverpool in Kemmel trenches (14th) then at 7.45 am took part in attack on Petit Bois. "C" and "D" Companies entered enemy's line at point of bayonet. Prisoners taken and position consolidated. "C" Company attempted further advance but forced back. Relieved by 2nd Suffolk during afternoon and moved back to position behind reserve trench. Later relieved by 1/10th King's Liverpool and to Kemmel. Casualties – Captain Hon. H.L. Bruce, Second-Lieutenant E.F. Mackenzie and 24 other ranks killed, Lieutenant T.S. Robson-Scott mortally wounded, 4 officers, 47 other ranks wounded, 28 missing. Private H.H. Robson awarded Victoria Cross for gallantry while rescuing wounded NCO under heavy fire. To Locre (15th). Visited by General Smith-Dorrien who commented – "Your charge was magnificent." To trenches at Kemmel (18th). Relieved by 1st Lincolnshire (21st) and to Westoutre. Casualties since going into line – 1 killed, 3 wounded. War Diary records (24th) – inter-company football match stopped due to bombing by enemy aircraft. To Kemmel trenches (27th). Relieved and to Westoutre (31st). Casualties since going into line – 5 killed, 2 wounded.

1/8TH BATTALION (TERRITORIAL FORCE)

AUGUST

Headquarters and "A" Company at Haddington, "B" Tranent, "C" Prestonpans, "D" North Berwick, "E" Dalkeith, "F" Loanhead, "G" Peebles, "H" Innerleithen. Part of Lothian Brigade with Scottish Coast Defences. Commanding Officer – Lieutenant-Colonel A. Brook,VD.

NOVEMBER

Received orders to proceed overseas (1st). Battalion strength made up to establishment by addition of 1 company from 1/6th Royal Scots at Edinburgh, and another supplied by 1/8th Highland Light Infantry from the Lanark area. Left Haddington for Southampton (2nd). Strength – 30 officers, 982 other ranks. Sailed SS *Tintorette* for France (4th), arriving Havre (5th). Entrained for St. Omer (6th). Arrived (7th) and from there marched to billets at Heuringhen. In his book *1914* Lord French remarks on the efficiency of the Territorials then in France and how the 1/8th Royal Scots were "so good" that they could soon be sent to the front. To Wallon-Cappel (10th), Merris (11th). Attached to 22nd Brigade, 7th Division. Began work digging communication trenches. To Fleurbaix (14th). Provided digging parties for front line La Boutillerie sector. Battalion's first casualty – Sergeant D. Grieve killed (15th). Began tours (under instruction) in trenches Touquet sector (16th). Relieved 1st Royal Welsh Fusiliers in Sub-Section No.6 (29th). Total casualties by end of month – 2 officers wounded, 2 other ranks killed, 8 wounded.

DECEMBER

Relieved by 1st Royal Welsh Fusiliers (8th). Relieved 1st Royal Welsh Fusiliers (14th). Captain T. Todrick killed. In support of attack by 2nd Queen's and 2nd Royal Warwickshire on German line near Bas Maisnil (18th). Battalion bombers employed and part of "A" Company. Lieutenant A. Burt killed, 2 others killed, 6 wounded. Relieved by 1st Royal Welsh Fusiliers (20th). Returned to trenches (24th). Draft of 1 officer and 82 other ranks arrived (25th). Relieved by 1st Royal Welsh Fusiliers (28th). Total casualties for month – 2 officers, 8 other ranks killed, 18 wounded, 2 missing. Strength – 23 officers, 858 other ranks.

Queen's (Royal West Surrey Regiment)

"Mons" "Retreat from Mons" "Marne, 1914"
"Aisne, 1914" "Ypres, 1914" "Langemarck, 1914"
"Gheluvelt"

1st Battalion

AUGUST

Bordon. Part of 3rd Brigade, 1st Division. Entrained for Southampton (12th) and sailed SS *Braemar Castle* for France. Officers – Lieutenant-Colonel D. Warren (Commanding Officer), Major H.C. Pilleau, DSO (Second in Command), Captains C.E. Wilson, E.B. Mathew-Lannowe, M.G. Heath, A.E. McNamara, C.F. Watson, S.F. Stanley-Creek, H.N.A. Hunter, F.C. Longbourne, A.M. Rose (RAMC, Medical Officer), Lieutenants R.L.Q. Henriques, M.V. Foy, B.M. Kenny, R.S. Pringle, J.D. Boyd, M.W.H. Pain, W.Hayes, H.E. Iremonger, G.H. Wallis (Quartermaster), Second-Lieutenants E.D. Drew, F.M. Eastwood, H.B. Strong, T.O.M. Buchan, H.J.P. Thompson, C. Bushell, V. Cooper. Arrived Havre during morning (13th) and to No. 6 Rest Camp. Entrained (15th) and via Rouen, Amiens and Arras arrived Le Nouvion 2.30 am (16th). Marched to billets at Leschelle. Moved via Le Nouvion and Barzy to Le Sart (20th), via Barzy, Beaurepaire, Cartignies and Dompierre to Les Bodelez (21st), via St. Aubin, Maubeuge and Bettignies to Croix-des-Rouveroy (22nd). Began entrenching 300 yards north of the Convent and on ridge just north of village. Later advanced to within ¼-mile of Mons and awaited orders. Returned to former positions after dusk. Ordered to retire (24th). Enemy cavalry patrol engaged – all men being hit by members of "B" Company at 400 yards. Battalion came under shell fire for first time. Fell back through Bettignies to Neuf Mesnil. Continued retreat via Hautmont, Limont-Fontaine, St. Rèmy, Dompierre and Marbaix to Le Grand Fayt (25th). To Favril (26th) and ordered to reinforce 1st (Guards) Brigade. Entrenched facing Landrecies then during afternoon ordered to retire. Fell back via La Groise to Oisy. At Oisy the Battalion suffered its first casualty. Lieutenant Pain being shot in the arm by a Frenchman who thought he was a German spy. To Bernot (27th) and during morning (28th) entrenched north of village. Relieved 1 pm and continued retirement via Ribemont, Sery and Brissy to Barisis. War Diary records that some 52 miles had been covered in a period of 16½ hours and with just 2½ hours rest. Two battalions had marched abreast most of the way. It was also noted that 8 miles of the journey had not been necessary, a Brigade Order having been mis-understood. In the several villages that the Battalion had passed through, one officer noted, the inhabitants showed a great deal of resentment. The retirement, they said, was leaving them to the mercy of the Germans. To Bertaucourt (29th), via St Gobain and Septvaux, to Brancourt (30th), via Anizy, Pinon and Soissons to Missy-aux-Bois (31st). German cavalry division reported moving towards Paris.

SEPTEMBER

Marched via the Forest of Villers-Cotterêts to bivouacs in the neighbour-hood of Le Ferté Milon (1st) and via Mareuil-sur-Ourcq and Varinfoy to Cregy (2nd). Crossed the Marne near Germigny and then via Sammeron to Perreuse Château. "A" Company remained at bridge to cover demolition party. Continued march via Aulnoy and Mouroux to bivouacs south of Coulommiers (4th) and via Maupertuis to Rozoy (5th). Draft of 90 men under Lieutenant W.A. Phillips arrived. Began advance towards the Aisne (6th). Moved to Les Hauts Grés Farm then to outpost positions north of Vaudoy. Two French civilians found killed. Both had been shot through the head, one man having had his hands tied behind his back. To Chauffry via Dagny and Chevru (7th) and via Choisy, La Boullaise, Jouy, Camp Martin and Grande March, to Hondevillers (8th). Second draft of 92 men arrived with Lieutenant F.W.H. Denton and Second-Lieutenant F.P.S. Rawson. Crossed the Marne at Nogent (9th) and moved on to Beaurepaire Farm 2½ miles north of Charly. Marched via Lucy, Torcy, Courchamps and Priex to Sommelans (10th), via Grisolles, Rocourt and Coiney to Villeneuve (11th), via Fere, Loupeigne, Bruys and Bazoches to Vauxcéré (12th). To Longueval (13th) and from there crossed the Aisne at Bourg. Moved to bivouacs on northern side of village. Marched via Moulins to Paissy (14th) and deployed north-east of the village. Later moved forward across the Chemin des Dames and into wood 150 yards north of road. Enemy's trenches noted on slopes ahead. Opened fire and inflicted heavy casualties on the enemy from 700-800 yards. Enemy returned fire and order given at 4 pm to fall back on the Chemin des Dames. Casualties – Lieutenant Henriques killed, Major Pilleau and Lieutenant Pringle mortally wounded, 8 officers wounded, 13 other ranks killed, 88 wounded, 39 missing. War Diary notes that British guns were just 30 yards to the rear – "they nearly blew our heads off each time they fired" noted one diarist. Road held all night – "D" and "C" Companies in front, "A" and "B" in support. Enemy attack repulsed 1 pm (15th). Casualties – 6 killed, 49 wounded. French on right retired (17th) and support companies sent forward to hold line to evening. Lieutenant-Colonel Warren killed by sniper, Captain Wilson mortally wounded. Enemy attack repulsed (18th). Relieved later and to Vendresse in reserve. Draft of 197 arrived under Lieutenants J.M. Rose-Troup and M.S. Pound. War Diary records (25th) British artillery shells falling short and causing 3 killed and 3 wounded among "C" Company. Enemy attacked at 4 am (26th). War Diary records that the advance was made while it was still dark, the Germans marching in fours across the Battalion`s front at a range of 200 yards. On the same day our artillery was again noted as firing short. Lieutenant Thompson and 20 men being wounded, 3 men killed. Relieved from firing line north of Troyon by 1st Coldstream (27th) and to billets at Oeuilly. Sir Douglas Haig visited Battalion (28th) and congratulated it on doing so well.

OCTOBER

To Verneuil (1st) – 2 companies moving into front line, 2 remaining in village as support. Colonel B.T. Bell, DSO joined and took over command (3rd). Enemy attack repulsed at 10 pm – 3 killed, 3 wounded. Lieutenant Foy killed by sniper (13th). Moved via Pont-Arcy, Vieil-Arcy and Yauxtin to Courcelles (16th). Entrained for Cassel (17th). Arrived (18th) and to billets at Hondeghen. To bivouacs in farm just west of Elverdinghe (20th). Marched via Elverdinghe and Boesinghe to Langemarck (21st) and deployed for attack on north- eastern side of village. "B" and "A" Companies in front line, "C" and "D" in support. Advanced under heavy fire during morning, digging in about 10.30 am. Fell back later with heavy casualties. Relieved during evening and to bivouacs just 400 yards south-west of Langemarck. Captain J.R.M. Thornycroft killed, Lieutenant Pound mortally wounded, 13 other ranks killed, 68 wounded, 6 missing. War Diary notes that most of the casualties were from shelling. Attached to 2nd Brigade, 1st Division (23rd) and advanced towards the Inn due north of Pilckem and on Bixschoote – Langemarck road. "A" Company on Right, "D" on left soon overran position inflicting heavy casualties on the enemy and releasing some 80 men of 1st Cameron Highlanders that had been taken prisoner. "D" Company then moved forward to ridge 400 yards north of the Inn and captured German trenches after hand to hand fighting. Over 100 prisoners taken. "A" Company held line running from the Inn to Langemarck road in support. An officer of the Battalion noted that at 5.30 pm firing was heard to the front and soon a group in column of fours approached from right front. The men were dressed in khaki and shouting in English. Suspecting that they were Germans, which they were, the officer gave the order to open fire. Another counter-attack repulsed later – Lieutenant M.D. Williams and 16 other ranks killed, 4 officers and 35 other ranks wounded, 89 missing. Repulsed 2 counter-attacks (24th) then relieved. Moved into billets at Hooge. Moved to wood near Bellewaarde

Farm (26th) then to another wood on north side of Veldhoek. To field near Bellewaarde Farm (27th) then Gheluvelt (29th). "D" and "C" Companies moved forward in support of 2nd Battalion, Queen's in line near Kruiseecke. "A" Company took part in failed attack on German line during afternoon. Second-Lieutenant Eastwood killed. Lieutenant Strong killed and Second-Lieutenant R.S. Schunck mortally wounded (30th). Colonel H.C. Wylly, CB noted in his history of the Queen's that 31st October "was one of the worst days experienced by the 1st Battalion during the whole war", some 624 men (including Captain Stanley-Creek, killed) becoming casualties during the fighting around Gheluvelt that day. Colonel Wylly gives the Battalion's strength after the battle as a total of 32. Most of these men being cooks and transport personnel.

NOVEMBER
Moved to support position at the Château near Gheluvelt (1st). To Bellawarde Farm (5th) and in support of attack by 1st Gloucestershire near Zwartelleen (7th). To Brielen (8th). Draft of 49 men received and Battalion organized into a single company. Strength – 2 officers, 179 other ranks. Removed from 1st Division and transferred to I Corps Headquarters. Marched via Poperinghe and Steenvoorde to Hazebrouck (21st). Several drafts arrived. Lieutenant-Colonel H. St. C. Wilkins assumes command.

DECEMBER
To Hinges (13th). Several drafts arrived and strength at (31st) – 26 officers, 450 other ranks.

2ND BATTALION

AUGUST
Robert's Heights, Pretoria, South Africa. Left for Cape Town (19th). Arrived (22nd) and embarked HMT *Kenilworth Castle*. Put out into Table Bay (23rd) and sailed for England (27th).

SEPTEMBER
Called at St. Helena (1st) and sailed again (2nd). Arrived Southampton (19th) and then to Lyndhurst. Joined 22nd Brigade, 7th Division.

OCTOBER
To Southampton (4th). Officers – Lieutenant-Colonel M.C. Coles (Commanding Officer), Major L.M. Crofts (Second in Command), Captain C.H.J. Wort (Quartermaster), Lieutenants C.R. Haigh (Adjutant),

A.C. Thomas (Transport Officer), R.L.G. Heath (Machine Gun Officer), F.G. Thatcher (RAMC, Medical Officer); "A" Company: Captains H.C. Whinfield, P.C. Esdaile, Lieutenants J.A.L. Browne, E.K.B. Furze, G.S. Ingram, Second-Lieutenant R.K. Ross; "B" Company: Major H.R. Bottomley, Captain H.F.H. Master, Lieutenant D.R. Wilson, Second-Lieutenants G.M. Gabb, C.H.B. Blount, J.G. Collis; "C" Company: Captains W.H. Alleyne, H.F. Lewis, Lieutenants E.W. Bethell, H.C. Williams, Second-Lieutenants R.H. Philpot, D.A. Brown; "D" Company – Captains T. Weeding, W.B. Fuller, Lieutenant G.A. White, Second-Lieutenants J.G.H. Bird, D. Ive. Battalion embarked in 2 parties – "A" and "B" Companies SS *Cymric* which sailed (5th), landed at Zeebrugge (6th) then by train to Oostcamp. "C" and "D" Companies sailed SS *Turkoman* (6th), landed (7th) and then to Oostcamp. To Bruges (8th) then to Nieuport Canal area. "C" Company in support at Istilles. To Ostend (9th), marching along railway line, then by train to Ghent. Arrived and to billets about a mile south of Hezewyek. Relieved Belgium troops in front of Melle (11th). Moving back to Ghent during night. To Hansbeke (12th) then via Lootenhulle to Thielt. To Roulers (13th), Ypres (14th). Men of "C" and "D" Companies fired on enemy aircraft which came down about 3 miles from town. To Zonnebeke (16th) and took up positions north-west of town along Langemarck road. To Dadizeele (18th) and took part in operations around Ledeghem. Captain Lewis killed (19th). Fell back to railway embankment near Zonnebeke, moving forward again to trenches east of the Passchendaele road during night (20th). Lieutenant Bethell killed (21st). Fell back to Zonnebeke during night and formed up near cross roads in centre of town. Casualties – 18 killed, 123 wounded, 37 taken prisoner. Took over line running south-east from level crossing south-west of Zonnebeke (22nd). Party of 250 men under Major Crofts (with 1st Royal Welsh Fusiliers) took part in raid on enemy line in Zonnebeke. Heavy fire forced withdrawal. "A" and "C" Companies to Veldhoek (24th) and began duties escorting prisoners to the rear. Rest of Battalion joined (25th). Moved forward to cross roads west of Gheluvelt (26th) then advanced. Soon forced to fall back to line in front of Gheluvelt-Zandvoorde road. Major Hon. Ralph Hamilton was serving in the area as an interpreter attached to the 7th Division and recalls in his diary (see *The War Diary of the Master of Belhaven*) how he was sent out to locate a French battalion to the left of 2nd Queen's. Making his way through the pitch dark night he eventually found the unit on the outskirts of Zonnebeke and returning to the Queen's line informed Colonel Coles. The two commanding officers were then brought together, and with Major Hamilton acting as interpreter, plans for the next day's operations were worked out. Recaptured trenches near Kruiseecke (27th) then to woods near Klein Zillebeke. To Veldhoek (29th) then moved forward to Gheluvelt. In action during morning and occupied a number of farms east of the Gheluvelt-Kruiseecke road. Reinforced by 1st Queen's during day. Casualties – 12 killed, 60 wounded, 20 missing. Captain Wilson killed, 90 other casualties (30th). Heavy shelling forced withdrawal to woods (31st). Casualties – 11 killed, 45 wounded, 22 missing.

NOVEMBER

Formed composite battalion with 1st Royal Welsh Fusiliers (1st). To billets in Hotel de Ville, Ypres (4th) then, due to heavy shelling, moved to positions 1½ miles outside town on Dickebusch. To bivouacs 1½ miles due north of Dickebusch (6th) then later in evening moved forward to assist 4th (Guards) Brigade in action at Zillebeke. Carried out successful attack (7th), driving the enemy back and capturing 3 machine guns. Held gains under heavy fire throughout day. Relieved and to Dickebush. Casualties – Captains Lewis, Master, Lieutenants Haig, Thomas, Wilson, Second-Lieutenants Ingram, Bird, Ive and 68 other ranks killed, 22 officers and 415 other ranks wounded, 163 men missing. To Merris (10th). Strength – 3 officers, 311 other ranks. Marched via Sailly and Fleurbaix to trenches at La Boutillerie (14th). Relieved by 2nd Royal Warwickshire (18th) and to Rue de Bataille in Divisional Reserve. War Diary records – "A good deal of stray bullets were flying about tonight as we left the trenches, every now and then we lose a man." Returned to trenches (20th). Relieved (23rd). War Diary records that at Rue de Bataille precautions were taken against frostbite. Many men were by then suffering with bad feet owing to the severe weather. To trenches (26th). Relieved (29th) – 2 companies to Rue de Biache, 2 companies to Rue de Bataille.

DECEMBER

To trenches just east of La Boutillerie (2nd). War Diary records white clothing being worn by raiding parties. Relieved and to Rue de Bataille (4th). To trenches west of La Boutillerie (8th). War Diary records (9th) the terrible condition of communication trenches. Three men had to be dug out of the mud during the night and it was noted that a preference was shown to walking in the open, and possibly be shot, rather than tackle the muddy communication trenches. Relieved and to Rue de Biache (15th). To trenches (18th) and with 2nd Royal Warwickshire took part in unsuccessful attack on German line near Bas Maisnil. Casualties – 8 officers, 89 other ranks. War Diary records (19th) a "local armistice." Parties from both sides came out to collect wounded and bury the dead. A German sniper, however, shot one man from the Battalion along with an officer from the 1st South

Staffordshire. Two officers and a party of 7 stretcher bearers were invited into the German trenches and were then taken prisoner. Relieved by 1st South Staffordshire (20th) and to Rue de Bataille. To trenches (23rd). During the armistice arranged for Christmas it was noticed that most of the Germans were from the 55th Regiment. A number of German Staff Officers came over who, the War Diary notes – "were quite a different class to the infantry officers, who were of a very low class." More German Staff Officers arrived (26th) and these, it was noted, were "immaculately dressed without a speck of mud on them." The Germans provided a list of British officers recently taken prisoner along with a request that relatives might be informed. Relieved by 1st South Staffordshire (28th) and to Rue Delpierre in reserve.

BUFFS (EAST KENT REGIMENT)

"Aisne,1914" "Armentières,1914"

1ST BATTALION

AUGUST

Fermoy, Ireland. Part of 16th Brigade, 6th Division. Left Ireland for England (12th), arriving Cambridge (19th). Billeted at Christ's College.

SEPTEMBER

To Southampton (7th) and embarked SS *Minneapolis*. Sailed for France (8th). Arrived St. Nazaire (9th) and to rest camp. Entrained (11th) and to Mortcerf. Began move forward (12th), marching via Crécy, Jouarres, Rocourt, Buzancy, Mont Notre Dame and arriving Courcelles (20th). Relieved 1st Northumberland Fusiliers and 4th Royal Fusiliers in front line trenches north-east of Vailly. Colonel R.S.H. Moody, CB in his war history of The Buffs, notes that the Battalion was on the left of 16th Brigade's line and holding positions on the crest of a plateau just beyond the Aisne. German line was between 200-700 yards away. Enemy attack repulsed – 2 officers wounded, 2 other ranks killed, 5 wounded.

OCTOBER

Relieved by French troops (12th) and to Bazoches. Entrained for Cassel (13th). Moved forward (17th) and took over Divisional Reserve positions at Bois Grenier. Later held line Croix Maréchal – Rue de Bois. With 2nd York and Lancaster advanced on Radinghem (18th). York and Lancaster records note that the battalions were divided by the Bois Grenier-Radinghem road. Village taken along with Château de Flandes. The latter, Colonel Moody records, ". . . . with severe hand-to-hand fighting." Fell back to wood south side of Radinghem after German counter-attack. Enemy attacked throughout day (20th) forcing withdrawal through Radinghem to Grande Flamengrie Farm during night. Casualties – Lieutenants J.D. Phillips, R. McDougall, R.S. Glyn and Second-Lieutenant M. Noott killed, Commanding Officer – Colonel J. Hasler and 3 other officers wounded, 17 other ranks killed, 57 wounded, 62 missing. The latter all believed killed. "A" and "C" Companies in action (23rd), engaged in hand-to-hand fighting during enemy counter-attack in front of Brigade line. Withdrew to line just south of the Le Touquet-La Boutillerie road (25th). "C" Company came under attack. Captain E.B. Chichester mortally wounded. "D" Company engaged enemy during evening. Casualties – Second-Lieutenant H.R. Stock and 5 other ranks killed, 2 officers, 20 other ranks wounded, 2 missing. Colonel Moody now records – "a long spell of comparative quite" in the trenches. Casualties averaging out to 2 killed, 5 wounded per day.

NOVEMBER
Relieved by 1st King`s Shropshire Light Infantry in trenches near Grande Flamengerie Farm (24th).

DECEMBER
Relieved 1st King`s Shropshire Light Infantry (9th), relieved by 1st King`s Shropshire Light Infantry (26th).

KING`S OWN (ROYAL LANCASTER REGIMENT)

"Le Cateau" "Retreat from Mons" "Marne, 1914" "Aisne, 1914" "Armentières, 1914"

1ST BATTALION

AUGUST

Dover. Part of 12th Brigade, 4th Division. Moved to Cromer in 2 trains (8th) and Norwich (10th). Billets in St. Andrews Hill area. To Horsham St. Faith (12th). "A"and "B" Companies billeted in the workhouse, "C" in the school, "D" in village. To Norwich (18th) and entrained for Wembley. Arrived 1.40 am and to camp in Neasden area. To Wembley (21st) and by train to Southampton. Embarked SS *Saturnia* and sailed for France 9 am (22nd). Arrived Boulogne 11 pm. Disembarked 6 am (23rd) and marched to rest camp at St. Leonards. Returned to Boulogne and entrained 9 pm. Strength – 26 officers, 974 other ranks. Arrived Bertry 10 am (24th) and to Ligny. Bivouacked north of village. Marched to Viesly during night. Came under shell fire during afternoon (25th) then at 9 pm moved via Béthencourt, Caudry and Ligny to Haucourt. Advanced (26th) moving via the Cattenières road and down slope across Warnelle Brook. Took up positions on high ground 6 am. Came under machine gun and shrapnel fire. Commanding Officer – Lieutenant-Colonel A. McN. Dykes, DSO killed. Colonel J.M. Cowper in his history of the King`s Own records that "C" Company were almost wiped out. Fell back to line in front of Haucourt. Another advance attempted about 8 am, but again driven back. Part of Battalion withdrew via Selvigny to Gouy. Remainder came under attack about 9.30 pm – enemy entering village but eventually driven out. War Diary records that the detachment in village retired about 11 pm, passing through German lines and rejoining rest of Battalion during afternoon (27th). Casualties – Lieutenant-Colonel Dykes, Captains F.G. Theobald, H. Clutterbuck, H.R. Sparenborg, Lieutenant C.S. Steel-Perkins and Second-Lieutenant L.S. Brocklebank killed, 4 other officers wounded, 2 missing, 431 other ranks killed, wounded or missing. Moved to cover withdrawal of 7th Division at Sancourt (28th). Later crossed the Sambre at Offoy then to Campagne. Continued retreat via Noyon to Sempigny (29th), to Fontenoy (30th) and to Verberie (31st).

SEPTEMBER

To Baron (1st) then marched through night to Dammartin. Left 10.30 pm (2nd) for Serris, marching via Lagny. "B" Company detached as escort to III Army Corps Headquarters. To Château Rothschild Ferrieres (4th) and during night to Brie-comte-Robert. Bivouacked 2 miles to the south on banks of the Yerres. Began advance (6th), Marching via Jossigny to Coupvray. Crossed the Grande Morin (7th) and to la Haute Maison. Continued advance (8th), moving in artillery formation north of la Haute Maison to Pierre Levée. Patrol under Lieutenant W.E.G. Statter engaged enemy with some casualties. Reached Jouarre about 12 am. As advance guard, went forward 1 pm towards La Ferté-sous-Jouarre. Part of "A" Company came under fire while crossing the Petit Morin. Two Uhlans killed and party advanced to crossroads in middle of town. "D" Company came forward under fire. Lieutenant L.S. Woodgate and 2 other ranks killed in the square. Colonel Cowper records that an attempt was made by Major R.G. Parker and some volunteers to reach Lieutenant Woodgate's body. The men had moved from the crossroads via back gardens on the right of the road. Moving into the square from the east side the party came under fire from across the Marne. Corporal J.C. Pike mortally wounded, Private S. Everson killed and Major Parker wounded. Battalion relieved by 2nd Royal Welsh Fusiliers during evening and fell back to reserve bivouacs. Moved forward to reserve positions near Luzancy (9th) and via Dhuisy and Coulombs to Vaux (10th). "B" Company rejoined from III Corps. Marched via Montigny to Billy-sur-Ourcq (11th) and via Tigny to billets in farm ½ mile north of Septmonts (12th). Moved to positions north of Billy-sur-Aisne (13th) and came under shell fire from direction of Croupy Venizel. Crossed the Aisne at Venizel and via Bucy-le-Long advanced to Ste. Marguerite. Dug in on hill north of village. German author Walter Bloem was with the 12th Brandenburg Grenadiers on the Chivres Spur and recalled the advance of the 12th Brigade in his book Vormarch (The Advance from Mons, 1914) – "Stretched out across the broad expanse of meadows between us and the river was a long line of dots wide apart, and looking through glasses one saw that these dots were infantry advancing, widely extended . . . A field battery on our left spotted them, and we watched their shrapnel bursting over the advancing line. Soon a second line of dots emerged from the willows along the river bank, at least ten paces apart, and began to advance. More of our batteries came into action; but it was noticed that a shell, however aimed, seldom killed more than one man, the lines being so well and widely extended. Our guns now fired like mad, but it did not stop the movement: a fifth and sixth line came on, all with the same wide intervals between and same distance apart. It was magnificently done."War Diary records being shelled nearly all day (14th), 2 men killed (15th), village heavily shelled (24th), enemy gun 1,000 yards due north "opened accurate fire" (29th).

OCTOBER

To trenches at Missy-sur-Aisne (2nd). Relieved and to Septmonts (6th). Moved forward to Chacrise (8th) and now in support of French troops holding line between Bucy and Ciry. Travelled in French lorries to Le Meux (11th), then by train to Hazebrouck (12th). Took part in attack on Meteren (13th). Leading company reached outskirts of Meteren about 2 pm. War Diary records heavy Maxim and rifle fire from the enemy ". . . who had excellent field of fire." Shelled at close range about 4 pm but trenches held. Relieved (14th) and to Bailleul. Casualties – Lieutenant A.G.A. Morris, Second-Lieutenant A. Waterhouse and 44 other ranks killed, 2 officers and 32 other ranks wounded and missing, 15 other ranks missing. Moved forward (15th) and held in support during 11th Brigade's attack on Erquinghem. To support line at Petit Pont (16th) and took part in attack on Le Touquet (18th). Moved forward via Ploegsteert to line on Le Bixet-Le Touquet road. War Diary records railway being taken "without much opposition." Later came under heavy fire from enemy trenches across river. Positions held from Le Touquet as far as crossroads by evening. Casualties – Major J.H. Morrah killed and 5 other ranks wounded. "C" Company moved forward to new line (19th) and came under attack at dawn (20th). Enemy gained strong hold in line and company forced to retire to line on Le Gheer-Le Touquet road. "A" Company later sent forward as reinforcement. Another counter-attack (21st) forced "A" and "C" Companies back 200 yards. Battalion relieved (22nd) and to bivouacs at Le Bizet. Casualties (20th-21st) – Major N.L.S. Lysons, Captain P.B. Lendon and Second-Lieutenant P. Heaney killed, 4 other officers wounded, 2 wounded and missing, 21 other ranks killed, 78 wounded, 76 missing. To la Chapelle d' Armentières (23rd). "D" Company in front line assisting 2nd Essex near railway. Relieved 2nd Lancashire Fusiliers in front line – Rue de Bois to Lille road during night (24th). Section of "D" Company sent to assist 2nd Durham Light Infantry in front line to left of railway (27th). Enemy attack repulsed. Casualties – 2 officers wounded 3 other ranks killed. Battalion relieved by 2nd Lancashire Fusiliers 6 pm and to la Chapelle d' Armentières. Relieved 2nd Lancashire Fusiliers in front line (29th).

NOVEMBER

Relieved by 2nd Essex and to la Chapell d' Armentières (6th). Went forward to Le Bizet (7th) in support of 1st Rifle Brigade holding line running from the Lys near Frélinghien via Le Touquet to cross roads about ½ mile south of Le Gheer. Took over line from 1st Rifle Brigade (10th). Relieved by 2nd Lancashire Fusiliers (29th) and to Armentières.

DECEMBER

Inspected by HM The King at Nieppe (2nd). Relieved 2nd Lancashire Fusiliers in trenches (3rd). Relieved by 2nd Lancashire Fusiliers and to Armentières (7th). Relieved 2nd Lancashire Fusiliers (10th). Second-Lieutenant R.A.C. Aitchison mortally wounded (13th). Relieved by 2nd Lancashire Fusiliers and to Le Bizet (15th). Relieved 2nd Lancashire Fusiliers (20th). Relieved by 2nd Lancashire Fusiliers and to Le Bizet (24th). Relieved 2nd Lancashire Fusiliers (28th).

NORTHUMBERLAND FUSILIERS

**"Mons" "Le Cateau" "Retreat from Mons"
"Marne, 1914" "Aisne, 1914" "La Bassée, 1914"
"Messines, 1914" "Armentières, 1914" "Ypres, 1914"
"Nonne Bosschen"**

1ST BATTALION

AUGUST

Cambridge Barracks, Portsmouth. Part of 9th Brigade, 3rd Division. Moved in 2 trains to Southampton (13th) and embarked SS *Norman*. Sailed for France 4 pm. Disembarked Havre 5 am (14th) and marched to rest camp. Officers – Lieutenant-Colonel H.S. Ainslie (Commanding Officer), Major C. Yatman, DSO (Second in Command), Captains H.S. Toppin, H.R. Sandilands, R.F. Gatehouse, J.H. Matthews, B.T. St. John, E.L.D. Forester, B.H. Selby, W.N. Herbert (Adjutant), A. Landen (Quartermaster), M. Leckie (RAMC, Medical Officer), Lieutenants R.M. Booth, H.L. Ovans, G.O. Sloper, C.T.S. Cogan, F.E. Watkin (Machine Gun Officer), H.O. Sutherland, R.T. Vachell, B.G.C. Hobbs, C.L.C. Hodgson, Second-Lieutenants L.A. Barrett, E.F. Boyd, B.G. Gunner (Transport Officer), E.E. Dorman-Smith, A.B. Surtees, E.S. Swaine (Cyclist Company), A.F. Geddes. Travelled by train via Rouen and Busigny to Landrecis (16th). Arrived 11.30 pm. Men billeted in French army barracks, officers at a girls` school. To Noyelles (17th), La Longueville (21st). Advanced towards Mons (22nd). Reached Genly then "B" and "C" Companies moved to left of line and taking up outpost positions on the Mons-Condé Canal running between Jemappes and Mariette. "A" and "D" Companies placed into Brigade Reserve at Cuesmes. War Diary records "C" Company coming under heavy shell fire about 11 am (23rd) and "B" Company around noon. Rifle fire followed from the front, the enemy massing in large numbers and bringing 2 field guns forward to within 150 yards. Withdrawal ordered. "A" and "D" Companies covering retirement from outskirts of Cuesmes. The Battalion eventually assembling at Frameries and taking up defensive positions. Casualties – 8 other ranks killed, 11 wounded. During the enemy`s attack on the bridgehead at Mariette 2 men, Privates Green and Batton, became isolated. Undetected they were able to observe the Germans marching across the bridge continuously for 3 hours before making an escape. War Diary records (24th) that the enemy opened with heavy shell fire about 3.30 am – ". . . the British guns being unable to respond for some time." An infantry attack about 7 am was held off, but troops on both flanks were forced to retire. The 9th Brigade was also ordered to fall back, moving via Frameries, where street fighting took place, to positions some 4 miles west-south-west of the town. Casualties – 2 officers wounded, 3 other ranks killed, 32 wounded. Moved on to Bermeries during evening. Continued retreat to Inchy (25th), taking up defensive positions south of the town (26th). War Diary records that these had been dug prior to arrival and were unsuitable. Began entrenching and improving line then came under bombardment. Enemy came forward in force about 2 pm and withdrawal ordered. Fell back under heavy fire to a field behind Audencourt. Retirement was over 600 yards of open ground. Casualties – 3 officers wounded, 2 other ranks killed, 18 wounded. Acted as rearguard to 9th Brigade, marching through night and arriving at Hargicourt mid-day (27th). Later moved on to Vermand. Resumed march 11.30 pm and arrived at Crisolles 3 pm (28th). Left bivouacs 6 pm (29th) and arrived at Bresson le Long 6.30 pm (30th). Moved to Vauciennes (31st).

SEPTEMBER
Continued retreat to Bouillancy (1st), Penchard (2nd), Villemareuil (3rd). Marched throughout night, arriving Châtres 7.30 am (4th). Advanced to Lumigny (6th) and La Martroy (7th). Moved forward 6 am (8th). War Diary records – ". . . engaged in a skirmish at Orly." Some prisoners taken. Machine guns in action with 8th Brigade. Billeted for night at Les Feuchères. Crossed the Marne at head of 9th Brigade (9th). War Diary records wood fighting throughout day delayed advance. Casualties – 3 killed, 12 wounded. Dug in for night near Ventrelett Farm. Moved forward 5.30 am (10th) and engaged enemy holding woods near Veuilly. "A" and "B" Companies led advance, "C" in support, "D" in reserve. War Diary records a stream waist deep in the middle of the wood had to be crossed. Several enemy snipers were killed and some prisoners taken. Reached Dammard about 4 pm. Moved to Grand Rozoy (11th) and Brenelle (12th). took up positions to the east covering advance of 3rd Division (13th). Later crossed the Aisne and moved into billets at Vailly. Moved forward in support of 4th Royal Fusiliers in line near Rouge Maison (14th). Enemy attacked in force at dawn forcing "C" Company on the right to retire. "A" and "B" Companies also driven back after engaging enemy in wood to the left. Battalion assembled in sunken road about 200 yards south of Rouge Maison. Casualties – Captains Toppin and Gatehouse killed, 4 other officers wounded, 7 other ranks killed, 80 wounded. Shelled throughout day (15th). Enemy attack during night repulsed. Casualties – Captain Matthews killed, Lieutenant Geddes and 3 men wounded. Positions held and improved

(16th-17th). Casualties – 3 killed, 12 wounded. Second-Lieutenant E.H. Tottie arrived with draft (16th). Observation post at corner of wood 300 yards to left of line came under attack about 4 pm (18th). Enemy gained hold, but later driven out. Casualties – 2 killed, 1 wounded. Came under attack (19th). Casualties – 3 killed, 14 wounded. War Diary records (20th) enemy snipers from north edge of wood caused high casualties – Second-Lieutenant Boyd killed, Captain Selby and Lieutenant Tottie mortally wounded, 3 other ranks killed, 5 wounded. Wood "cleared by maxim gun." Relieved by 4th Middlesex (21st) and moved back to Courcelles. Relieved 4th Middlesex at Vailly (26th), "C" and "D" Companies taking up forward position north of the village. "A" and "B" Companies attached to 16th Brigade (27th) and to positions 3 miles to the east.

OCTOBER

Relieved (1st). Battalion withdrew via Vailly, assembling south of the Aisne and then marching to billets at Augy. Moved to Cramaille (2nd), Troesnes (3rd), Crépy-en-Valois (4th), Moru (5th). Entrained for Abbeville at Pont-Ste. Maxence (6th). Arrived (7th) and marched via Grand Leviers to Pont-le-Grand. To Tollent (9th) and at midnight Ste. Austreberthe. Later travelled in buses to Sachin. Marched to Robecq (11th) and billeted for night behind Mt. Bernenchon south of the La Bassée Canal. Moved to Vieille Chapelle in support of 8th Brigade (12th), withdrawing to Paradis at dusk. Advanced to Zelobes (13th) then in afternoon took part in attack on Bout Deville. War Diary records – ". . . not much progress was made." Dug in on line of Rue de Ponch. Casualties – 8 other ranks killed, 1 officer, 18 other ranks wounded. Continued attack (14th) pushing enemy back from Bout Deville by late afternoon. Casualties – 4 killed, 33 wounded. Assisted French cavalry in taking Riez Bailleul during morning (15th) and, with 4th Middlesex and 1st Gordons, cleared enemy from Pont du Hem. Continued advance to the east, pushing all opposition back and occupying German trenches along Neuve Chapelle-Estaires road by dusk. Marched via Le Flenque to Fauquissart (16th) then "Z" and "W" Companies, with 4th Royal Fusiliers, took up positions for attack on Aubers. Attack cancelled due to fog and Battalion billeted at Fauquissart. Advanced 7 am (17th). Entering Aubers by 11 am. "W" and "X" Companies took up positions overlooking Fromelles on high ground to the north. Came under heavy shell fire. All attempts to enter village being driven back to line about 500 yards to he south. French artillery opened fire about 12.30 pm forcing the enemy from their cover. Captain H.R. Sandilands (later Brigadier) records in his war history of the 1st and 2nd Battalions that the Germans ". . . fled into the open to fall victims to the rifles of the Fifth." Relieved by 2nd Royal Irish

Regiment and to billets at Bas Pommereau. Casualties – 3 other ranks killed, 7 wounded. Went forward under heavy shell fire to Herlies 6 am (18th). "W" and "X" Companies went into reserve west of village, "Y" and "Z" dug in on ridge to the south west. Enemy observed in large number some 800 yards ahead in Le Pilly. "W" and "X" Companies attacked enemy line on Illies-Fournes road but soon ordered to withdraw. Casualties – 1 killed, 9 wounded. "W" and "Z" Companies took over defensive line west of Herlies (19th). War Diary records "Z" Company being shelled and both companies engaging the enemy throughout day. "X" and "Y" Companies also engaged on ridge and later forced to withdraw. Casualties – 2 killed, 30 wounded. Herlies heavily shelled 9 am (20th). Enemy came forward 10 am but driven back by rifle fire from "W" and "Z" Companies. Second-Lieutenant C.H. Van Neck and 8 other ranks killed, 3 officers and 41 other ranks wounded. Attack renewed in afternoon. Headquarters, "W" and "Z" Companies withdrew to line ½ mile from Herlies and across the Aubers road during evening. Marched to La Cliqueterie 10 pm (21st) then at dawn (22nd) to Piètre. "X" and "Y" Companies also withdrew and joined rest of Battalion at Piètre. Moved at 8.55 am to Bois de Biez, returning to Piètre during evening then at midnight to Divisional Reserve at Rue du Bacquerot. Captain Sandilands records that the Battalion's billets were "dangerously close to the front line" and shelter trenches were dug on the outskirts of the village. Two killed and 5 wounded from shelling (23rd). Moved to billets at Rouge Croix (24th). Casualties (21st-24th) – 6 killed, 13 wounded. Advanced 1 mile to support 2nd Royal Irish Rifles (25th). Battalion not required and ordered back to Rouge Croix. Relieved 1st Lincolnshire in trenches facing Neuve Chapelle early morning (26th). Second- Lieutenant A.V. Laws killed by sniper. This officer had recently been promoted from Company Sergeant Major. "Z" Company on right of line came under shell fire 3 pm followed by an infantry attack 3.30 pm. Enemy entered trenches on right, but driven off. Another attack during night also repulsed. War Diary records the gallantry of Lance Corporal Fish, who under fire put out a fire lit by the enemy under a gun limber, and Lieutenant C.F. Nunnerley (King's Own Yorkshire Light Infantry attached) who was killed while leading a charge. Captain Sandilands records that Captain Gordon rallied the survivors of Lieutenant Nunnerley's party and drove the enemy off "killing many." Another attempt to get forward was held up by wire – 3 men being killed and Captain Gordon receiving a bullet through his cap from a range of 15 yards. "Y" Company relieved "Z" in front line during night. War Diary (27th) records heavy sniping and Headquarters moved back 500 yards. Relieved by 2nd Gurkha Rifles during night (29th) and to Vieille Chapelle. War Diary records relief difficult and under fire. Casualties (26th-29th) – Captains J.M. Lambert and A. Barnsley (Lancashire Fusiliers attached), Lieutenants C. Leather and C.F. Nunnerley, Second-Lieutenants D.M. Coles and A.V. Laws killed, 121 other ranks killed, wounded or missing. Moved to billets in farms about 1½ miles north west of Estaires (30th), Lindenhoek (31st).

NOVEMBER
Took part in counter-attack on Wytschaete (1st), "W" and "X" Companies moving forward with 1st Lincolnshire on the right, "Y" and "Z" Companies in support. Captain Sandilands records seeing the Lincolnshire disappear into the darkness and wire holding up the advance. On the left, "X" Company came under strong rifle and machine gun fire from wood north-west of village. "W" Company also hit while moving forward between southern edge of wood and Kemmel-Wytschaete road. Withdrawal ordered. Relieved by 16th Lancers 11 am and fell back to Kemmel. Later, at 4 pm, moved to billets in farms between Mont Kemmel and Locre. Casualties – Captain R.S. Fletcher and Lieutenant E.J. Lamb (King's Own Yorkshire Light Infantry attached) killed, 2 other officers wounded and 1 missing, 83 other ranks killed, wounded or missing. Marched via Locre and Dranoutre to billets on south-western outskirts of Bailleul (3rd). Inspected by General Sir Horace Smith- Dorrien (4th). Moved to support positions 1 mile east of Ypres (6th). Took over trenches at Herenthage Wood on high ground over-looking Herenthage Château (7th). Positions held by "W", "X" and "Y" companies heavily bombarded 11.30 am. War Diary records that trenches were not deep enough and that several men were buried. Enemy attacked and 2 trenches on right of line lost. Counter-attack led by Captain Booth failed. Casualties – 2 officers and 153 killed, wounded or missing. War Diary records that line was readjusted during night and was then held by the whole battalion which now comprised about 200 all ranks. Captain Sandilands confirms this figure and points out that of the original officers that left England just 4 remained – Major Yatman, Captain Landen and Lieutenants Barrett and Gunner. Of the several officers later sent out or promoted from the ranks some 19 had become casualties. Enemy attack 5.30 pm (8th) repulsed with great losses. Captain Sandilands notes that the men "behaved with great coolness and judgement." Line held under shell and rifle fire (9th–10th). Enemy attack 8.30 am (11th) repulsed but 4th Royal Fusiliers line to the left taken. War Diary records Battalion now fired on from 15 yards. Also (12th) "quite day" – 2 of the 3 machine guns put out of action by rifle fire. Withdrew to new position in dugouts near gate leading to Herenthage Wood (13th). "W" Company assisted in retaking captured trenches in front of Herenthage Château (14th). Enemy attacked and took Château stables (15th). Party of 50 men under Company Sergeant Major

Gilborn counter-attacked and regained position. Headquarters, "W" and "Y" Companies relieved 10 pm by 5th Dragoon Guards and withdrew to positions 500 yards east of Hooge. "X" and "Z" Companies relieved by 2nd Dragoon Guards (16th). Moved to billets on main road near Hooge 8.30 am (17th). One officer and 100 men sent forward to Herenthage Wood during afternoon. Officer and 75 men returning same night. Moved to Herenthage Wood in support and reserve (18th). Relieved 2nd King`s Own Yorkshire Light Infantry in front line south of Herenthage Château 5.30 pm. Relieved 8.30 pm (19th) and moved back to reserve line. Relieved 11 pm (20th) and marched via Ypres and Dickebusch to Westoutre. Taking over billets about 1 mile west of town. Draft of 5 officers and 291 other ranks arrived (21st). War Diary records (25th) the issue of fur jackets and the "dilemma" of whether to wear them over or under the greatcoats. Inspected by Field-Marshal Sir John French (26th). Marched via Locre to trenches north of Kemmel (27th). Relieved and to Westoutre (30th). War Diary records casualties for November as 366 killed, wounded or missing.

DECEMBER
Continued tours Kemmel sector trenches throughout December. Captain Sandilands records that the programme was usually 3 days in line with 3 days in reserve, either at Locre or Westoutre. He also notes that the front line occupied by the Battalion was 560 yards in length and held by 395 men. This would be supported by a 130- yard line with 50 men and 200 yards of reserve dugouts holding 180 men. War Diary records (12th) the return of Lieutenant-Colonel Ainslie from sick leave, and the shelling of "W" and "X" Companies who lost 5 killed and 8 wounded. Battalion spent Christmas at Locre and returned to the trenches (31st). Its fighting strength being recorded as 772. Casualties for December – 8 killed, 11 wounded.

ROYAL WARWICKSHIRE REGIMENT

"Le Cateau" "Retreat from Mons" "Marne, 1914"
"Aisne, 1914" "Armentières, 1914" "Ypres, 1914"
"Langemarck, 1914" "Gheluvelt"

1ST BATTALION

AUGUST

Shorncliffe. Part of 10th Brigade, 4th Division. Headquarters, "A" and "B" Companies moved by train to York (8th) and moved into billets in the grandstand at Knavesmire Racecourse. Moved later to York railway station. "C" and "D" Companies moved same day to Cromer, joining rest of the Battalion (9th). Marched to Strensall Camp (14th). Returned to York (18th) and entrained for Harrow. Arrived 8 pm and marched to camp at Harrow Weald. To Southampton (21st). Arrived (22nd), embarked SS *Caledonia* and sailed for France. Arrived Boulogne 8 pm and remained on board. Moved to camp on outskirts of town (23rd). Left Boulogne by train 11.30 pm, arriving Le Cateau 10.30 am (24th) and marching forward to Beaumont. Moved via Viesly to St. Python during morning (25th). Withdrew later to defensive positions at Fontaine-au-Tertre Farm. Covered withdrawal of 18th Brigade, then at 11 pm fell back via Beauvois to Haucourt, taking up positions facing the Haucourt-Ligny road. War Diary records (26th) – heavy Maxim Gun fire on 1st King's Own and 2nd Lancashire Fusiliers holding ridge 800 yards to Battalion's front. Enemy later occupied ridge and the Warwickshires moved forward as reinforcement. Unable to hold their position, the men were forced to withdraw and dig in along the Haucourt-Ligny road. Battalion's left flank on the eastern edge of Haucourt, its right just beyond the Cattenières-Caullery bridlepath. Casualties – 7 officers, wounded, 40 other ranks killed, wounded or missing. Held line for rest of day having received no orders to withdraw. War Diary records that Major H.J. Poole become aware of a general retreat about 7.30 pm – the enemy at this time being on 3 sides of his position. The Battalion was now split up – records the War Diary (27th). "A" Company had moved off as escort to a battery of guns, while Major Poole's detachment, having got away marched via Caullery, Elincourt, Malincourt, Villers Outrèaux, Gouy, Bony, Ronssoy, Jeancourt, Bernes, Matigny, Noyon to Compiègne. The Commanding Officer – Lieutenant-Colonel J.F. Elkington, and 60 men fell back via Ligny to St. Quentin where at the Mayor's request he surrendered. This, however, was later withdrawn, and the Colonel – "left the town alone." The men, under Lieutenant C.P. Cowper, went on to Ham and from there, having been joined by another party under the Adjutant, Captain J.A.M. Bannerman, went by train to Compiègne. War Diary records (28th) that Lieutenant-Colonel Elkington, with 280 men, rejoined 10th Brigade at Voyennes. The records of 2nd Royal Dublin Fusiliers note how that battalion was temporally amalgamated with 1st Royal Warwickshire at Roisel (27th) then marching via Tertry, Monchy-Lagache, Guizancourt, Croix and Matigny, arrived at Voyennes 4 am (28th). Major Poole's party arrived at Rouen (29th) then proceeded to Le Mans to refit. Headquarters left Voyennes and arrived at Bussy (29th). Moved to Berneuil (31st).

SEPTEMBER

To Néry (1st) then withdrew later via Rully to Baron. Marched to Dammartin (2nd), Lagny (3rd), Magny (4th). Major Pool's party rejoined at Brie-compte-Robert (5th) and Battalion separated from 2nd Royal Dublin Fusiliers. Moved forward to Villers-sur-Morin (6th). Crossed the Petit Morin (7th) and took up positions on high ground north of Crécy covering the crossing of 4th Division. Moved later to Giremoutiers. Bivouacked for night at Hotel de Bois (8th). To Les Poupelans (9th), Hervilliers (10th), Villers-le-Petit (11th), Septmonts (12th). Crossed the Aisne at Venizel (13th) then to Bucy-le-Long. Relieved 1st Hampshire in firing line at Le Moncel (18th). War Diary records airship sighted near Bois-de-Chuny (29th).

OCTOBER

Relieved (6th) and marched via Bucy-le-Long, Venizel and Septmonts to Hartennes. To Rozet St. Albin (7th), Vauciennes (8th), Rully (9th), Verberie (10th). Entrained at Longueil (11th). Arrived St. Omer 5 am (12th), leaving in buses for Caestre 6.30 pm. Took part in the attack on Meteren (13th). Outskirts gained by 1 pm, then, War Diary records – held up due to lack of support. "C" and "D" Companies noted as moving forward later – taking several trenches, but with heavy loss. Withdrew during evening to reserve trenches. Casualties – Major W.C. Christie killed, Lieutenant C.G.P. Gilliat mortally wounded, 3 officers wounded, 42 other ranks killed, 85 wounded. Among the wounded officers was Lieutenant (later Field-Marshal) B.L. Montgomery. Moved into Meteren (14th). To Bailleul (15th), Le Leuthe (16th), Armentières (17th). Moved forward to firing line at Houpelines (18th) and in action throughout day. War Diary notes (21st) – "Battles raging all round – 11th and 12th Brigades get forward north-west of River Lys. 17th Brigade retired a little during the night to improve their line which left our right flank very much in the air." Captain C.A.S. Bentley mortally wounded (23rd). War Diary records (28th) – "We get 1 officer and 3 Germans at sniping and they only get 1 man of ours, (so we finished 3 up) – Fine." Attack by part of "D" Company during night (30th) failed.

NOVEMBER

Second-Lieutenant D.W. Rennie (Royal Fusiliers attached) killed (11th). Part of Battalion relieved by 2nd Argyll and Sutherland Highlanders (17th) and to Pont de Nieppe. Rest relieved by 2nd Leinster (18th). Casualties since 18th October – 2 officers, 11 other ranks killed, 2 officers, 61 other ranks wounded. To billets at Armentières (20th). Moved forward into Brigade Reserve trenches – St. Yves sector (21st). Relieved 2nd Royal Dublin Fusiliers in firing line (22nd). Relieved by 2nd Royal Dublin Fusiliers (26th) and to Brigade Reserve. To Pont de Nieppe (27th), Brigade Reserve (29th), firing line at St. Yves (30th).

DECEMBER

Relieved by 2nd Royal Dublin Fusiliers (4th) and to Brigade Reserve line. To Nieppe (5th), Brigade Reserve (7th). Relieved 2nd Royal Dublin Fusiliers in firing line (8th). Moved back to Brigade Reserve (12th), Divisional Reserve at La Crèche (13th). To Brigade Reserve at St. Yves (15th). Relieved 2nd Royal Dublin Fusiliers in firing line (16th). War Diary records (19th) – "Some casualties from our own gunners." Relieved by 2nd Royal Dublin Fusiliers (20th) and to Brigade Reserve. To La Crèche (21st), Brigade Reserve (23rd). Relieved 2nd Royal Dublin Fusiliers in firing line (24th). War Diary notes (25th) – "Local truce – intermingled between trenches – dead in front of trenches buried." Relieved by 2nd Royal Dublin Fusiliers (28th) and to Brigade Reserve. To La Crèche (29th).

2ND BATTALION

AUGUST
Malta.

SEPTEMBER
Arrived England (19th) and to Lyndhurst. Joined 22nd Brigade, 7th Division.

OCTOBER
To Southampton (4th) and embarked SS *Cymric*. Arrived Zeebrugge (6th) then by train to Oostcamp. Marched via Bruges to Zandvoort (8th), to Ostend (9th) then by train to Ghent. Bivouacked on outskirts of town. War

Diary records (10th) that heavy firing was heard during early morning – Belgian artillery moving up. Battalion advanced and took up entrenched positions – Belgian troops on the right, French on the left. Enemy opened fire about 8 pm – War Diary records that the French immediately withdrew – "to a position from where they could conveniently enfilade our line." Corporal R. Element wounded, Private J. Swift – "accidently killed by a man of the 1st Royal Welsh Fusiliers." Withdrew 8.30 pm (11th) and marched via Ghent to Hansbeke. To Thielt (12th), Roulers (13th), Ypres (14th), Zonnebeke (16th), via Veldhoek to Becelaere (18th). Took part in attack at Dadizeele (19th) – Charles Lethbridge Kingsford recording in his book *The Story of the Royal Warwickshire Regiment* that the village was passed without opposition, but as the Battalion approached Kezeberg it came under heavy shell-fire. Kezeberg was cleared, however, and the advance continued towards Kleythoek. Later ordered to retire and fell back to Zonnebeke. Captains G.R. Taylour, H.G. McCormick, Lieutenants J.E. Ratcliff and R.T. Stainforth killed. Enemy attacked at daybreak (21st). War Diary notes Battalion's first experience of German high explosive shells – "Black Marias" and a great many casualties. Retired later to railway crossing southwest of Zonnebeke. Captain C.O.H. Methuen killed. Took part in attack to recapture lost trenches (24th). Advanced through Polygon Wood – War Diary records that the enemy retired leaving many killed or wounded. Charles Lethbridge Kingsford noting that this was after hard and close fighting. Came under fire from enemy machine gun positioned in a farmhouse. This was taken and a further advance made. Lost trenches regained and an number of prisoners taken. Commanding Officer Lieutenant-Colonel W.L. Loring and Second-Lieutenant D. Dean killed. Over 100 other casualties. Bivouacked for night on the Menin-Becelaere road. Moved to Zandvoorde (26th), later taking part in unsuccessful attack on enemy positions south-east of Gheluvelt. Withdrew later to Klein Zillebeke. War Diary records British Aeroplane brought down by our own gunners. Took part in counter-attack (29th) – held up by heavy fire and forced to dig in. Held positions under heavy bombardment. forced to withdraw (31st) and ordered to hold new line at all costs. Charles Lethbridge Kingsford records that part of the Battalion was surrounded and cut off. Battalion strength in evening being just over 100. Trenches were held under constant attacks – servants, cooks etc being put into the line.

NOVEMBER

Relieved (4th) and to Ypres. Moved forward again (6th) and took part in successful counter attack north-west of Klein Zillebeke (7th). Relieved again and via Bailleul arrived at Merris (10th). To Sailly (14th) and relieved 2nd

York and Lancaster in trenches south of Fleurbaix (14th). Relieved 2nd Queen's in trenches at La Boutillerie (18th). Relieved by 2nd Queen's (20th) and to Rue de Bataille. Relieved 2nd Queen's (23rd), relieved by 2nd Queen's (26th) and to billets in Rue de Biache. Relieved 2nd Queen's (29th).

DECEMBER

Relieved by 2nd Queen's (2nd) and to Rue de Bataille. To trenches (5th). Relieved by 2nd Queen's (8th) and to Rue de Biache, relieving 2nd Queen's again (15th). Took part in unsuccessful attack on German line near Bas Maisnil (18th). War Diary records that "B" Company led on the right, "A" were to the left, "D" in the centre – Battalion advanced with steadiness, suffering very heavy casualties. The dead were later found only a few yards from the German trenches – the new Commanding Officer, Lieutenant-Colonel R.H.W. Brewis being among them. Relieved later and to Le Cron Ballot. War Diary records casualties – "as could be ascertained" as Lieutenant-Colonel Brewis, Captains C.A.R. Hodgson, R.J. Brownfield, Lieutenant G.B. Monk, Second-Lieutenants A.R.L. Tucker and B. Campbell killed. Three officers are recorded as wounded – one of these, Second-Lieutenant B.A. Standring, dying later, and 3 missing. Of the latter, both Lieutenant B.F.P. Bernard and Second-Lieutenant G.V. Pearce had been killed. Among the other ranks, some 363 were recorded as killed, wounded or missing. Moved back to firing line (20th). Relieved by 2nd Queen's (23rd) and to billets at Rue de Biache. To Le Cron Ballot (28th).

ROYAL FUSILIERS (CITY OF LONDON REGIMENT)

**"Mons" "Le Cateau" "Retreat from Mons"
"Marne, 1914" "Aisne, 1914" "La Bassée, 1914"
"Messines, 1914" "Armentières, 1914" "Ypres, 1914"
"Nonne Bosschen"**

1ST BATTALION

AUGUST
Kinsale, Ireland. Part of 17th Brigade, 6th Division. Sailed for Holyhead during third week of month and then to Cambridge. Camped on Midsommer Common then to Newmarket (31st).

SEPTEMBER
To Southampton (7th) and embarked for France. Arrived off St. Nazaire (10th). Disembarked (12th) and entrained for Coullomieres. Arrived (14th) and to camp. Began move towards the Aisne (15th). Arrived Dhuizel area (19th) and took over front line trenches in Soupir sector (21st).

OCTOBER
Relieved by 2nd Highland Light Infantry (1st) and to billets at Dhuizel. To Chassemy (4th) and relieved troops of 2nd Cavalry Brigade in front line trenches. Visited by General Sir Douglas Haig (5th). Relieved during evening (6th) and marched to Muret. Arrived about midnight and then to Droizy. Marched to Dampleux during night (7th) then to Orrouy (8th). To Le Meux (9th) and entrained early hours (10th). Arrived Wizernes (11th) and marched to Blandecques. Moved in afternoon to Faubourg de Lysel – "D" Company going into support line at Clair Marais. To St. Omer (12th) and then travelled by lorries to Hazebrouck. Billets found in the Town Hall. Held in reserve at Strazeele during attack on the Bailleul Ridge (13th). Advanced through Merris (14th) and then to Blanche-Maision. To Steenwerk (15th) then in evening to Bac St. Maur via Croix de Bac. War Diary records Bac St. Maur as being in "a filthy state." Some 3,000 Germans had just left, ransacking the town and destroying all they did not require. To La Vesée (17th) then in afternoon took over billets at la Chapelle d' Armentières. Moved forward into line – Le Fresnelle-Le Temple (18th) then later on to L'Epinette. Enemy engaged. War Diary records – "A hot fire was met – Germans were pressed back slightly into their trenches." Battalion

then ordered to entrench. Casualties – 4 other ranks killed, 2 officers, 27 other ranks wounded, 4 missing. Positions held under heavy shell fire (19th-23rd). War Diary notes – "We had orders not to retire under any circumstances." Relieved by 1st Royal Warwickshire (23rd) and marched to Fleurbaix. Later to Rue des Lombards and attached to 19th Brigade. Moved up to Rue du Petillon (24th) and took over support line behind 2nd Royal Welsh Fusiliers.

NOVEMBER

Captain H.J. Shaw killed (12th). War Diary records that the dugout where the officer was sleeping fell in. Relieved by 1st Leicestershire (13th) and marched via Fleurbaix to billets at la Chapelle d' Armentières. Casualties since 24th October – 16 killed, 82 wounded. Relieved 1st West Yorkshire in trenches south-east of la Chapelle d' Armentières – Porte Egal sector (14th). Began work digging communication trench back to la Chapelle d' Armentières Cemetery. Relieved by 3rd Rifle Brigade (21st) and moved back to la Chapelle d' Armentières. Continued work in communication trench to front line. War Diary records (26th) that work was completed and the trench was paved with stones. Relieved 3rd Rifle Brigade (28th).

DECEMBER

War Diary notes (1st) the issue of periscopes and 4 "Very" pistols. The former being – "Very useful but require to be made of stronger material." Private J.D.F. Murray accidently killed by man cleaning his rifle (4th). Relieved by 3rd Rifle Brigade (5th) and to la Chapelle d' Armentières. "A" Company to reserve positions at Desplanques Farm (11th). War Diary notes approximately 2,000 enemy shells fired into the Armentières area during night (14th). Relieved 1/16th London Regiment in line – Lille-Boulogne road on left to just east of Rue Au Bois on right (18th). Positions held under heavy shell fire. Relieved by 1/16th London (23rd) and to la Chapelle d' Armentières. Relieved 1/16th London (26th). War Diary gives total casualties for December as 14 killed or died of wounds, 18 wounded. Those for 1914 are recorded as 72 killed or died of wounds, 191 wounded.

4TH BATTALION

AUGUST

Parkhurst, Isle of Wight. Part of 9th Brigade, 3rd Division. Commanding Officer – Lieutenant-Colonel N.R. McMahon, DSO. To Southampton (13th) and embarked SS *Martaban* for Havre. In his war history of the Royal Fusiliers, H.C. O'Neill records that the battalion was well received by

French soldiers. The Fusiliers responded by whistling the *Marseillaise* followed by *Hold your hand out, naughty boy.* The French, thinking that the latter tune was the British National Anthem, bowed their heads. Moved to No.7 Rest Camp. War Diary records a very hot day – many men (mostly reservists) falling out during march. Entrained for Landrecies (16th) and from there marched to billets at Noyelles-sur-Sambre. To Taisnieres (20th), La Longueville (21st). Crossed Belgian border near Malplaquet (22nd). Outposts set up by "Y" (Captain L.F. Ashburner) and "Z" (Captain A.M. Byng) Companies guarding canal crossings (western face of canal bend) at Nimy just north of Mons. Orders received to hold these positions as long as possible. "X" Company (Captain L.W.Le M. Carey) in support near Nimy station, "W" Company (Captain M.L.S.O. Cole) in reserve just outside Mons. Strength – 26 officers, 983 other ranks. Battle of Mons (23rd). Two German cavalry officers wounded and captured. Private F. Gaunt saw one of the German officers and noted in his book *The Immortal First* that he was severely wounded – "He told our captain (Captain Ashburner) that he was a baron; he seemed to be rather old – about sixty years of age – and had a long beard. He looked very ill for the want of food; he told our captain he had only had chocolate for three days. Our officer was very kind to him, bandaging his leg and arm for him. He then asked if he could go back and pick up his helmet, which he was allowed to do, our captain assisting him over the barbed wire entanglements." Enemy attacked about 11 am. Most of Machine Gun Section (emplacements on railway bridge) killed or wounded – War Diary records Lieutenant M.J. Dease (Machine Gun Officer) and Private S.F. Godley displaying conspicuous gallantry in working the guns, both having been wounded. Machine guns put out of action by artillery fire and abandoned.

London Gazette, 16th November, 1914. Award of Victoria Cross – "Maurice Dease, Lieut., 4th Battn. Royal Fusiliers. . . .Though two or three times badly wounded, he continued to control the fire of his machine guns at Mons on 23rd Aug. until all his men were shot. He died of his wounds."

London Gazette, 25th Nov. 1914. Award of Victoria Cross – "Sydney Frank Godley, No. 13814, 4th Battn. Royal Fusiliers. . . ."For coolness and gallantry in firing his machine-gun under a hot fire for two hours, after he had been wounded at Mons on 23rd Aug."

Reinforcements sent up from support line. Captain F. Foster, Lieutenant E.C. Smith and Second-Lieutenant J.F. Mead killed. `Y` Company taken in rear. Battalion ordered to retire. Moved back through Mons during afternoon. War Diary notes withdrawal carried out with the greatest steadiness. Casualties – approximately 112 killed and wounded (including 7 officers). Most of the wounded taken prisoner. Arrived Ciply about 7 pm. Took up positions just north of Ciply (24th) and attached to 7th Brigade. Enemy attacked at dawn – Captain Byng`s company suffered 40 per cent casualties. Battalion retired through Genly then marched to Bermeries. To Inchy (25th). War Diary records much activity in the air during march. One German aeroplane brought down by rifle fire from battalion. Took over trenches south east of Inchy. H.C. O`Neill records that these positions had been dug by civilian labour and faced the wrong way. Relieved by 1st Northumberland Fusiliers (26th) and held reserve positions during battle of Le Cateau. Ordered to retire forming rearguard to 3rd Division. Marched through night to Hargicourt. To Vermand (27th), Marched via Ham to billets at Crissolles (28th). Private Gaunt recalls seeing "The Angels of Mons" on this day – "We had been harassed by the Germans all day and we lay down in the courtyard. It was between 6 and 7 pm. I was lying on my back half dozing, when I looked up, and saw in the sky a curious effect, which looked like a number of spirits or angel forms. Later on I mentioned it to others, and they said they had seen the same appearance." Retired through Noyon to Montois (29th). To Vauciennes (31st). Billeted in sugar factory.

SEPTEMBER
Continued rearguard action. To Bouillancy (1st), Penchard (2nd), Via Meaux to Le Mans Farm (3rd). Took up defensive positions south of La Haute Maison (4th). Retired during night to Châtres. To Lumigny (6th), La Martroy (7th), Les Fauchères (8th). Crossed the Marne and set up outposts (9th). Moved forward and engaged enemy near Veuilly (10th). Casualties – 4 officers wounded, 5 other ranks killed, 29 wounded. 600 prisoners taken. Reached Grand Rozoy (11th). To Brenelle (12th), Vailly (13th), crossing the Aisne at about 11 pm. Ordered to take up positions covering Vailly on heights north of village. Arrived at positions near Rouge Maison Farm just after midnight. One outpost, according to H.C. O`Neill, close enough to enemy lines as to hear them talking. Enemy attacked at dawn (14th) – line to the right gave way and forced to retire to sunken road about 200 yards south of Rouge Maison. Casualties – 4 officers killed, 1 wounded and approx. 200 other ranks killed, or wounded. Enemy attack during night repulsed with rifle fire and bayonet. Position entrenched and held under heavy shelling. Night attack (15th) repulsed. War Diary (16th) records position maintained – "all ranks doing splendidly" – enemy entrenched between 200 and 300 yards away. Enemy attacked after heavy shelling from short range (19th) – 50 casualties. War Diary notes confusion among the Germans

who suffered many casualties. Entry in War Diary (20th) headed "Alma Day" and commemorating regiment's involvement at the Battle of the Alma during Crimean War. About 20 casualties during enemy attack. Relieved by 1st Lincolnshire at 5 pm after 7 days in front line. Moved back across the Aisne during night then to Courcelles. Sir John French visited billets (21st) and congratulated all officers and men on their conduct at Rouge Maison – ". . . No troops in the world could have done better than you have. England is proud of you, and I am proud of you." Took up positions on high ground just north west of Vailly (25th). War Diary notes positions as "curious" – densely wooded in places, trenches facing in all directions and commanded by the enemy. There was no field of fire, but ground difficult for enemy to attack over.

OCTOBER
War Diary (2nd) records no enemy fire and that most of them seem to have gone. Relieved during evening. Marched through night via Braine and to farm just north of Servenay. Marched through night (3rd) to Troesnes. Moved during night (4th) through Forest of Retz to Crépy-en-Valois. To Roberval (5th), Longueil Pont (6th). Crossed River Oise and entrained for Ailly-sur-Somme. Continued journey to Pont Remy (7th) and then marched to Buigny St. Maclou. To Tollent (9th). Marched to Hesdin (10th) and from there in French lorries to Sains-les-Pernes. To billets south of canal at Robecq (11th), Vieille Chapelle and Brigade Reserve positions (12th). Withdrew during evening to billets at Le Cornet Malo. Took up Divisional Reserve positions at Vieille Chapelle (13th). War Diary records 7th and 8th Brigades heavily engaged on Bout de Ville – La Couture line. Major-General H.I.W. Hamilton (Commander, 3rd Division) killed by shrapnel (14th). Advanced on Bout de Ville at 1 pm (15th). Attached to 8th Brigade "W" and "X" Companies attacked through Pont du Hem and took objective (main road running south east from Estaires) with little opposition by 5 pm. Entrenched east of road with French on left. Advance continued (16th) – line reached east of Aubers astride Rue d' Enfer about 5 pm. Occupied Aubers without opposition (17th). Herlies taken at dusk with 10 casualties (including 1 officer killed) – "W" Company attacking via Aubers-Herlies road, remainder advancing through Le Plouich and Le Riez. Held forward line of houses and trenches on edge of village. Held Herlies during enemy attacks (18th) – 40 casualties. Heavy shell fire and village destroyed (20th) – H.C. O'Neill records the only building remaining intact being the convent behind the church. Part of Battalion retired to farm just west of Herlies. Retired to trenches half- mile east of Aubers running through Le Plouich and Ligny-le-Grand (21st). Casualties during fighting at Herlies –

5 officers and 150 other ranks. Withdrew during night (22nd) to Divisional Reserve billets at Pont-du-Hem. Re-took trenches recently captured by enemy (25th) – two companies attacking from Pont Logy towards Neuve Chapelle, one from the Fleurbaix-Neuve Chapelle road. Captain Sir Francis Waller mortally wounded while leading "Z" Company. Took part in failed night attack (26th) with high casualties. Renewed attack 10 am (27th) – driven back after severe fighting. War Diary (28th) records strength as just 8 officers and 350 other ranks. Relieved early morning (30th) and to Vieille Chapelle. Marched to billets at Doulieu. To Merris (31st).

NOVEMBER
Marched via Bailleul to billets just north of Locre (1st). To Bailleul (3rd). Inspected by General Sir Horace Smith-Dorrien (4th). Took over trenches east of Hooge south side of Ypres-Menin road, edge of Herenthage Wood (6th). Several enemy attacks repulsed (8th). One attack driven back by "Y" Company under Lieutenant Stapleton-Bretherton who charged the enemy. Most of company missing. War Diary records heavy shelling throughout – "This is much the most severe shelling I (Lieutenant G. Thomas-O'Donel) have seen during the war" (11th). Enemy attacked and entered line. Colonel (now Brigadier-General) McMahon killed. All other officers except Lieutenant Thomas-O'Donel and Second-Lieutenant C.T. Maclean casualties. Withdrew to reserve line (12th). Later sent forward to support trenches. Strength – 2 officers, 170 other ranks. To Divisional Reserve at Hooge (16th), trenches south of Hooge (19th). Relieved during night (20th) and to Westoutre. Major H. Hutchinson took over command (21st). To trenches at Kemmel (27th). Relieved during night (30th) and to billets at Westoutre. War Diary records that Battalion had lost about 1,900 men and 50 officers killed, wounded, missing or sick to date.

DECEMBER
Returned to trenches at Kemmel (6th). Relieved and to Locre (9th), trenches (12th), Westoutre (15th), trenches (21st), Locre (24th).

KING`S (LIVERPOOL REGIMENT)

"Mons" "Retreat from Mons" "Marne, 1914"
"Aisne, 1914" "Ypres,1914" "Langemarck,1914"
"Gheluvelt" "Nonne Bosschen"

1ST BATTALION

AUGUST

Talavera Barracks, Aldershot. Part of 6th Brigade, 2nd Division. Entrained at Farnborough for Southampton (12th). Embarked SS *Irrawaddy* and sailed for France. Arrived Havre (13th) and to rest camp at Ste. Adresse. Entrained at Havre (15th), travelling via Rouen to Busigny. Arrived (16th) and marched to Hannappes. To Landrecies (21st), Hargnies (22nd). Moved via La Longueville to Givry (23rd) and entrenched in chalk pit on northern side of village. "A" and "B" Companies sent forward to support 2nd South Staffordshire at Harmignies during afternoon. Rest of Battalion later moved out of chalk pit and dug in across the Givry-Villereille-le-Sec road. Came under shell fire. Fell back to high ground south-west of Givry (24th) then retired via Bonnet, Goegnies and Malplaquet to Bavai. "C" Company came under fire from German cavalry during morning (25th). Battalion later retired on Pont-sur-Sambe, then via Leval and Noyelles to Maroilles. Continued retreat via Le Grand Fayt, Prisches, Le Sart, Fesmy, Oisy and Etreux to Venerolles (26th), via Guise and Mont d`Origny to Lucy (27th). Moved at 4 pm to high ground west of Thenelles and dug defensive positions. Marched via Ribemont, Sery, Brissy, Mayot, Le Fère, Charmes, Andelain and Servais to Rouy (28th), via Barisis and Folembray to Coucy-le-Château (30th), via Soissons and Pommiers to St. Bandry (31st).

SEPTEMBER

Marched via Coeuvres and Villers Cotterêts to Pisseleux (1st) then ordered back to Assist 4th (Guards) Brigade under attack south of Villers Cotterêts. Enemy engaged and driven back. Battalion then marched back through Pisseleux to Thury. Casualties – approximately 70. Marched via Betz, Bois de Montrolle, Acy, Etrepilly, Barcy and Penchard to Trilbardou (2nd), via Meaux, Trilport, Montceau, Pierre Levée, Courte Soupe and La Brosse to Bilbarteaux-les-Vannes (3rd), via La Malmaison to Mouroux (4th), via Faremoutiers, Hautefeuille, Pezarches and Lumigny to Chaumes (5th). Began advance (6th), marching first to Chaubuisson Farm then in evening to Château-de-la Fontelle. Moved via Rigny, Pezarches, Touquin, La

Boissière and Chailly-en-Brie to St. Siméon (7th), via Voigny, Rebais, La Trétoire, Boitron, Petit Villers and Le Petit Basseville to La Noue (8th). Crossed the Marne at Charly (9th) then moved via Villiers and Domptin to Coupru. Moved forward via Marigny-en-Orxois and Bussiares (10th) then took part in the fighting at Hautevesnes. Enemy surrendered, 6th Brigade taking 400-500 prisoners. Later moved on to bivouacs at Chevillon, then (11th) via Priez, Sommelans, Breny and Qulchy to Cugny- les-Couttes, via Beugneux, Arcy, Branges, Jouaignes, Ouincy and Courcelles to Monthussart Farm (12th), via Vieil-Arcy to Dhuizel (13th). Crossed the Aisne at Pont Arcy (14th) then to Veneuil. Later took part in fighting on the Moussy Spur then dug in throughout the night. Held positions under shell fire. Enemy attacks repulsed (20th) – Captains A.K. Kyrke-Smith, F. Marshall, R.E. Tanner mortally wounded, Lieutenant M.R. Sweet-Escott and 21 other ranks killed, 2 officers, 38 other ranks wounded. Relieved by 1st Scots Guards (21st) and via Moussy to Oeuilly. To Moussy (26th) then to front line trenches. Casualties (26th-30th) – 9.

OCTOBER

Relieved by 2nd South Staffordshire (6th) and to Soupir. Casualties (1st-6th) – 25. Entrained at Fismes (15th) for Strazeele. Arrived (16th) and marched to Hazebrouck. To Godewaersveld (19th), Ypres then reserve positions at St. Jean (20th). Took up positions at Wieltje (21st), returning to St. Jean same night. Moved via Potijze to Zillebeke (22nd). "B" Company moved up into trenches on ridge between Zandvoorde and Hollebeke. Battalion returned to St. Jean (23rd). Commanding Officer – Lieutenant-Colonel W.S. Bannatyne mortally wounded (24th). Moved to high ground near Westhoek and relieved 1st South Staffordshire in firing line north of Polygon Wood then with 1st Royal Berkshire on the left attacked Molenaarelshoek. In his war history of the King's Regiment, Everard Wyrall notes that the Battalion advanced in good order. On the western side of Molenaarelshoek the enemy opened fire from heavily fortified buildings – "A" Company being "brought to a standstill by a perfect hurricane of bullets." The village was charged and enemy cleared. Hostile fire continued from several houses on the eastern side, however – "D" Company attacking, but unable to reach objective. Second-Lieutenant B.M.R. Denny mortally wounded, 24 other casualties. Battalion dug in during night north of village. Captain J.H.S. Batten killed by sniper (25th). Later, Lieutenant H.B. Wallace killed and 18 other casualties during attempt to get forward. Attacked again 5.30 am (26th). "D" Company clearing remaining Germans from Molenaarelshoek and advancing up to the Becelaere road. "B" Company also entered enemy's trenches. Casualties – Lieutenants P.T.

Furneaux and E.B. Baker killed, 5 officers wounded, 54 other ranks killed or wounded. Enemy counter-attack repulsed (27th). Relieved by 2nd Highland Light Infantry during night and to reserve positions near Polygon Wood. Moved up to north-west side of Polygon Wood (29th), Westhoek (30th). Moved forward to south-west corner of Polygon Wood (31st) and dug defensive positions.

NOVEMBER
Held positions under severe shell fire and several infantry attacks. Including that made by the Prussian Guard (11th). Relieved by French troops (16th). Casualties (1st-16th) – 120. Marched via St. Jean and Vlamertinghe to Zevecoten (20th), via Locre, Meteren and Flétre to Caestre (21st). Records note total casualties since 23rd August as 33 officers, 814 other ranks.

DECEMBER
Moved in buses to Béthune (22nd) then marched via Beuvry to Cambrin. Relieved 1st King's Royal Rifle Corps in trenches running from Béthune-La Bassée road to the La Bassée Canal (25th). Relieved by 2nd King's Royal Rifle Corps (26th) and via Cambrin, Beuvry and Le Quesnoy to Essars. To Locon (29th).

1/10TH (SCOTTISH) BATTALION (TERRITORIAL FORCE)

AUGUST
Headquarters – 7 Fraser Street, Liverpool. Part of Liverpool Infantry Brigade, West Lancashire Division. To annual camp at Hornby (2nd). Ordered to return to Liverpool (3rd). All ranks to headquarters (7th) and then billeted in Liverpool Stadium ("A" – "F" Companies) and the Shakespeare Theatre ("G" and "H" Companies). Entrained for Edinburgh (13th) and to camp at King's Park. Now part of Forth Defences.

OCTOBER
Entrained for Tunbridge Wells (10th). Battalion Headquarters at The Dell, Ferndale Road.

NOVEMBER
Entrained for Southampton (1st). Embarked SS *Maidan* and sailed for France. The 1/16th London Regiment were on the same ship and a member of that battalion, Leslie Walkinton, refers to the Liverpool Scottish in his book *Twice in a Lifetime* as – "a likely lot of Lancashire lads got up in kilts." Arrived Havre (2nd). Landed (3rd) and to No.1 Rest Camp. Entrained for

St. Omer (4th). Records show that during the journey, and while the train was halted outside Abbeville, Lieutenant N.G. Chavasse (Medical Officer) amused onlookers when he took a cold shower from a water tank at the side of the railway line. Noel Chavasse would later be awarded the Victoria Cross (twice) and the Military Cross. Arrived (5th) and to billets at Blendecques. To Hazebrouck (20th), Bailleul (21st). Paul Maze was a Frenchman attached to the 2nd Cavalry Division as a liaison officer and recalls in his book *A Frenchman in Khaki* seeing the Liverpool Scottish march through Bailleul. He had lived in England before the war and recognized among the Battalion a number of his old friends from the Birkenhead Park Rugby Football Club. Re-organized into 4 companies. Joined 9th Brigade, 3rd Division at Westoutre (25th). Began duty in trenches – Kemmel sector (27th). Positions recorded as being between 35 and 200 yards from the enemy. Captain Arthur Twentyman killed by sniper (29th). Ann Clayton in her book *Chavasse Double VC* recalls how it was Noel Chavasse who was sent out to bring in Captain Twentyman's body. In a letter he wrote – "At first the zip, zip of bullets hitting the sandbags close to one's head was rather disconcerting, then it became just part of the general environment. At one point we had to get past a gate where a sniper lay in wait. I went by doing the 100 well within 10 sec . . . We had to rest 5 times while crossing a ploughed field as the Captain was very heavy on the improvised stretcher (2 poles and a greatcoat)." Relieved and to Westoutre (30th).

DECEMBER

Continued duty in line, resting at Westoutre between tours. Kemmel Village is noted as being 1 mile from the front line and still containing numbers of civilians. The historian of the Liverpool Scottish, A.M. McGilchrist, recalls an incident regarding the church clock at Kemmel. It was noticed that although not working, its hands were not always in the same position. An investigation revealed that a civilian was using the hands, which faced the German line, to signal the enemy. Held line during 8th Brigade's attack on Petit Bois (14th). A.M. McGilchrist also makes mention of casualties due to sickness – mostly from frostbite. Upon entering the trenches for the first time on 27th November the strength of the battalion stood at 26 officers and 829 other ranks. By the first week of January this stood at 370 all ranks. Battle losses accounting for just 32.

NORFOLK REGIMENT

"Mons" "Le Cateau" "Retreat from Mons" "Marne, 1914" "Aisne, 1914" "La Bassée, 1914" "Ypres, 1914"

1ST BATTALION

AUGUST

Holywood, Belfast, Ireland. Part of 15th Brigade, 5th Division. Brigadier-General F.P. Crozier, CB, CMG, DSO was in Belfast at the time and he records in his book *A Brass Hat in No Man's Land* how he was asked to arrange the ceremony in which the Battalion's Colours were handed over to the authorities of Belfast Cathedral for safe keeping. Sailed SS *Anthony* for France (14th). Officers – Lieutenant-Colonel C.R. Ballard (Commanding Officer), Major J.B. Orr, DSO (Second in Command), Captain F.J. Cresswell (Adjutant), Lieutenant E. Smith (Quartermaster); "A" Company: Major H.R. Done, Lieutenants R.C. Nixon, M.D. Jephson, Second-Lieutenants G.N. Paget, A.E. Reeve; "B" Company: Captains R.H. Brudenell-Bruce, W.C.K. Megaw, Lieutenants M.F.R. Lightfoot, J.R. Holland, H.M. Openshaw, Second-Lieutenants O.S.D. Wills, F.C. Boosey; "C" Company: Captains C.E. Luard, DSO, T.R. Bowlby, Lieutenants G.C. Lyle, T.A.F. Foley, Second-Lieutenant R.W. Patterson; "D" Company: Captains E.N. Snepp, R.C. Clark, Lieutenants E.V.F. Briard, E.H.T.B. Broadwood, Second-Lieutenant J.B. Oakes. Landed Havre (16th) and to No.8 Rest Camp. Entrained for La Cateau (17th). Began move forward, arriving Dour (21st), Bois de Bossu (22nd). Advanced to positions along railway line south of the Mons-Condé, Canal. Moved back to Dour in Divisional Reserve (24th). Later sent forward to position west of Elouges – Battalion's right on the Elouges-Quièvrain railway line. Enemy attacked and withdrawal ordered to Bavai. Casualties – Major Orr, Captain Cresswell, Lieutenants Openshaw and Briard killed, 4 other officers wounded, approximately 250 other ranks killed, wounded or missing. Retreated via western edge of the Mormal Forest to Troisvillers (25th). Fell back to Reumont (26th) and later fired on advancing enemy from positions near Honnechy. Withdrew via Busigny to St. Quentin. Marched via Noyon to Pontoise (28th), Carlepont (29th), via Attichy to Croutoy (30th), to Crépy-en-Valois (31st).

SEPTEMBER

Continued retreat to Ormoy Villars (1st), Montgé (2nd). Crossed the Marne at Trilbardou (3rd) then via Esby to Montpichet. To Tournans (5th). Began advance, moving via the Forest of Crécy to La Celle (6th), via Tr,smes and Coulommiers to Boissy-le-Chatel (7th), Doué to Charnesseuil (8th). Crossed the Marne at Saacy (9th), moved forward and came under shell fire near Le Limon. Later took part in attack on Hill 189. Withdrew later to billets at Nampteuil. Advanced to Ste. Marguerite (13th). Moved through Missy (14th) and took part in attack on the Chivy Spur. Later fell back to Missy. Casualties – Captains Luard and Bowlby killed, 2 other officers wounded, approximately 100 other ranks killed, wounded or missing. Renewed attack 8 am (15th), but again forced to retire. Withdrew to line – Missy-Ste. Marguerite and later to Jury. Sent to Chassemy as reinforcement to 3rd Division. Second-Lieutenant A.M.A.I.deL.Teeling killed during bombardment (24th). Moved into billets at Vasseny (27th).

OCTOBER

Rejoined 15th Brigade at Droizy (2nd). To Corcy (3rd), Fresnoy-la-Rivière (4th), Verberie (6th). Entrained at Compiègne for Abbeville (7th). Moved forward, arriving Béthune (11th) and taking over front line trenches between Festubert and Givenchy. Took part in fighting along the La Bassée Canal. Later moved forward to positions near Violaines. Enemy attacked and broke through (22nd) forcing withdrawal to line in front of Festubert. Enemy attacked again (25th). Casualties – Lieutenant Foley and 20 other ranks killed, 30 wounded. Relieved and to billets in Festubert (26th).

NOVEMBER

Moved to Ypres area (13th) and took over trenches in Kemmel sector (18th). Relieved (23rd) and to Dranoutre.

DECEMBER

In trenches – Wulverghem sector. Battalion rested between tours at Neuve Eglise, Dranoutre and Bailleul.

LINCOLNSHIRE REGIMENT

"Mons" "Le Cateau" "Retreat from Mons"
"Marne, 1914" "Aisne,1914"
"La Bassée, 1914" "Messines, 1914"
Armentières, 1914" "Ypres,1914" "Nonne Bosschen"

1ST BATTALION

AUGUST

Victoria Barracks, Portsmouth. Part of 9th Brigade, 3rd Division. Entrained for Southampton (13th) and embarked SS *Norman.* Sailed for France 4 pm. Disembarked Havre during morning (14th) and to rest camp at Harfleur. Officers – Lieutenant-Colonel W.E.B. Smith (Commanding Officer), Majors C. Toogood, DSO (Second in Command), D.H.F. Grant, Captains F.W. Greatwood, H.C.W. Hoskyns, H.E. Dawson, F.C. Rose, R.E. Drake (Adjutant), G.K. Butt, G.M. Ellison, Lieutenants A.W.P. Peddie, L.M. Buller, C.C. Holmes, B.J. Thruston, E.L. Welchman, F.W. Masters (Quartermaster), Second- Lieutenants A.E.C. Baines, E.W. Wales, C. Hutchinson, R.FitzR.B. Herapath, A.P. Snell, W.M. Robertson, R.W. Cave-Orme, E. Barnes, H. Marshall, L.H. Trist. Entrained at Havre for Landrecies (15th). Arrived (16th) and to Dupleix Barracks. To Noyelles (17th), Leval (20th), Riez de l`Erelle (21st). Advanced to Frameries (22nd) then moved out to Cuesmes. In *The History of the Lincolnshire Regiment 1914-1918,* Major-General C.R. Simpson records the first shot fired by the Battalion – Captain Ellison shooting at an enemy aeroplane as it passed overhead. Moved forward towards Mons (23rd) and barricades set up on road leading into town. Opened fire on advancing enemy during afternoon. Received order to retire 6 pm and marched via Mesvin to Nouvelles. Later moved back via Ciply to Frameries and took up defensive positions in the orchard overlooking the Jemappes- Quaregon road. Enemy attacked about 4 am (24th). Lieutenant-Colonel Smith noted the good work of Lieutenant Holmes and the machine guns, who "fought to the last", and Private Stroulger who got many of the wounded away by bringing up a machine gun limber. Later withdrew to Eugies. Casualties (23rd-24th) – Lieutenants Buller and Welchman killed, Lieutenant Holmes mortally wounded, 1 officer wounded, 130 other ranks killed, wounded or missing. Continued retreat via Saars-la-Bruyere and Bavai to Bermeries. Moved through Gommegnies, Villereau, Le Quesnoy, Neuville, Solesmes and Neuvilly to Inchy (25th). Dug in 300 yards west of village and opened fire on advancing enemy during morning (26th). Casualties – 1 officer wounded, 93 other ranks killed, wounded or missing. Withdrew via Clary to Beaurevoir. Marched through Hargicourt and Villeret to Vermand (27th), via Estouilly and Ham to Crissolles (28th), via Noyon, St. Blaise, Pontoise, Cuts, Morsain and Vic-sur-Aisne to Ressons (30th). To Vauciennes (31st).

SEPTEMBER

To Bouillancy (1st), Penchard (2nd), billets in a farm between Vaucourtois and Maison Blanche (3rd). Moved via La Consuite (4th) and marching through night arrived at Liverdy 7.15 am (5th). Began advance (6th), marching first to Château de Lumigny. To La Bretonniere (7th), via Gibraltar and Orly to Les Feuchères (8th). To Bezu (9th). "C" and "D" Companies attacked and captured German guns west of village. However, British artillery, thinking the Lincolnshire were Germans, opened fire. Casualties – Captain Drake killed, 3 officers wounded, 30 other ranks killed or wounded. Arrived Dammard (10th) and to Grand Rozoy (11th). Marched via Braine, ordered with 1st Royal Scots Fusiliers to clear with the bayonet, then to Brenelle (12th). Crossed the Aisne at Vailly (13th) then to positions on ridge south-west of Rouge Maison Farm. Enemy attacked (14th). Major-General Simpson records that the Germans came on "wave after wave", many of the Battalion's rifles being clogged with mud, making rapid fire difficult. "D" and "B" Companies assisted 4th Royal Fusiliers in successful counter-attack. Machine guns situated in Rouge Maison Farm inflicted high casualties on "A" and "C" Companies. There were further casualties as Battalion fell back across the river to a railway cutting. Here the survivors came under heavy shell fire and later moved back across river to Vailly. Casualties – Captain Dawson, Lieutenant Peddie killed, 4 officers wounded, 180 other ranks killed, wounded or missing. The Medical Officer, Captain Kemp, and one other officer were recorded as wounded and missing. Moved forward to support positions north of Vailly (15th). Relieved 4th Royal Fusiliers in firing line (20th). Relieved by 2nd York and Lancaster (21st) and via Braine moved into billets at Courcelles. Relieved 2nd Royal Scots in front line (25th).

OCTOBER

Relieved (2nd) and moved back via Vailly and Braine to Servenay. To Troesnes (3rd), Crépy-en-Valois (4th), Rhuis then La Croix St. Ouen (5th). Entrained for Abbeville (6th), travelling via Amiens and Longpre, arriving (7th) and marching to Buigny. To Hesdin (10th) then in buses to Sachin. Marched to Busnes (11th). Moved forward to Vieille Chapelle (12th) then latter through La Couture to positions on the Richebourg St. Wasst road.

Advanced through Richebourg St. Wasst (13th) then back to La Couture. "A" and "B" Companies in support of 14th Brigade (14th). Battalion moved back to Vieille Chapelle (15th). Took over trenches near Rouge Croix during morning (16th). Later moved forward to Pietre and engaged enemy south of Aubers. La Cliqueterie Farm taken. Took part in attack on Herlies (17th). War Diary records that "A" and "B" Companies led the advance which was over 1,450 yards of open ground. Herlies was defended by strong entrenchments and barbed-wire. The attack moved forward in short rushes, the enemy firing into the Battalion with machine guns, rifles and artillery. Order given to charge at about 300 yards – ". . . the enemy commenced to waver and many were seen to leave their trenches. Battalion pressed home and crossed the entanglements and charged the trenches at the point of the bayonet." Relieved and to billets at La Cliqueterie Farm. Casualties – Captain C.G. Lyall killed, Lieutenant K.K. Peace (York and Lancaster attached) mortally wounded, 2 officers wounded, 83 other ranks killed or wounded. Relieved 1st Royal Scots Fusiliers in front line trenches facing Neuve Chapelle (19th). Line held under bombardment and infantry attacks. Withdrew positions 800 yards (22nd) and again (23rd). Lieutenant V.D.B. Bransbury and Second-Lieutenant R. Willis (York and Lancaster attached) killed (25th). Relieved by 1st Northumberland Fusiliers (26th) and to Rouge Croix. Moved forward again during afternoon and in support of 7th Brigade at Neuve Chapelle. Took part in attack (27th). War Diary records Battalion advancing only 800 yards then being forced to take cover behind walls, tree trunks or anything else available. Dug in after dark. Casualties – Lieutenant V.H. Hardy (York and Lancaster attached) and 13 other ranks killed, 4 officers, 70 other ranks wounded, 7 missing. Relieved by Indian troops (30th) and to Vieille Chapelle. Marched to Estaires same day. To Kemmel via Neuve Eglise and Lindenhoek (31st).

NOVEMBER
Took part in counter-attack on Wytschaete (1st). Moved forward 2 am on right of Kemmel-Wytschaete road with 2 companies of 1st Northumberland Fusiliers on the left. Captain H.R. Sandilands of the Fusiliers records seeing the Lincolnshire "disappearing into the darkness." War Diary records coming under fire south-west side of village, the enemy at this point having previously called out that they were Indian troops. Withdrew about 100 yards – Major-General Simpson recording that many deeds of gallantry took place while caring for the wounded. Battalion charged the enemy around dawn, but was again forced to retire with heavy casualties. Survivors held out in No Man's Land, coming under shell fire from both sides about 6.45 am. War Diary notes – "murderous fire" as what was left of the Battalion

"ran for our lives." Relieved and via Kemmel withdrew to Lindhoek. Casualties – Major C.C.L. Barlow, Captains R.N. King, L.deO. Tollemache, Second- Lieutenant Barnes killed, 3 officers wounded, 293 other ranks killed, wounded or missing. Moved to Bailleul. Marched via Dickebusch and Ypres to Hell Fire Corner (6th). Later took over reserve trenches south of the Menin road near Hooge. Took part in fighting at Nonne Bosschen Wood (7th-16th). Relieved and to Sanctuary Wood. Casualties – 20 killed, 88 wounded. Moved forward to Herenthage Château Wood (18th). Relieved 1st Royal West Kent in woods near Klein Zillebeke (19th). Relieved by French troops (20th) and to Westoutre. To Kemmel (27th) and relieved 2nd Oxfordshire and Buckinghamshire Light Infantry in trenches near Wytschaete. Relieved and to Westoutre (30th).

DECEMBER
To Locre (3rd). Relieved 1st Royal Scots Fusiliers in Kemmel area (6th). "A" and "B" Companies attacked enemy's line 10 pm (8th) but heavy fire forced withdrawal. Casualties – 2 officers wounded, 4 other ranks killed, 19 wounded, 11 missing. Relieved and to Locre (9th). Moved forward (14th) and in reserve during attack on Wytschaete. Moved back to billets at Kemmel about 4 pm. To Westoutre (15th), front line (21st), Locre (24th), front line (31st).

2ND BATTALION

AUGUST
Bermuda.

SEPTEMBER
Canadian Government sent Royal Canadian Regiment to relieve 2nd Lincolnshire (11th). Embarked SS *Canada* and sailed for Halifax, Nova Scotia.

OCTOBER
Embarked SS *Canada* again and sailed for England (3rd). Arrived Devonport and then to camp at Hursley Park, Winchester. Joined 25th Brigade, 8th Division.

NOVEMBER
Marched to Southampton (5th) and embarked SS *Cestrian* for France. Commanding Officer – Lieutenant-Colonel G.B. McAndrew. Arrived Havre (6th) and to rest camp outside of town. Entrained for billets at

Strazeele (9th). Moved to Laventie sector (14th) and relieved 1st Devonshire in trenches along the Fauquissart-Neuve Chapelle road. Came under heavy bombardment (15th). Lieutenant N.J.S. Huntington killed (17th). Other casualties for first tour in trenches 4 men killed, 17 wounded. Relieved 1st Royal Irish Rifles in "F" Lines (22nd). Raid carried out on German position known as "Red Lamp Corner" (23rd). Party of 8 men led by Lieutenant E.H. Impey entered enemy's trenches. White sheets (and according to the history of the 8th Division – ladies nightdresses) were worn as a form of camouflage in the snow. The enemy – black against the snow, made easy targets and the raiders retired without loss. Relieved by 1st Royal Irish Rifles (24th), returned to front line (27th), relieved (30th).

DECEMBER
8th Division visited by HM. the King accompanied by President Poincaré and General Joffre (1st). Guard of Honour commanded by Captain R. Bastard provided by 2nd Lincolnshire. Relieved 1st Royal Irish Rifles in front line (3rd). Relieved (6th), to front line (9th), relieved (12th).To "E" Line trenches (21st), relieved (23rd), to trenches (26th). Periods between tours in front line were spent at Fort d'Esquin, Laventie and Estaires.

DEVONSHIRE REGIMENT

"Aisne, 1914" "La Bassée, 1914" "Armentières, 1914"

1ST BATTALION

AUGUST

Jersey, Channel Islands. Embarked SS *Reindeer* (21st) and sailed for France. Officers – Lieutenant-Colonel G.M. Gloster (Commanding Officer), Major E.G. Williams (Second in Command), Captain L.E.L. Maton (Adjutant), Lieutenants W.A. Fleming (Machine Gun Officer), S. Downing (Quartermaster), Second-Lieutenant C. H. Gotto (Transport Officer); "A" Company: Captains N. Luxmoore, H.C. Whipple, Lieutenants A.F. Northcote, T.O.B. Ditmas, G.E. Dunsterville, Second-Lieutenant C.C. Haynes; "B" Company: Captains B.H. Besly, H.G. Elliot, Lieutenant G.A. Anstey, Second-Lieutenant A. Tillett; "C" Company: Captains T.B. Harris, G. F. Green, Lieutenants G.E.R. Prior, C.F.W. Lang, Second-Lieutenant V. A. Beaufort; "D" Company: Major C.C.M. Maynard, DSO, Captain D.R. Jeffreys, Lieutenants P.R. Worrall, S.H. Yeo, Second-Lieutenant W.J. Alexander. Landed Havre during night and marched 4.30 am (22nd) to No.1 Rest Camp. The Battalion was now divided and placed on Line of Communications work. "D" Company moved by train to Busigny during afternoon (22nd). Headquarters and "B" Company entrained for Amiens, one half of "C" Company to Boulogne, the other to Rouen (24th). "D" Company left Busigny in lorries for St. Quentin (25th) and then by train to Noyon (26th). Headquarters and "B" Company to Rouen (27th). "D" Company entrained at Noyon for Compiègne (29th) and then to Le Mans (30th). The Rouen detachment of "C" Company arrived at Le Mans same day.

SEPTEMBER

Headquarters and "B" Company at Rouen embarked SS *Teviot* (1st) and sailed (2nd) for St. Nazaire. Arrived (4th), landed (6th) and to bivouacs 2 miles outside of town. "A" Company, still at Havre, and the "C" Company detachment at Boulogne arrived St. Nazaire (7th). Left St. Nazaire by train (8th) and arrived Coulommiers (10th). The Le Mans detachment ("D" Company and half of "C") arrived same day. Battalion marched to Sarcy (11th), Monthires (12th), Oulchy La Valle (13th), Braine (14th). Joined 8th Brigade, 3rd Division and took over reserve positions on western side of the Vailly-Jouy road. Moved forward to front line (15th). Line held under heavy shell and machine gun fire. Medical Officer Lieutenant H.L. Hopkins killed (19th), Captain Elliot killed (20th). Relieved by 1st Royal Scots Fusiliers (26th) and to Courcelles. Total casualties – 2 officers, 12 other ranks killed, 8 officers, 81 other ranks wounded. Moved to Jury and joined 14th Brigade, 5th Division (30th).

OCTOBER

To Nampteuil (2nd), Longport (3rd), Fresnoy-la-Rivière (4th), Verberie (6th). Entrained at Longueuil-Ste. Marie for Abbeville (7th). Arrived 7 pm and to billets in Vauchelles-les- Quesnoy. To Vaux (8th), Dieval (10th). Marched via Camblain-Chatelain, Choques and Hinges to Locon (11th). Moved to Gorre in Divisional Reserve (12th). "A" and "B" Companies to Le Touret and attached to 15th Brigade. "C" and "D" Companies attached to 15th Brigade (15th), moved forward to Pont Fixe and relieved 1st Dorsetshire. "A" and "B" Companies rejoined. Moved forward to trenches on eastern side of wood to the south-east of Givenchy (16th). Took part in attack (17th) – "B" and "D" Companies advancing 5.30 am, but, War Diary records, were forced to fall back on account of lack of support. Casualties – 3 killed, 16 wounded. Supported French attack (18th). Digging in after dark at Canteleux. Casualties – 2 killed, 7 wounded. Captain H.A. Chichester killed, Lieutenant- Colonel Gloster and 1 other officer wounded, 3 other ranks killed, 10 wounded during enemy attack (20th). Trenches heavily shelled (21st) – 3 killed, 8 wounded. Enemy broke through at Violaines (22nd) and withdrawal ordered to Givenchy. Casualties – 6 killed, 11 wounded. Heavily shelled throughout day (23rd) – 4 killed, 19 wounded, 4 missing. War Diary notes the gallantry of Lieutenant R.E. Hancock who leaving the trenches carried a wounded man 100 yards to safety. Lieutenant D.A.L. Ainslie and 15 other ranks killed (24th), 29 wounded. Captain Besly and Lieutenant E.O. St.A. Quicke killed (25th). Relieved and to Festubert (26th). Relieved 1st Manchester in front line east of Festubert (28th). War Diary records positions as running south for about 700 yards from the road leading east and north-east from Festubert Church. Enemy attack repulsed (29th). Lieutenants Dunsterville and Hancock killed, 11 other casualties. Another attack driven back (30th). Casualties – 39 killed, 45 wounded. Relieved and to Gorre (31st).

NOVEMBER

Marched via Le Touret, La Couture and Vieille Chapelle to Lestrem (1st) and rejoined 14th Brigade. To Vieille Chapelle (3rd). Moved to Croix Barbée (4th) then later to La Couture. Returned to Vieille Chapelle (5th). Relieved 2nd Suffolk in trenches east of Chapigny, along the Fauquissart-

Neuve Chapelle road (6th). Relieved by 2nd Lincolnshire (14th) and via Lavente marched to billets in Estaires. Casualties since going into line – 2 killed, 11 wounded. Marched via Troubayard, Doulieu, Noote Boom and Bailieul to Meteren (15th). Took over trenches west of Messines (16th). Captain Whipple mortally wounded (20th).War Diary notes among the casualties (20th and 21st) – 1 "self inflicted" for each day. Also recorded (22nd) is the landing of an enemy aircraft 400 yards in rear of the firing line. A party from the Royal Flying Corps later arrived and removed the machine. Relieved by 1st East Surrey (28th) and via Neuve Eglise to St. Jans Cappel. Casualties since going into line – 1 officer mortally wounded, 1 wounded, 12 other ranks killed, 40 wounded.

DECEMBER
Marched via Bailleul and Le Leuthe to Neuve Eglise (4th) and relieved 1st Royal West Kent in trenches east of Wulverghem, between Wulverghem-Messines road and the River Douve. Relieved by 1st East Surrey (10th) and to Neuve Eglise. Casualties since going into line – 1 killed, 8 wounded. Began work digging reserve, support and communication trenches. "B" and "D" Companies relieved 1/5th Cheshire in front line trenches (16th). Battalion to St. Jans Cappel (17th). War Diary records (22nd) football match played against 14th Field Ambulance. Score – Devons 4 – RAMC 1. To Dranoutre (23rd) and took over trenches in Wulverghem sector, north of the Wulverghem-Messines road from 2nd Duke of Wellington's and 1/9th London. Relieved by 1st East Surrey (29th) and to Dranoutre. Casualties since going into line – 9 killed, 13 wounded. War Diary records (31st) that 4 men from each platoon received first lesson in the use of grenades at Headquarters, 59 Field Company, RE.

2ND BATTALION

AUGUST
Abbassia Barracks, Cairo, Egypt. Moved to Ismailia to guard Suez Canal towards end of month.

SEPTEMBER
Returned to Cairo (10th). Entrained for Alexandria (11th). Embarked SS *Osmanieh* and sailed for England (13th).

OCTOBER
Arrived Southampton (1st) and to Romsey. Later moved to camp at Hursley Park near Winchester. Joined 23rd Brigade, 8th Division.

NOVEMBER
To Southampton (5th). Embarked SS *Bellerophon* and sailed for France.
Officers – Lieutenant-Colonel J.O. Travers, DSO (Commanding Officer),
Major J.F. Radcliffe, DSO (Second in Command), Major J.D. Ingles
(Adjutant), Lieutenant G. Palmer, DCM (Quartermaster), Lieutenant C.A.
Sutton (RAMC. Medical Officer), Lieutenant H. Eardley-Wilmot
(Machine Gun Officer); "A" Company: Captains A.J.E. Sunderland, D.H.
Blunt, Lieutenants A.G.N. Belfield, F.R. Cobb (Signalling Officer), R.O.
Bristowe, F. J.C. Holdsworth (Transport Officer); "B" Company: Captains
G.I. Watts, M.I.G. Jenkins, Lieutenants R.P. Bates, R. H. Anderson-
Morshead, J.R. Cartwright, Second-Lieutenant G.C. Vaughan; "C"
Company: Major W. M. Goodwyn, Captain C.J. Spencer, Lieutenants R.G.
Legge, J.A. Park, R. B. Featherstone; "D" Company: Captains C.A. Lafone,
C.H.M. Imbert-Terry, Lieutenants O.M. Parker, J.A. Andrews, Second-
Lieutenants A.G. McMullen, H.J. Cox. Strength – 29 Officers, 983 other
ranks. Arrived Havre 9.40 am (6th) and marched to rest camp at Graville.
Entrained (8th) and travelled via Rouen, Abbeville, Calais and St. Omer to
Strazeele. Arrived during morning (9th) and marched to billets at Neuf
Berquin. To Neuve Eglise (11th) and under orders of Cavalry Corps took
over trenches opposite Messines Ridge (12th). Relieved by 2nd West
Yorkshire (13th) and to Neuve Eglise. Rejoined 8th Division at Estaires
(17th). To La Flinque (18th) and from there took over trenches south of
Rue du Bacquerot. Relieved by 2nd Scottish Rifles (21st) and to local
reserve billets at La Flinque. Casualties – 3 killed, 5 wounded. War Diary
records German aeroplane captured nearby. Relieved 2nd Scottish Rifles in
front line (24th). Relieved by 2nd Scottish Rifles (27th) and to Estaires in
Corps Reserve. Casualties – 4 killed, 6 wounded. Relieved 2nd Scottish
Rifles in font line (30th). War Diary records 54 men sent to hospital suffering
from frostbite.

DECEMBER
War Diary notes – "heavier sniping than usual" (2nd). Also shoulder straps
(57th Regiment) taken from dead Germans in front of Battalion`s trenches
(3rd). Relieved during evening by 2nd Scottish Rifles and to La Flinque.
Relieved 2nd Scottish Rifles (6th). Relieved by 2nd Scottish Rifles (9th) and
to Pont Rirchon in Divisional Reserve. War Diary records (10th) that whole
battalion went to Estaires for baths and a change of underclothing. Relieved
2nd Scottish Rifles in front line (11th). Relieved by 2nd Royal Berkshire
(14th) and to Brigade Reserve positions on La Bassée road – Red Barn.
Relieved 2nd West Yorkshire in front line (16th). Took part in attack on the
Moated Grange (18th) – "C" Company on left cut down by heavy enfilade

fire from their left – advance hampered by fences and barbed wire. Enemy had set fire to two haystacks which lit the ground. Captain Spencer, Lieutenants Featherstone and Legge killed. "D" Company on right took trench to the south then entered enemy's line east of Moated Grange. Position gained some 150 yards long – 30 prisoners taken. In their history of the 8th Division Lieutenant-Colonel J.H. Boraston, CB, OBE and Captain Cyril E.O. Bax note that the enemy were not expecting an attack and many of them were bayoneted in their dugouts. "B" Company followed and position consolidated. Relieved by 2nd West Yorkshire (19th) and to billets at Pont Rirchon. Casualties – 6 officers and approximately 120 other ranks. Relieved 2nd Scottish Rifles in front line (24th). War Diary records – "informal armistice" (25th) ". . . Germans got out of their trenches and came towards our lines. Our men met them and they wished each other a Merry Xmas, shook hands, exchanged smokes etc." Sniping began about 7.30 pm – 1 man killed, 1 wounded. Relieved by 2nd Scottish Rifles during evening (27th) and to La Flinque. Relieved 2nd Scottish Rifles (31st).

SUFFOLK REGIMENT

"Mons" "Le Cateau" "Retreat from Mons"
"Marne, 1914" "Aisne, 1914"
"La Bassée, 1914" "Givenchy, 1914"

2ND BATTALION

AUGUST

Curragh, Ireland. Part of 14th Brigade, 5th Division. Received order to mobilize (4th). Colours taken to Depôt at Bury St. Edmunds by Lieutenant N.A. Bittleston and 8 men. To Dublin in 2 trains (13th). Headquarters and right half of Battalion embarked SS *Lanfranc* and sailed for France 5.45 pm. Left half remained in Barracks at Dublin, sailing SS *Poland* 1 pm (14th). Arrived Havre. Strength 28 officers – Lieutenant-Colonel C.A.H. Brett, DSO (Commanding), Majors E.C. Doughty (Second in Command), A.S. Peebles, DSO, F.T.D. Wilson and S.J.B. Barnardiston, DSO, Captains E.E. Orford, E.E. Pearson, E.H. Reid, W.M. Campbell, A.M. Cutbill (Adjutant), L.F. Hepworth, W. Blackwell (Quartermaster) and E.C. Phelan (RAMC, Medical Officer), Lieutenants N.A. Bittleston (Machine Gun Officer), T.W. Reynolds and N.B. Oaks (Transport Officer), Second-Lieutenants J.B. Morgan, F.V.C. Pereira, E.H.W. Backhouse, R.G.C. Harvey, T.L. George, P.C. Nicholls, V.M.G. Phillips, F.C. Berrill, P.R.W. Carthew, H.P. James, G.H. Payne and E.G. Myddleton and 971 other ranks. Entrained for Le Cateau 3 am (17th) and then to billets at Landrecies. To St. Waast (21st), Hamin (22nd). "A" and "B" moved forward to positions on the Mons-Condé, Canal. Later relieved by 1st Duke of Cornwall's Light Infantry. "C" and "D" Companies moved up to canal to reinforce 1st East Surrey (23rd). Enemy engaged 4 pm – Battalion's first casualties – 1 officer wounded, 3 other ranks killed. Received order to retire during evening. Crossed the Haine and fell back to Hamin. Marched through night to Dour then to Bois-du Boussu. Took up defensive positions north of railway line. Continued retreat (24th) via Dour, Athis, Houdain, Prefeuillet to St. Waast and to Montat (25th). Later moved to Pont des Quatre Vaux and bivouacked at the crossroads just west of Le Cateau. Lieutenant-Colonel C.C.R. Murphy in his history of the Suffolk Regiment records that the Battalion moved off after 4 am (26th) on the east side of the road running south-west towards Reumont. At the crossroads south-west of Pont des Quatre Vaux Lord Douglas Malise Graham (ADC to Divisional Commander) arrived and remarked to Major Peebls, "You are going to fight it out here." Battalion dug in facing Le Cateau. No.15 Platoon opened fire on Uhlan patrol about 6 am. Later Brigadier-General S.P. Rolt (Commander 14th Brigade) came up and informed the Battalion – "You understand, there is to be no thought of retirement." Came under shrapnel and high explosive shell fire. Second-Lieutenant Myddleton killed, Lieutenant-Colonel Brett mortally wounded. Reinforcements could not get through but a small party of 2nd Argyll and Sutherland Highlanders eventually joined the Suffolks. Came under heavy fire from machine guns situated on the Le Cateau-Cambrai road. Enemy attacked in force at 2.30 pm from front and right flank. The Germans, Colonel Murphy records, shouting to the Suffolks and Highlanders to cease fire and surrender. Battalion eventually overwhelmed when enemy broke in from the rear. Withdrawal ordered and remnants of Battalion fell back via Bohain to St. Quentin. War Diary records roll call (27th) as 2 officers and 111 other ranks. There had been 720 casualties – officers killed being Lieutenant-Colonel Brett, Captain Reid, Second-Lieutenants Payne and Myddleton. Continued march to Ham and reached Pontoise during evening (28th). Strength of Battalion now 229 which was organized into a company under Lieutenant Oakes and attached to 1st East Surrey. Marched during night (29th) to Attichy and then to Crépy-en-Valois (31st). Colonel Murphy records 2 interesting coincidences. The Suffolk Regiment, as 12th Regiment of Foot, was present at the Siege of Gibraltar 1779-1783. As was one of the opposing German Regiments (Hardenberg's). Both were granted "Gibraltar" as a battle honour. Also at the Battle of Le Cateau, and in immediate support of the Suffolks, was No. 11 Battery, Royal Field Artillery. This battery along with the 12th Foot and Hardenberg's all fought at the battle of Minden in 1759.

SEPTEMBER
To Rouville then Nanteuil-le-Haudouin (1st), Montge (2nd). Crossed the Marne at Isles- les-Villenoy (3rd) and bivouacked at Bouleurs. Marched via Crecy (4th) and arrived at Favieres (5th). Took up outpost positions facing north-east. Advanced to Favieres (6th), where draft of 90 men under Captain A. Winn arrived, then moved on to Plessis St. Avoye. To Coulommiers (7th). In support of attack from Doue towards St. Ouen (8th). Continued advance during afternoon via Champtorel to Rougeville. Moved through Saacy (9th) and took part in attack towards Montreuil. War Diary records reaching top of a hill 1.30 pm then came under heavy fire from wood on the right. Range 150 yards. There was also shell fire from half left. Captain Winn killed. Withdrew to positions 200 yards south of wood 6.30 pm. Enemy retired during night. Moved forward via Montreuil to

St. Quentin (10th). Reinforcements arrived during march. War Diary gives strength now as 4 officers and approx. 480 other ranks. Organized into 4 companies (11th) then moved to Billy-sur- Ourcq. Battalion billeted in the church. Marched via Hartennes and Droizy to Chacrise (12th). To Serches (13th) and crossed the Aisne by rafts just above destroyed bridge at Venizel. Took up reserve positions just north of Missy-sur-Aisne. Draft of 14 officers arrived (16th). Began digging new trenches near railway line (22nd). Held reserve line under shelling and sniper fire until (24th). Then moved to Le Carrier. Draft of 2 officers and 168 other ranks joined. Strength now 20 officers, approx. 600 other ranks. Moved via Serches to Courville 4.30 am. (27th). Returned to Le Carrier same morning. Provided working parties to assist Royal Engineers in Serches. To Fere-en-Tardenois via Serches, St Maast and Acy (29th). Now serving as GHQ – Army Troops.

OCTOBER
War Diary records Guard of Honour practised daily in the event of a visit by the French President and that all badges and buttons were to be polished. "C" and "D" Companies sent to Braine (5th) and billeted in Belleme Château, 1 mile to the north-east. Attached to Headquarters, 1st Army Corps. Remainder moved in 2 trains to Abbeville (8th). Entrained for St. Omer (13th) then to billets at Caserne-de-la-Barre. "C" and "D" Companies rejoined (21st). Moved via Cassel to Vieille Chapelle in 34 motor buses (25th). Marched to Rouge Croix and attached to 8th Brigade, 3rd Division. Relieved 2nd Royal Scots in trenches along Fauquissart-Neuve Chapelle road (27th). War Diary records (29th) – "Great annoyance from snipers in the White House." Casualties (27th-30th) – 1 officer wounded, 4 other ranks killed, 7 wounded.

NOVEMBER
Relieved by 1st Devonshire (6th) and to Estaires. Moved to Vieille Chapelle (8th) and to Gorre (9th). Attached in support of French and Indian troops. War Diary records bad guiding by French soldier who caused ammunition cart to fall into a canal. The horses being drowned. "A" and "B" Companies attached to French brigade, "C" and "D" to 21st Indian Brigade in Givenchy sector. Concentrated at Gorre (11th) and to billets at Vieille Chappelle. Relieved 9th Gurkhas in trenches on western edge Estaires-La Bassée road – Neuve Chapelle sector (12th). Relieved by 1st Northamptonshire (14th) and to Lacouture. To Bailleul (15th). Relieved French troops in trenches east of Wulverghem (16th). Relieved by 2nd Royal Scots and to Neuve Eglise (21st). Relieved 4th Middlesex in trenches (24th). Relieved (27th) and to Westoutre. To billets in Sherpenberh (30th).

DECEMBER

War Diary records visit of HM The King (3rd), who with General Sir H. Smith-Dorrien went on to view the front line at Scherpenburgh Hill. Lieutenant-Colonel Murphy reminds his readers that this was the first occasion since the Battle of Dettingen in 1743 that a British Monarch had been present on a battlefield at time of war. Later took over trenches in Kemmel sector. The records of several battalions in the same area record the bad condition of trenches. Most knee-deep in water and in constant need of repair. War Diary records the deaths of 2 men (4th) after part of the Battalion's line collapsed. Also, on same day, an accident with a grenade that killed 1 man and badly wounded 3 others. Relieved (6th) and to Westoutre. To positions on Kemmel-Ypres road (14th) and in support during attack on Petit Bois. Moved forward 4.30 pm and relieved 2nd Royal Scots in captured trench. Captain A.H.W. Temple killed. War Diary notes that this officer fell into the arms of Private R.G. Girbow who next day in the same place was himself shot dead. Also recorded (15th) is the attempt by 80 Germans dressed in khaki to dig their way towards the Suffolk's line. They immediately offered to surrender when fired upon, but opened fire when men moved out to bring them in. Relieved 6 pm and to Locre. Casualties – 8 killed, 9 wounded. To trenches (18th). Headquarters at Pigsty Farm. Relieved (21st) and to Westoutre. Casualties – 1 killed, 8 wounded. Relieved 1/1st Honourable Artillery Company in trenches facing Spanbrock Moelen (27th). Headquarters at Vroilandhoek Farm. Relieved (31st) and to Westoutre.

1/4TH BATTALION (TERRITORIAL FORCE)

AUGUST

Headquarters, "A", "B", "C" and "D" Companies at Ipswich, "E" Company – Lowestoft, "F" Company – Halesworth, "G" Company – Framlingham, "H" Company – Leiston. Part of Norfolk and Suffolk Brigade, East Anglian Division. Battalion had arrived at Great Yarmouth for annual camp (31st July). Ordered back to Ipswich (1st). To War stations at Felixstowe (6th). Later moved to Shenfield, then Braxted, Peldon and Severalls.

NOVEMBER

Entrained at St. Botolph's for Southampton (5th). Sailed SS *Rossetti* (8th), arriving Havre (9th). Officers – Lieutenant-Colonel F. Garrett, T.D. (Commanding Officer), Majors F.W. Turner, T.D. (Second in Command), W. Dooley (Quartermaster), F. Pretty, Captains M.F. Mason, S. Garrett,

E.P. Clarke, E.L. Brown, F.S. Cubitt, F.J. Rodwell, H.D. Mitchell, R. Cockburn (Adjutant), J.D. Wells (Medical Officer), R.A. Parry, Lieutenants B. St. J. Glanfield, C. Catchpole, H. Pretty, H.F. Ling, H.K. Turner, M.A. Turner, J.W. Pain, Second-Lieutenants D.M. Ffrench, G.W. Stebbings, H.A. Row, L.J. Richards (Transport Officer), J.G. Frere, L.E. Milburn, R.S. Barnes, D. Pretty, H.M. Brown, F.J.C. Ganzoni. Entrained for St. Omer (13th) and from there marched to billets at Blendecques. To Lambres (30th).

DECEMBER
To Vieille Chapelle (4th) and attached to Jullundur Brigade, Lahore Division. Reorganized as 4 companies. To Béthune (11th), Beuvry (12th). "D" Company to trenches (14th). Remainder of battalion to Annequin (16th) and in reserve during attack on the Triangle between Béthune and La Bassée. Returned to Beuvry by mid-day. "D" Company relieved (17th) – casualties for first tour in the line – 1 killed, 2 wounded. To Cuinchy (20th) – "B" Company to front line across La Bassée Canal at Givenchy; "C" Company in support half- way up rise from canal to Givenchy; "D" in support trenches at brewery on far bank of canal; "A" in reserve at Cuinchy. "B" Company with 1st Manchester and two French territorial units attacked during afternoon and captured Givenchy along with 2 lines of trenches to the north-east. Enemy counter-attacks continued throughout night and next morning. Battalion to Beuvry (22nd), Allouagne (23rd).

PRINCE ALBERT`S (SOMERSET LIGHT INFANTRY)

"Le Cateau" "Retreat from Mons"
"Marne, 1914" "Aisne, 1914" "Armentières, 1914"

1ST BATTALION

AUGUST

Colchester. Part of 11th Brigade, 4th Division. Entrained for Harrow (17th) and camped on Harrow School playing fields. Entrained for Southampton (21st) and embarked SS *Braemar Castle*. Landed Havre (22nd) and to rest camp. Entrained for Le Cateau (23rd). Arrived 5 pm (24th) and marched to Briastre. "A" Company set up piquets on the Viesly and Solesmes roads. Moved forward to Solesmes (25th) – "C" and "D" Companies engaged enemy cavalry patrol. Later ordered to withdraw and during night marched via Viesly, Bethencourt and Beauvois to Fontaine-au-Pire. "A" and "B" Companies moved into defensive positions north-west of Ligny (26th). "C" and "D" Companies took up line at southern end of Beauvois and came under heavy shell fire. Later fell back to quarries near Fontaine. Enemy advanced and Battalion retired to Ligny. Major F.G. Thoyts mortally wounded. Everard Wyrall records in his war history of the Somerset Light Infantry that the Battalion reorganized at the eastern end of the village. The wounded being placed into the church, but could not be evacuated. Casualties are given as approximately 9 officers wounded, 19 other ranks killed, 150 wounded, 100 missing. Order received to retreat and Battalion withdrew after 5 pm in several parties. Commanding Officer, Lieutenant-Colonel E.H. Swayne fell back to Aubencheul while another detachment under Major C.B. Prowse moved via Clary and Elincourt to Serain. Colonel Swayne`s party came under fire from a British sentry near Vendhuilie (27th) then later marched via Roisel, Hancourt and Monchy-Lagache to Voyennes. Major Prowse joined his CO early (28th). Battalion left during morning, marching via Hombleux and Libermont to Campagne. Moved via Sermaize to Sempigny (29th) where a third party of 300 men under Lieutenant R.V. Montgomery rejoined. Continued retreat via Carlepont, Bailly, Tracy-le-Mont, Trosly and Breuil to Pierrefonds (30th), then via the Forest of Compiègne to defensive positions on high ground south of St. Sauveur (31st).

SEPTEMBER

War Diary records (1st) that Battalion marched at 7 am under orders to occupy a rearguard position. Headquarters, "A", "B" and "C" Companies noted as holding La Hautber Farm on the ridge north of Saintimes while the remaining company was – "...soon heavily engaged" on the right of 1st Hampshire north of St. Sauveur. Battalion formed up about 10 am and moved via .Rully to Rosieres. To Eve via Baron (2nd), Chanteloup via Dammartin, Juilly, St. Mesme, Claye-Souiccy and Lagny (3rd), Coupvray via Jossigny and Serris (4th). To billets at the Château la Mausadière near Chévry (5th). Began advance (6th), marching via Jossigny to Villeneuve-le-Comte. Moved through Tigeaux, Crécy and La Chapelle to Maisoncelles (7th) then via La Haute Maison, Pierre Levée and Signy Signets to the Château Venteuil at Les Corbier (8th). Crossed the Petit Morin at St. Martin (9th) then to Les Abymes. "C" Company later moved forward to assist 1st East Lancashires engaged at La Ferté. War Diary notes that the company ". . . did some damage at long range." Battalion moved forward to La Ferté (10th) then later via Porte-Ferrée and Cocherel to Chaton. To Vendrest (11th) then via Coulombs, Hervillers and St. Quentin to Passy. To Septmonts (12th) then at 10 pm to Venizel. Crossed the Aisne (13th) and took part in attack on Bucy-le-Long. Advanced to the north-west and objective taken without opposition. Battalion then established line in sunken lane facing Crouay. Here the men had their first meal since 2.15 the previous morning. Second-Lieutenant A.B. Read and 4 other ranks killed, 1 officer and 5 other ranks wounded from shell fire (16th).

OCTOBER

Relieved by French troops (6th) and to Buzancy. War Diary records that the Battalion assembled in a large cave. Began march to Vannette (7th), arriving (10th) and entraining for St. Omer (11th). Marched during morning (12th) to Blendecques then in afternoon travelled in buses to Hondeghem. Marched via Caestre to Flêtre (13th), Meteren to Bailleul (14th). Advanced on Erquinghem (15th) then moved via Nieppe to Armentières (18th). To Pont-de-Nieppe then Ploegsteert (20th). Moved to north-east corner of Ploegsteert Wood (21st) and took part in attack on Le Gheer. War Diary records that "A" Company supported by "B" advanced via the eastern edge of the wood. Captain W. Watson noted in a letter that the enemy were Saxons and cleared from the village "at the point of the bayonet." Casualties – 1 officer wounded, 7 other ranks killed, 19 wounded. Battalion relieved by 1st Hampshire from trenches running from St. Yves to River Douve (28th) and withdrew into reserve positions at the Château north of Ploegsteert Wood. Enemy broke through at St. Yves (30th) and Battalion went forward during evening to assist 1st Hampshire restore line. "C" company remained in firing line. Position held under heavy bombardment and infantry attack (31st).

NOVEMBER

Battalion relieved by 2nd Lancashire Fusiliers (2nd) and to bivouacs near Ploegsteert. Relieved 2nd Lancashire Fusiliers in trenches north-west of St. Yves (6th). Relieved by 3rd Worcestershire and 1st Rifle Brigade (13th) and to reserve positions in Ploegsteert Wood. To front line along eastern edge of Ploegsteert Wood (16th). Carried out tours in front line throughout month, resting at Pont-de-Nieppe and Armentières. Arrangements were made for the men to take baths and have their uniforms cleaned at Pont-de-Nieppe and details of this appear in a letter written by Lieutenant G.R. Parr (see Everard Wyrall history). He notes that the baths – 15 large vats (10 men to a vat), were situated in a linen factory and that the men, having removed their jackets and trousers, tied the garments together with their identity disk. The uniforms were then taken away for fumigation, washing, repair and ironing, while undergarments were boiled in disinfectant. These jobs, Lieutenant Parr records, were carried out by large numbers of local women.

DECEMBER

Continued duties in forward area – 6 days in firing line, 3 in support. Took part in attack on The Birdcage (19th). "B" Company led charge from eastern edge of Ploegsteert Wood at 2.30 pm. Everard Wyrall records that the enemy's line was some 120 yards away and that no sooner had the leading troops moved into No Man's Land – "sheets of flame leapt up from the German trenches and bullets from machine guns and rifles met the advance of the gallant Somersets." He also notes that several British shells fell among the men causing many casualties. Very few managed to reach the German lines – Captains C.C. Maud, R.C. Ore, Lieutenant Parr and Second-Lieutenant S.B. Henson all being killed at close quarters. Captain F.S. Bradshaw was mortally wounded. When the support company moved up about 5 pm the survivors of "B" Company were found in a house – the Somersets in one room, German troops in another. Casualties, other ranks – 27 killed, 52 wounded, 30 missing. Lieutenant R.L. Moore killed (20th). The War Diary of 11th Brigade provides approximate casualties since the Battalion landed in France as 36 officers and 1,153 other ranks. Of these, 8 officers and 131 other ranks had been killed.

PRINCE OF WALES`S OWN (WEST YORKSHIRE REGIMENT)

"Aisne, 1914" "Armentières, 1914"

1ST BATTALION

AUGUST
Lichfield. Part of 18th Brigade, 6th Division. To Dumfermline (7th). Moved to Cambridge (13th) and camped on Jesus Common.

SEPTEMBER
To Newmarket (7th) and entrained for Southampton. Embarked SS *Cawdor Castle* and sailed (8th) for France. Arrived off St. Nazaire (9th). Landed (10th) and entrained for Coulommiers (11th). Arrived (12th) and to billets at Croupet. Began march to the Aisne, arriving Bourg (19th). Moved forward and took over trenches along the Chemin des Dames above Troyon. French troops on right attacked about 5 am (20th) and forced to withdraw. "D" Company moved forward to protect Battalion`s right flank. French later returned to their line and mistaking "D" Company for the enemy opened fire causing several casualties. Enemy attacked again about 8 pm. War Diary records that a man came back from the front line and reported that the forward companies had been captured. Apparently, the enemy had come forward under a white flag. When the Sherwood Foresters went out to meet them they were surrounded and fired upon. Battalion relieved and moved back to Troyon. Casualties – Major A.W. Ingles, Captains M. Fisher, J.F. I`Anson, Lieutenants W.L. Eliot, T.G. Meautys, O.C.W. Thompson, Second-Lieutenant E.W. Wilson killed, 2 officers (including Commanding Officer, Lieutenant-Colonel F.W. Towsey) wounded, 8 officers missing, 71 other ranks killed, 110 wounded, 436 missing. Relieved 1st Durham Light Infantry in front line (24th). Relieved by 1st Loyal North Lancashire during evening (25th) and to Parnan. Casualties – 9 killed, 2 wounded. An officer of the relieving battalion noted that the West Yorkshire`s trenches were full of dead and it was impossible to dig without uncovering bodies. Moved forward to support line north-east of Troyon (28th).

OCTOBER
Relieved by 2nd Sherwood Foresters (1st) and to billets at Moulins. Later in evening to Vauxtin area. Marched via Braisne, Courville and Serches to Jury (2nd), via Largny and St. Sauveur to St. Remy (6th). Entrained at

Compiègne for St. Omer (9th). Arrived (10th) and to billets at Arcques. To Wardrecques (11th) then by lorries to Hazebrouck. To Vieux Berquin area (12th). Moved forward to La Couronne (13th) and at 1.30 pm began attack on German positions around Bleu and Bleu Farm. Village taken by 4 pm and line held throughout night. Casualties – Major H.T. Cliffe and 9 other ranks killed, 2 officers and 32 other ranks wounded. Advanced under fire to positions just under a mile north of La Verrier (14th). Second-Lieutenant J. Carew and 1 man killed, 1 officer and 4 other ranks wounded. To Steenwerck (15th). Continued advance and in reserve during the attack on Paradis Ridge (18th). Moved forward during night and relieved 3 companies of 1st East Yorkshire just south-west of Capinghem. Line held above Ennetières and on the Escobecques-Capinghem road. Enemy attacked in large numbers about 11.30 am (20th). War Diary records the withdrawal of regiment on Battalion's right (2nd Sherwood Foresters) and the enemy entering Ennetières. The Battalion became almost surrounded, 1st West Yorkshire's line held, however, and all attacks repulsed. Casualties – Lieutenant J. Lawson-Smith killed, Captain E.T. Welchman, Lieutenant B.D. Costin mortally wounded, 3 other officers wounded, 34 other ranks killed or wounded. Withdrew to Bois Grenier and Brigade Reserve during night (21st). Returned to front line on Rue du Bois before end of month.

NOVEMBER
Relieved by 1st East Yorkshire (3rd). Held line south-east of la Chapelle d' Armentières (17th-30th) then relieved by 2nd Durham Light Infantry and to billets at L' Armee.

DECEMBER
Returned to front line (5th). Captain A.R. Loveband killed (6th), Captain J.K. Clother killed (7th). Later relieved and to billets in Armentières. Moved to Erquinghem (16th). Relieved 2nd Leinster in trenches east of Armentières (26th).

2ND BATTALION

AUGUST
Malta.

SEPTEMBER
Embarked SS *Galicia* for England (14th). Arrived Southampton (25th) and to camp at Hursley Park near Winchester. Joined 23rd Brigade, 8th Division.

NOVEMBER

To Southampton (4th) and sailed for France. Lieutenant-Colonel G.F. Phillips in command. Arrived Havre (5th) and from there marched to No.6 Rest Camp. Entrained for Merville (9th) and took over billets near Neuve Berquin. To Neuve Eglise (11th) and came under orders of Cavalry Corps. Relieved 2nd Devonshire in line at Messines Ridge (13th). War Diary notes 3 men wounded (14th) – the first for the Battalion. Relieved by 2nd Middlesex (15th) and to Neuve Eglise. Rejoined 8th Division at Estaires (17th). Began tours of duty in line (18th) – 3 days in trenches, 3 in billets.

DECEMBER

Holding part of line Pont Logy-Chapigny almost 1 mile north of Neuve Chapelle (1st). From billets in Red Barn on Estaires-La Bassée road moved forward to front line (18th). In support of 2nd Devonshire attack on the Moated Grange. Party of bombers under Lieutenant F.J. Harrington took part of enemy's trench. Two companies began to dig communication trench to captured positions at 5.10 pm. Battalion ordered to take over 2nd Devonshire gains at 9.30 pm. Enemy counter-attacked 8 am (19th). Under strong bombing assault retired to original front line. Casualties – Major R.G. Cooper-King and Lieutenant B.H.G. Shaw killed, 2 other officers wounded, 120 other ranks killed or wounded. Relieved by 2nd Middlesex (21st) and to La Flinque. Returned to front line (25th). War Diary records that hardly a shot was fired during Christmas Day and British and German troops exchanged greetings. Also noted was battalion's first baths which were taken at Divisional Bath House in La Gorgue (29th).

EAST YORKSHIRE REGIMENT

"Aisne, 1914" "Armentières, 1914"

1ST BATTALION

AUGUST

York. Part of 18th Brigade, 6th Division. To Edinburgh (8th) then Cambridge (14th). Moved into camp on Jesus Common.

SEPTEMBER

To Newmarket (7th) and entrained for Southampton. Embarked SS *Cawdor Castle*. Sailed for France (8th). Arrived off St. Nazaire (9th). Landed (10th) and to Chantier rest camp. Entrained (11th). Reached Coulommiers (12th) and to billets in the sugar factory. Moved to Doue during night, Château Thierry (15th), Hartennes (16th), Chacrise (17th), Dhuizel (18th), Bourg (19th). Relieved 2nd Royal Sussex and 1st Loyal North Lancashire in trenches along the Chemin des Dames above Vendresse and Troyon. Enemy broke through on right of line (20th). "A" and "B" Companies went forward to counter-attack but soon forced to withdraw after encountering heavy shrapnel and machine gun fire. War Diary records action ceasing about 4.30 pm and original line held. Casualties – Captain E.L.P. Edwards, Lieutenant B.S.C. Hutchinson killed, Lieutenant-Colonel R.E. Benson (Commanding Officer) mortally wounded, 4 other officers wounded, 1 missing, 73 other ranks killed or wounded. Enemy continued shelling day and night. Lieutenant T.R. Bottomley killed (23rd). Relieved and to Troyon (24th) then to Moulins (25th). Took over support line just north of Vendresse.

OCTOBER

To Vauztin (1st) then via Braisne, Courville and Serches to Jury (2nd). Marched via Largny and St. Sauveur to St. Remy (6th). Entrained at Compiègne for St. Omer (9th). Arrived (10th) and to billets at Arcques. Later ordered forward to Racquinghem in support of French troops. Moved to Wardreques (11th) then in buses to Hazebrouck. Set up outpost line south-east of town. To Vieux Berquin area (12th) and La Couronne (13th). Took part in attack on enemy positions around Bleu and Blue Farm. "A" and "C" Companies moving forward 1.30 pm, "D" and "B" following in support. Bleu captured by 4 pm and line from village to La Couronne held throughout night. Casualties – 4 killed, 18 wounded. Advanced to positions around crossroads at Pont Wemeau (14th). To Steenwerck (15th) then in evening to billets at Petit Mortier. Advanced to positions behind Ennetières (17th) and took part in attack on the Paradis Ridge (18th). "A" and "D" Companies went forward 7 am. Objective taken by 10 am. Attacked Capinghem later in afternoon and immediately sustained high casualties from enfilade machine gun fire. Advance continued and line dug during night just west of village. "C" Company remained in line, but remainder relieved by 1st West Yorkshire and moved back to La Fleur d` Ecosse. Casualties – Captain A.H. Wilson and 12 other ranks killed, 2 officers, 52 other ranks wounded, 8 missing. "A", "B" and "D" Companies moved to positions on rear slope of the Paradis Ridge (19th) and dug in behind "C" Company in front line. "B" Company moved forward with Machine Gun Section to trenches on left of "C" Company during night. Enemy attacked in large numbers 8 am (20th). 2nd Leinster`s trenches overrun to the left at Premesques and "D" and "A" Companies sent to reinforce. Everard Wyrall in his war history of the East Yorkshire Regiment records that the 2 companies, with a party of Leinsters, were initially able to hold the German advance near the crossroads at Mont-de- Premesques. Later, however, "D" Company in its attempt to regain some of the lost ground, came up against a large number of the enemy and lost heavily. This gallant attack, Everard Wyrall notes, was led by Second-Lieutenant M.R. Pearse, who just before being killed was heard to call out to his men – "Come along lads; it is a fine thing to die a hero!" "A" Company had some success and with assistance from a company of 2nd Durham Light Infantry, held back any further advance by the enemy. Battalion ordered to retire just before midnight and fell back to Château Hancardry. Then via Rue du Bois withdrew into Divisional Reserve at Bois Grenier. Casualties – Captain F. Hind mortally wounded and taken prisoner, Lieutenants M.R. Pease, P. Clutterbuck and 3 other ranks killed, 2 officers, 81 other ranks wounded, 49 missing. Moved to Le Touquet during evening (21st), but returned to Bois Grenier same night. To Croix Blanche (22nd), returning to Bois Grenier (23rd). Relieved 1st Leicestershire in trenches east of Erquinghem-Armentières railway near Rue du Bois early (26th). Enemy attack on "C" Company's line beaten off (27th). Casualties – 1 officer wounded, 8 other ranks killed, 39 wounded, 1 missing. Another attack repulsed (28th) and during counter-attack "C" and part of "A" Company regained trenches north-east of railway belonging to 2nd Durham Light Infantry. Enemy casualties estimated at about 200. Relieved by 1st North Staffordshire during evening and moved back to L'Armée. Casualties – Major W.E. Campion, Captains B. Lawrence, E.W. Walker, Lieutenant H.S.F. Cosens, 30 other ranks killed, 1 officer, 40 other ranks wounded, 15 missing. To Chapel d` Armentières in Divisional Reserve (30th).

NOVEMBER

Chapel d`Armentières came under shell fire (3rd). Five killed, 23 wounded among "C" Company billeted in the brewery. Battalion later moved forward and via La Vesèe and La Guernerie took over trenches from 1st West Yorkshire on the Rue du Bois. War Diary records Battalion billeted between tours in the front line at Grispot, La Vesèe, Desplanque Farm and Armentières.

DECEMBER

Relieved 2nd Sherwood Foresters in front line on the Rue du Bois (7th). War Diary notes enemy trenches some 50 yards away. Relieved during night (11th) and to billets in flax mill north-west of Armentières station. Moved to Hoplines sector (26th) and took over trenches at Pont Ballot.

BEDFORDSHIRE REGIMENT

**"Mons" "Le Cateau" "Retreat from Mons"
"Marne, 1914" "Aisne, 1914" "La Bassée, 1914"
"Ypres, 1914" "Langemarck, 1914" "Gheluvelt"
"Nonne Bosschen"**

1ST BATTALION

AUGUST
Mullingar, Ireland. Part of 15th Brigade, 5th Division. To Belfast in 2 trains
(14th). Embarked SS *Oronsa* and sailed for France 3 pm. Officers –
Lieutenant-Colonel C.R.J. Griffith, DSO (Commanding Officer), Majors
C.C. Onslow (Second in Command), E. I. de S. Thorpe, W. Allason,
Captains J.C. Monteith, J. McM. Milling, C.H. Ker, R.J. McCloughin,
F.H. Edwards, C. Newington, J. Macready (Adjutant), P.J. Hanafin
(RAMC, Medical Officer), Lieutenants J.H. Mayne (Machine Gun
Officer), H. Courtenay, W.W. Wagstaff, C.E.G. Shearman (Scout Officer),
A.G. Corah (Cyclist Platoon), J.S. Davenport, S.A., Gledstanes, C. Pope,
W. St. J. Coventry (Transport Officer), W.A. Duke, A.E. Pierce
(Quartermaster), C.E. Goff (King's Liverpool Regiment attached), Second-
Lieutenants L.W. Rendell, W.A.B. Walker, V.C. Downes. Disembarked
Havre (16th) and to No.5 Rest Camp. A diary written by Lieutenant
Davenport (published in *The Story of the Bedfordshire and Hertfordshire
Regiment)* tells how the Battalion marched through Havre led by French Boy
Scouts. He also recalls the local people's desperation to obtain souvenirs.
Many of the men arriving at camp minus badges, buttons, shoulder titles
and even caps. Left camp 11.30 pm (17th) and marched to Havre station.
Left 5.45 am (18th) and travelled via Rouen and St. Quentin to Le Cateau.
Detrained and marched to billets at Pommereuill. To Commeqnies (21st).
An account written by Captain Macready of the Battalion's service during
1914 was also published in *The Story of the Bedfordshire and Hertfordshire
Regiment*. He recalls while on the march to Commeqnies seeing a signpost
for Malplaquet – 4 Kilometres and immediately remembered his regimental
history. The 1st Battalion had fought there in 1709 and the name borne on
their Colours – ". . . whatever happens, however frightened I may be" he
thought "I must not let down the men that fought at Malplaquet."
Lieutenant Davenport also mentions the battlefield, resting there and
receiving a "very fiery liquid to drink" from an old man. Moved forward
via Dours to Bois du Bossu (22nd). "A" and "B" Companies to Wasmes

(23rd) and dug trenches near the railway. "C" and "D" Companies to Paturage and dug line near the railway and facing east. "A" and "B" Companies came under fire from enemy field guns. Trenches noted as being very shallow and giving little protection. Captain Macready mentions the determination of the Officer's Mess Corporal – Corporal West, in bringing dinners up to the forward line under fire. Relieved and rejoined rest of Battalion at Paturage during morning (24th). Enemy advanced, but their attack beaten off with high casualties. Withdrew to Bavai then Le Cateau (25th). Took up position near Troisville and facing the Le Cateau-Cambrai road. Enemy attacked (26th). War Diary records troops on right driven back leaving Battalion exposed. There were, however, few casualties due to good trenches. Casualties – Lieutenant Wagstaff mortally wounded and 30 men. Eventually fell back to Estrees. Continued retreat via St. Quentin to Eaucourt (27th), Le Noyon and Pontoise (28th), Carlepont (29th), Croutoy (30th), Forest de Compiègne, Orrocqy and Bethisy St. Martin to Crépy-en-Valous (31st). Captain Macready records going to assist troops on the left who had come under attack during the night. Moving via a deep ravine to a line north of Crépy "C" Company then advanced and drove the enemy back.

SEPTEMBER

To Nanteuil (1st). Lieutenant Davenport records an incident involving Major Allason and Lieutenant R.A. West (North Irish Horse attached). Both mounted, the officers came across a German cavalry officer with his orderly. The two parties then charged each other with revolvers firing and swords drawn. Both Germans were brought down, the officer being killed. At Nanteuil a quantity of wine was taken from a cellar. However, a note was left requesting its owner to send his bill to the Officers' Mess when the war was over. This, Lieutenant Davenport points out, went to assisting the enemy with unit identification when they entered the village next day. To Vinantes via Montgé (2nd), Mont Pichet (3rd). Marched to Gagny via Tourant during night (4th). Advanced via Tournan, Villeneuve St. Denis and Mortcerf to La Celle (6th), Boissy-le-Chatel (7th), Doue then St. Cyr (8th). Enemy engaged and prisoners taken. Crossed the Marne at Saacy (9th) and moved on to Bézu. War Diary records enemy shelling and "B" Company coming under machine gun fire from a wood. Marched via Montreuill Aux Lions and Germinat to St. Quentin (10th). War Diary records – ". . . enemy apparently demoralized" – the area being covered with stores, equipment and greatcoats along with dead and wounded. To St. Remy (11th), L'Epitaphe (12th). Here, "A" and "B" Companies moved forward to the Aisne to escort artillery. To La Bigail (13th). War Diary records – "Germans holding line of River Aisne in force – artillery duel all day." Moved forward (14th) and crossed river to Missy. Took up support positions near railway. Heavy shelling all day (15th). Casualties – Captain McCloughin mortally wounded, 1 other officer wounded and about 35 other ranks. Captain Ker killed by sniper. Relieved during night by 1st East Surrey and moved back to bivouacs near Jury. Began tours of duty in trenches along Semoise-Soissons road and trench digging at Serches. Moved forward to line near Chivres (24th). War Diary notes position as being in a marshy wood which was impossible to dig deep. Relieved and to Jury (30th).

OCTOBER

Marched via Nampteuil to Launoy (2nd), Hartennes and Longport to Corcy (3rd) and during night (4th) via Villers Cotterêts to Vittain. To Busigny St. Pierre (6th) and via Saintaines and Verberies to Pont-Ste. Maxence (7th). Bivouacked in field near railway station. Entrained 4 pm and travelled through night via Creuil, St. Just, Amiens and Abbeville to Noyelles then marched via Neuilly to Millencourt. Moved via Agenvillers, Brailly and Boufflers to Genne-Ivergny (8th), Haravesnes (9th). Travelled in French buses (10th) via Fillievres, Linzeux, Croisette, Ramecourt, St. Pol and Brias to La Thieuloye. To Béthune (11th) and relieved French troops in trenches at Essars. Marched via Beuvry (12th) and took part in attack on Givenchy. War Diary records village and trench to the east occupied without much opposition. Shelled later – 17 casualties. Heavily shelled throughout day (13th) then enemy attacked. Withdrew 300 yards in rear of village and reformed on Pont Fixe road. Casualties – Second-Lieutenant Downes mortally wounded, 6 officers, 140 other ranks killed, wounded or missing. New line held (14th). Lieutenant Rendal mortally mounded while leading patrol into Givenchy (16th). Village found unoccupied except for snipers. "A" and "D" Companies advanced and occupied Givenchy. "B" Company sent to support 1st Cheshire at Violaines (19th). Lieutenant Coventry killed (23rd). Rest of Battalion to Chapelle St. Roch (22nd) and attached to 13th Brigade. Took part in attack on farm near Violaines. War Diary records – "Attack not pushed home and ordered to fall back at midnight." Withdrew to line south of Festubert-La Quinque Rue road about 1 mile east of Festubert. "B" Company attacked in support trenches (22nd). Heavy casualties and fell back to position near Rue d' Ouvert. Later rejoined Battalion. Line held and several attacks repulsed (23rd-26th). Second-Lieutenant Walker mortally wounded (26th). Relieved by 2nd Manchester and to billets at Gorre (27th). To Festubert in support during night (28th). Returned to Gorre next morning. "B" and "D" Companies sent forward to reinforce 2nd Manchester (29th). Upon arrival near the Manchester's positions,

Lieutenant Davenport recalls hearing cheering from the forward area. This was part of the Regiment's line being regained from the enemy. An action in which Second-Lieutenant J. Leach and Sergeant J. Hogan were awarded the Victoria Cross. Took over regained trenches – the parapets being rebuilt with the aid of German bodies. "B" and "D" Companies later relieved by Indian troops. Battalion moved forward again (30th) to assist Indian troops. War Diary records that it was difficult to ascertain which of the trenches were occupied by the Indians, and which by Germans. The enemy calling out "We are Gurkhas." Line finally established.

NOVEMBER

Relieved and to Gorre (1st). Returned to front line in support of Indians (2nd). Returned to Gorre 6 am (3rd) but back in trenches 4 pm. Relieved 9 pm (4th) and back to Gorre. Headquarters with "C" and "D" Companies to Locon (5th) and travelled (6th) in London busses via Lestrem, Estaires, Bailleul, Locre and Dickebusch to Ypres. On passing through Locre the Battalion came in contact with the 2nd Bedfordshire then *en route* to Bailleul from the front line. Marched through Ypres and via Hooge took over trenches in wood south of Ypres-Menin road at Gheluvelt. War Diary records that "A" and "B" Companies were already in line having arrived the previous day. Enemy gained part of line on left (7th). Trench reclaimed by counter attack. Casualties – 7 officers, 140 other ranks killed, wounded or missing. Enemy attacked (11th), Casualties – 5 killed, 17 wounded. Another attack (14th) – hand-to-hand fighting on right forced withdrawal 300 yards. Casualties – approximately 18 killed and wounded. Lieutenant Pope and about 10 men missing. Relieved by 2nd Worcestershire (19th) and fell back to wood near Hooge in support. Relieved by French troops (21st) and via Ypres and Vlamertinghe marched to Locre. To St. Jans Cappel (24th). To trenches north-west of Wulverghem via Dranoutre (28th).

DECEMBER

Relieved by 2nd King's Own Scottish Borderers (5th) and to Dranoutre in support. War Diary records that 3 officers and 200 men remained with the Borderers for 2 days as they were too weak to hold the line. Relieved 1st Norfolk in firing line at dusk (8th). Relieved by 1st Royal West Kent (10th) and to St. Jans Cappel. To Dranoutre (14th) then after dark to Neuve Eglise in reserve. To front line Wulverghem sector (17th). Half Battalion in trenches, rest in support at Neuve Eglise. Company of 1/6th Cheshire attached. Semaphore message received from German line (25th) indicating that they wound not fire today. Relieved by 2nd Duke of Wellington's (29th) and to Bailleul in Divisional Reserve.

2ND BATTALION

AUGUST
Robert`s Heights, Pretoria. Mobilized (10th). Embarked HMT *Kenilworth Castle* at Cape Town (22nd). Put out into Table Bay (23rd) and sailed for England (27th).

SEPTEMBER
Called at St. Helena (1st) and sailed again (2nd). Arrived Southampton (19th) and to Lyndhurst. Joined 21st Brigade, 7th Division.

OCTOBER
Moved by 2 trains to Southampton (4th). Half of Battalion sailed SS *Winefredian*. Remainder embarked SS *Cornishman* during following morning. Sailed (5th). *Winefredian* recalled off Ostend due to submarine alert and to Dover. Left 9 pm (6th) and arrived Zeebrugge 3.30 am (7th). Moved by train to Bruges then marched to billets at St. Croix. Rest of Battalion (*Cornishman*) arrived 6 pm. Officers included Majors J.M. Traill (Commanding Officer) and R.P. Stares (Second in Command), Captains C.C. Foss (Adjutant), H. Cressingham (Quartermaster), C.S. Garnett-Botfield (Machine Gun Officer) and W.G. Goudie (RAMC, Medical Officer). Company commanders were Captains F.M. Bassett, A.J. Patron, A.B. Lemon and A.G. Hall. To Clemskerke (8th), Hasebrouck (9th), Trois Rois (10th), Coolscamp (12th). War Diary records enemy Taube sighted. To Beverns (13th), Ypres and billets on Bailleul road (14th). Moved forward up Menin road (15th) and relieved 8th French Regiment. Position given as running from the 3- Kilometre stone on Menin road running south-south-west towards Zillebeke. Advanced to reserve positions at Gheluvelt (16th). Moved forward to 10-Kilometre stone on Ypres- Menin road (18th). "A" Company crossed road and took up position on edge of wood then came under fire from German field gun. Withdrew and dug in with right on 10-Kilometer stone. Casualties – Second-Lieutenant C.O. Bell and 2 other ranks killed, 3 officers, 21 other ranks wounded, 20 missing. Moved back to Gheluvelt in reserve (19th). Took over trenches near Veldhoek Château (20th). To Zonnebeke as reinforcement to 22nd Brigade (21st). Took up position at level crossing west of town. Returned to Veldhoek under heavy shell fire after 1 hour. Two platoons of "A" Company sent to assist 2nd Royal Scots Fusiliers during night. Returned next morning (22nd) under heavy shell fire. Lieutenant D.L.deT. Fernandez killed. Moved forward to Zonnebeke (22nd), but ordered back during march. Later, "C" Company sent to reinforce 2nd Royal Scots Fusiliers and "A" Company to 2nd

Yorkshire. "C" Company advanced (23rd). War Diary records that it almost reached the bend in the Poezelhoek road when heavy rifle and machine gun fire brought attack to a standstill. Lieutenant G.D.C. Wright killed. Later "B" Company came forward under heavy fire via west end of Gheluvelt. Moved through Château grounds north of village and was then hit by strong rifle and machine gun fire. Took up positions on edge of wood south of bend in Becelaere road. War Diary records "severe" losses. "D" company followed on, also under heavy fire, filling gap between "B" and "C" Companies. Position consolidated throughout night. Held line (24th). Detachments assisted 2nd Royal Scots Fusiliers in Château grounds and helped clear part of wood. Moved forward for attack on Becelaere (25th). War Diary records that it was dark and that – "the men behaved with great steadiness." Attack suspended and ordered to withdraw to start line. Captain Hall killed by sniper (26th). First draft of 20 men under Lieutenant D.G.C. Thompson arrived. Relieved by 1st Scots Guards during night and to Veldhoek. Later moved to bivouacs in wood near Hooge. Moved forward (27th) and relieved 1st Black Watch in line near Zandvoorde Château, Zandvoorde-Gheluvelt road. Relieved by 2nd Scots Guards and 1st Gordon Highlanders (28th) and via Gheluvelt to trenches near Zandvoorde. Took part in counter-attack on Kruiseecke Ridge (29th). Heavy shell, rifle and machine gun fire held up advance. War Diary records that the Battalion – "was now somewhat scattered and intermingled with other regiments." Later relieved and moved back into Brigade Reserve near Zandvoorde. Lieutenant E.E. Punchard killed and 6 other officers wounded. Germans entered Zandvoorde (30th) and Battalion came under fire from battery at 900 yards. Withdrawal ordered and fell back to line behind the Gheluvelt-Zandvoorde road. Part of "C" Company moved forward (31st) to occupy small wood 250 yards in front. War Diary notes severe losses – Majors Traill and Stares remaining in trenches and being killed at close range, Lieutenant H.C. Patterson killed in the wood, Captain E.H. Lyddon and Lieutenant W.C. Anderson missing. Both these officers had been killed. Fell back to position on Ypres-Menin road. Strength now 4 officers – Captains C.C. Foss, H. Cressinghem, Lieutenant S.D. Mills, Second-Lieutenant B.H. Waddy and between 350 and 400 other ranks.

NOVEMBER
Trenches shelled (3rd) and (4th). Some men buried, 1 man killed. Relieved by 1st Cheshire (5th) and to Herenthage Château. Marched via Ypres and Locre to Bailleul (6th). Took over billets in Rue de Lille. While at Locre the Battalion met the 1st Bedfordshire. The senior battalion arriving in London buses. To Ploegsteert (8th) and held in reserve near Château Rossignol. To

Bailleul (12th) and into billets near the Lunatic Asylum. Draft of 4 other ranks from 1/28th London joined as probationer officers. To Sailly (16th) and relieved 2nd Border in trenches south-west of Fleurbaix – La Boutillerie (17th). Relieved by 2nd Yorkshire (20th) and to Fleurbaix. To trenches (23rd), relieved (25th), to trenches (30th).

DECEMBER
Relieved (3rd). Inspected by Major-General T. Capper (GOC, 7th Division) (4th). He spoke of the recent fighting at Ypres and how the Battalion had been put to a severe test – "... holding the line against 3 times our own numbers." To trenches (6th), relieved (9th), to trenches (12th), relieved by 1st South Staffordshire (13th). To Pont-de-Nieppe (14th) in Corps Reserve. Returned to Fleurbaix (18th) and front line during evening. Relieved by 2nd Yorkshire (21st) and to Fleurbaix. To front line (24th). War Diary records Christmas Day (25th) and "The Truce." A report sent in by the Commanding Officer to Brigade Headquarters noted that about 8 pm on Christmas Eve the Germans began to sing. Lights were also seen on the parapets. Later, a voice called out in English with a request to meet in No Man's Land. This being with a view to making burial arrangements. Second- Lieutenant de Buriatt went out with 8 men and spoke to a German soldier. It was noted that he was not an officer and had lived in Brighton and Canada. Also observed were the shoulder numerals of the 15th Regiment and that red bands around the caps had been covered with grey cloth. On Christmas Day, a small party of Germans came out bearing a white flag. Burial arrangements were then made. The German trenches, the report noted, were strongly manned by young men between 19 – 25 years old. They were "well turned out and clean." A company sergeant major speaking to an elderly officer was informed that the Germans occupied very comfortable billets in a village to the rear. A passing German officer was described as "The Divisioner." Relieved by 2nd Yorkshire (27th) and to Pont-de-la-Justice. To trenches (30th). Germans noted as welcoming in the New Year at 11 pm (Berlin time).

LEICESTERSHIRE REGIMENT

"Aisne, 1914" "La Bassée, 1914" "Armentières, 1914" "Festubert, 1914"

1ST BATTALION

AUGUST

Fermoy, Ireland. Part of 16th Brigade, 6th Division. To Queenstown (14th). Embarked SS *Heroic, Londonderry* and *Kilkenny* (15th) and sailed for Holyhead. Moved by train to Cambridge and camp at Coldham Common. To Grantchester Common (27th).

SEPTEMBER

To Royston (7th) and by train to Southampton. Embarked SS *Braemar Castle* (8th) and sailed for France. Officers – Lieutenant-Colonel H.L. Crocker (Commanding Officer), Majors H. Stoney (Second in Command), B.C. Dent, Captains F. Le M. Gruchy, J. Bacchus, R.F. Hawes, L.S.D. Tollemache-Tollemache, A. T. Le M. Utterson, W.C. Wilson, M.G.B. Copeman, E.S.W. Tidswell (Adjutant), J.H. Greasley (Quartermaster), Lieutenants C.C. Rolph, H.B. Brown, J.T. Waller, T. Prain, J.W.E. Mosse, A. Weyman, J.G. Herring-Cooper, H.L. Bayfield, W.H.G. Dods, C. Smeathman, E.C. Lang (RAMC, Medical Officer), Second-Lieutenants H.N.H. Grimble, G.N. Wykes. Arrived St. Nazaire (10th) and to camp at Grande Marais. Moved by train to Mortcerf (11th). Began move forward to the Aisne (13th), marching via Crécy, Jouarres, Sancy, Château Thierry, Rocourt, Buzancy, Ambrief and Mont Nôtre Dame. Arrived Courcelles (20th). Relieved 3rd Worcestershire and 2nd Royal Irish Rifles in front line trenches near Vailly (21st).

OCTOBER

Relieved by French troops during night (12th/13th) and entrained at Fismes for Cassel. Casualties since going into line – Captain Hawes mortally wounded, 5 other ranks killed, 18 wounded. Later to Croix Blanche and moved forward to Bois Grenier (18th). Took up positions on line Rue du Bois – La Houssoie (20th) then in afternoon moved to Porte Egale area. Relieved 1st West Yorkshire in trenches, the Chemical Factory – Rue du Bois (21st). Colonel H.C. Wylly, CB in his war history of the Leicestershire Regiment, notes that a report was received from the Officer Commanding 1st Leicestershire stating that hostile shelling had compelled his battalion to evacuate the line from just south of the Rue du Bois to Le Quesne and that his men were lying in the open along the railway line. The enemy were forming up in considerable strength for an attack around the Le Quesne Distillery. Enemy attacked at dawn (26th). Colonel Wylly notes that – "The Leicester's line was intact from Rue du Bois to the barricade at the level crossing south of the station." Here ". . . close hand-to-hand fighting took place throughout the day." Later withdrew and Battalion located – Headquarters, "C" and "D" Companies at Grise Pot, "A" and "B" Companies Le Touquet. Casualties – Captain Gruchy, Lieutenants Prain and Dods killed, Lieutenant Smeathman mortally wounded, 47 other ranks killed, 5 officers, 134 other ranks wounded, 106 missing. Relieved by 1st East Yorkshire and to Bois Grenier.

NOVEMBER

For remainder of year carried out tours in front line – Porte Egale Farm, Rue du Petillon- Rouges Bancs, Le Touquet-Grand Flamengre Farm, Rue du Bois-Grande Flamanderie Farm. Billets and rest areas – Rue Dunquesne, Bac St. Maur, Fleurbaix and Grise Pot. War Diary of 1st Royal Fusiliers records that 1st Leicestershire relieved 1st Royal Fusiliers on 13th November in Rue du Petillon sector.

DECEMBER

Inspected by HM The King at Bac St. Maur (2nd). Captain P.E. Viney mortally wounded (14th). Sergeant E.B. Hayball, DCM served with "C" Company and recalls that trenches in the Armentières-Bois Grenier sector were taken over a few days before Christmas. He notes that the trenches held by "C" Company were knee-deep in water and – ". . . numerous things were floating about." Casualties for November and December – 24 killed, 26 wounded.

2ND BATTALION

AUGUST

Ranikhet, India. "C" Company at Delhi. Part of Garhwal Brigade, Meerut Division. Order to mobilize received (9th) and "C" Company recalled. Began march to Kathgodam (12th). Moved via Ratighat, Bhowali and Jeolikote. Arrived (15th) and entrained for Bareilly.

SEPTEMBER

Moved by train to Karachi (5th). Arrived (8th) and to rest camp. Headquarters, "C" and "D" Companies embarked SS *Devanha* (15th), "A" and "B" Companies SS *Elephanta* (16th). Sailed (21st). Officers – Lieutenant-Colonel C.G. Blackader, DSO (Commanding Officer), Majors H. Gordon, R.N. Knatchbull, DSO, Captains H.A. Grant, F.H. Romilly, L.B.C. Tristram, F. Latham (Adjutant), D.L. Weir, Lieutenants R. Le Fanu, M.K. Wardle, C. Chudleigh, R.H. Ames, G.P. D`A.G. Tunks, R.A.N. Lowther, H.C. Brodie (Quartermaster), Second-Lieutenants T.R. Grylls, G.A. Quayle, M.W. Seton-Browne, H.M. Raleigh, E.L. Wateridge.

OCTOBER

Arrived Suez (2nd), Port Said (3rd). Sailed for France (6th), disembarking Marseilles (12th) and marching to camp at La Valentine. Moved by train to Orleans (21st), Lillers (26th). To Calonne (28th). Moved forward via Gorre and relieved 3rd Worcestershire in firing line near Festubert (30th). Captain Tristram killed (31st).

NOVEMBER

"B" and "C" Companies relieved by 1st Seaforth Highlanders during night (17th). Second- Lieutenant Wateridge killed (20th). "A" and "D" relieved by 1st Manchester (22nd) and joined rest of Battalion at La Couture. Casualties since entering trenches – 2 officers killed, 2 wounded, 14 other ranks killed, 73 wounded. To Gorre (23rd). "B" and "C" Companies under Major Gordon moved forward and with 107th Pioneers attacked German held positions east of Festubert 4 am (24th). Lieutenant-Colonel W.B.P. Tugwell (107th Pioneers) records in his book *The History of the Bombay Pioneers* that the ground was covered with snow, trenches were ice-bound and a piercing wind was sweeping across the dreary flats around Festubert. The Leicesters, he notes, were on the right of the attack and had the shortest distance to go. Leading waves were soon met by a hail of bombs, rifle and machine gun fire. About a platoon of the Leicesters and 10 men of the 107th reached and occupied part of the objective. Report on attack notes – "the Leicesters effected a lodgment in the enemy`s trenches, but were hard pressed to retain it owing to heavy bombing. . . Captain Grant, killed whilst leading his company in the charge. Second- Lieutenant Seton-Browne was also killed at the head of his platoon just as he had reached the enemy`s trench". "B" and "C" companies withdrew 8.30 am (25th) and returned to Gorre. Battalion moved back to billets at La Couture same day. To front line east of Festubert (28th). Relieved during evening (30th) and to La Couture.

DECEMBER

"A" Company inspected by HM The King at Locon (1st). Colonel H.C. Wylly records in his war history of the 1st and 2nd Battalions, Leicestershire

Regiment that "A" Company was brought up to a strength of 100 by men from "D" Company. Carried out further tours in Festubert sector front line. Took over trenches in front of Rue des Berceaux from 2/3rd Gurkha Rifles (17th) but relief cancelled and Battalion withdrew to prepare for forth-coming attack. Took part in attack near The Orchard north-east of Festubert 3.15 am (19th). Several trenches and 2 Maxim Guns taken. Enemy later counter-attacked with bombs and forced withdrawal to start positions. General Sir James Willcocks was Commander of the Indian Army Corps and in his book *With The Indians in France* mentions the gallantry of several officers and men in the attack. One of these, Private W. Buckingham, would win the Victoria Cross in March, 1915. Moved back to Richebourg St. Vaast. Later rested at Lestrem and Robecq and by the end of the year billeted at Ecquedecques.

ROYAL IRISH REGIMENT

"Mons" "Le Cateau" "Retreat from Mons" "Marne, 1914" "Aisne, 1914" "La Bassée, 1914"

1ST BATTALION

AUGUST
Nasirabad, India.

OCTOBER
Embarked Bombay for England (13th).

NOVEMBER
Arrived Devonport (18th) and to Magdalen Hill Camp, Winchester. Joined 82nd Brigade, 27th Division.

DECEMBER
To Southampton and embarked for France. Strength – 26 officers, 910 other ranks. Commanding Officer – Lieutenant-Colonel G.F.R. Forbes. Arrived Havre (20th) and entrained for Arques.

2ND BATTALION

AUGUST
Devonport. Part of 8th Brigade, 3rd Division. To Southampton (13th) and embarked SS *Herschell*. Sailed for France (14th). Officers – Lieutenant-Colonel St. J.A. Cox (Commanding Officer), Majors S.E.St. Leger (Second in Command), E.H.E. Daniell, DSO, H.W. Long (RAMC, Medical Officer), Brevet-Major E.M. Panter-Downes, Captains G.A. Elliot, W. Mellor, J.S. Fitzgerald, I.B. George, Hon. F.G. Forbes, J. Richings (Quartermaster), Lieutenants F.C. Ferguson, M.C.C. Harrison, A.D. Frazer (Scout Officer), R.E.G. Phillips (Adjutant), P.J. Whitty (Machine Gun Officer), F.H.L. Rushton (Transport Officer), D.P. Laing, A.M.S. Tandy (Signals Officer), A.E.B. Anderson, E.C. Guinness, C.F.T.O`B. ffrench, Second-Lieutenants E.G.D.M. Phillips, C.B. Gibbons, J.D. Shine, K. Newton-King, C.G. Magrath. Arrived Boulogne and to rest camp. Entrained for Aulnoye (15th). Arrived (16th) and to Taisnières. To St. Remy (20th), via Maubeuge to Bettignies (21st). Took up positions (22nd) – Headquarters and "D" Company at St. Symphorien, "A" and "C"

Companies at Villers St. Ghislain, "B" Company at Givry. Moved forward (23rd) and took part in fighting on eastern outskirts of Mons. Heavily engaged around the cemetery before falling back to Nouvelles. Casualties – Captains Mellor, Forbes, Second-Lieutenants Gibbons and Shine killed or mortally wounded, 16 other ranks killed, 5 officers, 58 other ranks recorded as wounded and missing, Major Long and 226 other ranks missing, 1 officer taken prisoner. Marched via Bougnies, Genly and Bavai to Amfroipret (24th), via Le Quesnoy, Romeries, Solesmes, Viesly and Caudry to Audencourt (25th). Took part in fighting around Caudry (26th) – Major Panter-Downes mortally wounded. Received orders to withdraw at 4.45 pm and falling back from Audencourt moved via Clary and Malincourt to Beaurevoir. Continued retreat (27th), leaving at 2 am and marching to Vermand. Moved again at 11.15 pm, arriving Ham 9 am (28th). Left at 6.30 pm for Genvry. To Cuts (29th), Courtieux (30th), via Villers-Cotterêts to Vaumoise (31st).

SEPTEMBER
Marched via Levignen and Villers to Chèvreville (1st), via Monthyon to Iverny (2nd), via Penchard and Meaux to Vaucourtois (3rd). Took up outpost positions south of Previllers. Moved via Vancourtois and La Chapelle to Retal during night (4th). Began advance to the Aisne (6th), marching via Neufmoutiers, Les Meriers and Crevecoeur to Haure-Feuille. Via Coulommiers to Chauffry (7th). In support of the attack on Orly (8th) – 1 officer wounded, 2 other ranks killed, 28 wounded, 6 missing. Left Orly (9th) and marched via Bussieres, Saacy and Nanteuil to Crouttes. To Chezy, via Bezu-le-Guery, Marigny, Neuilly and Vinly (10th). In *The Campaigns and History of The Royal Irish Regiment* Brigadier-General Stannus Geoghegan records that at Chezy, the Battalion took charge of some 540 prisoners. The officers dining and billeting with those of the Royal Irish. To Oulchy-la-Ville via Dammard, Neuilly and Vichel (11th), via Courdoux, Launoy and Maast to Braine (12th). Came under shell fire while leaving Ancienne Wood about 8.15 am (13th). Crossed the Aisne south of Vailly during afternoon, still under heavy fire, and to St. Pierre. Took part in the fighting around the Château on high ground north of Vailly (14th) – Lieutenant Rushton killed. Relieved by 4th Royal Fusiliers (25th) and to Courcelles. Casualties (12th-25th) – 1 officer killed, 4 wounded, 10 other ranks killed, 57 wounded, 40 missing.

OCTOBER
To Longueil Ste. Marie (1st). Entrained for Noyelles-sur-Mer (5th). Arrived (6th) and to Le Titre. To Raye (9th), then by lorries to Tangry

(10th). Moved forward to billets in farm south of the La Bassée Canal (12th), Vieille Chapelle (13th). Advanced under heavy fire (14th) and dug in. Enemy driven out of Richebourg St. Vaast (15th). Relieved (17th) and moved back to Le Plouich. Casualties (13th-16th) – 2 officers wounded, 9 other ranks killed, 70 wounded, 18 missing. Took part in the fighting at Le Riez and Le Pilly (18th- 20th). Brigadier-General Geoghegan records that no information regarding the fate of the Battalion on the 20th October at Le Pilly is known. A report by a German officer of the 56th Regiment, however, tells how his unit (with the 16th Regiment) was informed that "an Irish infantry battalion" was at Le Pilly and well in front of the British line. Enemy artillery at Fournes was instructed to open fire on the Royal Irish – "pouring shrapnel on them at 2,000 yards." The German regiments eventually surrounded the survivors and note taking some 302 prisoners – most of whom were wounded and unable to walk. General Geoghegan gives casualties as Major Daniell, Captain A.W.S. Knox, Lieutenant Tandy, Second-Lieutenants J.R. Smyth, H.G.H. Moore and A.J.R. Anderson killed, the latter having joined the Battalion with a draft on the previous day. Other casualties are given as 11 officers, 561 other ranks wounded, missing or taken prisoner. The number killed was unknown. What remained of the Battalion – Second-Lieutenant and 135 other ranks, were subsequently sent to St. Omer where they served on Line of Communication duties. Refitted and again organized into 4 companies, 2nd Royal Irish joined 12th Brigade, 4th Division in March, 1915.

ALEXANDRA, PRINCESS OF WALES`S OWN (YORKSHIRE REGIMENT)

"Ypres, 1914" "Langemarck, 1914" "Gheluvelt"

2ND BATTALION

AUGUST
Guernsey, Channel Islands. Two companies on Alderney. Sailed SS *Sarnia* and SS *Vera* for Southampton (28th). Arrived during evening and to camp.

SEPTEMBER
Moved to Lyndhurst (4th) and joined 21st Brigade, 7th Division.

OCTOBER
To Southampton (4th). "A" and "B" Companies embarked SS *California* and sailed for Zeebrugge (5th). Arrived (6th) and to Bruges. "C" and "D" Companies sailed SS *Victorian* (6th). Battalion billeted in a tram company offices and sheds. Officers – Lieutenant-Colonel C.A.C. King (Commanding Officer), Majors W.L. Alexander, W.B. Walker, Captains T.W. Stansfield, DSO, A.L. Godman, H.W. McCall, B.S. Moss-Blundell, C.G. Jeffery, L. Peel, H. Levin, R.B. Corser, E.S. Winter (Medical Officer), Lieutenants C.G. Forsyth (Adjutant), A.E.G. Palmer, R.H. Phayre, F.C. Ledgard (Machine Gun Officer), H.S. Kreyer, E. Pickard (Quartermaster), Second-Lieutenants L.H. Marriage, W.A.A. Chauncy (Transport Officer), P.C. Kidd, W.A. Worsley, H.G. Brooksbank, R.H. Middleditch, M.D.W. Maude, W.H. Colley, R. Walmesley. To Clemskerk (8th), Bruges (9th), Beernem (10th), Coolscamp (12th), Roulers (13th), Ypres (14th). Lieutenant Pickard claims to have been the first within the 7th Division to fire on the enemy. Having been sent forward to organize billets for the Battalion at Kruisstraat, 2 Uhlans were sighted entering the village. Lieutenant Pickard, with his Quarter-Master Sergeant, opened fire hitting both men, who by then had turned and were galloping back down the Dickebusch road. Both were eventually collected and brought back to Kruisstraat by some Naval personnel in a lorry. "C" and "D" Companies moved forward to cover the Passchendaele road (15th). To Gheluvelt (16th) then advanced to positions on the crossroads at Nieuwe Kruiseecke. Colonel H.C. Wylly, CB in his history of the Green Howards, records how a patrol from "A" Company under Lieutenant Phayre encountered a party of Germans in a farmhouse. The men were given the opportunity to sur-

1. Private Andrew Gillespie, 10th (Scottish) Battalion, King's (Liverpool Regiment). Andrew Gillespie went overseas with the Liverpool Scottish on 1 November, 1914, and was commissioned into the 1/12th Battalion, Loyal North Lancashire Regiment, 2 November, 1915. *(Courtesy Simon Jervis)*

2. Company Quartermaster Sergeant Donald M. Hopping, 14th London Regiment (London Scottish), August, 1923. This long-serving member of the London Scottish went to France with his battalion on 15 September, 1914. His medals include the Queen's South Africa Medal (first from left) indicating service during the Second Boer War and the 1914 Star (second from left).

(Courtesy Simon Jervis)

3. Officers, 1st Battalion, East Lancashire Regiment, who embarked for France on 21 August, 1914 - (Back Row left to right) Second-Lieutenants W.A. Salt, R.Y. Parker, Lieutenants F.D. Hughes, H.T. MacMullan, Captain A. St. L. Goldie, Lieutenants E.B.M. Delmege, J.F. Dyer, W.E. Dowling, N.A. Leeson, H.W. Canton, Second-Lieutenant W.R. Tosswill; (Middle row left to right) Captains C.B. Walker (Army Service Corps attached), E.E. Coventry, G. Clayhills, DSO, Lieutenant F.E. Belchier, Major T.S. Lambert, Lieutenant-Colonel L.St.G. Le Marchant, DSO, Majors E.R. Collins, DSO, J.E. Green, Captain G.T. Seabroke, Lieutenant R. Longstaff; (Front row left to right) Second-Lieutenant G.H.T. Wade, Lieutenant C.E.M. Richards, Second-Lieutenant K.Hooper, T.H. Mathews, Lieutenants E.C. Hopkins, W.M. Chisholm, R.A. Flood (RAMC).

4. 1st Battalion, Manchester Regiment at Givenchy, 20 December, 1914. From the Painting by Fortunino Matania.

5. 1st Battalion, Rifle Brigade, Ploegsteert Wood, December, 1914.

render, but reused. Subsequently the building was set alight and after a
while the occupants came out. They had held on to the last possible
moment, some men having their boots badly burned. Asked why they would
not surrender the men told how they had been warned that if caught, the
English always shot their prisoners. It was noted that the Germans were
from the 19th Hussars and much was made of the fact that they had been
captured by the Yorkshire Regiment – the old 19th Regiment of Foot.
Moved to Becelaere in Brigade Reserve (18th). Returned to Nieuwe
Kruiseecke crossroads positions (19th). Came under heavy shell fire (20th)
– Second-Lieutenant Walmesley killed. Held line against shell fire and continuous enemy attack. Lieutenant Ledgard killed and Captain Jeffery
mortally wounded (22nd). Colonel Wylly records that some 96,000 rounds
of ammunition was brought up every night and on one occasion 6 waggons
had to come forward during the middle of the day. War Diary of 7th
Division records (23rd) – "The tenacity of this battalion (2nd Green
Howards) during this and the following days of heavy fighting was worthy
of all praise. Though subjected to violent shell fire and continued infantry
attacks, they fought steadily on. When blown out of one trench, they moved
on to the next, and never wavered." It was also noted by this, and other battalions, that the sandy soil in the area caused problems with the rifles.
Continuous shell fire sent up a great deal of dust, which got into the firing
mechanism causing bursts and jamming. Some men even found it impossible to fix bayonets. Second-Lieutenant L. Studley mortally wounded
(25th), Lieutenant Phayre killed (26th). Relieved by 1st Coldstream (27th)
and into reserve positions around Veldhoek. Later moved forward again to
front line. Returned to reserve lines (28th). "A" and "C" Companies sent
forward to support 2nd Royal Scots Fusiliers (29th). Enemy broke through
line on left at about 11 am and gained some ground. Colonel King then led
a counter attack in which former positions were reclaimed along with an
additional 200 yards. Major Walker killed. Colonel King, Captain E.S.
Broun and Second-Lieutenant F.C. Hatton killed by sniper (30th).
Withdrew to positions near Gheluvelt.

NOVEMBER
Relieved by 2nd Royal Scots Fusiliers (4th) and to reserve lines. Casualties
since 19th October – 10 officers killed, 18 wounded, 250 other ranks killed,
405 wounded. To Locre (5th), Bailleul (6th). Took over positions east of
Ploegsteert in support of 11th Brigade, 4th Division (8th). Strength – 3
officers, 220 other ranks. Relieved and to billets between Bailleul and
Neuve-Eglise (12th). To Sailly-sur-la-Lys (16th) and began tours in
trenches Fleurbaix sector.

DECEMBER
To Nieppe (14th). Returned to Fleurbaix sector (18th) and held in support during 22nd Brigade`s attack on Rouges Bancs. Carried out tours in line for rest of month.

LANCASHIRE FUSILIERS

"Le Cateau" "Retreat from Mons" "Marne, 1914" "Aisne, 1914" "Armentières, 1914"

2ND BATTALION

AUGUST

Citadel Barracks, Dover. Part of 12th Brigade, 4th Division. Major C.J. Griffin in Command. Moved by train to Cromer (8th). To Norwich (11th), Costessey (13th). Returned to Norwich (17th) and entrained for Wembley. Entrained for Southampton (21st) and embarked SS *Saturnia* (22nd). Arrived Boulogne (23rd). Strength – 27 officers, 974 other ranks. Transport – 2 officers, 70 other ranks, travelled via Dover to Havre. By train to Bertry (24th) then marched to Ligny. Advanced to Viesly (25th) but withdrew during night to positions just north-west of Ligny. Later took up line on high ground near Longsart Farm between Haucourt and Wambaix. Came under attack during early morning (26th) and later forced to fall back to positions on ridge south-west of Haucourt. Casualties – Captains A.S. Ward, DSO, R.H.M. Moody, R.Y.Sidebottom, Lieutenants D.E. Boyle, W.K. Humfrey and C.H. Bass killed. Major-General J.C. Latter, CBE, MC, records in his war history of the Lancashire Fusiliers that the number of other ranks killed was uncertain. Some 3 officers and 86 other ranks had been wounded with 6 officers and 402 other ranks listed as missing. Of the latter, 3 officers and 143 other ranks turned up later, but the remainder were thought to have been all killed. Moved during evening via Selvigny to Venduille. Major-General Latter also notes that during the fighting some 100 men under Lieutenant J. Smyth and Second-Lieutenant J.W. Evatt, became separated. The detachment with men from other regiments holding a line on the Ligny-Haucourt road and coming under attack several times. The party eventually withdrew to Caullery and after a 22-mile march rejoined 12th Brigade (27th). Battalion marched via Lempire to Ronssoy (27th) and dug defensive trenches. Later moved back to Hancourt then marched through night to Voyennes. Continued march (28th), reaching bivouacs at Muirancourt during evening. Marched via Noyon to Carlepont (29th), Tracy-le-Mont and Berneuil to Cuise Lamotte (30th), via the Forest of Compiègne. to Verberie (31st).

SEPTEMBER

Took up support position at Mont Cornon (1st) then continued retreat to Baron. Marched via Montagny and Eve to Dammartin (2nd) and through night via St. Mard, Messy, Claye-Souilly and Annet to Jossigny. Reached Ferrières and bivouacs in the grounds of Baron de Rothschild's estate (4th). To Pont Carr, (5th) then Brie-comte-Robert. War Diary notes – "End of retirement" and a distance of just over 146 miles having been marched since 25th August. Advanced via Pont Carr, to Serris (6th) then in afternoon to Villiers, via Sancy to La Haute Maison (7th), Jouarre then Courcelles (8th). Bivouacked on road at L' Hotel de Bois. Major-General Latter records that the battalion appears to have crossed the Marne (9th) in 2 sections. One party crossing via a weir and lock gates south-west of Charmigny then moving forward to the village itself and bivouacs on the Chamigny-La Ferté road. The second group came up between Luzancy and Charigny, crossing via the railway viaduct. The General also notes that a party of 12 Uhlans were engaged. Six prisoners were taken, one of which turned out to have worked in London before the war as a bus driver. Advanced via Dhuisy and Coulombs to Vaux (10th), Mareuil-sur-Ourcq, St. Quentin and Noroy to Chouy (11th), Septmonts (12th), Billy-sur-Aisne to Venizel (13th). Crossed the Aisne under heavy shell fire and via Bucy-le-Long advanced through Ste. Marguerite to a wood just east of the village. Came under rifle and machine gun fire from enemy trenches in front of Chivres and western slopes of the Chivres Spur. Held positions until relieved by 2nd Manchester during night. Withdrew to reserve lines at Ste. Marguerite. Casualties – Lieutenant C.E. Stuart killed, Second-Lieutenant J.S. Paulson mortally wounded, 14 other ranks killed, 3 officers, 53 other ranks wounded, 1 officer, 83 other ranks missing.

OCTOBER

Marched to Missy-sur-Aisne (2nd), Ciry and Sermoise (7th), Septmonts (8th), Chacrise (9th). Moved in lorries to Le Meux (11th) then by train to Hazebrouck (12th). Arrived 3 am (13th). Marched via Borre to Rouge Croix and during night advanced on Meteren. Enemy cleared from village. Casualties – Second-Lieutenant E.C. Mercer killed, 2 other ranks killed, 7 wounded. Relieved and to billets at Bailleul (14th). Moved to bivouacs on main road near Le Leuthe (15th) and to Ploegsteert sector (16th). Dug in between Nieppe and Ploegsteert on the Warnave Stream. Dug trenches between main road running from Ploegsteert to Le Bizet and Le Touquet during night (17th). Took part in attack on Le Touquet (18th). "B" and "C" Companies moved forward on left of Le Bizet-Le Touquet road, "A" in support, "D" in reserve. Major-General Latter notes that the village was strongly held and surrounded by trenches. Came under heavy artillery, machine gun and rifle fire from east bank of the Lys and Frélinghien. Railway line crossed by 10 am but leading companies held up by shrapnel fire on edge of La Touquet. This was noted as being from almost point-blank range. Le Touquet-Le Gheer road reached during afternoon – "B" Company digging in near level crossing. Le Touquet held by dusk. Battalion Headquarters set up at Pakenham Farm and Regimental Aid Post placed in the waiting room at Le Touquet station. Captain S.L. Lucas-Tooth killed by sniper (20th). Enemy counter-attack driven off (21st) – "B" Company receiving 32 casualties. Major-General Latter notes the good work done by the Battalion's machine guns and in particular that off Private J. Lynn. Private Lynn was to be killed near Ypres on 2nd May, 1915, being posthumously awarded the Victoria Cross for his gallantry that day. War Diary records that during the enemy's retreat ". . . our machine guns had the time of their lives." Relieved (22nd) and to Le Bizet. Casualties (17th-22nd) – 1 officer, 3 other ranks killed, 69 wounded, 7 missing. Relieved 2nd Leinster in trenches south-west of la Chapelle d' Armentières and running Rue du Bois to Lille road (23rd). Relieved by 1st King's Own (24th) and to Armentières. Billets in the brewery. Relieved 1st King's Own in trenches (27th). Enemy attack driven off (28th). Casualties – 4 killed 7 wounded. Captain W. Higgin-Birket was wounded in the head and while walking to the dressing station went missing and was never heard of again. Relieved by 1st King's Own and to Armentières (29th). Two companies sent up to trenches near Ploegsteert in support of 11th Brigade (30th). Remainder of battalion joined (31st).

NOVEMBER

Two companies moved forward to Messines road in support of 1st Somerset Light Infantry (1st). Battalion Headquarters at Hyde Park Corner. Took over trenches at St. Yves (2nd). Captain T.H. Sneyd and 4 other ranks killed, 19 wounded during shelling. To Ploegsteert Wood (6th). One company took part in counter-attack (7th). To reserve trenches at St. Yves (8th). In support of 2nd Argyll and Sutherland Highlanders in counter attack during night (9th), advancing between eastern edge of Ploegsteert Wood and St. Yves-Le Gheer road. Some ground taken but forced to retire after enfilade fire from the enemy. Casualties – 2 killed, 16 wounded. To trenches at St. Yves (11th), Ploegsteert Wood (15th). Relieved and to Le Bizet (20th). George Ashurst joined the Battalion while it was resting at Le Bizet and recalls in his book *My Bit* how the men's clothes were covered in mud and his friend's rifle looked like a long stick of clay. He was warned to expect shelling during the afternoon, a regular occurrence, and remembers hearing a bang and the sound of a shell coming in his direction. Emerging from a cellar George Ashurst saw that a house in the village had taken a direct hit. Its occupants, two women and a soldier, being blown to bits. Took over trenches at Le Touquet (21st). Relieved and to Nieppe (25th), returning to Le Touquet (29th).

DECEMBER
Relieved by 1st King's Own (3rd) and to Le Bizet (4th). Back to Le Touquet (7th). War Diary records (10th) trenches flooded – waist-deep in parts. Relieved by 1st King's Own and to Le Bizet (10th). Relieved 1st King's Own (15th), to Le Bizet (20th), Le Touquet (24th), Le Bizet (28th).

ROYAL SCOTS FUSILIERS

"Mons" "Le Cateau" "Retreat from Mons"
"Marne, 1914" "Aisne, 1914" "La Bassée, 1914"
"Ypres, 1914" "Langemarck, 1914" "Gheluvelt"
"Nonne Bosschen"

1ST BATTALION

AUGUST

Gosport. Part of 9th Brigade, 3rd Division. Entrained for Southampton (13th). Embarked SS *Martaban* and SS *Appam* and sailed for France. Arrived Havre (14th) and to rest camp. Entrained for Landrecies (16th). Arrived (17th) and to Noyelles. To Taisnieres (20th), La Longeuville (21st), Ghlin (22nd). Withdrew later to south bank of the Mons-Condé Canal and entrenched around Jemappes. Held off enemy attack (23rd) until approximately 3 pm, then withdrew via Flenu to northern edge of Frameries. Casualties – 2 officers wounded, 50 other ranks killed or wounded. War Diary records that the Germans then came on and opened fire from the coal dumps south of Frameries. There had been no time to entrench. Casualties – Captains T.A. Rose, DSO and J.E. Young killed, 100 other ranks killed or wounded. Withdrew to Bermeries (24th), Inchy (25th). Continued retreat through night (26th/27th) via Villeret to Vermand and (27th/28th) through Ham to Croissolles. To Montois (29th), Vauciennes (31st).

SEPTEMBER

To Bouillancy (1st), Penchard (2nd), Travenoterie (3rd), Liverdy (5th). Began advance towards the Aisne (6th), moving first to Lumigny. To La Bretonniere (7th). Engaged enemy at Orly (8th) – 2 killed, 22 wounded. Continued advance to Les Feuchères. Crossed the Marne at Nanteuil (9th) and then to Bezu. "C" and "D" Companies in support of 4th Royal Fusiliers at Veuilly (10th). War Diary notes – "mostly thick wood fighting." Over 600 prisoners taken. Later billeted at Dammard. To Grand Rozoy (11th). War Diary records (12th) – Battalion (with 1st Lincolnshire) to "clear Braine with the bayonet." Later moved to Brenelle. Crossed the Aisne (13th) and billeted in Vailly. In action around Rouge Maison (14th). Captain G.C. Briggs killed, 2 officers wounded, 8 other ranks killed, 67 wounded, 90 missing. Withdrew and entrenched. War Diary notes (20th) that the enemy had advanced their trenches during night and were now within 600 yards of the Battalion's line. Heavily shelled with shrapnel and high explosive. Casualties – 8 killed, 15 wounded. Relieved later and via Braine to billets at Courcelles. War Diary notes – "first rest since leaving Gosport." Moved forward (26th) and relieved 1st Devonshire in trenches west of Vailly. One company in the sugar factory. Casualties (26th-30th) – 3 killed, 10 wounded.

OCTOBER
War Diary notes that wooden crosses were placed over the graves of those killed around Vailly. Moved back to billets in Augy (2nd) then to Cramaille. To Troesnes (3rd), Crépy- en-Valois (4th), Moru (5th). Entrained at Pont-Ste. Maxence (6th). Arrived Rue (7th) and marched to billets at Buigny St. Maclou. To Tollent (9th), Hesdin (10th) then moved by lorry to Pernes. Marched via Burbure to Baquerollers Farm (11th). To Robecq (12th) then Vieille Chapelle. In reserve during attack on La Couture then to Locon. To Vieille Chapelle (13th). Moved forward (16th) to trenches near Rouge Croix then in support of 1st Lincolnshire during attack south of Aubers. Billeted for night at Chapigny. Moved to Bas Pommereau Farm (17th). Took part in attack on Château south of Herlies (18th). "A" Company leading, with "B" to the left, came under heavy fire and were forced to halt when within 500 yards of objective. "C" Company came forward and at 5.15 pm the attack was continued. This time being stopped some 60 yards from the enemy's positions. Received order to retire at 6 pm. Casualties – Captains Hon. J. Boyle, S.F.A. Hurt, Lieutenant J.G.S. Cozens-Brooke, Second-Lieutenant H.W.F. Barton killed, 4 officers wounded, 20 other ranks killed, 100 wounded. Relieved by 1st Lincolnshire (19th) and moved back to La Cliqueterie Farm. "A" and "D" Companies sent forward to support 1st Northumberland Fusiliers under attack at Herlies (20th) and sustained 19 casualties while covering that battalion's retirement (21st). Battalion withdrew to positions near Chapigny (23rd). War Diary records (26th) that the enemy had made new trenches 500 yards from those held by the Battalion. Attached to 8th Brigade (30th).

NOVEMBER
To Rue de Bacquerot then La Flinque (1st). Moved forward to reinforce 2nd Gurkhas (2nd). "C" Company went into firing line. Lieutenant Hon. R.S. Stuart killed. Relieved by 1st Duke of Cornwall's Light Infantry in trenches south-west of Rue du Bacquerot (7th) and to Les Lobes. Ordered to rejoin 9th Brigade. To Steenwerck (8th). Marched via Bailleul, Locre and Ypres to reserve positions just east of Hooge (10th). Took part in counter-

attack against Prussian Guard (11th). War Diary notes that the enemy were driven back and positions taken up about half-mile east of Herenthage Château. Lieutenants N.W.A. Henderson, G.S. Ness killed, Captain J.D. Tullis mortally wounded. "A" Company in action (12th), attacking German trench 300 yards to the front. War Diary records the operation as a failure – the men being dead tired and subjected to a close and heavy fire. Great difficulty was experienced in getting the company away. Second-Lieutenant C.A.K. Anderson killed, some 40 men missing. Battalion withdrew their line. Party attempted to clear enemy from the Château stables area (13th). Captain C.J.C. Barrett and Lieutenant C.J. Lyon killed. Casualties (11th-13th) – 6 officers killed, 5 wounded, 1 taken prisoner, 33 other ranks killed, 141 wounded, 103 missing, 13 taken prisoner. Relieved (15th) and to reserve dug-outs. Relieved (17th) and to Hooge. To Zillebeke (18th) and relieved 1st Royal West Kent in trenches. Relieved by French troops (19th). Withdrew to positions 1 mile east of Ypres, then marched via Vlamertinghe and Reninghelst to Westoutre. To Locre (27th). Attached to 7th Brigade (30th) and relieved 1st Dorsetshire in trenches west of Hill 75 in Kemmel sector.

DECEMBER
Relieved by 2nd Suffolk (3rd) and to Locre. Relieved 2nd Suffolk (6th), relieved by 1/1st Honourable Artillery Company (9th) and to Locre. Relieved 1/1st Honourable Artillery Company (12th), relieved by 1/1st Honourable Artillery Company (15th) and to Westoutre. Returned to firing line (21st), relieved (24th) and to Locre. To firing line in Lindenhoek sector (31st).

2ND BATTALION

AUGUST
Gibraltar.

SEPTEMBER
Returned to England and joined 21st Brigade, 7th Division at Lyndhurst Camp near Winchester.

OCTOBER
To Southampton (4th) and embarked – Headquarters, "C" and "D" Companies SS *Cymbrie*, "A" and "B" Companies SS *Lake Michigan*. Sailed (5th) and arrived Zeebrugge (6th). Moved by train to Bruges and then into billets at Ste. Croix. To Clemskerke (8th) and via Ostend to positions

around Meetkerke (9th). To Beernem via Ste. Croix (10th), Coolscamp (12th), De Ruiter (13th), Ypres (14th). Advanced to Wieltje (15th) and took up entrenched positions between the Ypres-Poelcappelle road and Ypres-Zonnebeke road. To bivouacs at Château Poezelhoek near Becelaere (16th). Moved forward to Tirhand (18th) and engaged enemy. Major Ian Forbes wrote that the Battalion was now constantly under fire and it was difficult to tell the difference between day and night. The enemy were persistent in their attacks, he recalls, and came on time after time; 4 or 5 to one as – ". . . rows and rows of cannon fodder." A ditch in front of the Battalion's line, roughly 6 feet deep, 10 feet across and about 100 yards long, became filled with German dead. Withdrew during evening (19th) and dug in on line between Reutel and Poezelhoek. Held line under constant bombardment and attack. War Diary records (21st) that "D" Company were enfiladed by machine gun fire and the enemy broke through between them and 2nd Yorkshire, forcing a withdrawal. "A" Company led counter-attack (22nd) but although the houses in Poezelhoek were cleared – was unable to regain lost ground. Major Forbes recalls the death of Captain F. Fairlie and that for days he could see the bodies of his men lying in front of the trenches. Lieutenant N. Kennedy also killed. War Diary records enemy attacking "C" Company's position 5.30 am (24th). Some 40 German prisoners were taken, but the company was eventually forced to retire having been reduced to a strength of 2 officers and 75 men. Battalion took up new line in Polygon Wood. In another attack, where the Germans were able to get around the Battalion's left, every available man fired on the enemy, Lieutenant H.W.V. Stewart noted as firing from behind a hedge and accounting for 11 men attempting to bring a machine gun into action against the Battalion. Lieutenant C.G.C. Mackenzie is also mentioned in the War Diary having led a bayonet charge after "B" Company's trenches were overrun. At 1 pm (25th) Company Sergeant Major Evans and 6 men went out into No Man's Land to collect and bury the dead. The party, only carrying shovels, were allowed to lay a number of men in a trench for burial, however, when an attempt to bring in Captain Fairlie's body was made, the enemy opened fire hitting 3 of CSM Evans's men. The War Diary records that soon after this the party returned with a German officer and 19 men as prisoners. Major Forbes recalls that this was achieved by the CSM rushing up to the building from where the enemy had fired and demanding that they surrender. The prisoners came in, Major Forbes notes – "like a pack of hounds in full cry. . . falling on their knees begging us not to shoot them." Second-Lieutenant C.McC. Alston killed. "A" and "D" Companies moved forward to reinforce 20th Brigade around Gheluvelt (26th), returning same night. Battalion relieved by 1st South Wales Borderers and moved back to bivouacs just south of Veldhoek, then (27th) to Sanctuary Wood. Advanced during evening via Gheluvelt and relieved 2nd Gordon Highlanders in trenches near Zanvoorde along the Kruiseecke Ridge. Major Forbes recalls that the line occupied was too long for the number of men available. Battalion's strength now about 500 after going into action on the 15th October with a strength of more than 1,000 men. "B" Company's line attacked throughout (29th) – Lieutenant Mackenzie killed. Ordered to retire (30th) and fell back to positions along the Gheluvelt-Zandvoorde road. Here the Battalion came under fire from a field gun placed about 900 yards away in Zandvoorde. War Diary records (31st) that the enemy broke through, surrounded then overwhelmed the Battalion's trenches. Lieutenant Stewart recalls that the enemy began shelling at 5 am, the infantry coming on about 4 hours later. No reinforcements could come forward, the ground to the rear being heavily bombarded – "No man could have lived on any square yard of the ridge behind us." War Diary notes that Commanding Officer, Second in Command, the Adjutant and 3 other officers were killed or captured. Casualties estimated at approximately 400 men.

NOVEMBER
War Diary gives position (1st) as wood ¼ mile south-east of Gheluvelt. Drafts arrived under 2 officers. Strength (3rd) – 4 officers, 183 other ranks. Relieved 2nd Yorkshire Regiment in forward trenches south-south-east of Gheluvelt (4th). Line held under attack and bombardment. Relieved by 1st Bedfordshire (6th) and to Locre. Later in afternoon to Bailleul. Moved into reserve trenches at Ploegsteert Wood (8th), support line (9th), back to reserve (10th). In support of 1st Somerset Light Infantry at St. Yves during afternoon, returning to Ploegsteert Wood (11th). To Bailleul (12th), Sailly (16th). Took over billets at crossroads on Fromelles road 1¼ miles south-east of Sailly. Moved to billets along the Rue Bataille between Quesnoy and Bataille (17th). Relieved 2nd Wiltshire in trenches Fleurbaix sector (20th). Relieved by 2nd Wiltshire (23rd), relieved 2nd Wiltshire (26th), relieved by 2nd Wiltshire (29th). Moved to new billets along the Rue de la Lys.

DECEMBER
Relieved 2nd Wiltshire (2nd), relieved by 2nd Wiltshire (5th), relieved 2nd Wiltshire (8th), relieved by 2nd Wiltshire (11th). War Diary records strength (12th) as 16 officers, 574 other ranks. To Pont de Nieppe (14th), billets along the Rue Biache in Bac St. Maur (18th). Later advanced to reserve positions at Croix Blanche. Took over billets along northern end of

Croix Blanche-Fleurbaix road (19th). Relieved 2nd Wiltshire in front line (21st). Relieved by 2nd Wiltshire (24th) and to Fleurbaix. Relieved 2nd Wiltshire (27th). Lieutenant K.C. Thompson mortally wounded (30th). Relieved by 2nd Wiltshire 5 pm.

CHESHIRE REGIMENT

**"Mons" "Le Cateau" "Retreat from Mons"
"Marne, 1914" "Aisne, 1914" "La Bassée, 1914"
"Armentières, 1914" "Ypres, 1914"
"Nonne Bosschen"**

1ST BATTALION

AUGUST

Londonderry. Part of 15th Brigade, 5th Division. Moved in 2 trains to Belfast (14th) and embarked SS *Nassilia*. Landed Havre (16th) and to rest camp. Entrained for Le Cateau (17th). Arrived (18th) and to billets at Pommereuil. To Gommegnies (21st), Bois de Boussu (22nd). "A" and "B" Companies moved forward (23rd) and dug defensive line near Wasmes. "C" and "D" Companies to Hornu, entrenching astride the Mons road. Withdrew to Dour (24th) then took up defensive positions at Audregnies. Came under attack from enemy advancing from Quiévrain and Bois de Déduit. Retired about 4.30 pm. to Bavai after some 4 hours continuous fighting. War Diary records that only 6 officers, 1 Warrant Officer and 199 other ranks were present at roll call. The Battalion' strength at 7.30 am having been 27 officers and 934 other ranks. Moved via Le Cateau to bivouacs at La Sotière (25th). Covered retirement of 15th Brigade east of Troisvillers (26th) then to Eaucourt. To Pontoise (28th), via Charlepont to Croutoy (29th), Crépy (31st).

SEPTEMBER

To Nanteuil (1st), Montg, (2nd), St. Germain (3rd). Gagny (4th). Began advance to the Aisne (6th) moving via Villeneuve-le-Comte and Mortcerf to Montlevon. To Boissy-le- Chatel via Trouchet (7th), Charnesseuil (8th), via Saacy to Bézu (9th), via Montreuil to Louvry (10th), St. Remy (11th), L'Epitaphe (12th), Serches (13th). Crossed the Aisne (14th) and to Ste. Marguerite. Later advanced on Missy and held positions under heavy shell fire. Relieved by 2nd Duke of Wellington's (16th) and moved back across the Aisne to Le Mesnil Mill. Took over billets at Le Mesnil (18th). Occupied trenches just south of the Aisne and at Serches. Moved forward to Ste. Marguerite (25th).

OCTOBER

Moved back to billets in Jury (2nd) then in evening to Droizy. To Longpont (3rd), via Corcy to Pontdrun (4th), Verberie (6th). Entrained at Pont-Ste.

Maxence for Abbeville (7th). Arrived during evening and marched to billets at Neuilly-l`Hôpital. To Boufflers (8th), Haravesnes (9th). To Fillièvres (10th) and from there travelled in buses to La Thieuloye. To Béthune (11th). Moved into firing line at Festubert (12th). "A" Company took part in attack on Rue d`Ouvert (13th). War Diary records the operation as unsuccessful, "A" Company moving back to rest of the Battalion entrenched on the Festubert-La Quinque road. Colonel A. Crookenden in his war history of the Cheshire Regiment notes that the objective was a large farm, Chapelle St. Roch, which was occupied and defended throughout the day. The enemy eventually surrounded the Cheshire and set light to the buildings. Casualties are recorded as 4 officers, 55 other ranks captured, 8 men wounded. Moved forward to Rue d`Ouvert (16th) then to Rue du Marais. Part of "A" Company engaged enemy along the Violaines road then rejoined Battalion at Rue du Marais. Took part in unsuccessful attacks towards Violaines (17th), moving into village during evening. War Diary records (19th) that Battalion attempted to occupy La Bassée without success. Casualties – 32. Held positions outside Violaines (20th). Enemy attack repulsed 3 pm. Casualties – 29. Another attack on La Bassée failed (21st). Captain F.H. Mahony mortally wounded, 9 other casualties. War Diary records (22nd) heavy attack by the enemy who took the trenches – "at the point of the bayonet." Battalion fell back on Rue du Marais under heavy fire. Retired later to bivouacs near Rue de Béthune. Casualties – Captain H.I.St.J. Hartford, Second-Lieutenant J.A. Greenhalgh killed, Captains L.A. Forster, W.S. Rich, Second-Lieutenant H.N. Atkinson mortally wounded, 18 wounded, 216 missing. To Le Touret (27th) then at 7 pm marched via Richebourg St. Vaast to St. Vaast. Moved into firing line at Pont Logy (28th). Relieved (30th) and to billets at Le Touret. Moved later to Calonne, then to Borre (31st).

NOVEMBER
To reserve billets south of Dranoutre (1st). Moved through Ypres (5th) and relieved 2nd Bedfordshire in trenches just south of the 6km stone on the Ypres-Menin road. Enemy attack repulsed on left (7th). Captain G.B. Pollock-Hodsoll (Suffolk Regiment attached), Second-Lieutenant G.R.L. Anderson killed, 34 other casualties. Withdrew line 150 yards (14th). Second-Lieutenant H.R. Stabled (Royal Fusiliers attached) killed, 31 other casualties. Relieved by 2nd Worcestershire (19th) and moved back into reserve dugouts. War Diary records total casualties since going into line as 35 killed, 99 wounded, 65 missing. To Locre (21st), Bailleul (24th).

DECEMBER

To Dranoutre (8th), St. Jans-Cappel (10th), Dranoutre (14th). Moved to
Neuve Eglise (17th) and began tours in firing line at Wulverghem – 2
companies in trenches, 2 at Neuve Eglise. Relieved (29th) and to Bailleul.

1/6TH BATTALION (TERRITORIAL FORCE)

AUGUST

Headquarters and 4 companies at Stockport, 2 at Stalybridge and 1 each at
Hyde and Glossop. Part of Cheshire Brigade, Welsh Division. Mobilized
(4th). All companies assembled at Headquarters (8th). To Shrewsbury
(9th), Church Stretton (22nd), Northampton (31st).

OCTOBER

At Great Brinton and Stonham for brief periods before returning to
Northampton.

NOVEMBER

To Southampton and sailed SS *Honorius* for France (9th). Sergeant J.A.
Boardman wrote in his diary that the *Honorius* was a cattle boat and full of
rats. Arrived Havre (10th) and to rest camp. Entrained for St. Omer. Arrived
(13th) and billeted in French Army barracks. Officers – Lieutenant-Colonel
G.B. Heywood (Commanding Officer), Majors H. Hesse, R. Rostron, J.
Rawlinson (Quartermaster), Captains F. Leah, W.D. Dodge, R. Kirk, J.M.
Diggles (Adjutant), H. Cooke, A.W. Smith, T. Gibbons, C.F. White,
Lieutenants J.C. Hoyle, G.E. Haworth, F. White (Machine Gun Officer),
W.R. Innes, J.E. Johnston, E.E. Spence (Transport Officer), R. Norman
(Scout Officer), C. Norman, J. Morris (Medical Officer), Second-
Lieutenants W.L. Read, S.A. Alexander, H.B. Burgess, R.R. Cooke, C.E.
Brockbank. To billets at Helfaut and Bilques (21st).

DECEMBER

To Hazebrouck (9th), Bailleul (10th). During an inspection, Lieutenant-
General H.L. Smith-Dorrien complimented the battalion on its turnout. He
also spoke at length to Sergeant P. Tanner, an ex regular soldier that had
served with Lord Roberts in Afghanistan back in 1880. Began duty in
Wulverghem sector (11th). Half battalion in front line, half in billets at
Neuve Eglise. Sergeant Boardman described the line as comprising very few
trenches, just sandbags built up into a parapet. Private W. Williamson
(battalion's first casualty) killed by sniper (12th). Re-organized into 4
companies (16th) and attached to 15th Brigade, 5th Division (17th).

Battalion historian Charles Smith records that during "Christmas Truce" (25th) both sides meet in No Man`s Land. Food was exchanged and a pig killed behind the lines by the Cheshires was cooked and shared with the enemy. He also notes that on 2nd September, 1918 the battalion captured the same trenches they occupied at Christmas, 1914. Relieved and to billets near Bailleul (28th). War Diary records that between 11th – 29th December some 120 men were sent to hospital suffering from frostbite or rheumatism.

ROYAL WELCH FUSILIERS

**"Mons" "Le Cateau" "Retreat from Mons"
"Marne, 1914" "Aisne, 1914" "La Bassée, 1914"
"Messines, 1914" "Armentières, 1914" "Ypres, 1914"
"Langemarck, 1914" "Gheluvelt" "Givenchy, 1914"**

1ST BATTALION

AUGUST
Malta.

SEPTEMBER
Sailed for England (3rd) and joined 22nd Brigade, 7th Division at Lyndhurst.

OCTOBER
Left for Southampton 9.30 pm (4th). Embarked SS *Winifredian* and sailed 8 am (5th). Ordered to return to England (6th), arriving at Dover 6 am. Sailed again 9 pm. Landed Zeebrugge 9 am (7th) and then by train to Oostcamp, 4 miles south of Bruges. Marched via Bruges, Vulvlage, Lempelher and Ostend to billets at Oudenburg (8th). One company placed on outpost duty at Westkerke. Entrained at Ostend for Ghent (9th). Arrived 6.30 pm and marched to bivouacs just over 1 mile south-west of town. Moved forward during early hours of morning (10th) and dug in south-east of Meirelbeke to cover French and Belgium troops in forward trenches. Took over front line during afternoon (11th) and held while line fell back. Withdrew during night via Ghent and Tronchiennes to Hansbeke. Arrived 7 am (12th) and covered retreat at canal crossings. Relieved by Northumberland Hussars 10.15 pm and retired to Thielt. Arrived 5.30 am (13th) and later withdrew to Roulers. Moved to Ypres (14th). War Diary records that 600 men (150 per company) travelled by train, while remainder marched with transport by road. The Diary also notes that the troops, when leaving the train at Ypres, opened fire on an enemy aeroplane which was "obliged to descend." Major C.H. Dudley Ward, DSO, MC, records in his history of the Royal Welch Fusiliers that the men were billeted in the Kaserne and spent the day (15th) in the orchards round Zillebeke. Returning to billets on the eastern side of Ypres during the evening. Advanced to Zonnebeke (16th). War Diary notes arrival at 6.20 am and learning from the inhabitants that a patrol of 17 Uhlans had withdrawn

from the village less than 20 minutes previously. Moved forward and took up entrenched positions midway between the 5th and 6th Kilo stones on the Wervicq-Passchendaele road. Major Dudley Ward notes that the centre of the line was about the Broodseinde crossroads. Moved to Veldhoek in reserve during morning (18th) and then forward to Becelaere after dark. Advanced to Dadizeele (19th) and formed up for attack on Kleythoek. War Diary records position as being on the Menin-Roulers road crossroads between the 5th and 6th Kilo stones. Moved forward 11.30 am on left of road – "A" and "D" Companies in front, "B" and "C" in support. Major Dudley Ward records heavy shrapnel fire as Battalion advanced across the fields and up a gentle slope. The enemy were retiring and as the Battalion passed through Kezelberg and pressed on Kleythoek in short rushes, they came under rifle fire. War Diary notes that the attack -"was very rapidly pushed home although there was no artillery support whatsoever. All but about three platoons of the supporting companies were in the firing line." Order received 12.40 pm to withdraw. Major Dudley Ward notes position as being within a short distance of the second milestone out of Menin, on the forward slope of the swell in the ground, overlooking the town. Retired via Dadizeele to Potteriyebug then through Terhand and Becelaere to trenches previously held at Broodseinde. Casualties – Captain J.H. Brennan, Lieutenant G.O. de P. Chance killed, 5 other officers wounded, 15 other ranks killed, 84 wounded, 11 missing. Major-General T. Capper (GOC., 7th Division) noted in his report that ". . . the battalion attacked Kleythoek with much gallantry and dash, and later on the same day acted with coolness and discipline under trying conditions." Line held under heavy shell and rifle fire throughout day (20th). War Diary records that the enemy`s attack recommenced at daybreak (21st). Their advance positions being within 100 yards of the Battalion`s trenches. German artillery is noted as firing with "extreme" accuracy. Many trenches being blown in as a result of shells bursting on the parapet. There was little support and supplies of ammunition difficult to bring forward. Message received at 3.30 pm to hold line at all costs. Enemy entered line about 6 pm – War Diary notes members of "B" and "C" Companies being taken prisoner. Battalion withdrew to secondary line some 250 yards to the rear then at 1.30 am (22nd) fell back to Eksternest in reserve. Casualties – Captains W.M. Kington, DSO, M.E. Lloyd, Lieutenant E.C.L. Hoskyns, Second-Lieutenant G.P.J. Snead-Cox killed, Captain W.G. Vyvyan mortally wounded and taken prisoner, 3 other officers wounded and 5 missing, 37 other ranks killed, 80 wounded and 213 missing. War Diary notes that due to records being lost in action, these numbers are only approximate – "The actual number being greater." Battalion strength – 6 officers and 206 other ranks. Moved forward during afternoon (22nd) to support position east of the Hannebeek River and running along a stream towards Gheluvelt. Withdrew to former line 8 pm. War Diary records (23rd) that a party sent out to collect the dead and wounded from Zonnebeke were fired on by a number of the enemy dressed in British uniforms. Second-Lieutenant H.T. Ackland-Allen killed. Battalion moved forward 2 pm and ordered to take up support position. War Diary notes that there were no tools available to entrench with and Commanding Officer ordered men back to their former positions. Strength now recorded as just over 400. Came under heavy shrapnel fire during afternoon (24th). This, War Diary notes, was as a result of information possibly supplied to the German artillery by a local spy. Casualties – 1 killed, 13 wounded, 2 missing. Moved at 3 pm to Veldhoek. War Diary records (25th) that 3 goats had "attached themselves" to the Battalion 3 days before. The animals refusing to leave and following the men everywhere. The Battalion was already in possession of 1 goat – The Regimental Goat. Draft of 90 men under Second-Lieutenant E. Proctor arrived (26th). Advanced with 2nd Royal Warwickshire for attack on enemy line south-east of Gheluvelt but forced to withdraw to trenches east of Veldhoek due to heavy shell fire. Second-Lieutenant Proctor and 10 other ranks wounded. Moved forward to trenches in front of Zandvoorde (27th). The men, War Diary records, occasionally being sent back to Zillebeke for a few hours' rest. Casualties (27th-29th) – 4 killed, 13 wounded, 6 missing. Enemy attacked daybreak (30th). Major Dudley Ward notes that the Battalion was just over 400 strong and scattered in short slits of trenches. There was no inter-communication, field of vision was short and it was impossible to know what was happening on either right or left. Advancing German infantry, however, were "mowed down" by rifle fire. War Diary records that – "Owing to the cavalry on the right giving way" the enemy were able to enfilade the trenches. Exact casualties were unknown – all officers and about 320 other ranks found to be missing. Survivors attached to 2nd Queens. Major Dudley Ward records that few details became available regarding the attack. He recalls a report given by Lieutenant A.E.C.T. Dooner who having been wounded saw the Commanding Officer, Lieutenant-Colonel H.O.S. Cadogan killed while attempting to come to his assistance. Lieutenant E. Wodehouse, who was wounded and taken prisoner, notes that the line held by the Battalion was about three-quarters of a mile long – "A" Company on the right, then "B", "D" and "C" on the left. German guns on Zandvoorde Ridge were firing point-blank into the trenches – ". . . No orders were received, so it was thought best to stay where we were, and about midday the whole battalion was either killed, wounded, or taken prisoner." He also noted that the opposing enemy were probably a regiment of Hanoverians and bore the word "Gibraltar" on their shoulder straps.

NOVEMBER

Draft of 109 men under Second-Lieutenant F.R. Orme arrived (5th). Attack on enemy line (7th) – objective taken and 3 machine guns captured but soon forced to retire due to heavy enfilading fire. Second-Lieutenant Orme and 13 other ranks killed, 20 wounded, 37 missing. Relieved (8th) and to billets in church at Locre. To Bailleul (9th). Draft of 2 officers and 99 other ranks arrived. To Merris (10th). Draft of 2 officers and 303 other ranks arrived. Further drafts arrived (12th/13th). Took over trenches at Touquet (14th). War Diary records that the Battalion had remained in the line continuously, companies resting in billets in rear of the trenches and being relieved by 1/8th Royal Scots. Casualties till end of month – 3 killed, 17 wounded, 1 missing.

DECEMBER

Relieved (4th) and to billets at Rue Biache. Returned to trenches (8th). Relieved by 1/8th Royal Scots (14th) and to Rue de Bataille. Moved forward to reserve positions for attack on enemy line near Bas Maisnil (18th). "C" and "D" Companies sent up in support about 5.15 pm, followed later by "B" Company. Returned to billets 6.30 am (19th). Casualties – Second-Lieutenant G.R. Gore mortally wounded, 1 other rank killed, 17 wounded, 3 missing. Relieved 1/8th Royal Scots (20th). Relieved (24th) and to Rue de Bataille. Casualties – 2 killed, 6 wounded. Relieved 1/8th Royal Scots (28th).

2ND BATTALION

AUGUST

Portland. To Dorchester (8th), Southampton (10th). Headquarters, "A" and "B" Companies embarked SS *Glengariffe* and sailed for France. Arrived Rouen (11th) and detailed for Line of Communications work. Detachment of "A" Company to Amiens (12th). "C" and "D" Companies arrived (13th). Rest of "A" Company to Amiens (14th). Battalion entrained for Valenciennes (22nd) and became part of 19th Brigade. Later moved forward and took up outpost line at Vicq. Advanced (24th). War Diary records that Battalion moved forward via Quiévrain, almost reached Elouges then retired via Rombies to entrenched positions north-east of Jenlain. One officer wounded, 17 other ranks missing. Moved back 5 am (25th) via Haussy, St. Python, Briastre and Neuvilly to Le Cateau. Battalion slept in the market square. War Diary records leaving Le Cateau 5.30 am (26th). Moved via Bertry and Montigny to position on the Bertry-Busigny road. Withdrew, reaching Estrées early morning (27th) and later marching via St. Quentin to Ollezy. Continued retreat via Noyon to Pontoise (28th), Couloisy (30th). Moved through the Forest of Compiègne (31st) to positions around the railway at Verberie.

SEPTEMBER
Continued retreat via Raray to Fresnoy (1st), through Montlongon Wood and Montagny to Dammartin (2nd), Lagny (3rd). Grisy (5th). Began advance to the Aisne, moving forward via Jossigny to Villeneuve St. Denis (6th), via Roman Villers to La Haute-Maison (7th). Came under shell fire while approaching Signy-Signets (8th). Moved forward later and engaged enemy in the streets of La Ferté-sous-Jouarre. Second-Lieutenant E.J.V. Collingwood-Thompson mortally wounded (9th). Relieved later by 1st East Lancashire and moved back via Signy Signets to Les Corbierre. Moved forward through La Ferté to Certigny (10th), Marizy Ste. Geneviève (11th), Buzancy (12th), Equiry (13th), via Rozières and Septmonts to Venizel (14th). Moved back to Septmonts (19th).

OCTOBER
To St. Remy (5th), Vez (7th) then to bivouacs in woods west of Bethisy St. Fiegu. Marched via Verberie to Longueill (8th) then to Estrées-St. Denis (9th). Entrained for St. Omer (10th). Arriving and marching to billets at Renescure. To St. Sylvestre (12th), Strazeeke (13th). moved through Bailleul (14th) and dug in to the south-east along the Bailleul-Nieppe road. Advanced on Steenwerck (15th), War Diary recording that "C" and "D" Companies eventually occupied the town and drove the enemy back. To Vlamertinghe (16th), Laventie (19th). Moved forward (20th) to firing line at Fromelles. Major C.H. Dudley Ward mentions in *Regimental Records of the Royal Welch Fusiliers* that the Battalion relieved French dragoons wearing brass helmets, horsehair plumes and Cuirasses. One member of the Battalion noted Fromelles as a "deserted village". the houses looking as though the occupants had just gone out for a few minutes. Withdrew about midnight (21st) to new line in front of La Cordonerie Farm. Positions held, repulsing several enemy attacks. Second-Lieutenant E.R.C. Stone killed (25th), Captain E.N. Jones- Vaughan and Lieutenant L.L. Stable killed (26th), Lieutenant T.L. Pritchard mortally wounded (27th). Enemy entered 1st Middlesex trenches on right (29th) and Battalion assisted in recapture.

NOVEMBER
Relieved by 2nd Scots Guards (14th) and to Sailly. Casualties since 21st October – 4 officers killed, 6 wounded, 54 other ranks killed, 185 wounded. Marched via Armentières to Houplines (17th) and took over firing line. Relieved by 1st Middlesex (25th) and moved back to billets in Houplines.

DECEMBER
Relieved 1st Scottish Rifles in trenches near Frélinghien (3rd). Captain C.I. Stockwell noted in his diary that the Battalion's right was against the houses of Frèlinghien. The enemy were occupying a brewery 150 yards away. War Diary records (22nd) enemy dead found belonging to the 133rd Saxon Regiment and – "practically a truce all day" (25th). Relieved by 2nd Durham Light Infantry (26th) and to Erquinhiem. Casualties since going into line – 3 killed, 10 wounded.

1/4TH (DENBIGHSHIRE) BATTALION (TERRITORIAL FORCE)

AUGUST
Headquarters at Wrexham and comprising 8 companies: "A" – Wrexham, "B" – Gresford, "C" – Ruabon, "D" – Denbigh, "E" – Coedpoeth, "F" Gwersylly, "G" – Rhosllanerchrugog and "H" – Llangollen. Part of North Wales Infantry Brigade, Welsh Division. Mobilized and to Conway then to Northampton (29th).

NOVEMBER
To Southampton in 2 trains (5th). Embarked HMT *Architect* and sailed 11.30 pm for France. Arrived Havre (6th) and to rest camp at Bleville. Entrained at Havre (8th) and travelled via Abbeville to St. Omer. Arrived 7.30 pm (9th) and moved into the old cavalry barracks. Moved to the infantry barracks (10th). To Heuringhem (11th) and organized into 4 companies. War Diary records – "Heard the guns in the battleline" (12th). Began a series of training programmes, mainly digging trenches, practising taking up outpost duties and attacks, route marches and musketry. While on a 7-mile march (15th) the War Diary recorded that most of the boots issued at Northampton – "Were of the most inferior quality." New rifles were also issued at Northampton and these were fired for the first time just outside Heuringhem (17th). The men received their first pay (20th). Trenches were dug along the canal bank at Wardrecque (26th) and the men's first rest day since landing in France was on (29th).

DECEMBER

Left Heuringhem (6th) and via Wardrecque marched to Hazebrouck. War Diary records that the advance party led by Major W.R. Wilson saw the bombing of the town by a German aircraft. Two bombs were dropped killing 9 soldiers and a number of civilians. Battalion now attached to 3rd Brigade, 1st Division. To Bailieul (7th). Dug trenches about 1½ miles north-west of town (8th). Carried out more battle training (9th-12th) and under orders to move at 2 hours notice (14th-19th). Case of scarlet fever reported and half of the Battalion isolated in their billets. Battalion moved to Merville (20th), Béthune (21st). Moved forward to Gorre and held in reserve during attack on Festubert. Came under fire for first time. Several casualties. Moved forward to bivouacs near Festubert (22nd) then to dugouts at southern end of town. Two companies moved into reserve trenches (23rd).

SOUTH WALES BORDERERS

"Mons" "Retreat from Mons" "Marne, 1914"
"Aisne, 1914" "Ypres, 1914" "Langemarck, 1914"
"Gheluvelt" "Nonne Bosschen" "Givenchy, 1914"

1ST BATTALION

AUGUST

Bordon. Part of 3rd Brigade, 1st Division. To Southampton (12th) and embarked SS *Gloucester Castle* for France. Officers – Lieutenant-Colonel H.E.B. Leach (Commanding Officer), Major A.J. Reddie (Second in Command), Lieutenants C.J. Paterson (Adjutant), R.B. Hadley (Machine Gun Officer), W.R. Wilson (Quartermaster), Second-Lieutenant J.R. Homfray (Transport Officer); "A" Company: Captains G.B.C. Ward, W.C. Curgenven, Lieutenants M.T. Johnson, C.J. Coker, C.K. Steward; "B" Company: Captains F.G. Lawrence, DSO, M.E. Yeatman, Lieutenants V.B. Ramsden, H.H. Travers; Second- Lieutenant H.D. Daws; "C" Company: Major W.L. Lawrence, Captain R.S. Gwynn, Lieutenant C.W. Anstey, Second-Lieutenants C.A. Baker, N.G. Silk; "D" Company: Major G.E.E. Welby, Lieutenant A.E.L. James, Second-Lieutenants M.G. Richards, C.C. Sills, J.M.L. Vernon. Arrived Havre (13th) and to rest camp. Entrained for Etreux (15th). Arrived (16th) and marched to billets at Leschelle. To Malgarni (20th), St. Aubin (21st). Marched via Maubeuge to Bettignies (22nd) then later via Villers-sire-Nicole to Givry. Moved forward (23rd) and held high ground near Vellereille-le-Sec. Relieved in afternoon and withdrew via Givry to defensive positions at Peissant. "D" Company fired on Uhlan patrol (24th). Battalion withdrew during evening and marched via Vieux-Reng and Bettignies to Neuf Mesnil. Continued retreat via Maubeuge and Marbaix to Le Grand Fayt (25th). To Favril (26th) then bivouacs on the Wassigny-Oisy road. Moved through Etreux and Guise to Bernot (27th), La Fère to Crépy (28th), St. Gobain Forest to Brancourt (30th), Soissons to Missy-aux-Bois (31st).

SEPTEMBER

To Fulames (1st), Cregy (2nd), via Meaux and Vendresses to Sammeron (3rd), through Mouroux to bivouacs south of Coulommiers (4th), Ormeaux and positions south-east of Rozoy (5th). Began advance (6th), marching through La Chapelle Iger and Bois Blandereau to Vaudoy then via Dagny and Leudon to Choisy (7th). Crossed the Grand Morin at Jouy (8th) then via Sablonnieres to Hondevillers. Crossed the Marne at Nogent (9th) then via Beaurepaire and Bontemps to Le Thiolet. To Sommelans (10th), Villeneuve (11th), Vauxcéré (12th). Marched through Longueval to bivouacs near Bourg (13th). Advanced west of Vendresse towards Chivy (14th) and took up positions along the Chivy- Beauln road. Came under heavy shell fire. Advanced again towards the slopes of the Chemin des Dames Ridge. Held positions north-west of Troyon against attacks (15th). Casualties – Captain Yeatman killed, Lieutenant Johnson mortally wounded, 18 other ranks killed, 1 officer, 76 other ranks wounded, 54 missing. Withdrew (21st) – 2 companies in trenches around the Quarries on the Mont Faucon Ridge, 2 in reserve around Vendresse. Casualties among other ranks now total 35 killed, 131 wounded. Enemy attacked in large numbers (26th) and broke through Battalion's line. In his war history of the South Wales Borderers, C.T. Atkinson records that much hand-to-hand fighting took place – the men picking up any weapon available. One man, he notes, used a table fork. Casualties – Major Welby, Lieutenant G.P. Blackall-Simonds and Second-Lieutenant Sills killed, Lieutenant Coker mortally wounded, 3 officers wounded, 87 other ranks killed, 95 wounded, 12 missing. Battalion received congratulations from Major-General S.H. Lomax. The Divisional Commander comparing the defence of the Quarries with that of the Regiment's stand at Rorke's Drift in Zululand, 1879. Relieved by 1st Cameron Highlanders (27th) and to billets at Coilly.

OCTOBER

Moved into support trenches at Vendresse (1st). Relieved by French troops (15th) and marched via Bourg to Lime. To Fère-en-Tardenois (16th). Entrained for Cassel (17th). Arrived (18th) and to billets at Hondeghem. To Poperinghe (20th) and moved forward via Boesinghe to Langemarck (21st). Took part in attack on Poelcappelle. Casualties – Captain Curgenven, Second-Lieutenant H.H. Watkins killed, 1 officer wounded, 19 other ranks killed, 62 wounded, 65 missing. Held line under heavy fire. Several infantry attacks repulsed. C.T. Atkinson records one officer's words – "they came on in masses of 200 and got simply cut to pieces." Relieved (24th) and to bivouacs near Hooge. "A" and "B" Companies relieved 2nd Royal Scots Fusiliers in trenches around Poezelhoek Château and "C" and "D" Companies to positions north of Zandvoorde (26th). Relieved (27th) and back to Hooge. Moved forward (29th) and dug in along the Gheluvelt-Poezelhoek road. Lieutenant Paterson mortally wounded. Took part in the fighting at Gheluvelt Château (31st), withdrawing to positions near Polderhoek Château about 5 pm. Major Lawrence and Captain I.B. Maxwell killed.

NOVEMBER

Relieved (1st) and moved back to reserve line at Sanctuary Wood. Moved forward into Herenthage Wood (2nd) – "A" Company taking part in counter-attack. Relieved by 1st Gloucestershire (4th) and back to Sanctuary Wood. Relieved 1st Irish Guards near Zillebeke (9th). Battalion's right on Zwartelleen. Enemy attack repulsed (11th). Lieutenant Homfray killed. Relieved (14th) and moved back via Hooge to Ypres. To Locre (15th), billets south-west of Bailleul (17th). Relieved 9th Lancers and 18th Hussars in trenches near Kemmel (23rd). Enemy attack on "C" Company's line repulsed (25th). Casualties 15 other ranks. Relieved during evening and to Oubtersteene.

DECEMBER

To Merville (20th). Advanced via Béthune and Gorre to Festubert sector (21st). Took part in attack to regain lost trenches. Objectives gained and held. Relieved by 2nd Royal Munster Fusiliers (24th). Casualties – 220 killed, wounded or missing. Returned to front line (26th). Relieved by 2nd Royal Munster Fusiliers (28th). Second-Lieutenant A.M. Farrier mortally wounded. Back to front line (30th). Second-Lieutenant R.D. Pryce-Jenkin killed (31st).

KING`S OWN SCOTTISH BORDERERS

"Mons" "Le Cateau" "Retreat from Mons"
"Marne, 1914" "Aisne, 1914" "La Bassée, 1914"
"Messines, 1914" "Ypres, 1914" "Nonne Bosschen"

2ND BATTALION

AUGUST

Dublin, Ireland. Part of 13th Brigade, 5th Division. Sailed SS *Gloucestershire* for France (14th). Arrived Havre (15th) and to No.3 Rest Camp. To Tréville (16th). Marched to Havre (17th) and entrained for Landrecies. Moved to billets at Maroilles. To Houdain (21st). Moved forward to Hainin (22nd) – 3 companies taking up defensive positions at Les Herbières covering road bridge and No. 4 Lock on Mons-Condé Canal. `D` Company entrenched off road north of bridge. Officers present in forward positions – Lieutenant-Colonel C.M. Stephenson (Commanding Officer), Majors A.E. Haig, E.S.D`Ewes Coke, C. Leigh, DSO, Captains L.D. Spencer, E.W. Macdonald, C.F. Kennedy, H. Cobden, G.W. Smith, R.C.Y. Dering (Adjutant), A. Murray (Quartermaster), Lieutenants J.B.W. Pennyman, G.H.M. Lindsay, J.R. Hamilton-Dalrymple, R.P.M. Bell, R. Joynson, R.H.P. Holme, Second-Lieutenants E.G. Miles, H.J. Harvey, G.P. Hammond, W.A.O. Rutherfurd, W.G.M. Shewen, G.B. Bayley, G.S. Amos, A.L.Y. Dering, T.F.P.B.J. Teeling. Enemy (Brandenburg Grenadiers) attacked (23rd) – first observed advancing about 1 pm diagonally south-west along road from Tertre. Battalion came under artillery fire. Enemy advance checked by rapid fire. Suffered high casualties but continued attack. Major Leigh mortally wounded. Casualties among other ranks estimated at between 40 and 100. Order received at sundown to retire. Moved via Boussu and bivouacked at Petit Wasmes. Continued retreat and bivouacked between Bavai and St. Vaast-la-Vallée (24th). Moved through Montayand then halted at positions on high ground 2 miles east of Troisvilles, 300 – 400 yards south of the Le Cateau – Cambrai road (25th). Captain Stair Gillon in his war history of the King`s Own Scottish Borderers notes that the trenches had been dug by French civilians and were generally too short and shallow. Battle of Le Cateau (26th). Came under heavy shelling from 6 am. Ordered to retire towards Troisvilles 3 pm. Most of "C" Company surrounded and taken prisoner. "A" Company halted at "The Tree" on sunken road (Le Cateau – Troisvilles road) and engaged advancing infantry at 900 yards range for almost one hour. Retreat continued via

Maurois and Bois-de-Gattigny. To Ollézy (27th), La Pommerave (28th), Jaulzy (30th), Crépy-en-Valois (31st).

SEPTEMBER
Took up positions in turnip fields off the Campiègne road by 7 am (1st). Engaged enemy until 10 am then ordered to retire. Fought rearguard action until reaching Silly-le-Long. To Coulommes (2nd). Continued retreat and in Presles by (5th). Ordered to advance (6th). Marched via Coulommiers to bivouacs near Boissy. Engaged enemy north-east of Doue about 9 am (8th) and later around Mauroy and St. Cyr. Bivouacked at night on heights north of the Grande Morin. Crossed the Marne at Saacy (9th) and bivouacked in woods. To Chézy-en-Orxois (10th), Hartennes (11th), Serches (12th), Sermoise (13th). Captain Murray fatally wounded by shell fire. In action around Missy (14th) – Second-Lieutenant Amos killed. Dug in during evening.

OCTOBER
Relieved (1st) and to Ciry. Continued march via Violaine, Hartennes and Largny arriving Fresnoy (5th). Entrained at Pont-Ste. Maxence for Abbeville (6th) and from there marched to billets at Noyelles-en-Chaussée. To Gueschart (9th), Haravesnes (10th). Moved during afternoon in French buses to Valhuon. To Verquin (11th). Moved forward to front line positions (12th) and took part in attack on Cuinchy. "D" Company on left encountered heavy fire. Engaged around Annequin (13th). Relieved by French troops and to Beuvry (15th). To Le Touret (16th) and then Richebourg St. Vaast in reserve positions. Relieved 1st Duke of Cornwall's Light Infantry in forward positions at Beau Puits (17th). Took part in attack on La Bassée (18th). Later took up positions near Le Bizet. Retired to Richebourg St. Vaast (23rd). Second-Lieutenant Bayley killed (26th). From Merville moved in buses to Wulverghem (31st) and then forward under heavy shell fire for attack on Messines. Advanced 300 strong south of the Wulverghem-Messines road at 1 pm. Engaged in heavy fighting around the convent – 140 casualties.

NOVEMBER
Retired to line of trenches east of Wulverghem 8 pm (1st). To Ypres (6th) and during night took over trenches at Nonne Bosschen Wood. In these positions came under almost continuous shelling for 13 days. Attack on "C" Company's line (11th) – enemy repulsed with high casualties. Another attack repulsed (17th). Relieved by 2nd Duke of Wellington's and to Hooge (19th). Casualties since entering line – 1 officer killed, 1 wounded, 18 other

ranks killed, 297 wounded. To Locre (20th), Neuve Eglise (28th). Took over trenches Wulverghem sector, north side of the Wulverghem-Messines road from 2nd Duke of Wellington's (29th).

DECEMBER

Relieved by 2nd Duke of Wellington's (1st). Located at Wulverghem, Neuve Eglise, Dranoutre, Lindenhoek and St. Jans Cappel. The War Diary of 1st Bedfordshire Regiment records that they were relieved by 2nd King's Own Scottish Borderers (5th) and 3 officers and 200 men had to remain in the trenches for 2 days as the Borderers were too weak to hold the line. War Diary records attack on enemy (14th-16th) and for a 13-day period in the line more than 230 casualties. Battalion was relieved in trenches north of the Wulverghem-Messines road by 2nd Duke of Wellington's (22nd) and at St. Jans Cappel (25th), according to War Diary – "did not fraternize with the enemy". Was at Neuve Eglise on New Years Eve.

CAMERONIANS (SCOTTISH RIFLES)

"Mons" "Le Cateau" "Retreat from Mons" "Marne, 1914" "Aisne, 1914" "La Bassée, 1914" "Messines, 1914" "Armentières, 1914"

1ST BATTALION

AUGUST

Glasgow. Entrained for Southampton (13th). Embarked SS *Caledonia* (14th) and sailed for France. Arrived Havre (15th) and to rest camp. Entrained (17th). Arrived Busigny and marched into billets at Maretz. Began work unloading trains. "A" Company to Valenciennes (21st) followed by rest of Battalion (22nd). Became part of 19th Brigade. Moved to outpost line at Vicq (23rd). Advanced later to positions along the Mons-Condé Canal near Condé. Order received to hold position at all costs. Ordered to retire 2 am (24th) and fell back to Jenlain. Withdrew via Haussy to Le Cateau (25th). Moved into billets at the goods station. Marched via Montigny and Berty to Maretz (26th) then through night to St. Quentin. Continued retreat to Ollezy (27th), Pontoise (28th), Carlemont (29th), Couloisy (30th), La Marbonniere (31st).

SEPTEMBER

Moved with 1st Middlesex to reinforce troops at Néry (1st). Continued retreat, reaching Eve (2nd) then to Dammartin. Left 1 am (3rd) for Lagny then to Chanteloup. To Grisy (5th). Moved forward via Jossigny to Villeneuve (6th), La Haute Maison (7th). War Diary records forming up for attack on Pierre-Levee (8th) – but enemy had retreated. Moved on to Signy-Signets. Heavily shelled from enemy holding north bank of the Marne. Relieved 1st Middlesex in forward positions (9th). Crossed the Marne at La Ferté-sous-Jouarre (10th) then to Certigny. To Marizy-Ste. Geneviève (11th), Buzancy (12th), Le Carrier d'Eveque (13th), positions 1 mile south of Venizel (14th). Covered 4th Division's crossing of the Aisne then moved to line south of Bucy-le-Long. To Septmonts (20th).

OCTOBER

To St. Remy (5th). Marched through night (6th) to Vez. To Bethisy St. Pierre (7th), Pont- Ste. Maxence (8th). Entrained at Estrées-St. Denis (9th). Arrived St. Omer (10th) then to Renescure. "B" Company to Lynde, "C" Company to Lenieppe (11th). To Borre (12th). 19th Brigade attached to 6th Division. To Rouge Croix (13th), Bailleul (14th), Steenwerck (15th), Vlamertinghe (16th). War Diary records (18th) – Battalion to "experiment" in getting into motor buses. Left Vlamertinghe in buses 2.30 pm (19th), arrived Laventie 8.45 pm. War Diary – "Going in buses not all quite simple." Marched to Fromelles (20th), Bas Maisnil (21st). "B" Company sent forward in support of 1st Middlesex. Heavily shelled and fell back later to trenches in front of La Boutillerie. Casualties – 1 killed, 13 wounded, 1 missing. Held positions under heavy shell fire and infantry attacks. Captain R.H.W. Rose and 14 other ranks killed, 2 officers, 35 other ranks wounded, 1 officer, 19 other ranks missing (22nd). Lieutenant J.F. Hewitt and 13 other ranks killed, 11 wounded (26th). War Diary ends October with a note to the effect that the men in the trenches are not supported adequately by artillery – "if all artillery officers would spend a little time in the trenches, they would realise this too."

NOVEMBER
Relieved (14th) and to Bac St. Maur. To Houplines (17th) and took over trenches near Frélinghien. War Diary notes that the enemy were just 80 yards away.

DECEMBER
Relieved by 2nd Royal Welch Fusiliers (3rd) and to Houplines. Took over trenches near Pont Ballot (11th). Relieved by 1st East Yorkshire (26th) and to Armentières.

2ND BATTALION

AUGUST
St. Andrew's Barracks, Malta.

SEPTEMBER
Sailed for Southampton (15th). Arrived and to camp at Baddesley Common near Romsey. Later moved to Hursley Pary, Winchester and joined 23rd Brigade, 8th Division.

NOVEMBER
To Southampton (4th) and sailed SS *Cornishman* for France. Arrived Havre (5th) and to No.6 Rest Camp. Entrained for St. Omer (8th). Moved to billets between St. Omer and Berquin (10th) and between Neuf Berquin and Estaires (11th). To Steenwerck (12th), Neuve Eglise (13th). Relieved 156th French Regiment in trenches south-west of Messines (14th).

Relieved by 4th Middlesex (17th) and via Neuve Eglise to billets in Estaires. Casualties – 1 killed, 5 wounded. To La Flinque (18th). Relieved 2nd Devonshire in front line Chapigny sector (21st). Relieved by 2nd Devonshire (24th) and to Estaires. Casualties – 1 killed, 4 wounded. Relieved 2nd Devonshire in front line (27th). Lieutenant A.W. Tomes (3rd Devonshire Regiment attached) accidentally killed. Relieved by 2nd Devonshire (30th) and to La Flinque. Casualties – 1 officer, 3 other ranks killed, 15 wounded.

DECEMBER

Took over front line from 2nd Devonshire (3rd). War Diary records (4th) "Cap shot off German – blue with red piping, probably Jiega." War Diary records (5th) that the Paybook, diary and letters of a dead German belonging to the 57th Regiment were brought in. Relieved by 2nd Devonshire (6th) and to billets at Pont Rirchon. Casualties – 1 killed, 5 wounded. Returned to trenches (9th) relieving 2nd Devonshire. Relieved by 2nd Devonshire (12th). Casualties – 1 killed, 2 wounded. One of the latter, War Diary records, was "accidentally self-inflicted." Relieved 2nd Northamptonshire in trenches north of Neuve Chapelle (14th). In reserve during attack on Moated Grange (18th), supporting attack made by 2nd Devonshire with covering fire from trenches. Dug trench during night connecting Battalion's left with 2nd Devonshire. Lieutenant C.R. Hopkins and 4 men killed, 4 wounded. Relieved by 1st Worcestershire (19th) and to Brigade reserve at Laventie. Total casualties – 1 officer, 7 other ranks killed, 1 officer, 10 other ranks wounded. Relieved 2nd Royal Berkshire in Chapigny sector (20th). Lieutenant T.E.D. Dunn mortally wounded (21st). Relieved by 2nd Devonshire (24th) and to La Flinque. Casualties – 1 officer, 3 other ranks killed, 13 wounded. Relieved 2nd Devonshire (27th) Relieved by 2nd Devonshre (30th) and to Pont Rirchon. Casualties – 2 killed, 1 officer, 13 other ranks wounded. War Diary records one of the latter being self-inflicted.

1/5TH BATTALION (TERRITORIAL FORCE)

AUGUST

Headquarters – 261 West Princes Street, Glasgow. Commanding Officer – Lieutenant- Colonel R. Jeffrey Douglas, C.M.G., T.D. Part of Scottish Rifle Brigade, Lowland Division. Assembled at Headquarters (5th). Billeted in Woodside and Willowbank Schools. To billets in Larbert and Carronshore (11th).

6. Postcard from the 'Daring Deeds' series showing Private J. Pym, 1st Battalion, Royal Berkshire Regiment, winning the Distinguished Conduct Medal during the fighting near Gheluvelt on 31 October, 1914.

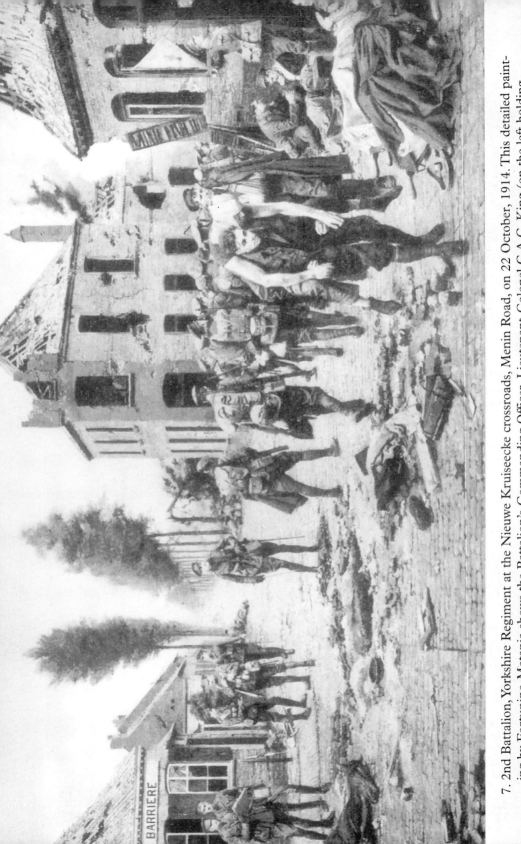

7. 2nd Battalion, Yorkshire Regiment at the Nieuwe Kruiseecke crossroads, Menin Road, on 22 October, 1914. This detailed painting by Fortunino Matania shows the Battalion's Commanding Officer, Lieutenant-Colonel C.A.C. King (on the left holding ...) who was killed on 30 October and Private Henry Tandy (on right carrying wounded man). This soldier later gained the

8. 10th (Scottish) Battalion, King's (Liverpool Regiment) having just arrived at Tunbridge Wells, 10 October, 1914. These Territorials landed in France on 2 November and would be in action before the end of the month.

(Courtesy David Barnes)

9. Private George Wilson, 2nd Battalion, Highland Light Infantry, winning the Victoria Cross during the fighting at the Tilleul Spur, 14 September, 1914.

10/11. Cigarette cards from the W.D. & H.O. Wills "Victoria Cross Heroes" series. Both Lieutenant M.J. Dease (left) and Private S.F. Godley (below) fought with the 4th Battalion, Royal Fusiliers, gaining their VCs at Mons on 23 August, 1914.

OCTOBER

Began duty on Tay defences (27th) billets at Broughty Ferry and Wormit.

NOVEMBER

Left Scottish Rifle Brigade and entrained for Southampton (2nd). Moved to rest camp on common. Sailed SS *Huanchaco* (4th). Arrived Havre (5th) and to rest camp. Battalion history notes new uniforms issued bearing brass buttons. These were replaced with black ones (as worn by rifle regiments) from the old uniforms. Entrained for St. Omer (6th). Arrived (7th) and marched to billets at Helfaut and Bilques. Battalion history records a "new recruit" joining at Havre railway station. He was a black and white collie which was soon named "Jock" and remained with the battalion until killed on the Somme in 1916. Also noted were numbers of French Territorials guarding the railways. Most were old men, some wearing medals for the Franco-Prussian War of 1870. At Helfaut a number of 1/28th London Regiment (Artists Rifles) cap badges were proudly displayed in the houses. The battalion had been in the village and had just left for the front line. Ordered to front line and to be attached to 19th Brigade, 6th Division. Marched to Hazebrouck. Battalion history notes German prisoners in the area and mentions that they were quite distinguishable from each other – "Domineering" Prussians, "Swashbuckling" Bavarians and "Docile" Saxons. Moved on to Bailleul and next day to Armentières. Began tours of duty in trenches – Houplines sector. Position running from Frélinghien – Armentières road to River Lys. War Diary of 2nd Argyll and Sutherland Highlanders records 1 company of Battalion being attached for instruction (28th). Frank Richards (2nd Royal Welsh Fusiliers) came in contact with the 1/5th Cameronians just after the battalion came to Houplines. In his book *Old Soldiers Never Die* he mentions that the old regular soldier generally did not have a high opinion of the Territorials. After a time, however, the 5th Cameronians were accepted and he noted that they were the best Territorial battalion that he ever saw . . . "we never worried if they were on the left or right of us in the line or in attacks."

DECEMBER

Inspected by H.M. King accompanied by the Prince of Wales (1st). Heavy shelling 7.30 pm (9th). Enemy attacked 20 minutes later but were beaten off. Relieved 2nd Argyll and Sutherland Highlanders in trenches near Pont Ballot road, Houplines sector (11th). Germans heard singing and brass band playing (24th). Firing ceased during morning (25th) and Germans left their trenches unarmed. Both sides met in No Man's Land and souvenirs exchanged. During afternoon, shot from right hit one man (Corporal W.S.

Smith) who died next day. Records shown that the Saxons opposite went to great lengths to let the Scottish Rifles know that it was a Prussian battalion that had fired the shot. Relieved and to Armentières (26th). Billeted in l' Hospice Civile. Casualties during period in trenches – 6 killed, 2 wounded.

ROYAL INNISKILLING FUSILIERS

"Le Cateau" "Retreat from Mons" "Marne, 1914" "Aisne, 1914" "Messines, 1914" "Armentières, 1914"

2ND BATTALION

AUGUST

Dover. Part of 12th Brigade, 4th Division. Moved by train to Cromer (8th), Norwich (10th). Entrained for Wembley (18th) and moved into camp at Neasden. Left Wembley by train (21st) and sailed from Southampton to France (22nd). Arrived Havre (23rd) and to rest camp. Entrained for Bertry (24th). Arrived (25th) and moved forward – Headquarters with "A" and "D" Companies to Ligny, "B" and "C" Companies to Bévillers then Beauvois. Withdrew to defensive positions – Headquarters, "A" and "D" Companies at Esnes, "B" and "C" Companies around Longsart Farm. War Diary records (26th) – enemy engaged at Esnes 8.05 am till 10.45 am, also 2.15 pm to 4.40 pm. Headquarters detachment withdrew to Ronssoy, other companies moved back to Le Catelet. Battalion assembled at Hancourt (27th) and at 11 pm began march to Voyennes. Halted just north of Voyennes during morning (28th) then sent via Martigny to cover retreat of 3rd Division across the Sambre near Offoy. Moved later to Campagne. To Chevilly (29th) then at 7 pm to Noyon. Marched through night via Carlepont to Trosly-Breuil. To Verberie (31st).

SEPTEMBER

Moved as rearguard 4 am (1st). War Diary records coming under attack by Germans at dawn. The machine guns engaging a party of cyclists and killing 6. Enemy then appeared to withdraw and moved off around on left flank. Sir Frank Fox records in his war history of the Royal Inniskilling Fusiliers that the Germans then opened an attack, forcing a retirement back through Verberie. Later, Captains S.G. Roe and J.H.R. Yardley led their companies back along the main road from the south end of the village. Here, a German field gun opened fire at a range of just a few hundred yards. Sir Frank notes that the shrapnel fire was deadly, the men forced to shelter against the walls of buildings as best they could. Advance continued however and the Battalion reached Baron at 3.30 pm. Casualties – 2 officers wounded, 1 man killed, 24 wounded, 25 missing. Marched through night (1st/2nd) to Dammartin. To Serris (3rd), Jossigny (4th), Brie-comte-Robert (5th). Advanced to Villiers (6th), Ferm Petit Loge (7th). Came under fire from enemy about 7 pm – Second-Lieutenant H.A. Boyd killed, 1 other officer wounded, 1 man killed, 19 wounded, 6 missing. Second-Lieutenant Boyd had joined the Battalion from England only hours before his death. Crossed the Petit Morin at Courcelles (8th). War Diary notes that Germans were still in the village as the Battalion approached. Bivouacked on the La Ferte-Bussieres road. Marched via Les Pouelain and Tartarel (9th), crossing the Marne at Saussoy railway bridge. Came under heavy shell fire and took up positions at Les Boissieres. To Montigny (10th) and bivouacked on the Montigny-Cerfroid road. To Marizy St. Mard (11th), via Chouy, Hartennes, Villemontoire and Septmonts to Billy-sur-Aisne (12th). One company took up positions covering the bridge at Venizel. Crossed the Aisne at Venizel (13th). Advanced under heavy shell fire and took up positions around Ste. Marguerite. Casualties – 5 killed, 44 wounded, 12 missing. Held line under shell and sniper fire. War Diary notes (24th) that neighbouring villages – Missy, Chivres and Bucy-le-Long had all been destroyed and were on fire. Casualties (14th-30th) – 1 killed, 22 wounded, 5 missing.

OCTOBER
Relieved (7th) and to Septmonts. To Chacrise (8th) then travelled in lorries to Longeuil (11th). Entrained (12th). Arrived Hazebrouck (13th) and moved forward towards Meteren. War Diary records coming into contact with the enemy about 3 pm – "fierce fighting, village taken during night." Casualties – 1 killed, 13 wounded. To Bailleul (14th). Left for Ploegsteert (15th), taking up positions just east of Le Gheer and facing Pont Rouge (17th). In support during attack (18th) then in evening to Houplines. Moved back to Le Gheer (19th). Enemy attacked 7 am (20th). War Diary records – "advanced posts driven in." Casualties – 6 killed, 16 wounded. Another attack on Battalion`s trenches (21st) recorded as unsuccessful – "We were driven back a few hundred yards where we held the enemy from 5.15 am till 12.30 pm, at which time we reoccupied our forward trenches." Relieved later and to Ploegsteert. Casualties – Captains D.G.H. Auchinleck, S.G. Roe, Second-Lieutenant A.G.M. Roberts killed, 2 officers wounded, 33 other ranks killed, 76 wounded, 41 missing. Moved to trenches north of the Armentières-Lille road (23rd). Enemy attack during morning repulsed. Casualties – 1 killed, 15 wounded. To Ploegsteert (30th), Messines (31st). War Diary records – heavy fighting at Messines and several trenches recaptured. Casualties – 9 killed, 20 wounded.

NOVEMBER
War Diary records – forward trenches being held, regiments on left retired without giving warning. Held on until midnight then fell back to 2nd line.

Casualties – Second-Lieutenant K.S. Aplin and 4 other ranks killed, 23 wounded, 6 missing. Took part in counter-attack to regain lost trenches on edge of Ploegsteert Wood (7th). War Diary records that 2 "desperate assaults" were made – both being repulsed. Casualties – Lieutenant J.R. Geoghegan, Second-Lieutenant A.T.L. Barton and 9 other ranks killed, 70 wounded, 16 missing. Held positions on edge of wood throughout day (8th) then returned to billets in Ploegsteert. Moved into support and reserve trenches in Ploegsteert Wood (9th). Assisted in another unsuccessful attempt to recover lost trenches (10th). Casualties – 2 killed, 3 wounded. To Le Bizet (11th) – 2 companies taking over part of line from Le Touquet railway towards the Warnave. To Nieppe (20th), Le Bizet (26th).

DECEMBER
To Bailleul (6th), Hazebrouck (7th), via St. Omer to Wisques (8th). Remained in Wisques to refit.

GLOUCESTERSHIRE REGIMENT

**"Mons" "Retreat from Mons" "Marne, 1914"
"Aisne, 1914" "Ypres, 1914" "Langemarck, 1914"
"Gheluvelt" "Nonne Bosschen" "Givenchy, 1914"**

1ST BATTALION

AUGUST
Bordon. Part of 3rd Brigade, 1st Division. Entrained for Southampton (12th) and embarked SS *Gloucester Castle*. Arrived Havre early morning (13th) and moved to No.1 Rest Camp on high ground north of town. Entrained at docks (15th) and via Rouen, Amiens, St. Quentin and Wassigny arrived Le Nouvion (16th). Marched through Forest of Le Nouvion to billets in Le Tilleul and Dohis. Began advance towards Belgium frontier (20th), billeting at Beaurepaire and then Doulers (21st). Marched via Maubeuge to Villers-sire-Nicole (22nd). During evening ordered to Haulchin and commenced digging defensive positions on northern edge of village. Stood by all day (23rd) – "D", "C" and "B" Companies holding front line north and north-east of Haulchin, "A" in support at Haulchin. War Diary records (24th) heavy rifle fire from the direction of Mons. Battalion's outposts made contact with German cavalry patrols. Received orders to retire from Haulchin at 7 am. "B" Company became separated and moved parallel with the Bavai-Binche road. Remainder of battalion withdrew on Croix-lez-Rouveroy then via Villers-sire-Nicole and Bettignies to Neuf Mesnil. "B" Company having rejoined, the Battalion continued its 200-mile march to the Marne moving to Le Grand Fayt (25th), Oisy (26th). Enemy engaged near Favril during march – Captain G.M. Shipway of "B" Company mortally wounded, 1 man killed and 29 wounded. To Bernot (27th), Bertaucourt (28th), Brancourt (30th), Missy-aux-Bois (31st).

SEPTEMBER
To Mareuil (1st), Cregy (2nd), Signy Signets (3rd), crossing the Marne at Germigny and billeting of a lake near Perreuse Château east of the village. To Moroux (4th), Rozoy (5th). Everard Wyrall in his war history of the Gloucestershire Regiment records that while at Rozoy the Battalion's strength was brought up to just above war establishment by the arrival of some 100 men. This, the first reinforcement since leaving England, was also accompanied by a small supply of shirts, socks and boots. By this time boots were in bad condition and a number of men were marching in bare feet.

Began advance towards the Aisne, marching via Courpalat to Vaudoy (6th), Dagny and Chevru to Choisy (7th). Crossed the Grand Morin at La Ferté Gaucher (8th) then via Hondevillers to bivouacs at Ferme de L'ile near Basseville. Crossed the Marne at Nogent (9th) and bivouacked at Le Thiolet. Continued advance via Torcy, Courchamps and Priez to Sommelans (10th), via Latilly, Grissoles and Coincy to Villeneuve (11th), via Fère-en-Tardenois, Loupeigne and Bazoches to Vauxcéré (12th). Crossed the Aisne at Bourg (13th). At Bourg, one diarist recorded, the French were pleased to see British troops. A villager had recently shot a German soldier and as a retaliation a number of men had been rounded up for execution. News of the proximity of the 1st Division had come just as the men were about to be shot. Reached Vendresse (14th), "B" and "C" Companies advancing during the afternoon and firing on the enemy who retreated up the slopes opposite. Later, "A" and "D" Companies moved to Divisional Reserve at Chivy, "B" and "C" moved forward through Chivy and dug in west of Troyon. "B" Company assisted in repelling German counter-attack (15th). Casualties (14th-15th) – Lieutenant R.K. Swanwick and 10 other ranks killed, 2 officers and 72 other ranks wounded, 2 men missing. "A" Company relieved "B" in front line (16th) and came under shell-fire at 6 am. Casualties – 3 killed. 9 wounded. Second-Lieutenant D. Baxter, Sergeant Durham and Drummer Fluck noted as doing good work throughout the day. Battalion assembled in Chivy (17th) and at 7.15 pm moved to Troyon. "C" and "D" Companies took up positions along the Chemin des Dames, "A" and "B" moved into support lines some 200 yards to the rear. Later "B" Company was sent forward to fill in a number of German trenches. Everard Wyrall notes that many of the enemy's dead were buried along with 3 machine guns. War Diary records – "mud is simply awful" and that it was still raining. Heavy, but ineffective, shell-fire all day (18th). Front line companies relieved (19th) and withdrew to quarries on ridge west of Troyon. Battalion relieved (27th) and withdrew to Bourg. To Pagnan (29th).

OCTOBER

To Moulins in Divisional Reserve (1st). Later "A" and "D" Companies sent forward as reinforcements to Chemin des Dames line north of village. Everard Wyrall records the following weeks as uneventful, just one shell hitting Headquarters and doing no damage. Marched via Bourg and Dhuizel to Paars (16th) and billeted in farms south of the village. Moved via Bazoches and Loupeigne to Fère-en-Tardenois (17th) and entrained for Flanders. Arrived Cassel (18th) and from there marched to billets at Longue Croix. To Poperinghe (20th). Strength – 25 officers, about 970 other ranks. Marched via Elverdinghe, Boesinghe and Pilckem to Langemarck (21st). Took part in fighting around Koekuit and Grutesaele Farm, driving back German counter-attack from Mangelaare. Captain W.A.M. Temple mortally wounded, 49 other casualties. After midnight withdrew to Varna Farm south-west of Langemarck. Enemy shell killed 5 and wounded 12 men of "A" Company (22nd). Two platoons of "A" Company and 1 of "D" in action on northern outskirts of Langemarck (23rd). Enemy withdrew just after 1 pm. Casualties – Lieutenants H.E. Hippiley and W.S. Yalland killed, Lieutenant D. Baxter wounded, 15 other ranks killed, 36 wounded. For their part in the action, Captain R.E. Rising was awarded the Distinguished Service Order and Lieutenant Baxter the Military Cross. Four other ranks were awarded Distinguished Conduct Medals, the citation mentioning that the men had helped repulse a very determined attack and defended their position after all officers had become casualties. In a letter, Brigadier-General H.J.S. Landon (Commanding 3rd Brigade) noted that the Gloucesters inflicted great losses on the enemy who had come to within 50 yards of their line. Each man had fired some 500 rounds and some had the bayonets shot off their rifles. Not a man retired. During afternoon, remainder of "A" Company successfully re-claimed trenches recently taken by the enemy. To bivouacs near Bellewaarde Farm (25th). Moved to Hooge (26th), digging shelter trenches in wood around the Château, then to positions north of Ypres – Gheluvelt road near Veldhoek. Holding position north of Veldhoek and support trenches on road running to south-west corner of Polygon Wood (28th). Took part in Battle of Gheluvelt (29th). "C" Company advanced on left of Gheluvelt Château grounds and eastern outskirts of village – Everard Wyrall notes early casualties among the officers and that the company "practically ceased to exist." "D" Company moved along the Menin road to within 300 yards of the Kruiseecke cross roads. Heavy shell fire and constant attacks from the north-east later forced withdrawal. "A" Company advancing behind "C" also suffered heavy casualties. "B" Company moved forward north of Gheluvelt Church, cross the Menin road east of village and advanced towards Kruiseecke. Withdrawal forced after strong enemy attacks. Battalion concentrated at Veldhoek. Casualties – Captain A.G. McBurn (East Surrey Regiment attached), Lieutenants H.K. Foster, A.D. Harding and 56 other ranks killed, 2 officers and 64 other ranks wounded, 2 officers and 34 other ranks taken prisoner. Position shelled (30th) – 7 killed, 5 wounded. In action again (31st) – western side of Gheluvelt astride the Menin road. Withdrew to Château grounds then counter-attacked. Later held barricade at Veldhoek crossroads. Casualties – Major R.M.S. Gardner killed, 69 other casualties.

NOVEMBER
Withdrew to Inverness Copse (1st). Seventy-six casualties during relief. To Sanctuary Wood (2nd) and during afternoon advanced towards Veldhoek. Engaged enemy then forced to retire back to Sanctuary Wood. Captain A.A. McLeod and 11 other ranks killed, 2 officers and 45 other ranks wounded, 2 men missing. Heavy shell fire (3rd) – 2 killed, 9 wounded. Relieved 1st South Wales Borderers in support positions on edge of Herenthage Wood (4th). Returned to Sanctuary Wood then during night took over front line east of Herenthage Wood. Heavy shell fire (5th) – 13 killed, 28 wounded. Relieved during night and to Railway Wood. To front line north of Zwartelleen (6th). Advanced (7th) and came under heavy fire from eastern side of village. Everard Wyrall records that many men were forced to lie down in the open all day unable to get back to their line. He also notes the deaths of Captain R.E. Rising and Lieutenant M. Kershaw and approximate casualties among the men as 43 killed, 47 wounded, 8 missing. At roll-call there were just 3 officers and 213 men present. A number of men were promoted in the field as there were no sergeants. Relieved and to Herenthage Wood (8th), Bellewaarde Farm (10th). Moved forward (11th) and took part in the fighting around Nonne Bosschen. During afternoon took up positions running from Inverness Copse to Verbeck Farm. Relieved (16th) and to Locre. To Outtersteene (17th), trenches near Wytschaete (21st). Relieved by 2nd Oxfordshire and Buckinghamshire Light Infantry (25th) and to Outtersteene. Casualties – 4 killed, 10 wounded. Everard Wyrall records that out of the 25 officers and 970 other ranks that took part in the Battle of Langemarck only 2 officers and 100 men remained. Casualties, since 19th October, had been 10 officers killed, 11 died of wounds, 3 taken prisoner, 1 sick; other ranks had suffered 189 killed, 413 wounded, 62 taken prisoner.

DECEMBER
To Merville (20th) and Béthune (21st). Advanced to Gore then Festubert and in afternoon took part in the attack on Givenchy. Think mud held up advance, rifles were clogged and, Everard Wyrall notes, it was impossible even to fix bayonets. Dug in during night on a line running from Le Plantin to La Quinque Eue. Casualties – Second-Lieutenant D.H. Wiggin mortally wounded, 5 officers wounded, 45 other ranks killed, 109 wounded, 4 taken prisoner.

2ND BATTALION

AUGUST
North China – Tientsin (2 companies), Peking (1 company), Shan-Hai-Kwan (1 company).

SEPTEMBER
Ordered to India. Embarked SS *Arcadia* at Ching-Wang-Tao. Received orders while at sea off Shanghai to proceed to England.

NOVEMBER
Arrived Southampton (8th) and to camp near Winchester. First at Hursley Park, then Magdalen Hill (13th). Joined 81st Brigade, 27th Division. The regimental history of the Gloucestershire Regiment for 1914-1918 by Everard Wyrall records the arrival while at Winchester of "Buller." This stray bull terrier appeared in the transport lines one night and was to remain constantly with the battalion throughout the war. Arriving back in England from South Russia in 1919.

DECEMBER
To Southampton (18th). Embarked SS *City of Chester* and sailed for France. Commanding Officer – Lieutenant-Colonel G.S. Tulloh. Arrived Havre (19th) and entrained for Aire-sur-la-Lys 4 am (20th). Arived 5 am (21st) and billeted in French Army barracks at Château Moine. Began work digging defensive positions around Boesghem (27th) and Pecqueur (28th). War Diary records that the boots issued at Winchester were beginning to break up. Continued entrenchments around La Roupie (29th).

WORCESTERSHIRE REGIMENT

**"Mons" "Le Cateau" "Retreat from Mons"
"Marne, 1914" "Aisne, 1914" "La Bassée, 1914"
"Armentières, 1914" "Ypres, 1914"
"Langemarck, 1914" "Gheluvelt" "Nonne Bosschen"**

1ST BATTALION

AUGUST
Cairo, Egypt.

SEPTEMBER
Sailed from Alexandria on SS *Deseado* for England (30th).

OCTOBER
Arrived Liverpool (16th). Entrained for Winchester (17th) and to camp at Hursley Park. Joined 24th Brigade, 8th Division.

NOVEMBER
Marched to Southampton (5th) and embarked SS *Maidan* for France. Officers – Lieutenant-Colonel A.E. Lascelles (Commanding Officer), Majors E.C.F. Wodehouse, DSO, G.C. Lambton, DSO, B.K.W. Bacon, Captains T. Fitzjohn, C. Richardson, J.H.M. Arden, F. St. J. Tyrwhitt, J.F.S. Winnington (Adjutant), C.S. Linton, D. King (Quartermaster), Lieutenants C.F.G. Crawford, J.F. Leman, J.S. Veasey, K.W. Wilkins, L.H. Ruck, J.M. Monk, H. Fitz M. Stacke, E.L.G. Lawrence, Second-Lieutenants F.C. Roberts, R.M. Slater, E.B. Conybeare, L.G. Phillips, M.A. Hamilton Cox, J.H. Tristram, H.P. Hartnoll, F. Darby, F.W. Young, D. King. Arrived Havre (6th). Disembarked (8th). Entrained for Berguette (9th). Detrained (10th) and to billets in railway siding. Marched via Merville to Neuf Berquin (11th). To front line (14th) marching via Estaires, Rouge Croix, Croix Barbée and St. Vaast. Took up positions facing Neuve Chapelle. Right of line being at Port Arthur and then running along western side of main road from La Bassée to Estaires as far as the crossroads at Pont Logy. In much of the line held there were no trenches, the men occupying the sloping embankment (10 feet high) and lying down on the top to fire. Came under heavy shell fire (15th). Casualties – 7 killed, 25 wounded. Shelling continued (16th-19th). Second-Lieutenant Slater mortally wounded. Other casualties – 12 killed, 27 wounded. Relieved by 1st

Sherwood Foresters during night (19th) and to La Gorgue. The march to La Gorgue is described as "painful", many of the exhausted troops suffering frostbite. War Diary describes the event as — "The retreat from Moscow." At an inspection (20th) one man in every 4 was found to be suffering from frostbite, some 150 cases being recorded as "serious." Battalion continued tours in front line, exchanging with 1st Sherwood Foresters and billeting in either La Gorgue, Estaires or Rouge Croix. Second-Lieutenant Darby killed (29th).

DECEMBER

Second-Lieutenant Hartnoll killed (12th). Major B.K.W. Bacon killed (13th). Casualties by middle of month — 39 killed, 74 wounded, 440 suffering from severe frostbite. In reserve during 8th Division's attack on Neuve Chapelle, marching from Estaires and holding positions at St. Vaast during night (18th/19th). Took over front line positions to the left of those previously held (19th). Relieved and to La Gorgue (22nd). Casualties — 2 killed, 17 wounded. To front line (25th). Captain H. Fitz M. Stacke, MC. in his war history of the Worcestershire Regiment refers to the Christmas truce as — "a strange sensation. . . the silence seemed unreal."

2ND BATTALION

AUGUST

Aldershot. Part of 5th Brigade, 2nd Division. Entrained for Southampton (13th) and embarked SS *Lake Michigan* and SS *Herlborough* for France. Officers — Lieutenant- Colonel C.B. Westmacott (Commanding Officer), Major E.B. Hankey (Second in Command), Captains G.E. Lea, M.R. Carr, C.E.L. Porter, E.L. Bowring, R.J. Ford, R.W. Pepys, R.H. Nolan (RAMC, Medical Officer), Lieutenants B.C. Senhouse (Adjutant), G.J.L. Stoney, E.C.R. Hudson, E.A. Haskett-Smith, C.C. Lilley, F.E. Myddleton-Gavey, H.S. Lowe, R.E. Vyvyan, A.W. Hudson, F.G.O. Curtler, C.M. Pope, J. Batchelor (Quartermaster), Second-Lieutenants G.A. Slaughter, T.H. Watson, F.F. Smythe, O.C. Guinness. Total other ranks — 977. Arrived Boulogne (14th) and to Marlborough Camp. Left camp at midnight (15th) and entrained for Wassigny. Arrived and marched to billets at Les Germain. Marched via Etreux to La Groise (21st) and set up outpost on the bridge at Catillon. Moved via Landrecies to Pont-sur-Sambre (22nd) and via Malplaquet to Bougnies (23rd). Advanced during night to Frameries, arriving about 1 am (24th) and "A", "C" and "D" Companies setting up a defensive line on the northern outskirts of the village. Came under shell fire at daybreak, shrapnel causing Battalion's first casualties. Enemy seen later advancing between Cuesmes and Flenu. Received order to retire about 8 am and fell back through Frameries. Captain H. Fitz M. Stacke, MC in his war history of the Worcestershire Regiment records that the village was heavily shelled during the withdrawal, the civilian population stampeding through the streets in a "terror-stricken mob." He also notes the staidness of the Battalion who formed up in fours just south of the main road, sloped arms and moved of – "exactly as if marching back to barracks at Aldershot." Moved back to Eugies, and prepared defensive line, then about 4.30 pm to Bavai. Continued retreat via Pont-sur-Sambre to Noyelles (25th). Arriving 10.30 pm then received order to return to Pont-sur-Sambre. Marched through night but ordered to halt just outside Leval. Continued retreat dawn (26th), marching via Marbaix to Barzy then via Boue, Etreux and Guise to billets at Mont d` Origny (27th). Marched via Ribemont, Hamegicourt and Danizy to billets at Servais (28th), Coucy le Château to Terny (30th), Soissons and Pommiers to Laversine (31st).

SEPTEMBER

Marched via Soucy to Villers-Cotterêts (1st) then moved to wood north-east of Villers-en-Potées. Halted for 2 hours awaiting attack then moved to Cuvergnon. Dug defensive positions on outskirts of village. Battalion now covering retreat of 2nd Division. Withdrew (2nd) via Betz, Etavigny, Vincy, Etrepilly, Barcy and Penchard to bivouacs at Chauconin. Marched to Meaux (3rd), crossed the Marne at Trilport then continued on via Monceaux to Petit Courois. Fell back to positions near Grand Bilbarteaux Farm 10.15 am (4th). Later, during evening, moved to defensive line running from Bois de Morillas to Maisoncelles. Withdrew to La Celle (5th), crossed the Grand Morin then via Mortcerf and La Houssaye to billets at Marles. Took up defensive line near Champlet during morning (6th) then at 4 pm advanced to Pezarches. Moved forward (7th) via Mauperthuis, Bertheuil, La Touche and Chailly-en-Brie to St. Siméon. Marched through Rebais (8th) then sent forward to banks of the Petit Morin near La Trétoire to assist 4th (Guards) Brigade. "A" and "B" Companies opened fire on enemy across river while "C" and "D" crossed to the left and drove enemy back towards the Marne via Sablonnières. Bivouacked for night at La Petite Basseville. Casualties – 11 killed and wounded. Crossed the Marne (9th) and to billets at Domptin. Advanced via Cupru to Monnes (10th), Neuilly-St. Front, Oulchy-le-Château to Beugneux (11th), Arcy, Jouaignes to Courcelles (12th). Crossed the Vesle and engaged enemy taking 107 prisoners. Continued on to Vieil Arcy then set up outpost line on slopes above Pont Arcy. Withdrew at dawn (13th) to Vieil Arcy. Moved forward 2.30 pm, crossed the Aisne at Pont Arcy and advanced through Moussy towards the Tilleul Spur. Crest occupied by 10 pm. Covered advance of 6th Brigade (14th). Captain Stacke noting the day as one of – "heavy and confused fighting." Enemy counter-attack along the spur from Courteçon just after noon driven back. Later moved forward and with 2 companies of 1st King's Royal Rifle Corps and 2nd Highland Light Infantry crossed the Chemin des Dames by 9 pm and set up positions on ridge overlooking Courteçon. Captain Stacke records the advance as being over ground covered with dead and wounded. Positions found to be unsupported on either side and withdrawal ordered. Fell back to southern end of the Tilleul Spur then to bivouacs at Moussy. Casualties – 11 killed, 58 wounded. Moved forward (15th) to Tilleul Spur. Heavily shelled – Captain Lea mortally wounded, 1 man killed, 7 wounded. Relieved by 2nd Connaught Rangers 7 pm. (16th) and to reserve at Verneuil. Casualties – 1 killed, 7 wounded. Relieved 2nd Highland Light Infantry in trenches on the Tilleul Spur (17th). Heavily shelled (18th). Direct hit on dug-out killing Captain Carr and Second-Lieutenant Smythe. "A" and "B" Companies relieved by 2nd Highland Light Infantry 7 pm and to Verneuil. "A" and "B" Companies moved forward in support of 6th Brigade (19th) and held in reserve throughout night. "C" and "D" Companies relieved and to Verneuil. Enemy attacked 6th Brigade's line (20th). "A" and "B" Companies sent forward to assist 1st King's Liverpool holding positions from canal to western slope of the Tilleul Spur. Advanced through woods and counter-attacked at 11 am. Enemy cleared from trench beyond wood then came under heavy fire from flank. Captain Stacke notes many casualties amoung the officers. Fell back to edge of wood and dug in. "C" and "D" Companies moved forward to Tilleul Spur. "A" and "B" Companies relieved (21st). Casualties – Lieutenant A.W. Hudson killed, Captain Pepys and Lieutenant Lowe mortally wounded. Two other officers wounded, 6 other ranks killed, 5 wounded, 16 missing. Battalion relieved by 1st Coldstream during evening and marched to Dhuizel. Billets at La Cour des Moines Farm. Village shelled (29th) and moved back to temporary billets at Vauxtin until after dark. To Vauxtin (30th) returning to Dhuizel after dark.

OCTOBER
Marched via St. Mard and Cys (1st) and relieved 1st Irish Guards in trenches to the east of La Cour de Soupir Farm. Relieved by French troops during night (13th) and via Soupir, St. Mard and Vauxtin to Vauxcer,. Marched via Perles to Fismes (14th) and then entrained for Hazebrouck. Arrived (16th) and to billets at Morbecque. To Godewaersvelde (17th), Poperinghe (19th) and via Elverdinghe and Boesinghe to Pilckem Ridge (20th). Advance to crossroads north of St. Julien (21st) and engaged enemy

at 9.30 am. Captain Stacke records confused fighting with small bodies of men firing from behind hedges. Troops forced to dig in and hold positions. Captain Nolan (Medical Officer), Lieutenant Curtler and 16 other ranks killed, 39 wounded, 3 missing. Digging continued throughout night. Came under heavy shell fire dawn (22nd). Several attacks by enemy driven back, Casualties – 2 killed, 4 wounded, 1 missing. Firing continued throughout night. Bombardment continued throughout (23rd). Trenches almost destroyed and men exhausted from lack of sleep. Casualties – 16 killed, 22 wounded, 10 missing. Captain Stacke notes that the missing were almost certainly killed and buried by the shell fire. Covered relief of 5th Brigade throughout night. Relieved at dawn (24th) and marched via St. Julien, Wieltje and St. Jean to bivouacs at Hell Fire Corner. After just 20 minutes rest ordered forward to assist 7th Division. Advanced along Menin road to Hooge then took up positions in line on western edge of Polygon Wood. Moved forward into wood with fixed bayonets but forced back to start line to reassemble. Went forward again and enemy engaged. High casualties from hand-to-hand fighting. Enemy retreated and pursued to eastern edge of wood where shrapnel and machine gun fire forced Battalion to dig in. Casualties estimated at around 200. Line held during attack of 4th (Guards) Brigade (25th). Casualties – 1 killed, 5 wounded from shell fire. Relieved (26th) and to bivouacs near south-west corner of Polygon Wood (Black Watch Corner). Moved to northern corner of wood (28th) and in reserve for attack by 5th Brigade. Moved into Divisional Reserve west of Polygon Wood (29th). Took part in the counter-attack at Gheluvelt (31st). "A" Company went forward 12.45 pm to positions on railway embankment north of Gheluvelt and maintained fire on enemy for 2 hours. Remainder of Battalion advanced to Black Watch Corner 2 pm. Captain Starke notes that a general retreat from the direction of Gheluvelt was taking place, the 2nd Worcestershire the only troops going forward. Continued into the Reutelbeek Valley then charged across the Polderhoek Ridge – "A" and "D" Companies leading, "B" Company in second line. Attacking strength about 370 all ranks. Leading troops soon hit by high explosive and shrapnel shells causing over 100 casualties. Survivors rushed down the slope towards Gheluvelt Château and with 1st South Wales Borderers cleared enemy from grounds. Line set up in sunken road beyond. "A" Company later moved forward and took Gheluvelt village. Retired during night along Menin road to Veldhoek then further back into reserve.

NOVEMBER

Advanced to Hooge Château (1st) then to reserve positions east of Zillebeke. Went forward into Bassevillebeek Valley (2nd). "A" Company took part in counter-attack during afternoon clearing enemy from the woods. Battalion moved back into reserve around midnight. Casualties (1st/2nd) – 2 killed, 21 wounded, 3 missing. Relieved by 2nd Duke of Wellington's (6th) and moved to west corner of Polygon Wood. Relieved 2nd Connaught Rangers in trenches north-east of Polygon Wood (8th). Captain Stacke records the shooting of a German patrol leader. The dead man being in possession of field glasses belonging to Captain Pepys who had been mortally wounded at the Tilleul Spur on 21st September. Relieved by French troops (15th) and via Zonnebeke marched along railway line to Railway Wood. Moved via Menin road (19th) and relieved 1st Bedfordshire and 1st Cheshire in trenches south of road near Gheluvelt. Relieved by French troops (21st) and marched via Hooge, Ypres, Vlamertinghe and Locre to Bailleul. Casualties (19th-21st) – 2 killed, 6 wounded.

DECEMBER
Travelled in buses during night (22nd) via Hazebrouck and Béthune to Zelobes then marched to billets at Lacoutre. Relieved 2/39th Garhwal Rifles in front line south of Port Arthur (27th). Trenches recorded as being in bad condition. Flooded and in parts waist deep in water and mud. Headquarters moved back to a farm near Richebourg l' Avou, due to shelling (30th).

3RD BATTALION

AUGUST
Tidworth. Part of 7th Brigade, 3rd Division. To Southampton (13th) and embarked SS *Bosnian*. Sailed for France (14th). Officers – Lieutenant-Colonel B.F.B. Stuart (Commanding Officer), Majors W.R. Chichester (Second in Command), H.D. Milward, Captains E.A.A. deSalis, DSO, L.C. Dorman, H.R. Eliott, C.C. Messervy, C.V. Beresford (Adjutant), T.H. Hughes, E.L.D. Brownell, A. Whitty (Quartermaster), P.S. Stewart (RAMC, Medical Officer), Lieutenants R.F. Traill, H.J.G. Gilmour, J.T. Goff, C. Henry, W.A. Underhill, S.A. Gabb, M.E.L. Clarke, Second-Lieutenants C.C. Harrison, S.A. Goldsmid, P. D. Harding, R.H.M. Lee, F.B. Harvey, I.T. Pritchard, L.F. Urwick, C.S. Morice, C. Tyson. Arrived off Havre (15th) then to Rouen (16th). Disembarked during evening and entrained for Aulnoye (17th). Marched to Marbaix (18th), Dumpierre (20th), via Maubeuge to Feignies (21st). Took up defensive positions at Ciply (22nd). Fired on advancing enemy during morning (24th) then withdrew via Noirchain, Genly, Bavai and St. Waast to Wargnies. Moved via Le Quesnoy, Solesmes, Viesly and Bethencourt to Caudry (25th). Came under fire during early morning (26th) – "B" and "C" Companies holding enemy

back with rapid and accurate fire. Battalion eventually fell back to high ground above Derrière le Tronquoy. Moved later to Montigny. Casualties – Lieutenant Clarke killed, 2 officers wounded, approximately 100 other ranks. Marched via Hargicourt to Vermand (27th) then through night via Ham to Tarlefesse. To Salency during afternoon (29th) then at 10 pm to Noyon. Continued retreat (30th) via Pontoise, Cuts and Camelin to Vic-sur-Aisne, via Mortefontaine, Taillefontaine and Emevilie to Coyolles (31st).

SEPTEMBER

To Levignen (1st) then at 4.30 pm moved via Boissy to Villers. Marched via Bouillancy, Fosse Martin and Douy to Marcilly (2nd). Later took up outpost positions with 1st Wiltshire running Barcy to St. Souppless. To Pringy (3rd) then via Meaux and Nanteuil to Sancy. Moved during night (4th) via Crécy then took up outpost positions near Les Chapelles Bourdon. Began advance to the Aisne (6th), moving into the Forest of Crécy then via Hautefeuille to Faremoutiers. To Les Petits Aulnois (7th), positions near Rebais then Bussieres (8th). To Bezu (9th) and moved forward via Ventelet Farm, Neuilly and Chézy to positions around Montmarlet and Montmarfoy (10th). Marched via Oulchy-le-Château to Grand-Rozoy (11th), Cerseuil (12th), Braine (13th). Crossed the Aisne (14th) and took up positions around Vailly. Moved forward to firing line (15th) – 3 killed, 25 wounded, 3 missing. Enemy attack repulsed (20th) – Lieutenants Gilmour, Henry and Harrison killed, 78 other ranks killed, wounded or missing. Relieved by 1st Leicestershire (21st) and to Braine. Took over outpost positions around Chassemy and covering the Condé bridge (22nd) Relieved by 2nd South Lancashire (24th) and to Augy.

OCTOBER

Relieved 1st Wiltshire at Chassemy (1st). Relieved by 18th Hussars (2nd) and moved back via Braine to Grand-Rozoy. Marched during night (4th/5th) to Coyolles, (5th/6th) to Saintimes, (6th/7th) to Pont-Ste. Maxence. Entrained for Pont Remy then marched to billets at Le Plessier. To Regnauville (8th), Hesdin (9th). Travelled in lorries to Pernes (10th) and took over outpost line from 2nd Royal Irish Rifles on high ground above village. Moved forward via Auchel, Zozinghem and Pont du Reveillon to Lannoy (11th) then Lacouture (12th). Took part in attack on Richebourg St. Vaast, coming under fire from houses situated along the banks of the Loisne, then forced to dig in. Captain Eliott and Lieutenant A. Northey killed and approximately 50 other casualties. Moved forward again (13th), entering the village and digging in on eastern side. Casualties – 8. Held position throughout (14th) – 8 casualties. Advanced (15th) and dug in after about half-mile. Captain Hughes killed, 26 other casualties. Went forward via Port Arthur (16th) and bivouacked on eastern side of Bois de Biez. Moved to Halpegarbe (17th) then fired on from enemy`s line at Le Hue. Second-Lieutenant F.L. Hastings-Medhurst and 1 other rank killed, 16 wounded. Relieved by 1st Royal West Kent (18th) and moved back past Neuve Chapelle to Pont Logy. Moved during evening to billets on western side of Bois du Biez. Relieved 1st Royal West Kent (20th). Enemy attacked (21st) and broke through Battalion`s line. "A strange dim battle ensued", records Captain H. Fitz M. Stacke in *The Worcestershire Regiment in the Great War* – "Parties of the enemy would loom out of the mist to be bayoneted or shot down at close quarters." The author also notes the work of 2 of the Battalion`s marksmen – Company Sergeant Major P.T. Bond and Sergeant J.R. Jewsbury who claimed more than 50 of the enemy. Lost trenches retaken before dark. Casualties – Lieutenant Underhill, Second-Lieutenants E.C.V. Battle and T.H. Galton killed, 4 officers wounded, 13 other ranks killed, 63 wounded, 29 missing. Withdrew after midnight to west side of Bois du Biez. Moved forward again 9.30 am (22nd) and from the crossroads at La Tourelle took part in attack on Rue du Marais. Held positions on northern side throughout day – 18 casualties. Later moved back to new line in front of Festubert. Relieved by 2nd Leicestershire (30th) and to Le Touret. Casualties (23rd-30th) – 17 killed, 47 wounded, 3 missing. Moved later to Lacouture then Merris.

NOVEMBER
Moved in buses to Neuve Eglise (1st). Later advanced via Le Romarin to positions just west of Ploegsteert. "D" Company moved up to south-east corner of Ploegsteert Wood in support of 1st East Lancashire. Rest of Battalion took over positions near La Hutte Château (2nd). "D" Company rejoined later and Battalion relieved 1st Hampshire in front line on eastern side of Ploegsteert Wood. Casualties (3rd-5th) – 9 killed, 23 wounded. "C" Company`s trenches overrun during attack (7th), survivors falling back into Ploegsteert Wood. Enemy checked on edge of wood after counter-attack. Relieved by 2nd Argyll and Sutherland Highlanders (8th) and moved into reserve positions near Butler`s House. Casualties – Captain A.S. Nesbitt, Lieutenant J.B. Vandeleur (Leicestershire attached), Second-Lieutenants Goldsmid, J.M. Atkin (Sherwood Foresters attached) killed, 2 officers wounded, 42 other ranks killed, 121 wounded, 39 missing. Relieved 1st Somerset Light Infantry in trenches north-West of St. Yves (13th). Relieved during night (16th/17th) and to Petit Pont. To Neuve Eglise (17th), La Clytte (19th), billets north of Kemmel (20th), Dranoutre (24th). Took over

front line trenches near Spanbroek Mill (26th). Relieved and to Westoutre (29th). Casualties – 2 killed, 8 wounded. To Locre (30th).

DECEMBER

To Westoutre (3rd), billets near Scherpenberg (6th). Moved into front line trenches near Spanbroek Mill (9th). Relieved and to Locre (12th). Casualties – 2 killed, 5 wounded. To front line at St. Vaast (15th). Relieved and to Locre (18th). To front line near Spanbroek Mill (24th).

EAST LANCASHIRE REGIMENT

"Le Cateau" "Retreat from Mons" "Marne, 1914" "Aisne, 1914" "Armentières, 1914"

1ST BATTALION

AUGUST

Colchester. Part of 11th Brigade, 4th Division. To Harrow (18th), Southampton (21st). Embarked SS *Braemar Castle* for France. Officers – Lieutenant-Colonel L. St. G. Le Marchant, DSO (Commanding Officer), Major T.S. Lambert (Second in Command), Lieutenants F.E. Belchier (Adjutant), R. Longstaff (Quartermaster), J.F. Dyer (Machine Gun Officer), H.T. MacMullen (Transport Officer), R.A. Flood (RAMC, Medical Officer); "A" Company: Captain G. Clayhills, DSO, Lieutenants N.A. Leeson, H.W. Canton, Second-Lieutenants W.R. Tosswill, K. Hooper; "B" Company: Captains E.E. Coventry, A. St. L. Goldie, Lieutenant E.M.B. Delmege, Second-Lieutenants R.Y. Parker, G.H.T. Wade; "C" Company: Major E.R. Collins, DSO, Lieutenants E.C. Hopkinson, W.E. Dowling, Second-Lieutenants T.H. Mathews, W.A. Salt; "D" Company: Major J.E. Green, Captain G.T. Seabroke, Lieutenants F.D. Hughes, W.M. Chisholm, C.E.M. Richards. Sailed for France (22nd). Arrived Havre and to rest camp. Entrained for Le Cateau (23rd). Arrived (24th) and to Briastre. Moved forward during night to positions south of Solesmes. Later withdrew to positions around Briastre then about 10 pm (25th) moved off via Viesly, Bethencourt and Beauvois to Fontaine-au-Pire. Engaged enemy from line on the Carrièrerec Ridge (26th). Later withdrew to Ligny. Casualties – Lieutenant Chisholm mortally wounded, 3 other officers wounded, 257 other ranks killed, wounded or missing. The confused situation in Ligny resulted in the Battalion being divided into 2 columns for its retreat south. To the east, one detachment under Lieutenant-Colonel Le Marchant marched via Clary to Elincourt, then on through Nauroy, Bellenglise and Vermand to Ham (27th), via Noyon to Sempigny (28th) then to Cloyes 29th). Major Green to the east, however, took a party of about 250 men out of Ligny, first through Selvigny and Malincourt to Lempire, then (27th) via Hervilly and Haucourt to Voyennes, via Hombleux and Esmery-Hallon to Freniche (28th) then to Pont L`Evêque (29th). This party eventually joined up with Lieutenant-Colonel Le Marchant (30th). Battalion moved through Carlepont (30th) then via Berneuil, and Attichy to Pierrefonds. Took up positions around St. Sauveur (31st).

SEPTEMBER

Engaged enemy during morning (1st) then retired through Vaucelles and Néry to Rosières. Moved via Montagny to Eve (2nd) then in evening marched through Dammartin to Lagny. To Coupvray (4th), via Serris and Jossigny to Chevry (5th). Advanced through Jossigny to Villeneuves-le-Comte (6th), via Crécy to Maisoncelles (7th), to Les Corbiers (8th). "A", "B" and "C" Companies advanced under fire from La Ferté (9th) and relieved 2nd Royal Welch Fusiliers in forward positions. Lieutenant-Colonel Le Marchant shot by sniper. Crossed the Marne during evening and took part in attack north of La Ferté (10th). Advanced later to billets at Rademont. Moved forward via Ocquerre to Vendrest (11th) then through Coulombs, Vaux and St. Quentin to Passy-en-Valois. Marched via Chouy, Villers-Helon, Vierzy and Rosières to Septmonts (12th), moving again at 11 pm to Venizel. Crossed the Aisne (13th) and took up positions around Bucy-le-Long.

OCTOBER

Relieved by French troops (6th) then march to Compiègne. . Entrained for Blendecques (10th) and moved in buses to Hondeghem (12th). To Flêtre (13th), via Meteren and Bailleul to Neuve Eglise (14th), Romarin (15th). In support of 12th Brigade at Le Bizet, moving into billets on eastern side of Armentières same day. Later dug trenches across the Armentières-Lille railway line. Moved into Divisional Reserve positions at la Chapelle d` Armentières (19th), trenches in Wez Macquart sector (20th). "B" Company remained in line between Wez Macquart and Porte Egale (21st), rest of Battalion moving via Armentières to Ploegsteert then taking part in attack on Le Gheer. Advanced 8.30 am through Ploegsteert Wood and engaged German patrol on southern edge. Enemy withdrew to positions across the Ploegsteert road which were then attacked by a party led by Lieutenant Hughes. Regimental records note that the enemy almost immediately surrendered, one man however firing and killing Lieutenant Hughes. "B" Company rejoined and trenches held around Le Gheer. Regimental records note several counter-attacks by the enemy – all of which were "defeated by rifle fire and very accurate artillery fire." "C" and "D" Companies moved back into reserve at Ploegsteert (25th), "D" returning to support line (28th), "C" taking over trenches running from the Le Touquet crossroads to the Warnave Brooke (30th). Second-Lieutenant G.H. Stanley, who had just been promoted from the ranks, killed (31st).

NOVEMBER

Captain Coventry killed by sniper (1st). Records note the first use by the Germans of a heavy trench mortar. Parts of "B" Company`s trench being blown in by a single shell and burying 3 men alive. Enemy attacked in large numbers (2nd). Lieutenants Delmege and Dyer noted for their work in repulsing assaults on their positions. Drummer S.J. Bent took charge of one part of the line that had lost its officers and was subsequently awarded the Victoria Cross. Casualties – Captain Clayhills, Second-Lieutenant Mathews and 16 other ranks killed, 11 wounded. Another trench mortar attack (3rd) buried 15 men, of which only 2 were dug out alive. Relieved by 1st Hampshire (4th) and to billets in farms west of Ploegsteert Wood. Began work digging trenches on Hill 63. Moved forward (7th) and took part in counter-attack through Ploegsteert Wood. Enemy forced to retire and positions around Le Gheer regained. Captain L.A.F. Cane killed. "B" Company later led attack on trenches to the north of Le Gheer but heavy fire brought the assault to a standstill. Casualties – 22 killed, 46 wounded. Lieutenant L.D. Waud killed by sniper (8th). Captain Goldie and Lieutenant H.M. Warner mortally wounded (14th). Captain T.H. Preston killed (17th). Later relieved by 1st Hampshire and to billets in Nieppe. Total casualties among other ranks since 8th November – 45 killed, 126 wounded. Relieved 2nd Essex in trenches running from the Le Gheer crossroads down to the Rive Warne (21st). Remained in same area for rest of year – 2 companies in front line, 1 in support at Lawrence Farm, the other in reserve in billets at Nieppe. Companies spent 3 days in the front line followed by 3 in support, 3 back in front line then 3 in reserve.

DECEMBER
Le Gheer area trenches.

2ND BATTALION

AUGUST
Wynberg Camp, South Africa. After mobilization at end of July manned coast defences at Cape Town and Simon's Bay. Relieved and battalion concentrated at Wynberg by (19th).

SEPTEMBER
Embarked SS *Dover Castle* at Cape Town (28th-29th).

OCTOBER
Sailed for England (1st). Arrived Southampton (30th). Entrained for Winchester and from there marched to camp at Hursley Park. Joined 24th Brigade, 8th Division.

NOVEMBER

Marched to Southampton and embarked SS *Lake Michigan* for France (6th). Commanding Officer – Lieutenant-Colonel C.L. Nicholson. Arrived Havre (7th) and to rest camp outside of town. Entrained for Merville (10th) and from there marched to billets at Neuf Berquin. To Estaires (14th). "A" and "B" Companies to front line attached to 25th Brigade. Remainder to billets at Pont du Hem. Relieved Indian troops of the Ferozepore Brigade in Neuve Chapelle sector near Pont Logy (15th). Relieved and to billets at Pont du Hem (18th). Took over trenches along western side of Estaires-La Bassée road between Pont Logy and Rue de Bois (19th). Continued 3-day duties in front line, resting in Divisional Reserve billets at Pont Rochon and Brigade Reserve at the Red Barn on Estaires-La Bassée road near Rouge Croix.

DECEMBER

Left Red Barn for Estaires (14th). To reserve trenches at Rouge Croix (junction of the Estaires-La Bassée road and Rue de Bacquerot) (18th). Moved northwards to reserve trenches along Rue de Bacquerot during night. To Red Barn (20th). Began 3-day tours in front line trenches (22nd).

EAST SURREY REGIMENT

"Mons" "Le Cateau" "Retreat from Mons" "Marne, 1914" "Aisne, 1914" "La Bassée, 1914" "Armentières,1914"

1ST BATTALION

AUGUST

Dublin, Ireland. Part of 14th Brigade, 5th Division. Embarked SS *Botanist* (13th). War Diary records packets of fruit cake and cigarettes taken on board as a gift to the men from friends in Dublin. Officers – Lieutenant-Colonel J.R. Longley (Commanding Officer), Major H.S. Tew (Second in Command), Captain F.H. Bowring (Adjutant), Captain W. Ford (Quartermaster), Lieutenant T.H. Darwell (Machine Gun Officer), Lieutenant E.G. Lawton (Transport Officer), Lieutenant Brown (RAMC, Medical Officer); "A" Company: Captains H.P. Torrens, Hon. A.R. Hewitt, Lieutenants D. Wynyard, H. St. G. Schomberg, G.R.P. Roupell; "B" Company: Captain E.M.Woulfe-Flanagan, Lieutenants G.E. Swinton, R.A.F. Montanaro, H.F. Stoneham, Second-Lieutenant O.M. Jones; "C" Company: Captains J.P. Benson, R.C. Campbell, Lieutenants W.G. Morritt, J.O.G. Becker, N.L. Ward; "D" Company: – Captains M.J. Minogue, H.H. Stacke, Lieutenant E.G.H. Clarke, Second-Lieutenants G.L. Relton, A.Adams. Arrived Havre (15th) and to No.1 Rest Camp. Entrained at Havre (17th) and travelled via Rouen, Amiens and Busigny to Le Cateau. Arrived 4 am and via Pommereuil marched to Biron Barracks, Laundrecies. "A" Company placed on outpost duty. War Diary notes the death by drowning of Private A. Walters ("C" Company) who was bathing in the canal. Marched via Forêt de Mormal to billets at Bermeries (21st). Moved forward into Belgium and to the Mons-Condé Canal. Took up positions in line from canal railway bridge near Les Hebrières to the Ville Pomeroeul road. Came under attack (23rd). Captain Benson and Lieutenant Ward killed. Machine Gun Section noted as doing excellent work from its position on the railway bridge. Also the steady firing of the men which did much to delay the enemy`s advance. Enemy came in on the right and forced withdrawal to south bank of canal. Railway and road bridges blown then Battalion fell back to positions south of the Haine. Later marched to Bois de Boussu. Casualties – 5 officers, 128 other ranks killed, wounded or missing. Moved into reserve at Dour (24th) then to Wiheries. Battalion split – "A" and "C" Companies under Major Tew marched to Eth and took over defensive positions just to the south from 4th Hussars and 16th Lancers. "B" and "D" Companies led by Lieutenant-Colonel Longley moved to St. Waast then (25th) formed rearguard to cover retirement of 5th Division. Marched via western edge of Forêt de Mormal and on to bivouacs just north-east off Le Cateau. "A" and "C" Companies (25th) marched to Briastre then in evening to Troisvilles. Next morning (26th) took up positions at junction of Montay-Reumont road with Troisvillers-Le Cateau road. The companies were facing north-east with 2nd Manchester on the right and 2nd King`s Own Yorkshire Light Infantry on the left. Came under heavy shrapnel fire. War Diary notes that the men held their ground despite this and several retirements on the right. Later, troops on the left withdrew and unsupported "A" and "C" Companies fell back, marching via Ferme Genève, Maretz and Estrees to St. Quentin. "B" and "D" Companies (26th) formed up for march 6.15 am then came under fire from eastern side of Le Cateau. Brigadier-General H.S. Sloman and Colonel H.W. Pearse in their war history of the East Surrey Regiment note that the attack was unexpected, and was made by German troops disguised in khaki uniforms. Formed firing line across Catillon road then withdrew south of railway line. Later attempted to move south of the town but met strong opposition from Germans concealed in a wood. "B" and "D" Companies, with 1 company of 1st Duke of Cornwall`s Light Infantry, delivered an attack but were beaten back. Eventually withdrew to Maurois then Ferme Genève. Moved on to St, Quinten (27th) then St. Simon. "A" and "C" Companies moved via St. Simon to Ollezy (27th) and the 4 companies were reunited at Noyon (28th). Battalion then bivouacked at Pontoise. The 2nd Suffolk had sustained severe casualties and survivors (just over 200 men) were attached. Continued march (29th) towards Carlepont, then (30th) to Attichy and bivouacked alongside of canal. To Raperie via Pierrefonds and Bérhancourt (31st). Regimental history records casualties during the Battles of Mons and Le Cateau and the Retreat from Mons as 2 officers killed, 3 wounded, 2 missing, 27 other ranks killed, 82 wounded and 117 missing. The authors also note that of the missing, both officers and some 50 men were recorded as wounded.

SEPTEMBER
Held position east of railway, just north of Crépy, to cover retreat of 13th Brigade (1st). Then withdrew to Nanteuil-le-Haudoun. To Montgé via Le Plessis (2nd). Memorandum to Brigade Major, 14th Infantry Brigade – "Will you kindly cause a telegram to be sent instructing Lieut. Brown RAMC to rejoin this Battalion as Medical Officer. He is now with No.2 Field Ambulance, which he joined on his own accord after losing the Battn. at Le

Cateau". Marched via Iverny, crossing the Marne near Meaux, to Bouleurs (3rd). To Tournan (4th) and took up outpost duty near Favières. Captain J.K.T. Whish with first draft of 98 men arrived (6th) then to Dammartin. To Coulommiers (7th). Moved forward via Dou, (8th) and then advanced for attack on St. Ouen. Passed through dense wood, where the men were required to moved in single file, and crossed the Petit Morin via a single boat. Continued advance and squadron of German cavalry engaged at top of ridge. Moved on and enemy trenches sighted ahead. Men were cheered, the War Diary records, by their Commanding Officer's promise that they would that day have the opportunity to get at the enemy with their bayonets. Attack held up, however, due to British artillery barrage. Moved to Rougeville and bivouacked for the night. Casualties – Captain Whish and 2 other ranks killed, 1 officer and 6 other ranks wounded. Lieutenants Lawton, Stoneham and Second-Lieutenant Relton arrived with draft of 111 men. War Diary notes that most of this party were from the Battalion`s transport and had been separated since the fighting at Le Cateau on 26th August. Crossed the Marne at Saacy (9th) and advanced towards Méry. Turned north along wooded slope towards Bézu then crossed St. Aulde- Belu road and began to climb wooded ridge. "B" and "D" Companies came under fire from enemy artillery across the valley on La Ferté road then trenches south of Bezu-Monreuil road. War Diary records that twice the Commanding Officer led forward reinforcements but as they reached the front line – ". . . were met by a perfect hail of bullets." Bivouacked along Bézu-St. Aulde road for night. Casualties – 20 other ranks killed, 5 officers and 95 other ranks wounded. In reserve and to bivouacs near St. Quentin (10th). To San Rémy (11th), Chacrise (12th). Crossed the Aisne at Venizel (13th) and advanced across the valley towards Ste. Marguerite under heavy shrapnel fire. Bivouacked on northern edge of wood just north of village. Advanced on Missy (14th). War Diary records that the move was over open country and across the enemy`s front. "B", "D" and "C" Companies in occupation of northern edge of village by midday, "A" Company fighting on eastern side. Three companies attacked enemy`s positions on wooded spur above Chivres. Moving forward at 4.30 pm strong opposition forced withdrawal during night to Ste. Marguerite. Casualties – Second-Lieutenant Relton and 15 other ranks killed, 2 officers and 81 other ranks wounded. To positions facing across the valley towards the Chivres spur north of Missy (15th). Later took up outpost duty at Missy – 2 companies on eastern side, 2 on the western perimeter. War Diary records heavy shelling and much sniping. Captain A. de V. Maclean killed and 20 other ranks wounded (19th). Captain Maclean had been among a party of 7 officers that had joined just 3 days previously. Battalion Headquarters destroyed by shelling (20th). One man killed, 20 wounded. Relieved by 1st Dorsetshire (23rd) and to Ste. Marquerite. To Jury (25th). Moved to Serces (27th) but returned to Jury same day.

OCTOBER

To Nampteuil (1st), Longpont (2nd), Fresnoy (3rd), Gilocourt (4th). Entrained at Longueil for Crécy (6th). Arrived 2.30 am (7th) then ordered on to Noyelles-sur-Mer. Detrained then marched via Abbeville to billets at Château Bois de L'Abbaye. To Vaulx via St. Riquier, Oneux and Yvrench-le-Ponchel (8th). To Diéval by motor buses (10th). Marched to Choques (11th) then took up positions on west bank of the Aire canal. Crossed canal via Avelette bridge (12th) and moved forward via Locon. Regimental history records that a great number of French cavalry were encountered along the road. There were regiments of Cuirassiers wearing steel breast-plates and red breeches and Chasseurs Alpins with tam-o'-shanters, knickerbockers and stockings. The men had been relieved by the British cavalry and were carrying their wounded in wheelbarrows. Arrived at forked road and went left towards Richebourg l'Avou, "D" Company and Machine Gun Section engaged enemy causing high casualties and putting 3 machine guns out of action. Dug in about a mile west of Richebourg l'Avou, after dark. Casualties – 1 officer wounded, 21 other ranks killed or wounded. Advanced towards Richebourg St. Vaast (13th). Came under fire from enemy holding several houses on right front. These positions cleared by artillery fire and advance continued. Dug in – positions facing east and crossing the Rue des Berceaux midway between Richebourg St. Vaast and Richebourg l'Avoue. Casualties 4 officers wounded, 42 other ranks killed or wounded. Enemy opened fire during evening (14th). Maxim gun mounted on motor car noted moving up and down road to rear of German front line. Casualties – 32 other ranks and Captain M.J. Minogue. This officer being the last of the captains and all companies, War Diary records, now commanded by subalterns. Moved forward to Ferme du Biez about 1½ miles east of Richebourg l'Avou, (16th). War Diary records Battalion's left in contact with the enemy and prisoners taken during advance. Took up positions at southern end of Lorgies (17th). Relieved by 2nd Manchester (18th) – "A" and "D" Companies remaining in support, "B" and "C" moving into Brigade Reserve at La Tourelle. "A" and "D" Companies rejoined (19th). Relieved 2nd Manchester (21st). "A" and "B" Companies in front line running to the south west from the Lorgies-La Bassée road, "C" Company in support on west side of road. Strong attack on left and "D" Company brought forward. Enemy driven back and "D" Company took up line east of road. Casualties – 5 killed, 16 wounded.

Maintained rifle and machine gun fire throughout day (22nd). Lieutenant N.L. Bridgland and 4 other ranks killed, 7 wounded. Withdrew at midnight to positions about 500 yards south of Richebourg l'Avou,. Trenches shelled. Casualties (24th-28th) – 8 killed, 37 wounded. Lieutenant M.S. Benning was mortally wounded (27th) having joined the Battalion just 2 days previously. War Diary records list of decorations awarded to the Battalion being published (29th). Among those listed were Sergeants H.W. Hunt (Médaille Militare and Mentioned in Despatches) and R.H. Hunt (Mentioned in Despatches) who were brothers from Chertsey in Surrey and had both been killed on 9th September. Relieved by 2nd/39th Garhwalis (30th) and via Les Glatignies to billets at La Coutre. Upon arrival 2 men were killed and 8 wounded from "D" Company when a shell hit the head of the Battalion.

NOVEMBER
To Lestrem via Le Touret (1st). Marched to Bailleul (2nd) but upon arrival rushed back to Lestrem in 33 motor buses. Took over billets in farms about 2 miles west of Vieille Chapelle (3rd). To Laventie (4th) and positions in close support of the Lahore Division. Returned to billets (5th). In a message to Division, Lieutenant-Colonel Longley requests that a report in the English papers to the effect Lieutenant J.R. Macfarlane had been wounded should be amended. This officer having in fact been returned to Base as "sick." Relieved 2nd Royal Scots in trenches at Fauquissart (6th). Relieved (14th) and to Estaries. Casualties since entering trenches – 2 killed, 23 wounded. To Meterin (15th) and relieved French troops of the 153rd Regiment in trenches west of Hill 75, east of Lindenhoek (16th). German line noted as being between 50-100 yards away and on slightly higher ground. Positions under constant shell fire. Second-Lieutenant H. Housecroft killed (19th). Relieved by 1st Dorsetshire (24th) and to Dranoutre. Casualties since entering trenches – 18 killed, 40 wounded. War Diary notes several men suffering from frostbite. War Diary records (27th) that – "the Staff had some misgivings" regarding the recent issue of winter clothing and how it was to be carried by the men. As an experiment, a Brigade Order was issued requesting the Battalion to detail 7 men, all to be in marching order, but with the following variations –

(a) One man wearing khaki jacket and greatcoat, whilst cardigan, extra shirt, and fur waistcoat are stowed in packs, and waterproof coat or sheet under flap of valise.

(b) One man wearing fur waistcoat (fur outside) and greatcoat, whilst cardigan, extra sheet and khaki jacket are stowed in pack, and water-proof coat or sheet under flap of valise.

(c) One man same as (b) but fur waistcoat to be worn fur inside.

(d) One man wearing khaki jacket and fur waistcoat (fur outside) over it, whilst cardigan, extra sheet and greatcoat are stowed in pack, and waterproof coat or sheet under flap of valise.

(e) One man same as (d) but fur waistcoat to be worn fur inside.

(f) One man same as (b) but without pack, and carrying cardigan in pocket of greatcoat and waterproof coat or sheet rolled and tied on to waist belly.

(g) One man same as (a) but without pack, and carrying cadigan in pocket of greatcoat and waterproof coat or sheet rolled and tied on the waist belt. Thick vest and pants to be worn in all above cases.

Total weight of Greatcoat, pack & kit, fur waistcoat, khaki jacket, cardigan, shirt and waterproof sheet given as just over 27 pounds.

War Diary (28th) records a visit by Sir Horace Smith-Dorrien (Corps Commander) who addressed each company in turn, pointing out that – "by containing the enemy here we had assisted the Russians on the Eastern Frontier." Relieved 1st Devonshire in trenches west of Messines, near Wulverghem (28th).

DECEMBER

Relieved by 1st Dorsetshire (1st) and via Neuve Eglise marched to St. Jans Cappel. Paraded for inspection by Sir John French (2nd). The Field-Marshal complimented the Battalion on its good work and made reference to the "terrible retirement" after Mons and Le Cateau, in which the Battalion had the brunt of the fighting, and – "in the Battle of the Marne", he said "you had to attack the most difficult section of the line." HM The King presented Distinguished Conduct Medals to several NCOs (3rd). To Neuve Eglise in Brigade Reserve (5th). Relieved 1st Devonshire in trenches east of Wulverghem between the Wulverghem-Messines road and the Douve River (10th). Relieved by 1st Dorsetshire (17th) and to St. Jans Cappel. Casualties since entering trenches – 13 killed, 34 wounded. Figures included Lieutenant W.H.M. Simpson mortally wounded. War Diary records that the number of men going sick had considerably increased due to weather conditions. Several cases of Enteric fever had also been noted. Captain and Quartermaster W.D. Ford left to join the 3rd Battalion in England (20th). He had completed 31 years with the 1st Battalion. Marched to Dranoutre (23rd) – the roads, War Diary records, being – "a sea of mud." Billets noted as "extremely dirty" – part of "A" and "C" Companies accommodation being condemned by the Medical Officer. Relieved 1st Devonshire in trenches (29th). War Diary notes condition of trenches as "deplorable" and in some places "nothing more but wide open drains with next to no parapet." Water was waist deep. Three men killed, 7 wounded (30th).

DUKE OF CORNWALL`S LIGHT INFANTRY

"Mons" "Le Cateau" "Retreat from Mons" "Marne, 1914" "Aisne, 1914" "La Bassée, 1914" "Armentières, 1914"

1ST BATTALION

AUGUST

Curragh, Ireland. Part of 14th Brigade, 5th Division. By train to Dublin (13th). Embarked SS *Lanfranc* and sailed for France. Landed Havre (15th) and to rest camp. Entrained during night (16th) and travelled via Amiens, Ham, St. Quentin and Bohain to Le Cateau. Arrived 6 pm (18th) and to billets at the Supérieure School, Landrecies. Moved forward to Pissotiau (21st). Marched to Sardon (22nd) then advanced to positions in defence of the Mons-Condé Canal around Le Petit Crépin. "A" and "B" Companies in forward line, "C" and "D" in reserve between the Haine river and Sardon. Section of "B" Company fired on enemy patrol 6 am (23rd) and again about 6.30. A wounded German cavalryman was later brought in and was noted in a diary kept by Lieutenant A.N. Acland as being very afraid and under the impression that he would be shot. He was unable, apparently, to understand why he was being treated kindly. War Diary records enemy advancing in great numbers from direction of Ville Pommeroeuil about 4.45 pm. Forward positions opened fire at 750- 800 yards and inflicted high casualties. Withdrawal ordered, and covered by 2nd Manchester, Battalion fell back across the Haine towards Dour. Casualties – 1 killed, 5 wounded. War Diary records that the British were no longer greeted with cheers and messages of welcome from the local population – now "...there were nothing but tears and mourning." Streams of people "all fleeing for safety" crowded the roads. Later took up line running from Bois du Boussu Halte on the left, across the Dour-Boussu road, to railway sheds on the right. Received orders to retire 11 am (24th) and moved via Blaugies to positions on high ground just west of St. Waast. Covered retreat of 14th Brigade at Bavi (25th) then at 6 pm moved to positions just east of Le Cateau. War Diary notes bivouacs were in a field at the fork-road on south-eastern outskirts of town. The men, drenched to the skin, received rations, the first since 8 pm the previous night. Formed up for withdrawal during morning (26th). Came under enemy fire from houses in Le Cateau 6.30 am and fell back to line south side of railway line. Still under fire, Battalion withdrew to Escaufort – "A" and "D" Companies via St. Souplet, "B" and "C" Companies through Fassiaux.

Later moved to positions south-west of Honnechy and covered retreat of 5th Division. Moved off 5 pm through Maretz to Estrées. Resumed retreat before dawn (27th), marching via Bellenglise, St. Quentin and St. Simon to Ollezy, via Villeseive and Ouiscard to Pontoise (28th), Bailly (29th). Crossed the Aisne at Attichy (30th) then to Croutoy. To Mermont (31st).

SEPTEMBER
Marched through Crépy-en-Valois to Nanteuil (1st), via Le Plessis to Montge (2nd), Cuisy, Iverny, Trilbardou, Esby and Couilly to Bouleurs (3rd). Moved off 11 pm and marched via Crécy to Favières. Arrived Tournan (5th). Began advance to the Aisne (6th), marching via Favières, Le Pilonnerie, the Forêt de Crécy to Le Plessis St. Avoue. Moved to bivouacs east of Coulommiers (7th). To Doue (8th) then advanced on St. Quen clearing enemy from village. Later bivouacked at Rouge Ville. Moved forward through Saacy and Mery (9th) to woods south-east of Caumont. "B" and "D" Companies came under fire from village. Continued advance and engaged enemy on the Pisseloup Ridge. Moved forward via Montreuil, Dhuisy, Coulombs and Brumetz to Chèzy (10th), via Neuilly St. Front to Billy- sur-Ourcq (11th), Chacrise (12th). Crossed the Aisne (13th) and to Ste. Marguerite. Took part in the attack on Chivres (14th) but heavy machine gun and rifle fire forced withdrawal to Missy. Casualties – Captain R.H. Oliver killed, Lieutenant O.D.M. Garsia and Second- Lieutenant C.E.Crane mortally wounded, 2 other officers wounded, 145 other ranks killed or wounded. Came under heavy shell fire 9.15 am (15th) and moved to west of village. Later fell back to Ste. Marguerite in reserve. Relieved 2nd Manchester in forward trenches (20th). Relieved by 1st Bedfordshire (24th) and moved back to billets at Ste. Marguerite. Moved at dawn (26th) to Jury.

OCTOBER
To Nanteuil (1st), Longpont (3rd), Fresnoy La Rivière (4th), Bethancourt (5th). Entrained at Le Meux for Abbeville (6th). Arrived during morning (7th) and marched to billets at Bellancourt. Marched during night (8th) to Vitz-Villeroy. To Haravesnes (9th) then travelled in buses to Dieval (10th). Advanced to Hinges (11th) and took up positions just west of La Quinque Rue (12th). War Diary notes line as almost parallel with the Rue de l'Epinette. Moved forward to line running La Quinque Rue to Rue de Bois (13th). Enemy attack repulsed (14th). To line on La Bassée-Estaires road (16th) and took part in attack (17th). "A" and "D" Companies moved forward 2.30 pm, "B" and "C" in support. War Diary records little resistance encountered until reaching Beau Puits. Then came under fire from houses and surrounding trenches. Relieved during night by 2nd King's Own

Scottish Borderers and moved back to crossroads 1 mile south-east of Richebourg l` Avoue. Moved forward again 4.30 am (18th) and in support of 2nd King`s Own Scottish Borderers attack on La Bassée. "C" and "D" Companies in support of 2nd Manchester during fighting at Les Trois Maisons (19th). Second-Lieutenant P.L. Elliott killed (20th). "A" and "B" Companies moved to Lorgies in support of "C" and "D" Companies. War Diary records that Lorgies was under shrapnel fire throughout the night. Also large numbers of the enemy moving along the Lille road towards La Bassée. Enemy attacked dawn (21st) and broke through on left of Battalion`s line. "D" Company became surrounded, almost every man (except one reserve platoon) becoming a casualty or taken prisoner. "A" Company came forward and with "D" Company reserve platoon opened fire on the enemy. Everard Wyrall in his war history of the Regiment, records how the Germans came on in close formation ". . . shooting rapidly, "A" Company poured such a heavy and accurate fire into the enemy that he first wavered and then had to retire hurriedly, leaving the ground covered with killed and wounded men." "B" Company also came under attack, but held line until dusk when ordered to fall back, the company having lost all its officers either killed or wounded. Battalion held line during night just east of the road running north-east from the eastern edge of Lorgies and near Richebourg l` Avoue. Casualties – Captains A.H.R. Romilly, L.D. Passy killed, 3 other officers wounded, 3 missing; 25 other ranks killed, 85 wounded, 148 missing. War Diary records that most of the missing are believed killed or wounded. Relieved by 2nd King`s Own Yorkshire Light Infantry (22nd) and moved back to reserve line at Ferme du Biez. Later moved forward to western side of Estaires-La Bassée road and began attack on enemy`s line at Rue du Marais. Advance held up on outskirts of village. Withdrawal ordered and moved back into reserve. "A" and "C" Companies moved forward to Richebourg l` Avoue (25th) in support of 2nd King`s Own Yorkshire Light Infantry. To billets in Rue du Bois (26th). One company in action south of La Quinque Rue (31st).

NOVEMBER
To Le Touret, then Lestrem (1st), Bailleul (2nd). Arrived 1 pm then ordered back to Lestrem. To Les Lobes (3rd) then in afternoon to Rue de Paradis. Returned to Les Lobes (4th), Rue de Paradis (5th), Les Lobes (6th). Relieved 1st Royal Scots Fusiliers in trenches south-west of Rue du Bacquerot, near Neuve Chapelle (7th). Enemy`s line recorded as being just 45 yards away. Relieved (11th) and to La Flinque. To Estaires (14th), Meteren (15th), via Bailleul and Dranoutre to Lindenhoek (16th). Relieved French troops in front line facing Messines Ridge (17th). Enemy began

shelling about 9 am (20th). War Diary records that the first 3 shells landed on the German's own line. Later, however, "A" Company took a number of direct hits – many men being blown to bits or buried alive. Casualties – 12 killed, 16 wounded, 1 missing. Bandsman Thomas Edward Rendle awarded the Victoria Cross for attending the wounded and rescuing buried men from the trenches while under shell fire. Enemy aircraft came down 400 yards in rear of firing line (22nd), its occupants being taken prisoner. Relieved (25th) and to Dranoutre. To St. Jans Cappel (26th).

DECEMBER
Marched via Bailleul and Neuve Eglise to Wulverghem (4th) and took over front line trenches facing La Petite Douve Farm. Relieved during night (17th) and to St. Jans Cappel. To Dranoutre (23rd). Relieved 2nd Manchester in front line just south-west of Wulverghem (29th).

2ND BATTALION

AUGUST
Hong Kong – Headquarters and 2 companies at Murray Barracks, 1 company at Peak and 1 at Kowloon. Battalion occupied in rounding up German residents who were interned at Stone Cutters Island and in the military prison. Detachment (Captain E.B. Ward, Lieutenant J.E. Marshall, Sergeant Blackburn and 105 other ranks) served on HMS *Triumph*. Ship left Hong Kong to join Fleet at Tsing-Tau. Arrived Wei-hai-Wei (24th) and detachment ordered to return to Hong Kong.

NOVEMBER
Battalion arrived Devonport from Hong Kong (3rd) and moved to camp at Winchester. Joined 82nd Brigade, 27th Division. Strength (23rd) – 21 officers, 881 other ranks. Commanding Officer – Lieutenant-Colonel H.D. Tuson.

DECEMBER
To Southampton (19th) and embarked for France. Arrived Havre (21st). Entrained for Arques and from there marched to Wardrecques. Billeted in two factories.

DUKE OF WELLINGTON'S (WEST RIDING REGIMENT)

"Mons" "Le Cateau" "Retreat from Mons" "Marne, 1914" "Aisne, 1914" "La Bassée, 1914" "Ypres, 1914" "Nonne Bosschen"

2ND BATTALION

AUGUST

Portobello Barracks, Dublin. Part of 13th Brigade, 5th Division. To Alexandra Basin (13th) and embarked SS *Gloucestershire*. Sailed for France 2.20 am (14th). Landed Havre (15th) and bivouacked for night at docks. Marched to Bleville Camp (16th). Entrained for Landrecies (17th) and then to billets at Marouilles. To Bavai (21st). Marched via Dour and Boussu to St. Ghislain (22nd). Helped support positions to 1st Royal West Kent at the Mons- Condé Canal. Retired during evening to Hornu. Billets in Market place. Moved forward (23rd) and in action along canal at St.Ghislain. Later withdrew via Hornu to Wasmes. Casualties – 3 officers wounded, 7 other ranks killed, 24 wounded, 1 missing. Came under heavy shell fire (24th). Enemy attacked later and hand-to-hand fighting took place when the battalion became almost completely surrounded. Brigadier-General C.D. Bruce, CBE recalls in his war history of the Regiment a number of first-hand accounts from those present at Wasmes – "I saw the Germans charge the platoon, who fought to the last with the bayonet, and were all either killed or wounded. The Germans were piled up in heaps all around them. All our officers were either killed or wounded. . . .Sergeant Spence ordered us to fix bayonets and to cut our way back" (Corporal J.G. Williams). Casualties – Major P.B. Strafford, Captain C.O. Denman-Jubb, Lieutenant L.E. Russell killed, Lieutenant J.H.L. Thompson mortally wounded, 3 other officers wounded, 2 missing, 37 other ranks killed, 35 wounded, 244 missing. Survivors withdrew via Bavai then (25th) took up positions on high ground south-west of Le Cateau. Held support line during fighting (26th). Ordered to retire 4 pm and moved back via Maretz to Estrées. Continued retreat via St. Quentin and Ham to Ollezy (27th), Noyon to Pontoise (28th), Attichy to Jaulzy (30th), to Crépy-en- Valois (31st).

SEPTEMBER

Enemy attacked about 6 am (1st). Later withdrew via Cuisy and Coulommes, arriving Tournan (5th). Advanced to Villeneuve (6th),

Guerard (7th) then via Boissy le Chatel to St. Cyr. To Rougeville (8th), Le Limon (9th), Crezy (10th), Hartennes (11th), Serches (12th), Ciry (13th) then Sermoise. Came under heavy shell fire from across the Aisne. Casualties – 4 killed, 19 wounded, 4 missing. Crossed the Aisne (16th) and to Missy. Relieved by 2nd King's Own Yorkshire Light Infantry (24th) and moved back into reserve at La Corbinne Wood.

OCTOBER
Relieved by 2nd Durham Light Infantry (2nd) and to Violaines (3rd). To Hartennes (4th), Largny (5th), Fresnoy (6th), Verberie (7th). Entrained at Longueil For Abbeville (8th). Arrived and to billets at Noyelle. Marched via Guescart and Harravesnes to positions south of the Conchy-Hesdin road (9th). Travelled in buses via St. Pol to Dieval (10th). Marched via Béthune to Vaubricourt (11th). To Beuvry, then Annequin (12th). Relieved by French troops (14th) and to billets at Le Quesnoy. Took up positions on the Festubert-Gorre road (15th), then trenches at Rue d' Ouvert (16th). Took part in attack on Violaines (22nd). Withdrawn 2 am (23rd) and dug in. Relieved by 2nd Black Watch (29th) and to Rue de Béthune. Casualties since 22nd October – 13 killed, 32 wounded. Black Watch War Diary records trenches taken over as being 1,000 yards east of Le Plantin. Moved forward to trenches at Festubert (30th) and in support of 1st Bedfordshire. Relieved (31st) and returned to billets.

NOVEMBER
Marched to Estaires (2nd) then in buses to Bailleul. Moved to billets near Dranoutre (4th). Major E.G. Harrison's diary records that Battalion's stength was now 15 officers and 800 other ranks. Moved through Ypres (5th) and took over trenches either side of the Ypres- Menin road, half-mile east of Hooge. Took over trenches near Hermitage Château (6th). Took part in attack to regain trenches north side of Menin road lost by Zouaves regiment (8th). Major Harrison records that the first advance by "C" Company was repulsed. One officer being killed, another mortally wounded and a third missing. There being no officers, Sergeant Alfred Edward Taylor took command and with Sergeant Ernest Pogson led "C" Company into a second assault. The trenches were regained and both NCOs were eventually awarded Distinguished Conduct Medals. Casualties – 3 officers, 87 other ranks. Moved to new positions at Veldoek Château (10th). Major Harrison records the close proximity of the two Châteaux, the woods belonging to each being divided by the Ypres- Menin road and the drive gates being exactly opposite each other. Enemy attacked about 8 am (11th). Major Harrison records – ". . . but we managed to repulse them and gained back

the ground very nearly as far as our old firing line, which we could have gained had the troops on our left been up with us." Casualties – 7 officers, approximately 380 other ranks. Withdrew to support trenches either side of Veldhoek Château (13th). Major Harrison recalls that he sent back (14th) for a draft of 75 men recently arrived from England. Marching up from Hooge the party was shelled and only 42 arrived at the Battalion's line. Relieved by 11th Hussars in trenches east of Veldoek Château 11 pm (15th) and moved back to Menin road. Total casualties since 5th November – 14 officers, 387 other ranks. Fighting strength – 4 officers, 280 other ranks. Moved back to trenches (17th), but later relieved by French troops and to dug-outs near Hooge Château. Relieved 2nd King's Own Scottish Borderers in trenches at Nonne Bosschen Wood (19th). Relieved by French troops midnight (20th) and marched through Ypres to Locre. Relieved 2nd Manchester in trenches Wulverghem sector, north side of Wulverghem-Messines road (27th). Two killed, 5 wounded from sniping (28th), 1 killed, 3 wounded by shell fire (29th). Later relieved by 2nd King's Own Scottish Borderers and to billets at Neuve Eglise. Two companies remained in support.

DECEMBER

Relieved 2nd King's Own Scottish Borderers (1st). Relieved by 2nd Manchester (5th) and marched via Neuve Eglise and Bailleul to St. Jean Capel. To Dranoutre (10th). Relieved 1st Royal West Kent in trenches – Wulverghem sector (13th). Major Harrison records that the German trenches on the left were within 25 yards. There was constant sniping "and even throwing mud at each other." Relieved by 1st Royal West Kent (16th) and to support positions near Lindenhoek on the Dranoutre road. To billets in Dranoutre (19th). Returned to support line (20th), Dranoutre (21st). Relieved 2nd King's Own Scottish Borderers in Wulverghem sector (22nd). Trenches north of the Wulverghem-Messines road. Relieved by 1st Devonshire (23rd) and to Divisional Reserve at Revetsberg. To trenches south side of Wulverghem-Messines road (29th). Relieved during evening (31st) by 1st Royal West Kent and to Neuve Eglise.

BORDER REGIMENT

"Ypres, 1914" "Langemarck, 1914" "Gheluvelt"

2ND BATTALION

AUGUST
Pembroke Dock. Colours deposited in Carlisle Cathedral for safekeeping by Lieutenant C. Lamb and Second-Lieutenant T.J. Clancey. Entrained for Southampton (28th) and placed in 20th Brigade, 7th Division.

SEPTEMBER
Marched to camp at Lyndhurst (5th).

OCTOBER
To Southampton (4th). Sailed for Belgium in 2 ships, "A" and "B" Companies – SS *Turkoman,* "C" and "D" Companies – SS *Minneapolis* (5th). Officers – Lieutenant- Colonel L.I. Wood (Commanding Officer), Majors J.T.I. Bosanquet, W.L. Allen, DSO, Captains G.E. Warren, L.E.H. Molyneux-Seel, R.N. Gordon, E.H.H. Lees, C.G.W. Andrews (Adjutant), C.A.J. Cholmondeley, Lieutenants H.A. Askew, C. Lamb, P.J. Egerton, H.V. Gerrard, W. Watson, J.B.B. Warren, F.W. Mitchell (Quartermaster), Second-Lieutenants H.F. Chads, T.H. Beves, G.W.H. Hodgson, C.H. Evans, H.L. Chatfield, C.G.V. Surtees, T.J. Clancey. Lieutenants H.P.O. Sleigh, E.C.Clegg, A.B. Johnson, M.S.N. Kennedy. "C" and "D" Companies arrived Zeebrugge (6th). Entrained for Bruges and from there marched to billets at St. André. Headquarters at The Rosary. "A" and "B" Companies disembarked (7th) and then to St. André. One officer records that the people of St. André treated the men well and that cap and collar badges were given as souvenirs. Marched to Leffinghe (8th). To Ostend (9th) and entrained for Ghent. Moved to Destelbergen same afternoon. Line of outposts set up facing east by "B", "C" and "D" Companies. "A" Company in reserve at village. Relieved by French Marines and to Somergem (11th) then to Thielt (12th). Enemy aircraft brought down by fire from brigade (13th). Continued march to Roulers then to Ypres (14th), Zillebeke (15th). Enemy engaged en route by party led by Lieutenant Lamb (Scout Officer) – 8 Uhlans killed and 2 prisoners taken. After inspecting an advanced post at Zillebeke, Lieutenant Edgerton became lost in the fog and was accidently shot by a sentry. He later died in hospital at Ypres. Moved to billets at Zandvoorde (16th) and dug trenches on north side of village in

support of 2nd Scots Guards. To ridge near Kruiseecke (18th). War Diary (19th) notes Brigade advance on Menin – came under heavy shrapnel fire at America, battalion fell back at 3 pm and entrenched on Kruiseecke Hill. "D" Company left in support at America. "D" Company to Kruiseecke Hill (20th). Colonel H.C. Wylly in his war history of the Border Regiment notes 2nd Border's front as covering some 2¼ miles and impossible to connect all companies, platoons and sections by trenches. He also notes positions as being along the Zandvoorde road where it cuts the Kruiseecke-Wervicq road. Second-Lieutenant Clancey killed (22nd), Captain Gordon killed (23rd). Enemy began attack (24th) – Battalion (with 20th Brigade) received order that – "trenches were to be held at all costs." Records show that brigade had no support or reserve, save two platoons of 2nd Border. Battalion's positions came under heavy bombardment – trenches being commanded on three sides by enemy artillery, particularly from guns situated on America Ridge about 1 mile to the south east. One officer calculated some 1,500 enemy shells during a 10-hour period. Colonel Wylly notes that it was impossible to leave the trenches by day, rations and supplies having to be brought up by night. There were no telephonic communications – messages being carried by runners, and enemy snipers were operating from 300 yards. Machine-gun section blown out of its position during night and one gun buried. Detachment under Lieutenant Watson forced to retire to second position. Lieutenant Watson led his party back during night (25th) and upon seeing the enemy advancing in large numbers moved his gun to a more forward position where his section inflicted high casualties from 300 yards throughout next day. Party of some 200 Germans entered line to the left of "B" Company and indicated that they wished to surrender. However, when Major Allen and six men moved out to bring them in he was killed with one other man. Front-line trenches held by "A" and "B" Companies taken (26th) – 70 survivors driven to the rear. Captains C.G.W. Anderson, Cholmondeley, Lees and Lieutenant Warren killed. Later, with Headquarters personnel, held off further enemy advance. "C" Company under Captain Molyneux-Seel brought up in support. Battalion ordered to retire to Zandvoorde during evening. "C" Company marching on into Ypres. Concentrated at Zonnebeke (27th) – strength 12 officers and 538 other ranks. Ordered to advance in support of 2nd Gordon Highlanders (29th). Moved forward with left on Ypres-Menin road towards Kruiseecke Hill. Came under heavy shell, machine gun and rifle fire at first ridge – Lieutenant-Colonel Wood and Captains Molyneux-Seel and Warren wounded. Command passed to Captain Askew. One officer who recorded the advance up the hill into Gheluvelt noted that positions were held for more than an hour before being reinforced. Advance continued on north slope of hill through village. German reinforcements sighted moving along Menin road in fours some 1,200 yards off. Machine-guns set up in a ploughed turnip field and opened fire. Retired after ammunition ran out. The same officer records his retirement with the machine guns into a sunken road in the rear where he found Captain Warren and Lieutenant Hon. Simon Fraser (2nd Gordons) – "I was sitting between Fraser and a lance-corporal of ours when a shell burst killing them both instantaneously." Battalion ordered to support cavalry advance east of Hooge (30th). Positions held in woods north west of a Château near Zonnebeke. Returned same night to Hooge-Ypres-Menin crossroads and entrenched on west side. Heavily shelled throughout day (31st). Moved during night to positions at Klein Zillebeke.

NOVEMBER
Heavily shelled during day (1st). Parties led by Lieutenants Lamb and Watson engaged enemy with great effect. Battalion on extreme right of 20th Brigade (2nd). Shell fire put last machine-gun out of action – Lieutenant Watson wounded. Enemy attacked – fire held until last moment – Germans driven back with great casualties. Further attack also saw great loss among the enemy who entered line on Battalion`s right. Sergeant Booth left his position under heavy fire and with men brought up from reserve managed to keep line intact. Lieutenant Gerrard killed, Second-Lieutenant Hodgson mortally wounded, 14 other ranks killed, 35 wounded. Relieved at night and moved back to woods near Ypres in Brigade Reserve. Message to Commanding Officer from GOC 7th Division (Major- General T. Capper) – "Stout action of The Border Regiment in maintaining its trenches throughout the day, although unsupported on its right, is much commended. Congratulate Border Regiment from me and tell them I am making a special report on their conduct through Corps Headquarters." Also received from GOC via Brigade Commander – "2nd Battalion Border Regiment. This Battalion held a portion of the Kruiseecke position in front of Ypres during which it was exposed to particularly heavy shell fire for 3 days and nights. Many of the trenches were blown in, but no trench was given up by any portion of this battalion. On 2nd November this Battalion formed the right of the Brigade at Veldhoek. Owing to troops on the right giving way the enemy was able to occupy some woods and so surround the right of The Border Regiment. Nevertheless the Battalion held its line for some hours until the enemy could be driven from these woods by relieving troops. During the fighting this Battalion lost very heavily. The devoted and firm conduct of this Battalion repeatedly called forth the admiration of the Brigadier and of officers in other battalions in the same brigade; and I,

myself, can testify to its fortitude and determination to maintain its position at all costs; a spirit which saved a difficult and critical situation. It is impossible to praise this Battalion too highly for its firmness and battle discipline." Received first reinforcement of 98 men under Captain N.F. Jenkins. Moved via Ypres (then under heavy bombardment) to Locre (5th). To Meteren (6th). Casualties figures for period 18th October-7th November – 9 officers and 79 other ranks killed, 6 officers and 259 other ranks wounded, 5 officers and 253 other ranks missing. One officer – Second-Lieutenant Evans was, according to Colonel Wylly's history, wounded and captured on 26th October and was shot by the Germans after attempting to defend a man who was being ill- treated. To Bac St. Muir (14th) and to trenches at "La Boutillerie." Relieved by 2nd Bedfordshire (17th) and to Sailly. Further drafts received at Sailly. Moved into trenches at Rouge Bancs near La Cordonnière Farm (21st). Relieved (24th) and to billets in Sailly. To trenches (26th). Relieved (28th).

DECEMBER

H M The King decorated Lieutenant (now Captain) Lamb (1st) with the Distinguish Service Order for gallantry while leading scouting parties at Kruiseecke. To trenches same night. Draft of 4 officers and 570 other ranks arrived from England. Relieved (4th), to trenches (6th). Battalion now maintaining 2 companies in trenches, 2 at Sailly. Attack on German lines by "A" and "C" Companies 6.15 pm (18th) – left of advance on road running south east of La Cordonnière Farm, right on Sailly-Fromelles road. Heavy casualties from German fire and own barrage. Enemy trenches reached but forced to retire. Survivors collected by Captain Warren and with two platoons of "B" Company resumed attack. Checked by un-cut wire and again forced to withdraw. Captain Askew killed in enemy's line. His cap returned by the Germans with note informing the battalion that they had buried the body and put up a cross to the memory of – "a very brave British officer." Captain Lamb fatally wounded Other casualties – Lieutenant Kennedy and Second- Lieutenant N. Castle wounded, 110 other ranks killed, wounded or missing. "A" and "C" Companies retired to Sailly. Lance-Corporal Brewer and Private Clare awarded Distinguished Conduct Medal for bringing Captain Lamb in under heavy fire. Two Victoria Crosses awarded – Privates Abraham Acton and James Smith – "For conspicuous bravery on 21st December, at Rouges Bancs, in voluntarily going from their trench and rescuing a wounded man who had been lying exposed against the enemy's trenches for 75 hours, and on the same day again leaving their trench voluntarily, under heavy fire, to bring into cover another wounded man. They were under fire for 60 minutes whilst conveying the wounded men into safety." *(London Gazette,* 18th February, 1915). Captain S.H. Worrall arrived (24th) and took over command (25th). Enemy requested (and were granted) an armistice for the purpose of burying the dead.

1/5TH (CUMBERLAND) BATTALION (TERRITORIAL FORCE)

AUGUST
Headquarters – Workington, "A" Company – Whitehaven, "B" and "C" Companies – Workington, "D" Company – Cockermouth, "E" Company – Egremont, "F" Company – Wigton, "G" Company – Frizington, "H" Company – Aspatria. To Barrow (5th).

OCTOBER
To Southampton (25th) and embarked SS *Manchester Engineer.* Landed Havre (26th) and to No.1 Rest Camp. Strength – 30 officers, 878 other ranks. Detachments from "C" and "F" Companies to St. Omer (27th) for duties escorting German prisoners to Havre. "A" Company to Nantes, "B" and "G" Companies to Le Mans, "H" Company to Rouen (28th). "D" and "E" Companies to No.7 Camp (30th). Detachments of "D" and "E" Companies to Abbeville (31st).

NOVEMBER
Battalion Headquarters moved from No.1 Rest Camp to Rue Raspail, Havre (2nd). War Diary notes (same day) that since arrival in France the main duties of the Battalion had concerned the movements of German prisoners. It is also recorded that due to the "unwillingness" of the Cumberland and Westmoreland Territorial Force Association, the Battalion had proceeded abroad badly clothed. The problem, however, was remedied to a great extent by the Battalion itself, but for future reference, the Diary records, ". . . .it would be as well for the County Association to store clothing, boots etc. instead of trying to hoard money." There are no further entries in the War Diary until 31st March, 1915 when it notes that the Battalion is to be relieved from it`s lines of communication duties. Some 2,000 prisoners, it records, had been escorted to England.

ROYAL SUSSEX REGIMENT

**"Mons" "Retreat from Mons" "Marne, 1914"
"Aisne, 1914" "Ypres, 1914" "Gheluvelt"
"Nonne Bosschen" "Givenchy, 1914"**

2ND BATTALION

AUGUST

Woking. Part of 2nd Brigade, 1st Division. Moved by train to Southampton (12th) and embarked SS *Olympia* and SS *Agapenor*. Sailed for France, arriving Havre (13th) and marching to Bleville Camp. Entrained for Etreux (14th). Marched to Esqueheries (16th), Avesnes (21st), via St. Reminal-bati, Maubeuge to Villers-sur-Nicole (22nd), Rouveroy (23rd). War Diary records that the German bombardment of Mons could be clearly seen. Began advance about 9.30 pm, bivouacking for night along the roadside just outside Givry. Moved forward to Bonnet (24th) and entrenched. Later to billets at Feignes. To Marbaix (25th), via Favril to Pit Cambresis (26th), via Wassigny and Hannappes to Hautville, Fressancourt (28th), via Premontre to Anizy (30th), via Soissons to Verte Feuille (31st).

SEPTEMBER

Continued retreat (1st), arriving Vareddes (2nd). Marched via Ferere to Romeny (3rd), to Aulnoy (4th), Bernay (5th), via Rozoy to Vaudoy (6th), to Jouy-sur-Moring (7th), Flagny (8th), La Croisette (9th). Marched on Preiz (10th). War Diary records that the enemy were fired upon from high ground just before the village. After passing through Preiz, "B" Company leading the advance came under heavy artillery fire. The forward troops being just 750 yards from the German lines. The Battalion was then shelled by British artillery. War Diary suggests that the gunners mistook the Sussex for Germans as they were wearing (presumably grey) waterproof sheets. Enemy opened up with heavy rifle fire and Battalion forced to retire to line across the Preiz-Coincy road. Casualties – Captain A.E. Jemmett-Browne and 18 other ranks killed, 2 officers, 83 other ranks wounded. Moved back to Raissy during evening. To Coincy (11th), Paars (12th). Passed through Bourg (13th) and enemy engaged. Casualties – 1 killed, 7 wounded. Later moved into billets at Moulins. Advanced to Vendresse (14th) in support of attack on high ground above Troyon. War Diary records the capture of 250 prisoners who, while coming forward under a white flag, were fired upon by their own side. Casualties – Lieutenant-Colonel E.H. Montresor, Major

M.E. Cookson, Captain L. Slater, Lieutenants Hon. H.L. Pelham, E.C. Daun, W.S. Hughes and 11 other ranks killed, 3 officers and 79 other ranks wounded, 114 missing. Battalion dug in and held positions under shell fire and infantry attacks. Relieved by 1st East Yorkshire (19th) and to outpost line in caves at Paissy. Assisted in regaining trenches lost on right by 1st West Yorkshire (20th). Relieved by 1st Northamptonshire and to Pargnan. To Moulins in reserve (23rd), returning to Pargnan same night. Took over front line trenches at Troyon (25th). Relieved by 1st Loyal North Lancashire early morning (28th). Relieved 1st Northamptonshire in front line (29th). Casualties since 25th September – 6 other ranks killed, 2 officers, 43 other ranks wounded.

OCTOBER
Relieved by 1st Loyal North Lancashire (5th). War Diary records (7th) that the enemy opened fire on some dummy trenches near the Battalion's position. A number of dummies had been made and one of these, a man reading the *Daily Mail*, was noted as having over 40 bullets in him. Later came under bombardment from "Bolos" – Captain R.J.P.D. Aldridge and 5 other ranks killed, 3 officers, 16 other ranks wounded. Later relieved 1st Northamptonshire in front line. Relieved from Troyon sector during night (15th) and to Vauxcéré. Casualties for month – 1 officer, 14 other ranks killed, 3 officers, 34 other ranks wounded. Entrained at Fismes 3 am (17th). Remained on train throughout day, moving via Amiens, Boulogne and Calais (18th) and arriving at Cassell early morning (19th). Moved to Elverdinghe (20th), Boesinghe (21st), Ypres (25th). Bivouacked near Haalte (26th) then advanced to trenches at Herentage Château Wood (27th). To Polygon Wood (28th). Withdrew to Château Wood after enemy attack (29th). Moved forward with 1st Northamptonshire to Bodmin Copse during morning (30th). Lieutenant-Colonel H.T. Crispin killed during advance. Moved into Shrewsbury Forest (31st). War Diary records – "The enemy came on in large numbers as far as the 5 Cross Roads: here we met him and drove him back." Records of the Northamptonshire Regiment note that much hand-to-hand fighting took place and the German dead were lying in heaps. Later attacked enemy in Bodmin Copse but forced to dig in on edge of Shrewsbury Forest. Casualties (30th/31st) – Lieutenant-Colonel Crispin, Lieutenant E.A. Lousada, Second-Lieutenants L.R. Croft, F.C.J. Marillier and C.F. Shaw killed, 394 other ranks killed, wounded or missing.

NOVEMBER
Moved back into reserve positions (2nd). Relieved 1st Northamptonshire in front line during night (4th). Moved (7th) and in action near Klein

Zillebeke. Second-Lieutenant G. Moore killed and approximately 20 others killed, wounded or missing. Relieved (9th) and to support line. Moved to Herenthage Château Wood (11th) in support of 1st (Guards) Brigade. Relieved from trenches just west of Veldhoek (14th) and to billets in Westoutre (16th). To Strazeele (17th), Hazebrouck (19th).

DECEMBER

Moved in buses to Zelore (21st) then marched forward to Le Touret. Relieved Seaforth Highlanders in front line trenches – Fleurbaix sector (22nd). War Diary records that the trenches were flooded. Some of the Battalion standing waist-deep in water. Relieved by 1st Grenadier Guards (23rd) and to Le Hamel. Casualties – Lieutenant C.F. Verrall killed, 1 officer wounded, 28 other ranks killed, wounded or missing. Relieved 2nd South Staffordshire in trenches near running from north bank of the La Bassée Canal to just south of Givenchy (26th). Second-Lieutenant A.L. Silvester killed, 4 other ranks killed, 7 wounded, 10 missing during attack (31st).

HAMPSHIRE REGIMENT

"Le Cateau" "Retreat from Mons" "Marne, 1914" "Aisne, 1914" "Armentières, 1914"

1ST BATTALION

AUGUST

Colchester. Part of 11th Brigade, 4th Division. Moved to Harrow (18th). Entrained for Southampton during early hours morning (22nd). Embarked SS *Braemar Castle* and SS *Cestrian* and sailed for France. Officers – Lieutenant-Colonel S.C.F. Jackson, DSO (Commanding Officer), Major F.R. Hicks (Second in Command), Captains G.F. Perkins (Adjutant), Williams (RAMC, Medical Officer), Lieutenants J. Le Hunte (Machine Gun Officer), G.L. Edsell (Transport Officer); "A" Company: Captains F.C. Moore, J.C.F. Richards, Lieutenants V.A. Cecil, E.M.S. Kent, Second-Lieutenant G. Nicholson; "B" Company: Captains N.E. Baxter, R.W. Harland, Lieutenants E.J.W. Dolphin, A.P. Knocker, Second-Lieutenant D.H. Cowan; "C" Company: Major N.W. Barlow, Captain P.M. Connellan, Lieutenants W.D.M. Trimmer, G.T. Rose, Second-Lieutenant L. Sweet; "D" Company: Captain Hon. L.C.W. Palk, Lieutenants B.B. von B. lim Thurn, S.V. Halls, G. Griffiths, Second-Lieutenant H.C. Westmorland. Arrived Havre (23rd) and to rest camp at Bleville. Entrained at Havre (24th) and to Le Cateau. War Diary records Battalion's first casualty during journey – a man falling from a truck while the train was passing through a tunnel. In his war history of the Hampshire Regiment, C.T. Atkinson records that the accident occurred while the Adjutant's groom was attempting to calm the officer's frightened horse. Arrived early morning (25th) and to Solesmes to cover retirement of 5th Division. Dug in south of the village near Bellevue Farm. War Diary records that the position – "was an impossible one to defend – very exposed to artillery fire and difficult to retire from." Fell back to Briastre during afternoon and then at 10.30 pm retired. "A" and "D" Companies holding village as rearguard until midnight. War Diary records that withdrawal was via Bethencourt and that the men rested in the streets and houses of Beauvois and Fontaine-au-Pire during the early hours (26th). Moved at daybreak to the north-west. War Diary records that the battalion took the wrong road – Lieutenant-Colonel Jackson having to ask a French peasant directions to Haucourt. Came under shell and rifle fire while moving east of Fontaine-au-Pire where, War Diary records, German cavalry had apparently surprised the rest of 11th Brigade and the Battalion's transport. "B" Company covered retirement, engaging the enemy and wiping out a platoon of Jäger. Half of "B" Company under Captain Baxter became separated and joined up with 1st Somerset Light Infantry. Battalion took up positions astride the Warnelle Ravine railway and facing north-west towards Cattenières. "C" and "D" Companies situated on higher ground north of the railway came under continuous artillery and infantry fire. C.T. Atkinson notes that a sunken lane leading down to the railway provided a certain amount of cover. Enemy advanced up railway line close enough to call out "Retire" – a few men, C.T. Atkinson records, being deceived. Battalion ordered to fall back during afternoon. Casualties noted from artillery fire while climbing the slope leading up to Ligny. Held line in rear of village and advancing enemy driven back. Withdrew during evening via Caullery to Clery then through night to Serain. Casualties – Lieutenant Kent and Second-Lieutenant Cowan killed, Major Hicks, Lieutenant Cecil wounded, Captains Baxter, Williams, Lieutenants Rose, Halls, Griffith, Le Hunte missing, 46 other ranks killed or missing, 126 wounded. The Medical Officer, Captain Williams, had remained behind with the wounded. C.T. Atkinson records that during the retreat Lieutenant Le Hunte and the machine gun section reached Clery and were taken prisoner. The machine guns, however, were hidden from the enemy by a civilian, M. Fernaud Lerouf, who after the war returned them to the Battalion. Lieutenant Le Hunte having the pleasure of collecting the guns himself in 1921. Marched via Beaurevoir to Nauroy (27th). Enemy artillery opened fire from about 1,000 yards. "A" Company moved forward and took up positions north and east of Nauroy and opened fire on the enemy's guns. Remainder of Battalion retreated and became split up. One party moved via Le Verguier and Tertry, another through Vermand. "A" Company were also divided, Lieutenant-Colonel Jackson being wounded and taken prisoner. War Diary records Headquarters as being at Freniches (28th) and a move via Noyon to Sempigny (29th) where the Battalion was concentrated. Reached Pierrefonds (30th). Marched through the Forest of Compiègne (31st) and took up line covering St. Sauveur.

SEPTEMBER
Retired to Vaucelle (1st) and came under attack from dismounted German cavalry. Fell back via Néry to Rosieres. "C" Company acting as rearguard engaged enemy during retreat. C.T. Atkinson notes hand to hand fighting in a turnip field. Marched via Montagny to Eve (2nd) then throughout night via Dammartin, Juilly, Messey, Lagny, Chanteloup to Château de Fontenelle. Moved to Coupvray (4th) and (5th) marched via Serris, Jossigny, Ferrieres, Ozoir-la-Ferriére to Chevry. Two companies moved to

outpost positions at Gretz. Advanced via Jossigny to Villeneuve-le-Comte (6th), Crécy to Maisoncelles (7th), La Haute Maison, Pierre-Levee, Signy-Signets to Les Corbières (8th). Took up positions on high ground near Ventemi Château (9th) and covered advance of 1st Rifle Brigade across the Marne. Moved forward during night to north bank of the river – 2 men being drowned while crossing. Advanced through La Ferté-sous-Jouarre (10th) then via Cocherel to Chaton. Advanced via Vendrest, Coulombe and St. Quentin to Passy (11th), Villers-Helon, Villemontoire and Rozières to Septmonts (12th). Went forward during night via Billy- sur-Aisne to Venizel. Crossed the Aisne and took up positions around La Montagne Farm, on high ground north of Bucy-le-Long. War Diary records that trenches were under continuous shell fire and that wet weather made conditions "very trying." Enemy brought up heavy guns (16th), which in conjunction with observation aircraft, fired with "amazing accuracy and caused a good deal of loss in our trenches." Casualties (13th-17th) – 11 killed, 66 wounded. Relieved by 1st Royal Warwickshire (18th). War Diary records (18th- 30th) that the Battalion was – "practically unmolested by the enemy." Positions had been improved daily and were strong. Supplies were plentiful and regular. Casualties – 5 wounded.

OCTOBER
Relieved by French troops during evening (6th) and marched via Venizel to Ville Montoire. To Billy-sur-Ourcq (7th), via Villers-Cotterêts to Vez (8th), Béthisy-St.-Martin (9th), via Béthisy-St.-Pierre to Noyvillers (10th). To Estrées-St.-Denis (11th) and entrained for Wizernes. Arrived about 10 pm and to billets at Oiselle. Travelled to Hondeghem in lorries (12th). Advanced via Caestre to Flêtre (13th) and through Meteren to Bailleul (14th). Took up positions about 2 miles south of Bailleul (15th) then in evening received orders to attack Nieppe. Moved forward – "B" Company in front, "C" on the right flank, "D" on the left, "A" in reserve. War Diary records that leading troops came under machine gun fire from houses upon reaching the village. The enemy were eventually cleared from the area and the Battalion entrenched. C.T. Atkinson records just 12 casualties and that Lieutenant Knocker, while leading his platoon on to the enemy 1st position at the bridge, fell into a cesspit in order to escape being hit by machine gun bullets. Moved forward again after dusk (16th). "C" and "D" Companies gained the river bank with little opposition, but "A" in the centre was held up and about 10 pm the flank companies were ordered to fall back to set up a new line with "A". C.T. Atkinson notes that the line held ran from Erquinghem along the railway line to the Nieppe-Armentières road. Relieved (18th) and via Pont de Nieppe went into billets at the goods station,

Armentières. "A", "B" and "C" Companies moved to support positions east of Armentières (20th). Captain Connellan killed. "A" and "C" Companies moved forward to support trenches around St. Yves during morning (21st). Rest of Battalion took over billets in Ploegsteert during evening then at night relieved 1st King's Own in trenches at the crossroads near Le Touquet. "B" Company opened fire on advancing enemy and brought attack to a halt. Battalion relieved (22nd) and moved back to Bois de Boulogne. Relieved 1st Somerset Light Infantry in front line east of Ploegsteert Wood (28th). Line held was approximately 2,000 yards and ran from the Douve via St. Yves to Le Gheer. War Diary notes that the whole Battalion, with the exception of 1 platoon of "A" Company, were in the firing line. "B" on the left followed by "C", "D" then "A". German trenches ran parallel and were about 1,100 yards away. Enemy bombarded Battalion's trenches between 6.30 am and 4.40 pm (30th) then attacked in large numbers. C.T. Atkinson records that the enemy were checked nearly everywhere except for the left centre where dead ground helped the Germans get forward. Heavy losses were incurred at a forward post held by Lieutenant Trimmer and No.10 Platoon. The party were overwhelmed and the attacking force entered "C" Company's line. "A" Company of the 1st Somerset Light Infantry were sent up and together with the survivors of "C" Company were able to prevent any further gains by putting up a barricade across the trench. War Diary records casualties amoung No.10 Platoon as Lieutenant Trimmer and 12 other ranks killed, Lieutenant Wade and 20 other ranks wounded, 40 missing. Other casualties were Captain Harland and 3 other ranks killed, 16 other ranks wounded, 1 missing. Another enemy attack (31st) driven off.

NOVEMBER
Further attacks (1st and 2nd). Part of "D" Company's line being taken (2nd) but recaptured by party of 40 men led by Captain Unwin. Relieved by 3rd Worcestershire during night and to billets at Ploegsteert. C.T. Atkinson gives casualties since going into the line on 28th October as 2 officers killed, 5 wounded (including Lieutenant H.A.B. Harrington mortally wounded), 46 other ranks killed, 121 wounded, 51 missing. He notes that of the latter many were probably buried under blown-in trenches. "B" Company moved into reserve trenches on the Ploegsteert road just west of Le Gheer (3rd). "A", "C" and "D" Companies relieved 1st East Lancashire in firing line (4th). Position running from the Le Gheer crossroads down to the River Warne. C.T. Atkinson records – "2 quiet days" (5th and 6th) and Germans seen dressed in kilts attempting to enter line held by the Scottish Rifles. "B" Company relieved "A" Company in firing line (7th). Enemy later attacked and entered trench of battalion on the left at Ploegsteert Wood.

"A" Company counter-attacked from reserve line and led by Captains Unwin and Dolphin cleared them from the area. Casualties – Captain Dolphin killed, Captain Unwin and 2 other officers wounded, 16 other ranks killed, 18 wounded, 18 missing. C.T. Atkinson records that Captain Dolphin was shot as he went forward to receive the surrender of a number of men calling out – "don't shoot." He also notes that of the officers that came out from England, only the following remained alive or unwounded – Captain Perkins, Lieutenant (now Captain) lim Thurn and Lieutenant Edsell. War Diary records – "snipers very active" – 3 killed, 4 wounded (8th), 7 wounded (9th). Relieved during night (14th) by 1st East Lancashire and to Ploegsteert. Relieved 1st East Lancashire (17th). Firing line now just north of that previously held and directly in front of Le Gheer. One company of 1/5th London attached. War Diary notes (19th-30th) – 1 company in firing line, 1 company in support, 1 company in reserve at Ploegsteert, 1 company at Nieppe. The latter rested there for 4 days while the remainder were relieved every 24 hours. Casualties – 1 officer wounded, 9 other ranks killed, 8 wounded.

DECEMBER
War Diary records (1st-18th) – "Practically no fighting" and flooded trenches in constant need of repair. Casualties- 11 killed, 27 wounded. Assisted 1st Somerset Light Infantry and 1st Rifle Brigade in attack on German House and The Birdcage (19th). Casualties – Major G.H. Parker and 15 other ranks killed, 25 wounded. "Nothing of importance" recorded (20th-31st). Company in firing line working night and day pumping and bailing water from flooded trenches. Casualties – 1 officer wounded, 4 other ranks killed, 6 wounded. All from snipers. Some 179 men had been sent to hospital sick during December. C.T. Atkinson records that at the end of 1914, 6 of the original officers were now present – Lieutenant- Colonel Hicks, Major Palk, Captains lim Thurn and Knocker, Second-Lieutenants F. Fidler and S. Sparke (both commissioned in October). There were also 366 other ranks still remaining from those that had left England with the Battalion in August. Total casualties in 1914 amounted to 8 officers killed, 6 missing, 15 wounded, 265 other ranks killed or missing, 390 wounded.

SOUTH STAFFORDSHIRE REGIMENT

**"Mons" "Retreat from Mons" "Marne, 1914"
"Aisne, 1914" "Ypres,1914" "Langemarck, 1914"
"Gheluvelt" "Nonne Bosschen"**

1ST BATTALION

AUGUST
Pietermaritzburg, South Africa. To Cape Town (21st) and embarked HMT *Briton* (24th). Sailed for England (27th).

SEPTEMBER
Arrived Southampton (19th) and marched to Lyndhurst Camp in the New Forest. Joined 22nd Brigade, 7th Division.

OCTOBER
To Southampton (4th) and embarked SS *Lake Michigan*. Strength – 29 officers, 1,113 other ranks. Sailed (5th), remaining in Dover Harbour until next day. Arrived Zeebrugge (7th). Moved by train to Bruges then into Oostcamp. Later to Lophem. "A" and "B" Companies setting up outpost line. Moved to positions at the canal just outside Ostend (8th). To Ostend (9th) and entrained for Ghent. Took up defensive positions covering canal bridge at Saynaerde (10th). Moved forward to positions south of Hansbeke (11th), withdrawing later through Saynaerde and Ghent to Hansbeke. Continued retreat (12th) via Bellem, Asltre, Ruywselde to Thielt. To Bevering (13th), via Roulers to Ypres (14th). Moved forward to entrenched positions at Zonnebeke (15th). To trenches around Molenhoek (18th). Moved forward (19th) through Strooiboomhoek to Dadizeele and in reserve during 22nd Brigade's attack on Kleyhoek. Later withdrew, covering retirement of 7th Division from positions in front of Strooiboomhoek then via Molenhoek to former positions at Zonnebeke. Lieutenant-Colonel Hon. Ralph Hamilton records (see *The War Diary of the Master of Belhaven*) how he stood on the crest of a small rise just behind the South Staffordshire's line. The country to the front, he noted, much resembled Essex and Suffolk. War Diary records (20th) Germans advancing to within 500 yards of Battalion's trenches. Enemy broke through on the left (21st) and Battalion forced to withdraw loosing its transport along with most of its stores and officers' kits. Lieutenant F.L. Holmes killed. Dug in around Veldhoek. War Diary records that in addition to loss of transport etc. most of the men were

now without greatcoats and equipment. Advanced to support positions in Polygon Wood (23rd). "B" Company took part in attack (24th). Captain J.S.S. Dunlop killed while leading the charge. Moved to Kruiseecke and in action attached to 20th Brigade (25th/26th). Casualties – Captain C.G. Ransford, Lieutenants F.R.J. Tomlinson, L.C. Moore-Radford and C.R.C. Bean killed. 8 other officers wounded. War Diary gives approximate casualties among other ranks as 80 killed, 360 wounded and prisoners. Held positions in Gheluvelt area. Second-Lieutenant G. Archer-Shee mortally wounded during attack (30th), Major J.F. Loder-Symonds killed (31st).

NOVEMBER
Took part in successful attack on enemy's line north-west of Klein Zillebeke (7th). Captain J.F. Vallentin killed and subsequently awarded the Victoria Cross. Battalion relieved and eventually moved to billets at Merris. In his history of the South Staffordshire Regiment, Colonel W.L. Vale records that when the Battalion left the trenches just 78 of the 1,100 other ranks that were present at the start of the fighting around Ypres remained. To Merville (11th).

DECEMBER
Moved forward (13th) via La Gorgue, Estaires and Sailly to billets in farm just outside Fleurbaix on Bac St. Maur road. Two companies moved forward and relieved 2nd Bedfordshire in trenches south-west of Fleurbaix – La Boutillerie (17th). In support of attack made by 2nd Royal Warwickshire (18th). Withdrew to farm just outside Fleurbaix on Bac St. Maur road. (19th). Lieutenant H.R.S. Bower killed while helping to clear wounded from No Man's Land (20th). Relieved 2nd Queen's in firing line. Relieved by 2nd Queen's (24th) and to billets at Le Cron-Ballot. Relieved 2nd Queen's (28th). War Diary records (30th) the flooding of Battalion's trenches around Well Farm. Water 4 feet deep in places.

2ND BATTALION

AUGUST
Aldershot. Part of 6th Brigade, 2nd Division. Entrained for Southampton (12th). Embarked SS *Irrawaddy* and sailed for France. Arrived Havre (13th) and to No.1 Rest Camp. Entrained for Wassigny (15th). Arrived (16th) and marched to billets at Iron. To Landrecies (21st), Hargnies (22nd), via Givry to Harmignies (23rd) and came under enemy fire. Received order to retire (24th) and fell back via Bonnet and Aulnois to Bavai. Dug defensive positions throughout night. Enemy engaged (25th) while covering retreat of 1st

Royal Berkshire and 1st King`s Royal Rifle Corps. War Diary records – very little firing and no casualties. Moved back later to Maroilles. Marched via Le Grand Fayt and Etreux to Venerolles (26th). To Mont d`Origny (27th), Amigny (28th). "A" Company to Condren (29th) to guard bridge. "D" Company entrenched along the road from Sinceny. To Ambleny (31st).

SEPTEMBER

Marched via Villers Cotterêts (1st), returning later to support 4th (Guards) Brigade then under attack. Continued march to Thury. To Trilbardou (2nd), Bilbarteaux-les-Vannes (3rd), Voisins (4th), Chaumes (5th). War Diary records that the Battalion had marched a total of 236 miles since 21st August. Advanced via Chaubuisson to Château-de-la-Fontelle (6th), via Touquin, La Boissière and Chailly to position just south of St. Siméon (7th), via Rebais, La Trétoire and Boitron to La Noue (8th). Crossed the Marne at Charly (9th) then via Villiers and Domptin to Coupru. Enemy engaged just south of Hautevesnes (10th). War Diary records that a German column was surprised about 8.45 am. "B" and "D" Companies were in action and the fight lasted about 2½ hours. Some 450 prisoners taken. Casualties – 2 officers wounded, 1 man killed, 5 wounded. Moved on to Chevillion. Went forward via Sommelans, Latilly, Breny, Oulchy-le-Château and Cugny-les-Couttes to Wallée (11th). To Monthussart Farm (12th), Vieil-Arcy (13th), Moussy in Brigade Reserve (14th). Two officers wounded during bombardment (15th). To Soupir as reserve to 4th (Guards) Brigade (16th). Returning to Moussy same day. To Soupir (18th) and held in support during enemy attack (19th). Relieved 1st King`s Royal Rifle Corps in firing line (20th) – 2 companies in trenches, Headquarters and 2 companies in Soupir. Enemy attacked forward companies ("A" and "B") during night (21st). Casualties – 2 wounded. Battalion relieved (22nd) and to Bourg. To Soupir (23rd) – "B" and "C" Companies to firing line. Medical Officer – Lieutenant W.O.W. Ball killed by shell while attending wounded (25th). "A" and "D" Companies moved out of Soupir (27th) and took up support line.

OCTOBER

"A" and "D" Companies joined "B" and "C" in firing line (1st). Relieved by 1st King`s Royal Rifle Corps (4th) – "B" and "C" Companies marching back to support line, "A" and "D" Companies to wood 1 mile north of Soupir. Battalion moved to Moussy (6th), "B" and "C" Companies remaining there in support while "A" and "D" relieved 1st King`s Liverpool in trenches west of Beaulne. Relieved by 148th French Regiment during night (15th/16th) and to Fismes. Entrained and arrived Strazelle (17th).

Marched to Hazebrouck. To Godewaersveld (19th), Ypres (20th). Moved forward to reserve positions just north of Wieltje (21st), moving 7 pm to Potijze. To Pilckem (23rd) and took part with 1st Queen's in attack to regain forward trenches. War Diary records that "A" and "D" Companies led and were involved in severe fighting before objectives were gained. Second-Lieutenant B.J.H. Scott killed, 3 officers wounded, 40 other ranks killed or wounded. Battalion withdrew to reserve positions just north of Pilckem. Withdrew via Pilkem and Frezenberg to positions on high ground north of Westhoek (24th). "C" Company moved forward in support of 1st King's Liverpool north of Polygon Wood (25th). Moved up to line 50 yards in front of the Broodseinde-Becelaere road (26th). Attacked during morning (27th). War Diary records that the enemy were driven back, but with heavy losses. Dug in on high ground west of Keiberg. Captain C.H. Thomas mortally wounded, Lieutenants F.E. Robinson and D.T.F. Fitzpatrick killed. Line held (28th-29th). Enemy attack repulsed after severe fighting (30th).

NOVEMBER
Positions held under heavy shell fire (1st-11th). Enemy broke through French line on Battalion's left (12th). War Diary records situation as critical – "but we held our own." Withdrew into Brigade Reserve (13th). "A" and "D" Companies sent forward in support of 2nd Highland Light Infantry at north-east corner of Polygon Wood, along the Passchendaele-Becelaere road. Battalion relieved 2nd Highland Light Infantry (14th). Relieved by 139th French Regiment (15th) and to Hooge. Marched via St. Jean to billets north-west of Ypres (16th), via Vlamertinghe, Reninghelst and Westoutre to Caestre (18th).

DECEMBER
Moved in London buses to Béthune (22nd) then marched to Beuvry. Took over trenches running from north bank of the La Bassée Canal to just south of Givenchy. Relieved by 2nd Royal Sussex (26th) and to Essars. To billets south of Locon (29th).

DORSETSHIRE REGIMENT

"Mons" "Le Cateau" "Retreat from Mons" "Marne, 1914" "Aisne, 1914" "La Bassée, 1914" "Armentières, 1914"

1ST BATTALION

AUGUST

Belfast, Ireland. Part of 15th Brigade, 5th Division. Embarked SS *Anthony* (14th) and sailed for France. Officers – Lieutenant-Colonel L.J. Bols, DSO (Commanding Officer), Majors R.T. Roper (Second in Command), J. Kearney (Quartermaster), Captain A.L. Ransome (Adjutant), Lieutenant C.H. Woodhouse (Machine Gun Officer), Captain B.H.V. Dunbar (RAMC, Medical Officer); "A" Company: Captains W.A.C. Fraser, R.G.M. Hyslop, Lieutenants J.M. Pitt, C.O. Lilly, F.D.S. King, Second-Lieutenant G.S. Shannon; "B" Company: Captains H.S. Williams, A.R.M. Roe, Lieutenants C.F.M. Margetts (Transport Officer), J.R. Turner, C.G. Butcher; "C" Company: Major C. Saunders, Captain J. Kelsall, Lieutenants A.S. Fraser, W.A. Leishman, Second- Lieutenants G.A. Burnand, L. Grant-Dalton; "D" Company: Captains W.T.C. Davidson, F.H.B. Rathborne, Lieutenants R.E. Partridge, A.K.D. George, A.E. Hawkins. Arrived Havre (16th) and to No.8 Rest Camp. Entrained (17th) for Le Cateau. Arrived (18th) and marched to Ors. Moved forward to Gommegnies (21st), via Bavai, Houdain and Athis to Dour (22nd). Headquarters, "C" and "D" Companies moved forward via Bois de Boussu (23rd) then turning off the road travelled along the railway line to positions at bridge on north side of Wasmes. Dug in facing Hornu. Fired on advancing enemy during afternoon and evening. "A" and "B" Companies later came forward in support. Came under shell and machine gun fire (24th) and engaged enemy again at about 200 yards. Withdrawal ordered and fell back via Blaugies and Athis to St. Waast. Casualties – 3 officers wounded and taken prisoner, 12 other ranks killed, 49 wounded, 69 missing. Moved back (25th) and dug defensive positions around Troisvillers and La Sotière. Retired to Ponchaux (26th), via Estrées and St. Quentin to Eaucourt (27th), Guiscard and Noyon to Pontoise (28th), to Carlepont (29th), via Attichy to Croutoy (30th), to Crépy-en-Valois (31st).

SEPTEMBER
Moved to Duvy (1st) then via Ormoy to Nanteuil. To Montgé (2nd).
Crossed the Marne at Trilbardou (3rd) then through Esby to Montpichet.
To Gagny (5th). Captain A.B. Priestley arrived with draft of 90 men. Began
advance towards the Aisne (6th), marching via Montcerf to positions just
south of Villeneuve. Moved via Trésmes and Coulommiers to Boissy-le-
Chatel (7th), via Doué to Charnesseuil (8th). Crossed the Marne at Saacy
(9th) then at 11.30 am led 15th Brigade's attack on the Pisseloupe Ridge.
Came under shell fire near Le Limon then from Bézu. "D" and "C"
Companies commenced assault on Hill 189. Captain Ransome records that
the attack took place over stubble fields and in full view of machine guns
hidden in woods on either flank – "The Companies gained ground slowly
by rushes, combined with rifle fire, but as a frontal attack unsupported by
artillery it was doomed to failure from the outset." Lieutenant George
mortally wounded. "B" Company advancing through the Bois des Essertis
were also unsupported and after heavy fighting were forced to dig in.
Captains Roe and Priestley both mortally wounded. Battalion withdrew
after dark to bivouacs near Bézu." Casualties – 3 officers mortally wounded,
7 other ranks killed, 31 wounded, 4 missing. Moved forward via Dhuisy,
Germigny, Gandelu and Chezy to billets at St. Quentin Farm (10th). To
St. Remy (11th). Advanced to Ferme de l'Epitaphe (12th), withdrawing to
Nanteuil same day. Crossed the Moulin des Roches during night
(13th/14th) and advanced to Ste. Marguerite. To Missy during afternoon
(15th), moving back to Jury early morning (16th). Relieved 1st East Surrey
in forward trenches at Missy (23rd).

OCTOBER
Relieved and to Jury (1st). To Launoy (2nd), Corcy (3rd), Fresnoy la Rivière
(4th), Verberie (6th). Moved to Compiègne. (7th) and entrained for
Abbeville. Detrained at Pont Remy (8th) and marched via Abbeville to
Neuilly. Moved later in evening to Genne Ivergny. To Haravesnes (9th),
returning to Genne Ivergny during morning (10th). To Haravesnes again
10.30 am then by buses to La Thieuloye. Arrived 5.30 pm and marched to
Béthune. "B" and "C" Companies took up outpost line running from Gorre
to Fin-de-Roi. Took part in fighting along the La Bassée Canal (12th-13th),
advancing from positions along the Pont Fixe-La Plantin road and engaging
enemy in front of Givenchy. Withdrew to Pont Fixe (13th). Casualties –
Major Roper mortally wounded, Captain Davidson, Lieutenants J.A.F.
Parkinson, Pitt, T.S. Smith killed, 7 officers wounded, 4 missing, 14 other
ranks killed, 122 wounded, 280 missing. The bodies of some 130 of the latter
were later found by a burial party. The war history of the Dorsetshire

Regiment recalls how a number of Germans came forward from Givenchy carrying lances and were at first taken to be French cavalry. Another group, about a battalion, advanced with hands held up as if to surrender. The Battalion ceased fire in order to allow the men to come in, but upon reaching the Dorsetshire line, the Germans rushed their positions and opened fire. The history also notes how Lieutenant-Colonel Bols fought alongside of Lieutenant Pitt, the officers taking up rifles from the dead and firing into the oncoming enemy. The Colonel was wounded and subsequently taken prisoner. However, having been told to lie on a stretcher and wait to be attended by a doctor, he managed to escape back to his battalion at Pont Fixe. Relieved by 1st Devonshire (15th) and via Gorre to Loisne. To Rue de Béthune in Divisional Reserve (16th), Festubert (17th), billets in Rue d`Ouvert, Chapelle St. Roch (18th). Moved forward into close support positions near Violaines (20th) then in evening withdrew to Rue du Marais. Enemy broke through 1st Cheshire`s line at Violaines (22nd) and Cheshires fell back to new line being dug by company of 1st Dorsetshire – Regimental History records – "Our composite company, who were digging in rear, could do nothing; as the remains of the Cheshires started falling back on them." Withdrew to La Quinque Rue then at 8 pm to Festubert. Casualties – 7 killed, 24 wounded, 103 missing. Took over billets at Rue de Béthune. Moved to Le Touret (27th) then advanced on Richbourg l`Avou,. Took up positions close to the La Bassée-Estaires road (28th) then to Richbourg St. Vaast. Withdrew to billets in the Rue de l`Epinette (29th). Moved to Calonne (30th), Strazeele (31st).

NOVEMBER
Travelled in buses to Neuve Eglise (1st). Moved forward to positions in Ploegsteert Wood (2nd). Relieved (19th) and via Petit Pont to billets at Dranoutre. Relieved 1st East Surrey in trenches west of Hill 75 (24th). Relieved by 1st Royal Scots Fusiliers (30th) and to Dranoutre.

DECEMBER
Carried out tours in trenches Wulverghem sector throughout month. Battalion rested at Neuve Eglise, Dranoutre and Bailleul.

PRINCE OF WALES'S VOLUNTEERS
(SOUTH LANCASHIRE REGIMENT)

**"Mons" "Le Cateau" "Retreat from Mons"
"Marne, 1914" "Aisne, 1914" "La Bassée, 1914"
"Messines, 1914" "Armentières, 1914" "Ypres, 1914"
"Nonne Bosschen"**

2ND BATTALION

AUGUST

Tidworth. Part of 7th Brigade, 3rd Division. To Southampton (13th). Embarked SS *Lapwing* and sailed for France. Arrived Havre (14th) then via River Seine to Rouen. Moved into rest camp at Mont St. Aignan. Entrained for Busigny at Rouen (16th). Arrived and to billets at Aulnoye. To Marbaix (17th), St. Hilaire (20th), Feignies (21st), Frameries (22nd) and billeted in the railway station. To Ciply during morning (23rd) then took up defensive positions on low ridge between Ciply and Frameries. War Diary records that Belgian civilians assisted in digging trenches. Enemy attacked about 5 am (24th). War Diary records that troops on the left in Frameries were driven out and Battalion's trenches enfiladed. "C" and "D" Companies who – "after suffering great loss were compelled to retire." High casualties were inflicted from German machine guns situated along the railway line. Battalion fell back and bivouacked some 3 miles to the west of St. Waast. Moved back (25th) via Le Quesnoy to Solesmes and there came under attack. Held positions till dark then withdrew to Caudry. War Diary records that the Battalion had – "suffered severely." Came under attack again (26th), withdrawing to Vermand during evening. Marched through night via Ham to Tarlefesse (27th/28th). To Salency during afternoon (29th) then to Noyon. Continued retreat via Pontoise, Cuts and Camelin to Vic- sur-Aisne (30th), via Mortefontaine, Taillefontaine and Eméville to Coyolles (31st).

SEPTEMBER

To Villers (1st), Pringy (2nd), via Meaux and Nanteuil to Sancy (3rd). Marched by night via Crécy and the Forest of Crécy to Châtres (4th). In his book *"Ich Dien" The Prince of Wales's Volunteers (South Lancashire) 1914-1934* Captain H. Whalley-Kelly records the Battalion's casualties throughout the retreat from Mons as 5 officers, 149 other ranks killed, 7 officers, 301 other ranks wounded or missing. This total, he notes, is greater than that incurred by the Regiment for the whole of the Peninsular War.

Began advance to the Aisne, marching via the Forest of Crécy to Faremoutiers (6th). Moved forward around 5 am (7th). War Diary notes several casualties throughout day during "wood fighting." Withdrew about 4 pm then to Les Petits Aulnois. Marched via Rebais to Bussieres (8th). Crossed the Marne and to Bezu (8th). To Montmafroy (10th), via Dammard and Neuilly to Grand-Rozoy (11th), to Cerseuil (12th), Braine (13th). Moved through Brenelle (14th), crossed the Aisne east of Vailly and took up Brigade Reserve positions. Two companies moved forward to reinforce firing line facing Rouge Maison (19th). Enemy attacked in large numbers (20th) and rest of Battalion (less 1 platoon) sent forward to reinforce firing line. Casualties – Second-Lieutenants E.G. Watson, D.S. Wallace and G.A.B. Birdwood killed, 4 other officers wounded, 141 other ranks killed, wounded or missing. Battalion (less "A" Company) relieved (21st) and withdrew during night to billets in Augy. "A" Company rejoined (23rd). Relieved 3rd Worcestershire in outpost positions around Chassemy (24th). "A", "B" and "D" Companies in woods north-west of village covering the bridge at Condé. Relieved (26th) and to Augy.

OCTOBER

To Grand-Rozoy (1st), Beugneux (2nd). Returned to Grand-Rozoy 6.30 pm then marched through night to Noroy. To Vaumoise (3rd), Saintines (4th). Left 11 pm (5th) and to Longueil Ste. Marie. Entrained for Rue (6th). Marched to Ouville (7th) then marched through night to Regnauville. Moved in lorries to Pernes (9th). Marched to Hinges (11th) then to trenches near Lacouture (12th). Moved forward to St. Vaast (13th), advanced to positions north of Richebourg St. Vaast (15th). War Diary records advance continued north-east (16th) and by night Battalion in vicinity of Neuve Chapelle. Relieved later by 1st Wiltshire and moved back to billets in Neuve Chapelle. Moved up in support of 3rd Worcestershire in firing line at Halpegarbe (17th). Enemy attacked (20th), War Diary notes "heavy losses", and again (21st) – "considerable" casualties, "large numbers" reported missing. Captain A.T. Gibson killed. Survivors withdrew to billets near western edge of Bois du Biez. Moved to billets at Richebourg St. Vaast (23rd). Went forward (26th) and placed into support positions. Took part in attack on Neuve Chapelle (27th). War Diary records assault as unsuccessful and Battalion withdrew to positions about 400 yards behind those previously held. Second-Lieutenant E.A. Mitchell killed. Relieved by Indian Troops (28th) and moved back to Richebourg St. Vaast. Returned to support line near Neuve Chapelle during afternoon. Relieved and back to Richebourg about 4 pm (29th). Came under heavy shell fire and withdrew to Lacouture. To Doulieu (30th), Merris (31st).

NOVEMBER

To Locre (1st). Moved forward towards Ypres (5th), later taking over Brigade Reserve trenches near Hooge. Relieved 2nd Royal Irish Rifles in firing line (7th). Moved back to reserve (9th), firing line (11th). Captain S. Duncan (Gloucestershire Regiment attached) killed (13th). Withdrew into reserve (14th). Shell landed on dugout occupied by Lieutenant-Colonel M.C.A. Green and Lieutenant B.V. Fulcher (17th) killing both officers. War Diary records that the Battalion now had just 2 officers. Relieved by French troops (20th) and to Westoutre. To Locre (27th). Relieved 1/10th King's Liverpool in trenches east of Kemmel (30th). War Diary records strength now as 9 officers, approximately 340 other ranks.

DECEMBER

War Diary records (2nd) – a "regrettable incident" in which a hand grenade being prepared was accidently dropped. The explosion mortally wounded Captain E. Robson, killed a corporal and wounded 2 others. Relieved (3rd) and to Westoutre. Moved to billets in farms about 1½ miles west of Westoutre (4th). To Locre (6th), Bailleul (8th). Various drafts arrived and War Diary records Battalion's strength (22nd) as 16 officers, 979 other ranks. An interesting survey was undertaken with a view to establishing how many of the men of the Battalion were from Lancashire. The findings were – Blackburn (13), Burnley (9), Leigh (3), Liverpool (291), Manchester (79), Preston (17), Prescott (2), Rochdale (3), St. Helens (168), Southport (17), Warrington (47), Wigan (83), Widnes (47). Total 779. The remaining 200 men were from – London (35), Birmingham (32), other places (133). To firing line south-east of Kemmel near Lindenhoek (24th). Relieved by 1st Gordon Highlanders (27th) and to Westoutre. To Locre (31st).

WELSH REGIMENT

"Mons" "Retreat from Mons" "Marne, 1914" "Aisne, 1914" "Ypres, 1914" "Langemarck, 1914" "Gheluvelt" "Nonne Bosschen" "Givenchy, 1914"

2ND BATTALION

AUGUST

Bordon. Part of 3rd Brigade, 1st Division. Entrained for Southampton (12th) and Embarked SS *Braemar Castle* for France. Officers – Lieutenant-Colonel C.B. Morland (Commanding Officer), Major O.B. Pritchard (Second in Command), Captain W.H. Ferrar (Adjutant), Lieutenants R.M. Hill (Quartermaster), G.D. Melville (Machine Gun Officer), Second-Lieutenant G.D. Partridge (Transport Officer); "A" Company: Captain L.I.O. Robins, Second-Lieutenant H.G.A. Corder, W.G. Hewett, W.T. Wootton; "B" Company: Captains C.R. Berkeley, DSO, M. Haggard, Lieutenants W.S. Evans, H.N. Walker, Second-Lieutenant G.R. Fitzpatrick; "C" Company: Captains W.A.G. Moore, H.C. Rees, Lieutenants Hon. W.Fitz R. Somerset, Second-Lieutenants F.W. Ford, J.J.C. Cocks; "D" Company: Major J.H. Kerrick, Captain P.L.W.Powell, Lieutenants C.A.S. Carleton, J.N. Gilbey, Second-Lieutenants W. Owen, B.V.T.B. Hambrough. Arrived Havre during morning (13th) and to No.6 Rest Camp. Entrained for Etreux (15th) then to billets at Leschelles. To Dompierre (21st), via Maubeuge to Grand Reng (22nd) then – Headquarters, "A" and "B" Companies at Fauroeulx, "C" and "D" Companies at Peissant. "C" and "D" Companies relieved by 1st South Wales Borderers (23rd) and rejoined Battalion at Fauroeulx. Fired on enemy patrol during morning (24th) then withdrew via Croix and Rouveroy to Neuf Mesnil. Continued retreat via Maubeuge and Marbaix to Le Grand Fayt (25th). Later took up support positions at Landrecies. Marched to Favril then Petit Le Cambresis (26th). Engaged enemy cavalry patrols near La Neuville (27th) then moved via Iron and Guise to Bernot. To Berteacourt (28th), Brancourt (30th), Missy-aux- Bois (31st).

SEPTEMBER

To Villers-Cotterêts (1st), Cregy (2nd), La Ferte-sous-Jouarra (3rd), Mouroux (4th), Rozoy (5th). Began advance to the Aisne, marching to Vaudoy (6th), Choisy (7th), via St. Siméon, Rebais and Sablonnieres to billets at Bassevelle Farm (8th). Crossed the Marne at Nogent (9th) then via Charly to Le Thiolet. To Sommelans (10th), Villeneuve (11th), Longueval (12th). Crossed the Aisne at Bourg (13th). Took part in attack towards the Chemin des Dames (14th). Heavy casualties while advancing across the Chivy Valley. Dug in on the Beaulne Ridge. Captain Haggard mortally wounded, Major Kerrich, Second-Lieutenants Fitzpatrick and G.O. Birch killed. Captain Haggard's gallantry was noted during the day. He led a charge with 3 men on a machine gun and was wounded while some 30 yards ahead of the nearest man. In his book on the Victoria Cross, Sir O'Moore Creagh recalls the words of a private of the Battalion who was also hit and lying close to Captain Haggard – "Near me was lying our brave captain, mortally wounded. As the shells burst over us, he would occasionally open his eyes between the spasms of pain, and call out weakly: 'Stick it the Welsh!' Captain Haggard was eventually brought in by Lance-Corporal William Fuller, who under tremendous fire carried the officer to shelter and dressed his wounds. For his gallantry, William Fuller was awarded the Victoria Cross. Held positions against attack (15th). Withdrew during night (20th) to Beaulne then to reserve positions at Vendresse (25th). "A" and "C" Companies moved forward (26th) to reinforce 1st South Wales Borderers under attack at the Quarries on Mont Faucon Ridge. Captain H.C. Davies killed. Took over front line (27th).

OCTOBER
Relieved by French Troops (15th). Casualties since 14th September – 5 officers, 50 other ranks killed, 6 officers, 132 other ranks wounded, 28 missing. Entrained for Hazebrouck, arriving (19th) and moving forward to Poperinghe. In reserve during Battle of Langemarck (21st), moving forward later and taking up positions in centre of line just north-east of the village. Enemy attack repulsed (23rd). Captain Rees noted that between 400-500 casualties were inflicted on the enemy, with no loss to the Battalion. Relieved during night and to positions near Hooge. Thirty-nine men of "C" Company killed or wounded by a single shell during relief. To Ypres (24th). Moved forward to Bellewaarde Lake in support (26th). Later dug in on the slopes of Kruiseecke Hill. Withdrew to Hooge (27th). Moved forward again and took part in fighting around Gheluvelt (29th-31st). Lieutenant-Colonel Morland mortally wounded, Captain W.A.G. Moore and Lieutenant J.H.W. Nicholl killed.

NOVEMBER
Relieved by 1st Royal Berkshire in Herenthage Wood (1st) and moved back to Sanctuary Wood. Took part in fighting at Herenthage Wood (2nd-4th). Captain Ferrar and Lieutenant Partridge killed. Relieved and to Bellewaarde

Farm. To front line (7th). Relieved and to Sanctuary Wood (8th). Took part in fighting at Shrewsbury Forest (10th-14th). Lieutenant C.V.P. Cornelius killed. Relieved (15th) and via Ypres to Locre. Casualty figures for the period 22nd September to 14th November are given in Major-General Sir Thomas O. Marden's history of the Welch Regiment as 5 officers and 197 other ranks killed, 16 officers and approximately 400 other ranks wounded. One officer and 45 other ranks had been taken prisoner. The General points out that Captain Rees was the only officer that left England with the Battalion who remained unwounded.

DECEMBER

Moved to Merville area (20th) then forward via Béthune and Gorre to Festubert sector. Took part in attack to regain lost trenches (21st-22nd). Second-Lieutenant J.R.B. Weeding killed, 123 other casualties. Remained in area holding front and support trenches. Captain H.F. Herd killed (27th).

1/6TH (GLAMORGAN) BATTALION (TERRITORIAL FORCE)

AUGUST

Headquarters – Swansea, "A" Company – Maesteg, "B","C","D" Companies – Swansea, "E" Company – Hafod, "F" Company – Neath, "G" Company – Clydach, "H" Company – Gorseinon. Part of South Wales Brigade, Welsh Division. Returned from camp at Portmadoc. Mobilized (4th) then took up war stations at Mumbles Head, Swansea Docks, Briton Ferry and Port Talbot.

OCTOBER

Sailed for France (28th). Landed Havre (29th). Strength – 28 officers, 812 other ranks. Began Line of Communications duties.

BLACK WATCH (ROYAL HIGHLANDERS)

**"Retreat from Mons" "Marne, 1914" "Aisne, 1914"
"La Bassée, 1914" "Ypres, 1914"
"Langemarck, 1914" "Gheluvelt" "Nonne Bosschen"
"Givenchy, 1914"**

1ST BATTALION

AUGUST

Oudenarde Barracks, Aldershot. Part of 1st (Guards) Brigade, 1st Division. Entrained at Farnborough (13th). Arrived Southampton and embarked SS *Italian Prince*. Landed Havre (14th) and to rest camp at Harfleur. Officers – Lieutenant-Colonel A. Grant Duff, CB (Commanding Officer), Major J.T.C. Murray (Second in Command), Captain C.J. Coppinger (RAMC, Medical Officer), Lieutenants G.B. Rowan-Hamilton (Adjutant), F.G. Chalmer (Machine Gun Officer), F. Anderson (Transport Officer), W. Fowler (Quartermaster); "A" Company – Major Lord George Stewart-Murray, Lieutenants V.M. Fortune, R.C. Anderson, Second-Lieutenants J.E.H. Rollo, R.G. Don; "B" Company – Captains Hon. M.C.A. Drummond, C.A. de G. Dalglish, Lieutenants E.H.H.J. Wilson, L.R. Cumming, Second-Lieutenants J.L. Rennie, P.E.A. Blair; "C" Company – Captain W. Green, Lieutenant W.D. Allan, Second-Lieutenants P.K. Campbell, N.J.L. Boyd; "D" Company – Captains H.F.S. Amery, A.D.C. Krook, Lieutenant R.E. Anstruther, Second- Lieutenants K.S. MacRae, G.W. Polson. Other ranks – 1,031. Entrained at Havre for Le Nouvion. Major-General A.G. Wauchope,CB records in his war history of the Black Watch, that during the journey the train stopped at Arras. A large crowd had gathered especially to see the battalion, which they referred to as "The famous Waterloo Black Watch." Arrived Le Nouvion 1 am (17th) and marched to billets at Boué. At Boué, General Wauchope records, a mess-cart and horse were acquired. The latter being named "Allez- vous-en" and returning home with the battalion after the war having been wounded 3 times. Moved forward to Cartignies (21st) and via Dompierre, Doulers and Maubeuge arrived Grand Reng 1 am (23rd). Took up defensive positions between the 19 and 17 kilometre stones on the Beaumont-Mons road during evening. Ordered to retire (24th). Fell back first to Villers-sire-Nicole then via Bettignies and Feignies to billets at La Longeuville. Continued retreat via Hautmont and Limont Fontaine to Dompierre (25th), Marbaix to La Grand Fayt (26th). Relieved troops of 6th Brigade in defensive line. Later moved to billets at La Petit Cambresis. Took up positions covering retreat of 1st Brigade north of Etreux (27th). Records note each unit passing through, but no sign of 2nd Royal Munster Fusiliers. Later withdrew through Etreux, coming under heavy shell and rifle fire on road between village and Iron. Casualties – 7 wounded, 3 missing. Continued march via Iron and Guise to billets in La Jonqueuse. At La Jonqueuse, General Wauchope records, the fate of the Royal Munsters was learnt. Just 1 platoon surviving the battalion's action that morning near the Sambre-Oise Canal. Marched via Ribemont and La Fère to the St. Gobain Forest (28th). Here, General Wauchope records that one soldier informed the Medical Officer that there was something wrong with his foot, and he was unable to march. When his boot was removed, a bullet fell out, the man having been hit the previous day on the road between Etreux and Iron. He also notes that the men, in order to lighten their loads, were given permission to hand in their greatcoats. These, however, could not be carried on the transport and were burned. Marched via Septvaux and Brancourt to Allemant (30th), via Soissons to Missy-Aux-Bois (31st).

SEPTEMBER
Covered retreat of 4th (Guards) Brigade at Villers Cotterêts (1st). Withdrew later via La Ferté Milon and bivouacked on high ground south of village. To Varreddes (2nd) then bivouacked on high ground near Chambry. Crossed the Marne (3rd) and into billets at La Ferté-sous-Jouarre. To Coulommiers (4th). "A" Company engaged party of 6 Uhlans during night on the Coulommiers-Jouarre road, killing one and taking remainder prisoner. Also captured – one horse who was named "German Jimmy" and remained with the battalion throughout the war. In 1925, General Wauchope records, the animal was alive and well and living in Scotland. Moved via Mauperthuis to Nesles (5th). Began advance (6th), marching through Rozoy to Voinsles. Five men wounded from shell fire. Later moved to positions at Gloise Farm. Marched via Amillis, Chevru and Choisy to bivouacs near Le Temple (7th), via Jouy to Bellot (8th). Came under artillery fire from woods on high ground across the Petit Morin. Advanced through village. Crossed the river and "B" Company, supported by "C", engaged the enemy at Sablonnières. Village cleared and 40 prisoners taken. Captain Dalglish mortally wounded, Lieutenant Wilson killed, 8 other ranks killed, 17 wounded. Continued advance and bivouacked at Hondevillers. Crossed the Marne at Nogent (9th) then marched via Charly-sur-Marne to bivouacs at La Nouette Farm. Moved via La Thiolet, Torcy and Courchamps to Latilly (10th), to Trugny (11th), via Fère-en-Tardenois and Mont Nôtre Dame to Bazoches (12th), Vauxcéré and Longueval to Bourg (13th). Moved forward in support of 2nd

Brigade, taking up positions in the caves on Paissy Ridge. Five men wounded from shell fire during advance. Went forward through Moulins and Vendresse in support of attack (14th). Leading battalions of 1st Brigade – 1st Coldstream and 1st Camerons, came under heavy fire during advance up the Vendresse Ridge. Battalion then split up in order to support. "A" and "C" Companies held position east of the sugar factory on the Chemin Des Dames throughout day. "D" Company moved up the Chivy Valley and were overwhelmed by large numbers of the enemy. Lieutenant- Colonel Grant Duff killed during strong counter-attack. Fell back after dark and began to dig in. Casualties in addition to Lieutenant-Colonel Grant Duff – Major Lord Stewart- Murray, Lieutenant Cumming, Second-Lieutenant Don killed, Second-Lieutenant Boyd mortally wounded. Six other officers wounded, 40 other ranks killed, 112 wounded, 35 missing. "C" Company supported by "D" moved forward again (15th). Came under fire and forced to retire. Second-Lieutenant Polson killed. Line held. Relieved (19th) and to billets at Oeuilly. To Verneuil (21st) and took over trenches near Beaulne in the Chivy Valley. Relieved by 1st Cameron Highlanders (24th) and to Cretonne Farm near Vernuil. To Chivy Valley (28th).

OCTOBER
Relieved (15th) and via Bourg to Blanzy. Marched to Fismes (17th) and entrained for Hazebrouck. To Poperinghe (20th) and via Elverdinghe and Boesinghe to Brigade Reserve positions at Pilkem (21st). Three companies moved forward during afternoon (22nd) to assist 1st Coldstream under attack at Korteeker Inn. "A", "B" and "D" Companies reaching the line of the Steenbeek and holding off any further advance by the enemy. Machine guns, War Diary records, inflicted high losses on the enemy from a windmill on the Langemarck-Bixschoote road. Moved to positions at Remi Farm and held off further enemy attacks (23rd-24th). Captain E.F.M. Urquhart and Lieutenant C.L.C. Bowes-Lyon killed. Relieved and via St. Jean, Zillebeke to Verbranden Molen. Casualties – 2 officers killed, 5 wounded, 29 other ranks killed, 40 wounded, 3 missing. Moved forward along Menin road (26th) and took part in attack on Kruiseecke. Retired to Gheluvelt but at 4 pm moved forward again. Digging in on line along the Zandvoorde-Gheluvelt road. "A" Company in front line heavily shelled (27th) – over half becoming casualties. Battalion relieved by 2nd Bedfordshire during evening. Headquarters with "A" and "D" Companies marching via Gheluvelt and relieving 2nd Grenadier Guards in trenches near Polderhoek Château. "B" and "C" taking up line 1 mile east of Gheluvelt with right on the Menin road. Enemy attacked "B" and "C" Companies early morning (29th). Survivors, mostly wounded, fell back and

joined Headquarters. "A" and "D" Companies repulsed attack during the day. Line now held running through Gheluvelt. Positions held at south-west corner of Polygon Wood (31st). Battalion Headquarters at Verbeek Farm. Casualties (26th-31st) – Captain P.L. Moubray, Lieutenant A.C.R.S. Macnaughton, Second-Lieutenants D.S.S. Smurthwaite and P.E.A. Blair killed, Captain Sir E. Stewart-Richardson mortally wounded, 4 officers wounded, 1 missing, 71 other ranks killed, 18 wounded, 71 missing.

NOVEMBER
Enemy attacked down the Menin road (2nd). "A", "C" and "B" Companies took part in counter-attack and held up advance. Casualties – Lieutenant R.P.D. Nolan killed, Captain Amery mortally wounded, 2 officers wounded, 5 other ranks killed, 34 wounded, 21 missing. Most of the latter believed killed. War Diary records heavy shelling (3rd-6th) – 23 killed, 22 wounded, 6 missing. "A" and "B" Companies assisted 1st Loyal North Lancashire in counter-attack near Inverness Copse. Line regained and held. War Diary records – "heaviest bombardment yet experienced" between 7-10 am (11th). Enemy (Prussian Guard) attacked and broke through on right of "D" Company. Headquarters overrun, "A" and "B" Companies suffering heavy casualties. "C" Company came into action and divided attacking force into small parties. Later, at 3.30 pm, 1st Northamptonshire with party of 1st Black Watch advanced from Nonne Bosschen Wood and cleared enemy from Verbeek Farm and south-west corner of Polygon Wood. The latter being recorded as gallantly held by a party under Lieutenant Anderson and later named "Black Watch Corner." Casualties – Lieutenant J.W.L. Sprot, Second-Lieutenants N. McNeil and A.S. Lawson killed, 4 officers wounded, 18 other ranks killed, 52 wounded, 49 missing believed killed. A.S. Lawson had left Aldershot with the battalion as Regimental Quartermaster Sergeant and had been promoted in the field. Withdrew (13th) to Sanctuary Wood then Hooge Château. Casualties (12th-14th) – 9 killed, 30 wounded. Marched to Westoutre (15th), Borre (16th).

DECEMBER
Visited by HM The King (3rd). Moved to Merville (20th), Béthune (21st). Later moved forward into support positions at Cuinchy. Took over front line from 1st Coldstream at Rue d'Ouvert north of Givenchy (22nd). Second-Lieutenant A. McAndrew killed (24th). Alister McAndrew left Aldershot with the battalion as Company Quartermaster Sergeant of "B" Company and had been promoted in the field. Relieved by 1st Coldstream and to Cuinchy (25th). To Annequin (27th). Relieved 1st Coldstream in firing line (28th). Major-General Wauchope provides casualty figures for

1914 in his book as – Officers: 20 killed, 29 wounded, 1 missing; Other Ranks: 344 killed, 457 wounded and 148 missing.

2ND BATTALION

AUGUST
Bareilly, India. Detachments at Ranikhet. Part of Bareilly Brigade, Meerut Division.

SEPTEMBER
Entrained for Karachi (3rd), arriving (6th). Embarked SS *Elephanta* (16th) and sailed (21st). Captain A.G. Wauchope, DSO (later Major-General) was a member of No.3 Company and recorded in his war history of the Black Watch that on leaving India the 2nd Battalion comprised 24 officers. Of these, some 13 officers were killed during the war, the remainder, except one, being wounded at least once.

OCTOBER
Arrived Suez (2nd), Port Said (3rd). Lieutenant-Colonel W. McL. Campbell, MVO arrived from England and took over command. Sailed for France (6th). Disembarked Marseilles (12th) and to camp at La Valentine. Officers – Lieutenant-Colonel W. MacL. Campbell, MVO (Commanding Officer), Major C.E. Stewart (Second-in-Command), Captain C.R.B. Henderson (Adjutant), Captain Dawson (RAMC, Medical Officer), Lieutenant J. Anderson (Quartermaster), Rev. A. Macfarlane (Chaplain); No.1 Company: Captains G.C.S. McLeod, C.E. Strahan, Lieutenants A.C. Denison (Machine Gun Officer), D.C. Hamilton-Johnson (Transport Officer), Second-Lieutenant W.D. MacL. Stewart; No.2 Company: Captains R.E. Forrester, P.G.M. Skene, Lieutenant K.R. Gilroy; No.3 Company: Captains A.G. Wauchope, DSO, D. Campbell, Lieutenants J.N. Inglis, J.A. Durie, I.B. McLeod; No.4 Company: Major H.H. Sutherland, Captain H.F.F. Murray, Lieutenants A.H.C. Sutherland, K. Buist, N. McMicking. Major Stewart was sent to 1st Black Watch to replace Lieutenant-Colonel A. Grant Duff who had been killed. Moved by train to Orleans (20th). Lieutenant Buist, with 80 men, remained at Marseilles as first reinforcement. The detachment, however, was later sent to 1st Black Watch to replace casualties at Ypres. Moved by train to Berguette (26th) – strength 19 officers and 824 other ranks. Arrived (27th) and to Robecq. Moved forward via Gorre (28th) and took over front line trenches from 2nd Duke of Wellington's 800 to 1,000 yards east of Le Plantin (29th). Private D. McInroy killed by sniper – the Battalion's first casualty.

NOVEMBER

Headquarters with Nos 1 and 2 Companies transferred to trenches north of Rue La Quinque – Festubert sector (2nd). Captain Forrester led a raid on enemy positions with 20 men of No.2 company (9th). Ten Germans killed after hand-to-hand fighting. Captain Forrester and 2 men wounded. Headquarters, Nos 1 and 2 Companies relieved by 1st Seaforth Highlanders (17th) and to Divisional Reserve at Le Hamel. Moved to Gorre (21st), Le Hamel (22nd) and Zelobes in Corps Reserve (23rd). Nos 3 and 4 Companies remained in line carrying out several raids on enemy positions. Relieved by Connaught Rangers (24th) and rejoined rest of Battalion at Zelobes. Reinforcement of 300 men sent up to line at Centre Section opposite Festubert (25th-26th). Captain Strahan killed (27th).

DECEMBER

Line held at Festubert included Picket House and Hell Corner. Also The Glory Hole which was within 12 yards of a German sap head. Captain (now Major) Wauchope records a great deal of fighting with grenades. The Germans, he notes, being – "superior both in equipment and training." Relieved and to Annezin in reserve (13th). To Essars (15th), Annezin (17th), Essars (18th), Le Touret (19th). Moved up to reserve line at Rue de l' Epinette (21st). Nos. 3 and 4 Companies under Captain (now Major) Wauchope sent forward to reinforce 1st Seaforth Highlanders near Picket House. Returning (23rd) – Lieutenant W.E. Maitland (Seaforth Highlanders attached) mortally wounded, Major Wauchope wounded. To Le Touret (24th), Paradis (25th), Ecquedecques (26th), Amettes (27th). Major Wauchope provides casualty figures for 1914 in his book as – officers: 2 killed, 7 wounded; Other Ranks: 56 killed, 122 wounded and 1 missing.

1/5TH (ANGUS AND DUNDEE) BATTALION (TERRITORIAL FORCE)

AUGUST

Headquarters at Arbroath and companies at Kirriemuir, Forfar, Montrose, Brechin, Arbroath (2) and Dundee (2). Part of Black Watch Brigade, Scottish Coast Defences. Assembled (5th) and to war stations – Tay Defences.

OCTOBER

Entrained for Southampton (29th).

NOVEMBER

Sailed SS. *Architect* for France (1st). Disembarked Havre (2nd). Officers – Lieutenant- Colonel H. Scrymgeour-Wedderburn (Commanding Officer), Major Lord P. Glamis (Second in Command), Major H.F. Blair-Imrie, Captain G.F. Bowes-Lyon (Adjutant), Lieutenant A. Hall (Quartermaster), Captain A.W. Duke (Machine Gun Officer), F.N.E. Kitson (Transport Officer), Major G.F. Whyte (Medical Officer). No. 1 Company: Captains J.B. McNab, T. Aubertin, Lieutenants R.F. D. Bruce, J.W.N. Gordon, I.M. Bruce-Gardyne, Second-Lieutenant Hon. J.H. Bowes-Lyon; No. 2 Company: Captains T. Lyell, A.H.M. Wedderburn, Lieutenants J.F. Dickson, J.H. Campbell, H.S. Queckett, G.M. Adams; No. 3 Company: Captains J.D. Duncan, J.A. Wilson, Lieutenants J. Murray, W.C.O. Barrie, L.A Elgood; No. 4 Company: Captains J. Cruickshank, W.L. Mitchell, Lieutenant A. Dickie, Second-Lieutenants H.R. McCabe, R.M. Leslie. Entrained for St. Omer (4th) and from there marched to billets at Blendecques. To Thiennes (12th), Neuf Berquin (13th). Attached to 24th Brigade, 8th Division. To Estaires (14th) and began instruction in front line trenches along the Estaires-La Bassée road opposite Neuve Chapelle. Companies were attached to the 1st Sherwood Foresters and the Commanding Officer of that battalion, Colonel W. Marshall, recalls in his book *Memories of Four Fronts* how one day he found that the Highlanders had deepened their trenches by about a foot, removed the fire-step and increased the height of the parapet by more than 12 inches. The men were now some 8 feet below ground. Colonel Marshall asked the officer in charge of the Black Watch how he proposed to deal with an enemy attack if his men could not see over the parapet? He relied – "Oh! we'll get on the top."

DECEMBER

As with other battalions during this period, the men of 1/5th Black Watch were effected by conditions in the trenches – frostbite etc. When the right half of battalion came out of the trenches (9th) only 150 men would be fit for duty.

OXFORDSHIRE AND BUCKINGHAMSHIRE LIGHT INFANTRY

"Mons" "Retreat from Mons" "Marne, 1914" "Aisne, 1914" "Ypres, 1914" "Langemarck, 1914" "Gheluvelt" "Nonne Bosschen"

2ND BATTALION

AUGUST

Albuhera Barracks, Aldershot. Part of 5th Brigade, 2nd Division. Colours taken to Depot at Cowley Barracks by Second-Lieutenants F. Pepys, A.H. Barrington-Kennett and F.W.C. Chippindale (5th). Inspected by HM The King (12th). The following list appears under the heading of – "Officers taking the Field" in *The Oxfordshire & Buckinghamshire Light Infantry Chronicle 1914-1915* – Lieutenant-Colonel H.R. Davies, Major A.J.F. Eden ("C" Company), Captains E.F. Villers, DSO (1st Royal Sussex, attached to "A" Company), H.L. Wood ("B" Company), G.A. Sullivan (Assistant Provost Marshal, 2nd Division), A.H. Harden ("D" Company), H.M. Dillon ("A" Company), R.C. Evelegh ("C" Company), G. Blewitt ("D" Company), P. Godsal ("B" Company), Lieutenants R.B. Crosse (Adjutant), W.E.C. Terry (Staff Captain, 5th Infantry Brigade), W.G. Tolson ("D" Company), R.G. Worthington (Scout Officer), J.A. Southey (Machine Gun Officer), C.S. Baines ("B" Company), R.J. Brett (Transport Officer), R.M. Owen ("A" Company), H. Mockler-Ferryman ("C" Company), G.M.R. Turbutt (In charge of 1st Reinforcement), A.V. Spencer ("D" Company), Second-Lieutenants F. Pepys ("A" Company), J.S.C. Marshall ("B" Company), A.D. Tylden-Pattenson ("C" Company), P.F. Newton-King ("D" Company), P.G. Girardot ("C" Company), G.T. Button ("B" Company), A.H. Barrington-Kennett ("C" Company), Captain A.S. Field (Quartermaster), Captain L.V. Thurston (RAMC, Medical Officer). Entrained for Southampton (13th). Embarked SS *Lake Michigan* and sailed about 8 pm. Arrived Boulogne about 2.30 pm (14th) and marched to rest camp. Extracts from Colonel Davies's private diary are quoted in the Regimental Chronicle for 1914-15 and he recalls that the rest camp was 2 miles outside of town and close to the Colonne de la Grande Armée memorial. Entrained (16th) and travelled via Amiens, Albert, Arras, Douai and Cambrai to Wassigny. Marched to Mennevret (17th). Carried out 10-mile route march via Tupigny and Verly (18th). Marched via Hannappes, Etreux and Oisy to La Groise (21st), via Landrecies and

Maroilles to Pont- sur-Sambre (22nd). Moved to Genly (23rd). Arrived 3 pm and soon ordered on to Bougnies. Advanced again during evening to Frameries and then into reserve positions in the square at Pâturages. Moved to defensive positions near La Bouverie early morning (24th) and covered retirement of 2nd Worcestershire and 2nd Highland Light Infantry. Later withdrew via Eugies to Sars-la-Bruyère and took up rearguard positions – "B" and "C" Companies on right near the village, "A"and "D" Companies on western side of Bois de Montreuil. Moved to bivouacs at Bavai 5 pm. Continued retreat to Pont-sur-Sambe (25th) and then took up defence of 4 bridges – "D" Company, Aymeries; "A" Company, Aulnoye; "B" Company, Berlaimont railway bridge; "C" Company, Sassegnies railway bridge. "A" and "D" Companies relieved by French troops about 4 pm and took up outpost positions running from Monceau to Leval – "D" Company on right, "A" on the left. "A" and "D" Companies moved back (26th) to relieve French from the Aymeries and Aulnoye bridges. Colonel Davies records that the take over was difficult as he did not have the necessary password. He also notes that the French officer did not know of the relief and was unaware that the Aymeries bridge should be guarded at all. Withdrawal ordered, "A" and "D" Companies collecting "B" and "C" on the way. Colonel Davies records that the French had blown up the Berlaimont bridge and 2 officers – Captain Godsal and Second- Lieutenant Button, had been wounded by fragments from the explosion. He also notes the Battalion`s first casualty from enemy action – a signaller named Giles who had received a rifle bullet in the groin. The 3 men were taken in a motor ambulance to the nearest field hospital, but this was to be captured by the Germans the same evening. Battalion arrived Leval about 4.30 pm then moved on via Taisnieres and north-east of Le Grand Fayt to Barzy. Marched via Boué, Etreux, Guise and Mont d`Orgny to Neuvillette (27th), via La Fère to Servais (28th). Rested at Servais (29th). Continued retreat through Barisis and Coucy-le-Château to Terny (30th). Crossed the Aisne at Pommiers (31st) then on to Laversine.

SEPTEMBER

Continued march via Boursonne and Villers-Cotterêts to Cuvergnon (1st), Betz, Acy-en- Multien, Etrépilly and Chambry to Chauconin (2nd), Meaux, Trilport, Montceaux, Pierre Levée to Le Petit Courrois (3rd). Three companies took up rearguard positions near La Ferté during morning (4th) – "A" Company around L'Hôtel des Bois, "C" Company with Headquarters at La Fringale on left of main road, part of "B" Company on the right of road, remainder to the south. Enemy seen moving in large numbers eastward along the Montmirail road. Battalion later assembled and marched via

Le Gros Chêne and Pré-aux- Rats to Le Charnois. Arrived 1 am (5th) and bivouacked in a field at Le Fay Farm. First reinforcement of 90 men under Lieutenant Turbutt arrived. During the march to Le Fay the rear of the Battalion was approached by 2 men of the German Death's Head Hussars. Lieutenant Owen records that he saw the cavalrymen and invited them to surrender. The Germans complied, their lances being taken by 2 men of the Battalion and one of the horses by Lieutenant Owen. Marched via Tresmes, Faremoutiers, Hautefeuille and Lumigny to Champlet (5th). "A" and "B" Companies set up outposts on the Marles- Lumigny road, "D" Company at edge of woods around the Château of Lumigny. Colonel Davies records that the Battalion had now marched 178 miles since the 24th August with very little sleep and in broiling hot weather. Began advance (6th) moving to bivouacs just north-east of Pézarches. Marched via Mauperthuis, Saints, Beautheil, Chailly to St. Siméon (7th) then via Rebais to La Trétoire (8th). Second reinforcement under Captain C.G. Higgins arrived. Crossed the Petit Morin and halted. "D" Company sent to the east of Orly and engaged enemy in woods. One man, Private A.F. Allen, killed. Private Allen was not only the first man of the Battalion to be killed in the Great War, but also the first of the Regiment. Colonel Davies notes that he was buried on the side of the La Trétoire-Orly road close to where he fell. "D" Company returned to Battalion and advance continued to La Belle Idée. Moved off 11.30 am (9th), marching via Pavant and crossing the Marne at Charly and bivouacking at Domptin. Advanced towards Bussiares (10th) then ordered to move through Breuil and Cointicourt and attack the ridge beyond. Major Eden records in his diary that "B" and "C" Companies were involved. Colonel Davies notes that there were few of the enemy to deal with and these all fled. Upon reaching the ridge the Battalion came under shell-fire for the first time. Casualties – 1 man of "D" Company killed, 4 wounded. Moved on to bivouacs at Monnes. Continued via Neuilly-St. Front, Nanteul and Oulchy-le-Château to Beugneux (11th). Marched through Lime and Courcelles (12th) then just past Monthussart Farm "D" Company opened fire on party of Germans retreating from the west. These immediately surrendered and some 107 prisoners were taken. Later, "A" Company fired on patrol of Uhlans who were also in retreat. Continued march and billeted at Vieil Arcy. Crossed the Aisne at Pont Arcy (13th) and took up line running from Ferme-de-Metz to Soupir. "D" Company held reserve positions with Headquarters near the canal bridge west of Moussy. "A" Company fired on by German cavalry patrol early morning (14th). Came under heavy shell fire later in the day. Major Eden records that great damage was done and casualties among "A" and "B" Companies who were out in the open. Casualties – 4 killed, approximately 40 wounded. Moved during evening to Soupir. Rested in reserve throughout (15th). "C" and "D" Companies moved forward to support 4th (Guards) Brigade at La Cour-de-Soupir (16th). During the evening a shell landed among "C" Company killing Lieutenant Worthington, Lieutenant Mockler-Ferryman, Second-Lieutenant Girardot and 8 other ranks and wounding Captain Higgings, Captain Evelegh, Second-Lieutenant Tylden-Patterson and 8 other ranks. The Company were bivouacked in a large cave near La Cour-de-Soupir and were hit just as they were leaving to form up outside. Battalion moved up and relieved 2nd Grenadier Guards at La Cour-de-Soupir (17th) – "B" and "D" Companies taking over the trenches. "A" were placed at Chavonne and came under attack during day. There were no casualties and the Company rejoined the Battalion at La Cour-de-Soupir (18th). Came under attack during afternoon (19th). Enemy driven back without loss, but Captain Evelegh killed, Second-Lieutenant Barrington-Kennet mortally wounded and some 35 other casualties from shell fire. Two casualties from enemy sniping (20th). Relieved by 2nd Leinster during night (21st) and marched via Chavonne and Vieil Arcy to 1st Corps Reserve at Dhuizel. Reinforcement of 120 men under Second-Lieutenant D.H.W. Humfrey arrived (22nd). Second-Lieutenant F.W.C. Chippindale arrived from England (24th) and Captain A.W.N. Ponsonby (27th). Moved to Bourg (29th).

OCTOBER
Relieved 2nd Leinster in front line at La Cour-de-Soupir (1st). "B" Company shelled during morning (3rd) – casualties – 3 killed and 19 wounded. "A" Company casualties from shelling (4th) – 1 killed, 9 wounded. Captain E.H. Kirkpatrick, Lieutenant C.F. Murphy, Lieutenant M. ff. R. Wingfield, Second-Lieutenants H.V. Pendavis, G.W. Titherington and L.A. Filleul (Somerset Light Infantry, attached) arrived (8th). Relieved by 254th French Regiment during night (13th) and marched via Soupir and Mard to Vauxcéré . To Fismes during afternoon (14th) and entrained. Travelled via Amiens, Boulogne, Calais and St. Omer to Hazebrouck. Arrived 11.30 pm (15th) and marched to billets at Morbecque. Moved via Hazebrouck and Steenvoorde to Godewaersvelde (17th) and to Poperinghe (19th). Major Eden provides the following as a list of officers then present with the Battalion – Lieutenant-Colonel H.R. Davies (Commanding Officer), Major A.J.F. Eden (Second in Command), Lieutenant R.B. Crosse (Adjutant), Lieutenant J.A. Southey (Machine Gun Officer), Lieutenant R.J. Brett (Transport Officer), Captain A.S. Field (Quartermaster), Captain L.V. Thurston (RAMC, Medical Officer); "A" Company: Captains E.H. Kirkpatrick, H.M. Dillon, Second-Lieutenants F. Pepys, D.H.W. Humfrey, H.V. Pendavis; "B" Company: Captain H.L. Wood, Lieutenants C.S.

Bains, G.M.R. Turbutt, Second-Lieutenants J.S.C. Marshall, L.A. Filleul; "C" Company: Captain A.W.N. Ponsonby, Lieutenant C.F. Murphy, Second-Lieutenants A.D. Tylden-Patten, G.W. Titherington, F.W.C. Chippindale; "D" Company: Captain A.H. Harden, Lieutenants W.G. Tolson, A.V. Spencer, M. ff. R. Wingfield, Second-Lieutenant P.F. Newton-King. Moved forward via Elverdinghe to trenches near Pilckem (20th). Formed up on Langemarck- Zonnebeke road (21st) – Battalion's left on the Lekkerboterbeck, "C" and "D" Companies in front line, "A" and "B" Companies in support. Moved forward for attack under heavy fire. In his book *The First Seven Divisions* Lord Ernest Hamilton records that the Battalion was held up just short of the Haanebeck (Lekkerboterbeck) stream by a long hedge, interwoven with barbed wire. There was an open gate in the middle of the hedge which the leading companies attempted to pass through. "Every officer and man" Lord Hamilton notes, who attempted the passage of the gate "was mown down by machine gun fire." Attack held up by enfilade fire from the left. German trenches some 300 yards ahead near Langemarck. Colonel Davies records that he reached a position at the farm on the St. Julien-Poelcappelle road subsequently known as "New House." He notes that the Battalion had had it's – "first big fight", the men "advancing splendidly", officers and NCO's doing their duty "magnificently." Casualties – Captain Harden, Lieutenants Turbutt, Murphy, Second-Lieutenant Filleul killed, Second-Lieutenant Marshal mortally wounded, 5 other officers wounded, 61 other ranks killed, 143 wounded. Three men were missing believed killed. Enemy attacked about 5.30 pm (22nd). Colonel Davies records that men of "C" Company situated on the St. Julien-Poelcappelle road where the Lekkerboterbeek crossed the road opened fire on the enemy who withdrew. Casualties – 7 killed, 8 wounded. German casualties found next morning to be about 70 killed, 4 wounded. Enemy attacked at 5.30 pm (23rd) and were again driven back. Casualties – Captain Ponsonby and Second- Lieutenant Humfrey wounded, 2 other ranks killed, 5 wounded. Relieved by French troops during night and marched via St. Jean and Potijze to the railway halt at Hell Fire Corner on the Ypres-Menin road. Arriving 5 am (24th). Later moved forward to western side of Polygon Wood – "B" Company in support of 20th Brigade in trenches north-east end of wood. Remaining 3 companies ordered down to Menin road during afternoon to take up support positions at cross roads near the 9th kilometre stone just beyond Gheluvelt. Later returned to Polygon Wood and moved to Veldhoek. Relieved Scots Guards in trenches north-eastern sector of Polygon Wood (25th). "B" Company rejoined. Moved to Glencorse Wood in reserve (26th). Colonel Davies records that upon arrival the Battalion was immediately sent back to Polygon Wood to act as support to 6th Brigade but returned to reserve same night. Battalion again sent up to Polygon Wood (27th), returning same day. Took over trenches north-east corner of Polygon Wood (28th). Came under heavy shell fire – 1 man killed, 18 wounded including Lieutenant Wingfield. Moved to reserve line at north-west corner of Polygon Wood (29th). Moved to reserve position west of Zwarteleen (30th) and dug trenches overlooking the road and railway line. "A" and "B" Companies sent forward during night to trenches near Groenenberg Farm. "C" and "D" Companies moved to Shrewsbury Forest (31st) and were later joined by "A" and "B" Companies who had retired from advancing enemy. Enemy engaged and driven back. Casualties – 9 killed, 36 wounded.

NOVEMBER

Positions in Shrewsbury Forest held under heavy shell fire (1st) then withdrawal to road at north-west edge of wood ordered. "D" Company took part in counter-attack and some ground retaken. Battalion Casualties – 17 killed, 48 wounded, 9 missing. Enemy attack driven off by "D" Company (2nd). Two companies moved up to forward line during night. Enemy approached to within 30 yards of line held by "A" Company (3rd) and were driven off by Second-Lieutenants Pepys and Pendavis with 2 men – Hall and Merry. Some 30 of the enemy were killed, Pepys and Pendavis later being awarded the Distinguished Service Order and Hall and Merry the Distinguished Conduct Medal. Several shells fell on the Battalion's Transport back at Hell Fire Corner wounding 1 officer and 4 other ranks. Second-Lieutenant J.B.M. Ward arrived during night with draft of 120 men. Nine wounded from shelling (4th). Enemy attack driven off (6th). Casualties – Second-Lieutenant Ward and 1 man killed, 6 wounded. Relieved by 1/14th London early morning (9th) and marched via Zillebeke to Corps Reserve bivouacs near Verlorenhoek. Moved forward to Westhoek (11th) and took part in attack on Nonne Bosschen Wood. "A" and "B" Companies led assault, followed by "C" and "D", and cleared the enemy from their trenches. Colonel Davies records that the Germans, men of the Potsdam Guards, had very little fight in them as they had been under artillery fire for some time. They either ran off or surrendered. Casualties – 5 killed, 22 wounded. Battalion assembled to the east of southern edge of the wood. Dug trenches between Nonne Bosschen Wood and Polygon Wood (12th). Positions shelled throughout day – Second-Lieutenant Pepys and 8 other ranks killed, 14 wounded. Relieved during evening (14th) by 1/1st Hertfordshire and to Molenaarelsthoek. Moved to trenches near Westhoek (15th). Relieved during evening (16th) and via Potijze to Ypres. Took over billets near canal on north-west side of town. Casualties – 2 killed, 3 wounded from shells while waiting near Ypres for directions to billets. Marched via Westouetre and Locre to Bailleul (18th). Relieved 1st Gloucestershire in trenches near Wytschaete (25th). Relieved by 1st Lincolnshire during night (27th) and to Bailleul.

DECEMBER

Moved by motor buses via Hazebrouck and Merville to La Coutre (23rd). Relieved 39th Gharwal Rifles in trenches near Richebourg St. Vaast (27th). British shell fell short (28th) killing 1 man and wounding another. Relieved during evening (29th) by 1/9th Highland Light Infantry and to billets at Richebourg St. Vaast. Relieved 2nd Highland Light Infantry in trenches (31st). *The Oxfordshire & Buckinghamshire Light Infantry Chronicle 1914-1915* provides the following information regarding the Battalion's service in France and Belgium during 1914: Casualties – 3 officers killed, 18 wounded; 150 other ranks killed, 450 wounded; admitted to hospital for sickness – 459; reinforcements – 25 officers, 952 other ranks; honours bestowed – 5 Distinguished Service Orders, 1 Legion of Honour, 1 Médaille Militaire, 8 Distinguished Conduct Medals, 4 promoted from the ranks to Second-Lieutenants.

ESSEX REGIMENT

"Le Cateau" "Retreat from Mons"
"Marne, 1914" "Aisne, 1914" "Messines, 1914"
"Armentières, 1914"

2ND BATTALION

AUGUST
Chatham. Part of 12th Brigade, 4th Division. Entrained for Cromer (7th).
To Norwich (10th), Harrow (18th). Entrained at Wembley Park for
Southampton (22nd). Embarked SS *Corsican* and sailed for France. Officers
– Lieutenant-Colonel F.G. Anley (Commanding Officer), Major G.M.
Tufnell (Second-in-Command), Captains W.M.C. Vandeleur, F.W.
Moffitt, C.F.de B. Boone, A.C. Halahan, C.J. Ryan, W.J. Maule, L.C.
Brodie, L.O.W. Jones (Adjutant), Lieutenants J. Vance, G.C. Binstead,
A.E. Maitland, A.F.H. Round, R.V. Read, J.W. Atkinson, A.J.R. Waller,
S.G. Freestone (Quartermaster), G.R. Howard, G.E.A. Northey, A.
Gardiner, J.G.H. Kennefick, Second-Lieutenants B.S. Smith-Masters,
N.M.S. Irwin, W.P. Spooner, J.P. Pearce. Landed Havre (24th) and to No.2
Rest Camp. Entrained same night for Bertry near Le Cateau. Arrived (25th)
and later marched via Montigny, Caudry and B,thencourt to bivouacs near
Prayelle. "A" and "B" Companies moved to Longsart, "C" and "D" back
to Béthencourt then via Ligny and Hancourt to Esnes. Enemy attacked "A"
and "B" Companies' positions on the Longsart Ridge (26th). "C" and "D"
Companies moving forward in support. Withdrawal ordered and Battalion
fell back to positions on the Hancourt-Esnes road. Came under shell fire
and about 5 pm and later retired via Selvigny to Vendhuille. Casualties –
Captain Vandeleur, Lieutenant Northey killed, Lieutenant Round mortally
wounded, 90 other ranks killed, 1 officer, 40 other ranks wounded, 98
missing. Retreated via Ronssoy, Râperie and Hervilly to Hancourt (27th).
Moved off again 10.30 pm and marched through night via Vraignes,
Mérancourt, Monchy-Lagache, Croix-Molignaux, Matigny and Voyennes,
arriving Sancourt 10 am (28th). Continued retreat, marching at 2 pm via
Offoy and Esmery-Hallon to bivouacs at Campagne. Moved through
Chevilly, La Cressonière, Sermaize, Noyon, Pont- l`Evâque and Sempigny
to Les Cloyes (29th), via Bailly, Tracy-le-Mont and Berneuil to Breuil
(30th), via Neufontaines to Verberie (31st).

SEPTEMBER

Marched via St. Vaast-de-Longmont to Ducy Baron (1st), via Montagny and Les Plessis to Dammartin-en-Goële (2nd). Continued through night via Juilly, Nantouillet, St. Mesmes, Messy, Claye-Souilly, Annet and Thrigny to Lagny. Marched (3rd) from Serris via Jossigny to Ferrières. Battalion bivouacked on the estate of Baron Rothschild. John Burrows in his history of the 2nd Essex, tells how a very "muddy and dirty" individual, dressed in the uniform of a French army private, informed Colonel Anley that dinner for the officers would be served at the Château. The soldier turned out to be no other than the Baron himself. Marched via Pontcarr, and Chevry to Brie-comte-Robert (5th). Began advance to the Aisne (6th), arriving at La Haute Maison (7th) and La Ferté (8th). John Burrows records street fighting took place at La Ferté and the enemy cleared from south side of town. Crossed the Marne at Chamigny (9th) and bivouacked on road ¼ mile to the north-west. To Cerfroid (10th), Noroy (11th), L'Evêque (12th). Moved through Billy-sur-Aisne (13th), crossed the Aisne at Venizel then via Bucy-le-Long advanced on Ste. Marguerite. Dug in on high ground north of the village during night. Casualties – 10 killed, 32 wounded. Held positions under shell fire. Casualties (15th-30th) – 4 killed, 51 wounded. Captain de B. Boon mortally wounded.

OCTOBER

Relieved (1st) and via Ste. Marguerite to Missy-sur-Aisne. To Septmonts (7th). Travelled in buses to Le Meux (11th) and from there by train to Hazebrouck. Moved forward to Rouge Croix (13th) then took part in attack on the Meteren Ridge. Enemy trenches taken north of village. Casualties – 4 killed, 21 wounded. Moved forward to Bailleul (14th) and to Le Leuthe (15th). Marched via Petit Pont to Ploegsteert Wood (16th) then back via Ploegsteert and Gouplines into reserve at Armentières (18th). Back to Ploegsteert (19th). "D" Company took part in fighting around Le Gheer (21st). Lieutenant Vance killed, 68 other casualties. Battalion moved to Messines sector, "B" Company taking part in successful counter-attack at Despierre Farm (22nd). Relieved by 1st Connaught Rangers (23rd) and to positions north-west of Messines in support of 1st Cavalry Division. Moved later to trenches at Le Bizet. Relieved and to Armentières (26th). "A" and "B" Companies to trenches outside Chapelle d'Armentières (27th). Battalion took over firing line south of Pont Edal Farm railway crossing (28th). Enemy attack repulsed (31st).

NOVEMBER
Attack on "D" Company's line repulsed (4th). Relieved later and to Chapelle d'Armentières. Relieved 1st King's Own in trenches at Chapelle d'Armentières (6th). Battalion's line on the Lille road just north of Rue du Bois. Enemy attack on left repulsed (11th) – 2 killed, 12 wounded. Relieved by 2nd Leinster (13th) then to trenches running from the Le Gheer cross-roads to the River Warnave. Relieved by 1st East Lancashire (21st) and to line running from the Warne to Le Touquet. 1/2nd Monmouthshire attached for training (22nd). Captain A.H.P. Rose killed.

DECEMBER
Relieved by 1/2nd Monmouthshire (2nd) and via Ploegsteert to Armentières. Carried out further tours in firing line, being relieved by 1/2nd Monmouthshire and resting at Le Bizet and Nieppe.

SHERWOOD FORESTERS (NOTTINGHAMSHIRE AND DERBYSHIRE REGIMENT)

"Aisne, 1914" "Armentières, 1914"

1ST BATTALION

AUGUST

Bombay and Deololi, India. Placed on war footing and by (8th) providing guards at Bombay Docks, Butcher Island Wireless Station, Elephata and Fort Colaba.

SEPTEMBER

Embarked SS *Thongwa* (2nd) and sailed for England (3rd).

OCTOBER

Arrived Plymouth (2nd). Entrained for Romsey (3rd) and from there marched to camp at Hursley Park near Winchester. Joined 24th Brigade, 8th Division. Records note that the battalion spent 3 weeks in their foreign service khaki drill uniforms, no service dress being available.

NOVEMBER

Marched to Southampton (4th) and embarked SS *Cardiganshire*. Officers present – Lieutenant-Colonel W.R. Marshall (Commanding Officer), Majors C.R. Mortimore, L. St. H. Morley, Captains S.M. Castle, M.B. Webb, H.B.T. Hume, H.B. Dixon, M.K. Hodgson, W.T. Stackhouse, A.E. Bankhead-Browne (4th North Staffordshire attached), W.P.A. Campbell (4th South Staffordshire attached), H.L. Howell (RAMC, Medical Officer), Lieutenants R.L. Sherbrooke, J.A.M. Lang, R.B. Young, R.E.F. Wyncoll, G.S. Dobbie, A.J. Goodwyn, A.H. Jackson, J.P. Wylie, R.H. Stranger (Adjutant), L. Wright (Quartermaster), J.H.M. Douglas (Transport Officer), MacL.P. Dilworth (Machine Gun Officer), Second-Lieutenants J.E. A. O'Dwyer, E.M. Williamson, C.R. Chambers, F. Wells, W.M. Smalley, G.S. Shacklock, J.A. Walker. Sailed for France (5th). Arrived Havre and to No.6 Rest Camp. Entrained for Merville (9th). Detrained (10th) and to billets at Neuf Berquin. Lieutenant-Colonel Marshall recalls in his book *Memories of Four Fronts* the keenness of the French to obtain from his men mementos such as cap badges and buttons. The British soldier was indeed constantly pestered by local people with cries of "Souvenir, Souvenir" everywhere he went. One day at Merville, a lorry ran over and killed a pig. The driver, the Colonel recollects, stopped his vehicle got out, and placed the dead animal inside. He then drove off waving his hand at the angry crowd and saying "Souvenir, Souvenir." Moved via Estaires to billets near Vieille Chapelle (14th). To Brigade Reserve billets near Pont-du-Hem (15th) – "A" and "C" Companies going into front line tenches along the Estaires-La Bassée road facing Neuve Chapelle. Companies attached to 2nd East Lancashire and 2nd Northamptonshire. Regimental historian – Colonel H.C. Wylly records the words of a platoon commander who noted ammunition being wasted at an incredible rate and that 98 percent of "A" and "C" Companies had never been under fire. First casualty (17th) – Private Backhouse of "C" Company killed. Battalion relieved 1st Worcestershire in front line (19th) and carried out 3-day tours in the trenches, resting at Red Barn and Rouge Croix. Lieutenant Dilworth shot (20th) while inspecting a house some 40 yards in front of the trenches. Captain Campbell killed (22nd) during attempt to bring in his body. Captain Hodgson notes in a letter (25th) that with a few exceptions the Germans are poor shots. Colonel Wylly records – "Hodgson had bad luck to meet one of the `exceptions` – being slightly wounded (26th)." Withdrew to billets near Estaires end of month. Casualties for November – 2 officers and 16 other ranks killed, 2 officers and 66 other ranks wounded, 1 man missing.

DECEMBER

Lined streets of La Gorgue upon visit of HM The King (1st). Returned to trenches. Second-Lieutenant Smalley killed by sniper while at Port Arthur (9th). Lieutenant-Colonel Marshall recalls that the shot came from the same house that Lieutenant Dilworth was inspecting when he was killed. He also notes that another bullet from the same building hit a cigarette case in his breast pocket. Fortunately only producing a slight flesh-wound. Captain Hodgson in a letter recalls the Colonel's lucky escape mentioning that bullets cut straps on his chest, smashed a button and made a graze below his heart. Relieved and to Estaires (14th). Here boxes and parcels sent out by the people of the City and County of Nottingham were distributed. To Red Barn (18th) and then to trenches. War Diary records (24th) the men started on some of the 1,100 plum puddings sent out from Nottingham. Christmas truce (25th). Lieutenant Dilworth's body collected and buried. Relieved 2nd East Lancashire in front line during night. End of month, War Diary records casualties – 3 officers and 31 other ranks killed, 5 officers and 101 other ranks wounded.

2ND BATTALION

AUGUST

Sheffield. Part of 18th Brigade, 6th Division. To Edinburgh (7th). Billeted in the Cavalry Barracks, Piershill then later to camp at King's Park. Moved to Cambridge (13th).

SEPTEMBER

To Newmarket (7th) and entrained for Southampton. Embarked SS *Georgian* and sailed for France (8th). Officers – Lieutenant-Colonel C.R. Crofton-Atkins (Commanding Officer), Majors P. Leveson Gower (Second in Command), R.J.F. Taylor, Captains B.G.V. Way, MVO, C.C. Parkinson, MVO, R.S.Popham, DSO, G.F. Luther, J.H. Mathias, W.R. Friend (Adjutant), F. Tomlinson (Quartermaster), R.D. O'Connor (RAMC, Medical Officer), Lieutenants G.D. Edwards (Brigade Machine Gun Officer), L.A. Bernard, B.C. Ash, J. MacD. Needham, R.R. Shawcross (Machine Gun Officer), P.M. Murray, Second-Lieutenants H.L. Paddock (Transport Officer), R.E.C. Weigall, I.G. Macbean, H.B.D. Willcox, W.A.W. Crellin, R.D.P. Milner, J.D'A. Whicher, H.L.C. Smith, B.G. Allen. Arrived off St. Nazaire (9th). Landed (10th) and entrained (11th) for Coulommiers. Arrived (12th) and to billets at Douai. Began move towards the Aisne, marching via St. Cyr, Manteuil Sur Marne, Romeny, Château Thierry, Chacrise, Dhuizel. Arrived Bourg (19th) and relieved 1st Black Watch in trenches near Vendresse. Later relieved by 1st Gloucestershire and to reserve line just north of Troyon. Enemy broke through front line (20th) and "A" and "C" Companies went forward to counter-attack. Colonel H.C. Wylly, CB records in his war history of the Sherwood Foresters that German machine guns were quickly brought into action, many casualties being caused not only in the leading companies, but also "B" and "C" coming up in the second line. Battalion pushed on and eventually cleared enemy from 1st West Yorkshire trenches. Captain Friend killed (21st). Line held until relieved (22nd) then moved back to Brigade Reserve at Troyon. Casualties – Lieutenants Bernard, Ash, Murray, Second-Lieutenant Milner killed, 8 other officers wounded, 44 other ranks killed, 165 wounded. Colonel Wylly brings his readers' attention to the fact that exactly 60 years ago to the day – 20th September, 1854, the Battalion (then 95th Regiment) had stormed up the slopes of the Alma. This action in the Crimea being likened to events of 20th September, 1914 and the climb up to the trenches on the Chemin des Dames. Coincidentally, Colonel Wylly notes, the casualties figures at the Alma were almost identical – 6 officers killed, 11 wounded; 46 other ranks killed, 168 wounded. Withdrew to billets at Pargnan (24th).

OCTOBER
Relieved 1st West Yorkshire in support line north-east of Troyon (1st). Later moved to Vauxtin area. Marched via Braisne, Courville and Serches to Jury (2nd). Marched via Largny and St. Sauveur to St. Remy (6th). Entrained for St. Omer (9th). Arrived (10th) and to billets at Arques. Marched to Wardrecques (11th) then by lorries to Hazebrouck. To Vieux Berquin area (12th). Advanced to Steenwerck (15th) then in evening crossed the Lys and cleared enemy from Sailly. Later dug in 300-400 yards south of town. Continued advance and relieved 2nd Durham Light Infantry east and south sides of Ennetièrs during night (18th). Enemy attacked (20th) and ordered to fall back to high ground at La Vallée. Retiring troops later became surrounded and forced to surrender. Survivors of Battalion – 2 officers, 49 other ranks, held ridge near the windmill at La Vallée and drove off German's last attack at 7.30 pm. Later moved back to Fetus, then Bois Grenier. Brigadier-General W.N. Congreve, VC (18th Brigade Commander) wrote to the Colonel of the Regiment and noted how 2nd Sherwood Foresters had held their line at Ennetièrs under constant attack for 48 hours and on 20th October were – ". . . just worn out and over-whelmed by superior numbers." Colonel Wylly refers to a German book – *Die Schlachten und Gefechte des Grossen Krieges* that gives the attacking force on 20th October at Ennetières and La Vallèe as 1 division plus 1 infantry brigade. Colonel Wylly also points out the difficulty of determining casualties for the period (18th-20th). Much of the Battalion's documents and rolls being lost. He provides the following figures, however, as approximately correct – Captain G.L. Anson, Second-Lieutenant Smith, A.G. Browne killed, 3 other officers wounded, 10 captured. Of the other ranks, 710 were either killed, wounded or taken prisoner. Headquarters and transport details later joined the 2 officers and 49 other ranks at Bois Grenier, bringing total strength up to 4 officers and 253 other ranks. Drafts received (26th) and (30th).

NOVEMBER
Began tours in trenches around Rue du Bois during first week.

DECEMBER
Relieved by 1st East Yorkshire (7th). Later moved to Pont de Nieppe and held in reserve for attack by 4th Division. Returned to billets in Armentières (23rd). Took over trenches in Houplines sector during last days of the month.

LOYAL NORTH LANCASHIRE REGIMENT

"Mons" "Retreat from Mons" "Marne, 1914" "Aisne, 1914" "Ypres, 1914" "Langemarck, 1914" "Gheluvelt" "Nonne Bosschen" "Givenchy, 1914"

1ST BATTALION

AUGUST

Tournay Barracks, Aldershot. Part of 2nd Brigade, 1st Division. Entrained at Farnborough for Southampton (12th). Embarked SS *Agapenor* and sailed for France. Officers – Lieutenant-Colonel G.C. Knight (Commanding Officer), Majors W.R. Lloyd, A. Burrows, Captains G.T. Body, R.H. Watson, H.L. Helme, A. W. Colley, L.T. Allason, B.J. Wakley, R. Howard-Vyse (Adjutant), W.C. Nimmo (RAMC, Medical Officer), Lieutenants E.J.W. Spread, G.H. Goldie, H.R. Loomes, J.G. Halsted, E.F. Cunningham, F. Robinson, R.C. Mason, J.G.W. Hyndson, E. Wilkinson (Quartermaster), Second-Lieutenants S.H. Batty- Smith, H.L.L. Knowles, N. Collins, W.R.L. Calow, C.E. Wallis, G.C. Kingsley. Arrived Havre (13th) and to rest camp. Entrained for Le Nouvion (14th). Arriving (15th) and marching to billets at Esquehéries. Advanced via Le Nouvion, Fontanelle and Floyon to Avesnes (20th). To Villers-sire-Nicole (22nd), Givry (23rd). Withdrew via Villers-sire-Nicole and Battignes to Feignies (24th), via Maubeuge to Marbaix (25th), Le Grand Fayt and Favril to Oisy (26th), Wassigny, Venerolles, Hannappée, Vadencourt and Noyale to Hauteville (27th), Lucy to Fressancourt (28th), to Anizy-le-Château (30th), via Soissons to Villers-Cotterêts (31st).

SEPTEMBER

Continued retreat via Meaux and La Ferté, arriving Aulnoy (4th). To Bernay (5th). Began advance (6th), crossing the Marne at Nogent (9th). In reserve during the fighting around Priez (10th). Casualties – 3 other ranks killed, 2 officers, 24 other ranks wounded. Lieutenant-Colonel Knight mortally wounded by shrapnel. Moved forward to Coincy (11th), Paars (12th). Crossed the Aisne at Bourg (13th) then to billets at Moulins. Advanced to Vendresse (14th) then took part in attack on Troyon. Casualties – Major Lloyd, Captains Body, Watson, Helme, Howard-Vyse, Lieutenants Goldie, Loomes, Mason and Robinson killed or mortally wounded, 5 officers wounded, over 500 other ranks killed, wounded or missing. Colonel H.C. Wylly in his history of the Loyal North Lancashire

Regiment notes that many of the casualties were from "B" Company, 3 out of 5 officers and 175 out of 200 other ranks being lost. He also records that the positions held were – "tolerably quiet" (15th), the Battalion's trenches being just below the crest of the hill. Enemy attack repulsed (16th). Relieved by 1st East Yorkshire (19th) and via Vendresse moved into billets at Pargnan. Relieved 1st West Yorkshire in front line (25th).

OCTOBER
Shell landed at door of Officers' Mess (7th) killing Captain Allason and Second-Lieutenant Calrow and wounding 2 others. Relieved by French troops (15th) and marched via Vendresse, Bourg and Longueville to Vauxcéré. Entrained at Fismes for Cassel (18th). Marched via Steenevoorde and Poperinghe to Boesinghe (20th) then forward via St. Jean to Pilckem (22nd). Took part in attack (23rd), Battalion charging forward with 2nd King's Royal Rifle Corps and with fixed bayonets cleared the enemy from their trenches. Some 600 prisoners taken. Held gains until relieved by French troops during night (24th). Moved back through Pilckem to Ypres. Casualties – Captain E.C. Miller and Second-Lieutenant Kingsley killed, 4 officers wounded, 178 other ranks killed, wounded or missing. Advanced through Hooge to Herenthage Château Wood (27th). Moved forward with 2nd King's Royal Rifle Corps during afternoon (29th). Came under heavy shell fire and attack held up just east of Gheluvelt. Dug in during night north of village. Line held under heavy shell fire throughout (30th). Withdrew to Hooge (31st) then advanced again 9 am. Took part in attack on enemy positions around Gheluvelt. Lieutenant Wilkinson killed. Colonel Wylly records that the assault was successful, a bayonet charge inflicting heavy casualties on the enemy. He also notes considerable losses among the Battalion. Casualties uncertain, but estimated at approximately 8 officers and 400 other ranks. Relieved during night and to Hooge.

NOVEMBER
Captain H.F.B. Ryley killed (2nd), Major A.J. Carter, DSO, Captain J.F. Allen (4th). Relieved 1st Royal Berkshire in front line (7th). Came under attack (8th). Enemy gained some ground, but later reclaimed by counter-attack. Captains A.G.M. Slade and A.L. Prince killed. Relieved during night (9th) and to trenches near Hooge. Took part in counter attack near Nonne Bosschen (10th). Moving back into reserve after dusk. Relieved (14th) and to billets at Vlamertinghe. Later moved to Hazebrouck.

DECEMBER

Moved in buses to Vieille Chapelle (21st) then advanced to Le Touret. Took part in attack to regain lost trenches near the orchard north-east of Festubert. Went forward 7.20 pm and objective gained within the hour. Casualties – Captains G.H. Smart (West Yorkshire attached) and G.M. Graham (Worcestershire attached) killed, 4 officers wounded, 408 other ranks killed, wounded or missing. Relieved and to Essars. Later to Cambrin.

NORTHAMPTONSHIRE REGIMENT

**"Mons" "Retreat from Mons" "Marne, 1914"
"Aisne, 1914" "Ypres, 1914" "Langemarck, 1914"
"Gheluvelt" "Nonne Bosschen" "Givenchy, 1914"**

1ST BATTALION

AUGUST

Blackdown. Part of 2nd Brigade, 1st Division. Entrained at Frimley for Southampton (12th) and embarked SS *Galeka*. Sailed for France 5 pm. Arrived Havre early morning (13th) and to No.2 Rest Camp just north of Le Hanail on the Octeville road. Officers – Lieutenant-Colonel E.O. Smith (Commanding Officer), Major H.H. Norman (Second in Command), Captains H. Lloyd (Adjutant), B.B. Dickson (Machine Gun Officer), Lieutenants E.G. Warren (Transport Officer), A. Hofman (Quartermaster); "A" Company: Captains R.E. Gordon, G.W. Hunt, Lieutenants C.L. Wauchope, C.H. Bacon, Second- Lieutenant L.H.B. Burlton; "B" Company: Captains E.L. Hughes, E.E. White, Lieutenants G.M. Fraser, W.J. Jervois, G.G.B. Paget; "C" Company: Captains R.B. Parker, G.M. Bentley, Lieutenants J.H. Farrar, E.J. Needham, Second-Lieutenants A.S.G. Jarvis, C.G. Gordon; "D" Company: Captains H. Cartwright, J.A. Savage, Lieutenant G.St.G. Robinson, Second-Lieutenants G.D. Gordon, A.N. Sherriff. Entrained for Etreux (15th). Arrived (16th) and to Esqueheries. To Etroeungt (21st), via Beaufort and Maubeuge to Villers-sire- Nicole (22nd). To Rouveroy (23rd). Later "A", "B" and "C" Companies moved forward via Givry to Vellereille-le-Sac in support of 1st Royal Berkshire. Retreated via Givry to Maubeuge (24th), to Marbaix (25th), to Favreuil then Oisy (26th), Wassigny (27th). Enemy patrol engaged. Later came under shell fire and infantry attack. Retreated during afternoon to Hauteville. At Hauteville the Royal Scots Greys were seen. The men having been in action throughout the retreat from Mons were cheered by the Battalion as they passed by. It was noted in the Regimental records that the grey horses had been covered in some kind of wash giving them a khaki appearance. Moved to high ground near Thenel (28th) and covered retreat of 1st Division across the River Oise. Later withdrew to Ribemont then La Fère. Marched via the Forêt de Coucy to Anizy le Château (30th) then via Soissons to bivouacs near Corcy (31st).

SEPTEMBER

To Mareuil and blew up bridges over the River Ourcq (1st), bivouacs north of Meaux (2nd), La Ferté then Romemy (3rd), Aulnoy (4th), Bonnay (5th). War Diary notes that losses at this time were not more than 70. Began advance and marched to Pezarches (6th), via Mauperthuis and Chailly to St. Siméon (7th), La Tretoire then Rebais (8th). Crossed the Marne at Nogent (9th) and moved forward. Took part in the attack on Priez (10th) – "A" and "B" Companies advancing during evening to occupy positions on ridge east of Rassey. Casualties – 5 officers wounded, 3 other ranks killed, 20 wounded. Moved forward to Coincy (11th), Paars (12th), Moulins (13th). Took part in attack on Troyon (14th). War Diary notes that when dusk fell, "B" Company had fought its way up to the Chemin des Dames. Casualties – Captain White, Lieutenant Paget killed, 4 officers wounded, 102 other ranks killed, wounded or missing. Battalion dug in and held positions. Captain Gordon killed (15th). Enemy attacked and took some ground (17th). Trenches retaken after bayonet charge by "C" Company. Captain Parker killed. Second-Lieutenant Burlton was in charge of "B" Company when the Germans opposite indicated that they wished to surrender. His account of the incident is recorded in *The Northamptonshire Regiment 1914-1918* and tells how both sides eventually met in No Man's Land. There were some 70 men from the Battalion and approximately 400 Germans. Some of the enemy handed over their rifles but one man opened fire and shot one of the Northamptons. Second-Lieutenant Burlton immediately complained to the German officer in charge, but he replied that Burlton was in fact his prisoner. Hand-to-hand fighting broke out -"The men used their butts and bayonets lustily." Observing the situation, 1st Queen's opened fire with their machine guns which cut through the German troops forcing the survivors to run back to their lines. A second offer to surrender by those that remained was ignored. Another officer, Captain Savage, was involved in the same incident and was shot in the back while returning from negotiations with the enemy troops opposite. Second-Lieutenant Gordon was also killed. Relieved (19th) and to billets at Pargan. Carried out further tours in firing line, resting between reliefs in the caves at Paissy.

OCTOBER

Relieved by French troops during night (16th) and to billets at Vauxere. To Fismes (18th) and entrained for Cassel. Marched via Poperinghe to Elverdinghe (20th) and through Ypres to Pilckem (21st). Took part in counter-attack (22nd). Captain W.R. Russell killed. Held trenches against several attacks. Medical Officer Captain M.J. Lochrin killed (23rd). Relieved by French troops during night (24th) and moved back into billets at Pilckem. Casualties – Captain Bentley mortally wounded, 6 officers wounded, approximately 150 other ranks killed, wounded or missing. To Ypres (25th). Moved forward to Hooge (26th) then positions at Harenthage Château Wood (27th), Western edge of Polygon Wood (28th). Returned to Harenthage Château Wood (29th). Took part in fighting at Bodmin Copse and Shrewsbury Forest (30th/31st). Second-Lieutenants Sherriff and Jarvis killed, 100 other casualties.

NOVEMBER
Relieved in Shrewsbury Wood by 2nd Royal Sussex (4th) and withdrew to close support positions. To front line (7th). Relieved (8th) and to reserve trenches just south of Hooge. To support line (9th), eastern edge of Nonne Bosschen Wood (11th). Took part in attack on Polygon Wood, leading companies coming under machine gun fire from houses south of the Reutel road. Enemy attacked and line held. Major Norman killed. Relieved (15th) and to Vlamertinghe. Regimental history records that Battalion now comprised just 350 other ranks and 5 officers – Lieutenant Farrar, Second-Lieutenant C.S. Cowley, the Quartermaster, Lieutenant Hofman and the new Medical Officer, Lieutenant W.J. Adie. Lieutenant Lewis of the Royal West Kent Regiment was attached. Marched to Westoutre (16th), Strazeele (17th), Hazebrouck (19th).

DECEMBER
Moved in buses to Vieille Chapelle (21st) then marched forward to Le Touret. Later took part in operations to regain lost trenches near La Quinque Rue. "A" and "D" Companies moving forward at 7 pm and gaining objective by 10 pm. Second-Lieutenants J.T.R. Pastfield (Middlesex Regiment attached) and G.C. Wainwright killed, approximately 60 other casualties. "D" Company held off German counter attack (22nd). Relieved and to Essars. Took over trenches east of Givenchy (26th).

2ND BATTALION

AUGUST
Mustapha Barracks, Alexandria, Egypt. The regimental history notes the training of Europeans residing in Alexandria and the rounding up of a number of spies. There is also mention of 3 officers who had proceeded home on leave just before war was declared. Their German East Africa vessel changing course from Southampton to Hamburg. While at Marseilles, however, the officers left the ship and made their way across France.

OCTOBER

Sailed for England SS. *Deseado* at beginning of month. Arrived Liverpool (16th) and entrained for Winchester. Marched to camp at Hursley Park and joined 24th Brigade, 8th Division.

NOVEMBER

Marched to Southampton (4th) and sailed SS *Turcoman* for France. Arrived Havre (5th) and marched to rest camp outside of town. Officers present – Lieutenant-Colonel C.S. Prichard (Commanding Officer), Major C.E. Higginbotham (Second in Command), Captain H. Power (Adjutant), Lieutenant R. Mayes (Quartermaster), Lieutenant U. Rastrick (Machine Gun Officer), Lieutenant B.O. Smyth (Transport Officer), Lieutenant O. Ryan (RAMC, Medical Officer); "A" Company: Captains J.I. Wood-Martin, O. Oakes (Yorkshire Regiment attached), Lieutenants St. J.C. Stocker, S.H. Sprey-Smith, Second- Lieutenant G.A. Parker; "B" Company: Captains L.J. Robinson, L.A. Haldane, Lieutenants A.D. Middleton, R.E. Lucy, Second-Lieutenants C.Z. de la P. Beresford, E.B.L. Rushton; "C" Company: Captains A.G.C. Capell, C.D. Elston, Lieutenants S.H. Beattie, R.D. Lake, G.T. Shaw, Second-Lieutenant C. Belding; "D" Company: Captains C.R.J. Mowatt, C.H.R. Watts, Lieutenants H.W. Jackson, W.G.A. Coldwell, O.K. Parker, Second-Lieutenant G.D. Gordon. Entrained for Merville (9th) and from there marched to billets at Vieux Berquin. Relieved 2nd Suffolk in front line trenches along western edge of the Estaires-La Bassée road facing Neuve Chapelle (14th). First tour in trenches lasting 7 days. At Brigade Reserve billets at Red Barn the men were able to remove their boots for the first time in over a week. Next day more than 100 went sick with frostbite. Returned to trenches and carried out tours in the line for remainder of year. Rest areas at Red Barn, Estaires and La Gorgue. Much detail regarding life in and out of the trenches is provided by regimental records (compiled under direction of the Regimental History Committee). On one occasion an alleged spy was captured by "C" Company. Wearing a dark blue greatcoat and speaking with difficulty, the captive turned out to be a British soldier wounded in the mouth and on his way to a first-aid post. Loopholes placed in the parapet proved to be dangerous, enemy marksmen managing to hit their targets through these with ease. Casualties due to weather conditions and mud, however, are noted as being – "worse even than the risk from a sniper's bullet." Minor cases of frostbite were not excused duty in the trenches. "Slow marching parties" were organized which would set out for the line some 2 hours before the main body. Cooking arrangements were difficult and the men usually made their own arrangements. One party had constructed a fireplace out of what they thought were bricks. The material turned out to be hair-brush bombs caked in mud. The introduction of "Jam Tin Bombs" is noted and these were nicknamed "Ticklers Artillery" after a jam manufacturer of that name. Also mention is the issue of the battalion`s first "Stove-Pipe" trench mortar which – "after 3 or 4 rounds assumed the shape of a soda-water bottle and was not used again."

DECEMBER
Lieutenant U. Rastrick killed (14th).

PRINCESS CHARLOTTE OF WALES`S
(ROYAL BERKSHIRE REGIMENT)

"Mons" "Retreat from Mons" "Marne, 1914" "Aisne, 1914" "Ypres, 1914" "Langemarck, 1914" "Gheluvelt" "Nonne Bosschen"

1ST BATTALION

AUGUST

Mandora Barracks, Aldershot. Part of 6th Brigade, 2nd Division. Entrained at Farnborough for Southampton (12th). Embarked SS *Ardmore* and sailed for France. Officers – Lieutenant-Colonel M.D. Graham (Commanding Officer), Majors H.M. Finch (Second in Command), D.B. Maurice, DSO, F.F. Ready, DSO, A.S. Turner, Captains T.E.C. Hunt, B.G. Bromhead, L.H. Birt, H.H. Shott, DSO, Lieutenants E.A.B. Orr, U.S. Hopkins, C.W. Frizell, P.J. Reeves, C.St.Q.O. Fullbrook-Leggatt, C.P. Wheeler, J.H. Woods, A.A.H. Hanbury-Sparrow, A.H. Perrott (Adjutant), F. Batt (Quartermaster), G.H. Bishop, Second-Lieutenants T.V.B. Denniss, A.P.J. Hibbert, E.E.N. Burney, J. Ranson, Y.R.D. Wigan, G. Moore. Arrived Rouen (13th) and to Camp de Bruyères. Entrained at Rouen for Wassigny (15th). Arrived and marched to Venerolles. To Landrecies (21st), Hargnies (22nd). Moved forward via Gognies towards Mons, digging in around Villereuile-le-Sec by afternoon (23rd). Came under shell fire – 1 officer, 3 other ranks wounded. Ordered to retire and moved back via Havay to defensive positions at Bavai. Moved at 3 am (25th) via Pont-sur-Sambre to Maroilles. "B" and "D" Companies moved during night to the Sambre river crossing west of Maroilles. Took up positions by the Rue des Juifs and engaged enemy. Major Turner taken prisoner, Captain Shott killed, 1 officer wounded, 2 other ranks killed, 35 wounded, 22 missing. Withdrew later then (26th) marched via Prisches, Le Sart, Fesmy, Oisy and Etreux to Venerolles. Continued retreat via Guise to Mont d`Origny (27th), via Ribemont, Sery, Brissy, Brissy-Choigny, Le Fère, Charmes, Andelain and Servais to Chauny (28th), via Barisis and Folembray to Coucy-le-Château (30th), via Soissons and Pommiers to St. Bandry (31st).

SEPTEMBER

Marched via Coeuvres, Villers Cotterêts and Pisseleux to Thury (1st) then 2 companies sent back to assist 4th (Guards) Brigade under attack south of Villers Cotterêts. Enemy engaged and driven back – casualties – 24. To

Trilbardou (2nd), via Meaux to Bilbarteaux- les-Vannes (3rd), via La Malmaison to Mouroux (4th), Chaumes (5th). Began advance (6th) marching to Chaubuisson Farm then in evening to Château-de-la-Fontelle. Moved via Rigny, Pezarches, Touquin, La Boissière and Chailly-en-Brie to St. Siméon (7th), via Voigny, Rebais, La Trétoire, Boitron, Petit Villiers and Le Petit Basseville to La Noue (8th). Crossed the Marne at Charly (9th) then moved via Villers-sur-Marne and Domptin to Coupru. Moved forward via Marigny-en-Orxois and Bussiares (10th) then took part in the fighting at Hautevesnes. Enemy surrendered, 6th Brigade taking 400-500 prisoners. During the affair at Hautevesnes the 3rd Division`s guns shelled a party of British troops thinking they were Germans. Lieutenant Perott was among those killed. Later moved on to bivouacs at Chevillon, then (11th) via Priez, Sommelans, Breny and Oulchy to Cugny-les- Couttes. At Breny a detachment of Senegalese cavalry passed through mounted on fine Arab horses with high saddles. The men were dressed in bright scarlet robes and turbans and armed with antique pistols, daggers and scimitars. The party, which was led by a French Cuirassier in full dress uniform, was referred to by the men of 6th Brigade as "The Circus." Marched via Beugneux, Arcy, Branges, Jouaignes, Quincy and Courcelles to Monthussart Farm (12th), to Vieil-Arcy (13th). Crossed the Aisne at Pont Arcy (14th) then to Veneuil. Later took part in fighting on the Moussy Spur then dug in throughout the night – Battalion Headquarters at La Metz Farm. Casualties – Second-Lieutenant R.G.B. Perkins killed, 40 other casualties. Held positions under shell fire and several infantry attacks. Casualties (15th-21st) – 116 killed or wounded. Relieved (21st) and via Moussy to Oeuilly.

OCTOBER
Relieved from firing line by French troops (13th) and to Bourg. Entrained at Fismes (14th) for St. Omer then to Hazebrouck. To Godewaersvelde (19th), Ypres (20th), via St. Jean to Wieltje (21st). "B" Company moved to Zonnebeke to dig trenches (22nd). Rest of Battalion to Frezenberg. "B" Company rejoined (24th) then moved forward to positions north of Polygon Wood. Took part in attack on Molenaarelshoek. Moved forward on left of 1st King`s Liverpool at 3.30 pm, advancing under heavy fire from village to line on the Broodseinde road. Lieutenant L.C. Nicholson killed. Positions held. Captain O. Steele killed by shell (25th). In support of attack by 1st King's Liverpool on right (26th). Relieved during night (28th) and moved back to Brigade Reserve near Polygon Wood. Casualties (24th-28th) – 1 officer, 29 other ranks killed, 5 officers, 79 other ranks wounded. "B" Company in action (30th). 6th Brigade War Diary notes that the company did – "very good service" and cleared the enemy from several houses on the

Becelaere road. "A" and "B" Companies moved up into Polygon Wood (31st) then going forward towards Gheluvelt engaged enemy near the railway west of village. Withdrew later to Polygon Wood.

NOVEMBER

Relieved 2nd Welch in Herenthage Wood (1st). Held positions under constant bombardment and infantry attacks. Relieved by French troops (15th) and to Hooge. To Ypres (17th), Caestre (18th).

DECEMBER

Moved in buses to Béthune (22nd) then forward to trenches at Givenchy. Captain G.R. Wyld (Wiltshire attached) killed (24th). Relieved (26th) and to Essars.

2ND BATTALION

AUGUST

Jhansi, India.

SEPTEMBER

Moved to Deolali (4th) and after 5 days to Bombay. Arrived (14th) and embarked SS *Dongola*. Sailed for England (20th).

OCTOBER

Arrived Liverpool (22nd). Entrained for Winchester and then to Hursley Park Camp. Joined 25th Brigade, 8th Division.

NOVEMBER

Marched to Southampton (4th) and embarked SS *Kingstonian* for France. Arrived Havre (5th) and marched to rest camp outside of town. Strength – 30 Officers: Lieutenant-Colonel E. Feetham (Commanding Officer), Major J.G.R. Walsh (Second in Command), Captains A.G. Macdonald ("A" Company), W.B. Thornton ("C" Company), G.P.S. Hunt ("D" Company), A.E.F. Harris ("B" Company), G.H. Sawyer, A.J. Fraser, T.R. Aldworth (Adjutant), H.S. Lickman (Quartermaster), Lieutenants M.C. Radford, R.G.C. Moody-Ward, C. Nugent, D.A. MacGregor, A.D. Gordon (Machine Gun Officer), E.F. Eagar, W.A. Guest-Williams, G.C.O. Mackwood, G.C. Hodgson, A.H. Saunders (Transport Officer), Second-Lieutenants G.F. Gregory, H.R.W. Wood. Attached: Captains A.P. O'Connor (RAMC, Medical Officer), G.R. Wyld (3rd Wiltshire), L.W. Kentish (5th Royal Fusiliers), Second-Lieutenants N. West (1st Royal

Berkshire) and A.G.I. Owen, R. Crowley, A.B. Raynes, G.S. Middlemiss (all Royal Sussex). Other ranks – 978. Entrained for Strazeele (9th) and from there to billets at Merville. To Estaires (14th) and from there took over front line trenches at Fauquissart. Shared these positions with 2nd Rifle Brigade, resting between tours at Laventie.

DECEMBER
At Estaires (7th-9th). Occupied trenches at Rue Bacquerot (14th-20th). In front line at Fauquissart (25th). Captain Ralph Verney records in his book *The Joyous Patriot* that – "the Berkshires were full of the armistice" when his battalion (2nd Rifle Brigade) relieved them on (26th).

QUEEN`S OWN
(ROYAL WEST KENT REGIMENT)

"Mons" "Le Cateau" "Retreat from Mons"
"Marne, 1914" "Aisne, 1914" "La Bassée, 1914"
"Messines, 1914" "Ypres, 1914"

1ST BATTALION

AUGUST

Richmond Barracks, Dublin, Ireland. Part of 13th Brigade, 5th Division. Embarked SS *Gloucestershire* (13th), strength 26 officers, 1,015 other ranks. Officers – Lieutenant- Colonel A. Martyn (Commanding Officer), Major P.M. Buckle, DSO (Second in Command), Captain G.B. Legard (Adjutant), Lieutenants H.G. Rogers (Quartermaster), D.J. Johnston (Machine Gun Officer), W. Newton (Transport Officer), W.P. Crocker (RAMC, Medical Officer); "A" Company: Captains G.D. Lister, G.F. Keenlyside, Lieutenants P.F. Wilberforce-Bell, C.K. Anderson, Second-Lieutenants S.K. Gore, A.A.E. Chitty; "B" Company: Major C.G. Pack-Beresford, Captain W.C.O. Phillips, Lieutenants F. Fisher, D.C.C. Sewell, Second-Lieutenant M.F. Broadwood; "C" Company: Major P. Hastings, Lieutenants W.V. Palmer, C.A.M. Holloway, W.K. Ames, J.H. Whitehouse; "D" Company: Captains R.G.M. Tulloch, H.D. Buchanan-Dunlop, Lieutenants H.B.H. White, N.J.P.K. McClennand. Sailed for France 2.20 am (14th). Landed Havre during afternoon (15th) and marched to rest camp (16th). Entrained for Landrecies (17th). Arrived about midnight and to billets at La Basse Maroilles. Marched to Houdain (21st), Doué (22nd). "C" and "D" Companies took up positions on the Mons-Condé Canal, north and north-east of St. Ghislain – "C" at the road bridge, "D" on the railway crossing. "A" Company came forward from Hornu (23rd). Crossed canal and engaged advancing enemy from crossroads south of Tertre. The German writer Walter Bloem was present during the action south of Tertre (1st Battalion, 12th Brandenburg Grenadier Regiment) and recorded later in his book *The Advance from Mons, 1914* how he saw the 1st Royal West Kent coming on – "The Brandenburgers deployed and advanced by rushes, fired at by an always invisible foe and losing men every time they rise. . . the enemy seems to have waited for the moment of a general assault. He had artfully enticed us to close range in order to deal with us more surely and thoroughly. A hellish fire broke loose and in thick swathes the deadly leaden fire was pumped on our heads, breasts and knees.

Wherever I looked, to the right and left, nothing but dead, and blood-streaming, sobbing, writhing wounded." Captain Lister who led "A" Company, was wounded and taken prisoner during the action. He records how he arrived at the canal bridge about 7.50 am. Moving forward with some men from the 19th Hussars, he then observed the advancing enemy – 400-500 strong on the eastern side of the road alone. Fire was immediately opened and heavy losses were noted. Lieutenant Anderson was killed and "A" Company eventually fell back. Enemy came forward and shelled Battalion's positions at close range. Received order to retire about 7 pm, moving via St. Ghislain to Wasmes. Enemy attacked about 10 am (24th). Major Pack- Beresford, Captain Phillips, Second-Lieutenant Broadwood killed, Lieutenant Sewell mortally wounded. Fell back during afternoon to St. Waast La Vallée and marched (25th) via western edge of Forêt de Mormal to bivouacs about 2 miles south-west of Le Cateau. Held support line during fighting (26th). Covered withdrawal of forward troops then moved back via Maretz to Estrées. Continued retreat (27th) via St. Quentin and Ham to billets near Ollezy. To La Pommeraye (28th), Jaulzy (30th), Crépy (31st).

SEPTEMBER
Enemy attacked 9.30 am (1st) and withdrawal ordered. Major Hastings and Second- Lieutenant Ames killed. Moved back to Silly-le-Long. To Cuisy (2nd), Coulommes (3rd), Tournan (4th). Began advance, marching to Villeneuve then Dammartin (6th), via Coulommiers to Boissy-le-Chatel (7th), St. Cyr to bivouacs near Noisement (8th), Saacy (9th), Montreuil, Gandelu to Chezy (10th), Dammard, St. Remy to Hartennes (11th), Chacrise, Serches to Ciry (12th). Lieutenant Palmer recalls in his diary that there was no room in Ciry and the Battalion had to march back to billets at Serches. Moved forward to Sermoise (13th) then "B" and "C" Companies advanced on the bridge at Missy-sur-Aisne. "B" Company soon came under fire – Captain Fisher and Lieutenant H.J. Vicat killed. The latter had only joined the Battalion less than a week previously. Battalion crossed the Aisne during night. Moved forward from river bank (14th) and dug in either side on road leading from the bridge into Missy – "A" and "B" Companies on the right, "C" and "D" on the left. Held positions under shell and sniper fire. Casualties since 23rd August – 9 officers killed, 2 wounded and taken prisoner, 4 wounded. Major C.V. Molony in his war history of the Battalion records casualties among other ranks as about 390. Some 31 of these being killed, and 96 wounded in the trenches at Missy.

OCTOBER

Relieved (2nd) and to Couvrelles. To Maast-et-Violaine (3rd), Hartennes (4th), Largny (5th), Fresnoy (6th). Entrained at Pont-Ste. Maxence (7th) for Abbeville. Arrived (8th) and marched to Gueschart. Moved during night (9th) to Haravesne then by lorries to Valhuon (10th). Marched to Drouvin (11th), Beuvry (12th). Advanced on Vermelles in afternoon. Major Molony records that no Headway could be made, the Battalion incurring more than 50 casualties. Relieved by French troops (14th) and moved back to Annequin then Quesnoy. To Richebourg St. Vaast (16th). Moved forward to Neuve Chapelle in support of 7th Brigade (17th) and during night relieved 3rd Worcestershire in front line facing Illies. Relieved by 3rd Worcestershire (20th) and moved back during night to billets near Bois de Biez. Sent forward during afternoon to trenches near Lorgies as reinforcements to 2nd South Lancashire. Withdrew during night (23rd/24th) to positions north-east of Neuve Chapelle. Battalion`s line lay between the La Bassée and Largies roads and was held under constant shell, machine gun and rifle fire. Enemy attacked (26th). C.T. Atkinson in his war history of the Queen`s Own, records that "D" Company on the right of the Battalion`s line took the main force of the assault, but – ". . . unshaken by the shelling, shot steadily and straight at the advancing enemy, met with the bayonet the few Germans who reached the parapet." Casualties – Captain A.C. Beeman, Second-Lieutenant J.M. Harding killed, Captain Keenlyside mortally wounded, over 50 other ranks killed or wounded. Another attack (27th) – casualties included Major Buckle killed and Captain Legard mortally wounded. Captain E.M. Battersby and Second-Lieutenant Gore were killed (28th). Relieved by 1st Seaforths (30th) and moved back via Le Touret to Merville. Of the 14 officers that went into action, just 2 remained alive or unwounded. The casualties among the other ranks while at Neuve Chapelle were estimated at around 450. The Battalion's discipline, determination and courage throughout the fighting was recognized at all levels. Lord Ernest Hamilton noted in his book *The First Seven Divisions* how – "the West Kents immortalised themselves" while General Sir H. Smith-Dorrien speaking directly to the Battalion said – "I am perfectly certain there is not another battalion that has made such a name for itself as The Royal West Kents. Everybody is talking about you. They say: 'Give them a job, they will do it; they never leave the trenches'." Some 2 years later, Major Molony records, a conversation that took place between the Second in Command of one of the Regiment`s Kitchener`s Army battalions just out from England, and a Quartermaster Sergeant. The officer enquired as to how the men managed to loose so many cap badges. The NCO then revealed that they were in fact selling their badges to the Australian troops next to them in the line for 5 shillings. Astonished at this, the officer pointed out that the badges were only worth a few pence, and asked why would anyone want to pay 5 shillings – "That doesn'tt matter sir", replied the Sergeant, "What they want is to get from a battalion actually on service the cap badge of the Neuve Chapelle Regiment." Moved to Coutre Croix (31st).

NOVEMBER
To Dranoutre and attached to 15th Brigade (1st). Moved to Neuve Eglise (3rd). Took over support trenches near Wulverghem (7th) then returned to Neuve Eglise. To trenches again (11th), being relieved during night (12th). Marched through Ypres and Zillebeke (13th) then took over front line trenches in woods near Klein Zillebeke. Now attached to 7th Brigade. Second-Lieutenant M.H. Thompson mortally wounded from shell (17th). Enemy attacked trenches to the right and left of Battalion's line (17th). Major Molony records how "C" Company fired into the attackers to their right and inflicted high casualties. He also notes that the Germans came forward arm-in-arm, to within a yard or two of the British tenches – "They made no attempt to fight and, judging from their actions, must have been heavily drugged, as they did not seem to know what they were doing." Relieved (19th) and to positions in front of Ypres. To Dranoutre (20th). Casualties (13th-19th) – 1 officer, 14 other ranks killed, 39 wounded. Major Molony notes that the majority of these were from snipers. Took over trenches east of Wulverghem running between the Wulverghem- Messines road and the River Douve (27th).

DECEMBER
Relieved by 1st Devonshire (4th). Casualties – 9 wounded. Carried out further tours in Wulverghem sector (10th-13th) and (16th-19th). The Battalion had relieved 2nd Duke of Wellington's and records note that the change-over took over 3 hours due to condition of the trenches. Waist-deep in mud, several men had to be pulled out with ropes. Rest periods spent at Bailleul and St. Jans Capelle. Casualties (10th-19th) – 11 killed, 19 wounded. Relieved 2nd Duke of Wellington's in trenches south side of Wulverghem-Messines road (31st).

KING`S OWN (YORKSHIRE LIGHT INFANTRY)

**"Mons" "Le Cateau" "Retreat from Mons"
"Marne, 1914" "Aisne, 1914" "La Bassée, 1914"
"Messines, 1914" "Ypres, 1914"**

2ND BATTALION

AUGUST

Dublin, Ireland. Part of 13th Brigade, 5th Division. Embarked SS *Buteshire* (14th) and sailed for France. Officers – Lieutenant-Colonel R.C.Bond (Commanding Officer), Majors C.A.L.Yate, H.E.Trevor, C.E.Heathcote, Captains L.Simpson, MVO, C.H.Ackroyd (Adjutant), A.C.G.Luther, A.R.Keppel, J.E.Simpson, W.E.Gatacre, R.S.Ledgard (Green Howards attached), Lieutenants B.N.Denison, C.H.Rawdon, W.H.deW.Unett, W.d`E.Williams, T.Reynolds, G.C.Wynne, C.E.D.King, C.Helm (RAMC, Medical Officer), H.L.Slingsby, J.B.L.Noel (East Yorkshire attached), A.E.Bentham (Quartermaster), Second-Lieutenants J.Pepys, J.B.Noel, T.B.Butt, H.B.Hibbert, A.F.Ritchie, H.J.Hardiman (East Yorkshire attached). Landed Havre (16th). Entrained for Landrecies (17th), arriving (18th) and marching to billets at La Bassée Maroilles. Moved forward via Bavai to positions near Taisnières (21st). To Boussu (22nd). Advanced to close support positions behind 2nd King`s Own Scottish Borderers (23rd) and assisted in defence of road and railway bridges at St. Ghislain. Lieutenant Pepys killed. Withdrew to Wasmes after dark. Enemy attacked (24th) and withdrawal ordered. Fell back to Bavai. Casualties since (23rd) – 1 officer killed, 27 other ranks killed or wounded. Moved to defensive trenches west of Le Cateau (25th). Order received from Brigade Headquarters instructing the Battalion – "There will now be NO retirement for the fighting troops; fill up your trenches with water, food and ammunition, as far as you can." Enemy attacked (26th). Positions held until eventually surrounded on three sides. There was much hand-to-hand fighting. Lieutenant-Colonel Bond records in his war history of the Regiment – "There was no surrender. The occupants of the trenches were mobbed and swamped by the rising tide of grey-coated Germans." Fighting ceased about 4.30 pm and survivors withdrew along the Reumont road to Estrées, then (27th) to Ollezy. Lieutenant-Colonel Bond records that the surviving officers were Major Heathcote, Captain J.E. Simpson, Lieutenant Williams, Second- Lieutenant Slingsby, the Quartermaster, Lieutenant Bentham and Medical Officer Lieutenant Helm. Total casualties – 18 officers, 582 other ranks. Later, 310 men were reported to be prisoners of war, some 170 of these having been wounded. For their gallantry at Le Cateau Major Yate and Lance-Corporal Frederick William Holmes were awarded the Victoria Cross. Marched via Noyon to bivouacs near Pontoise (28th), via Attichy to Faulzy (30th), Crépy-en-Valois (31st).

SEPTEMBER

Continued retreat via Nanteuil to Silly-le-Long (1st), Cuisy (2nd). Crossed the Marne at Isles-les-Villenoy (3rd) and billeted at Couilly. Marched during night to Tournan. Began advance, marching through Villeneuve to Dammartin (6th), Coulommiers to Boissy-le-Chatel (7th). Cleared enemy from St. Cyr (8th) then to bivouacs near Rougeville. Crossed the Marne at Saucy (9th) then advanced via Chaumont, Montreuil, Coulombs and Brumetz, arriving Chézy (10th). To Hartennes (11th), via Droizy to Serches (12th). To Ciry (13th) in support of 2nd King's Own Scottish Borderers and 1st Royal West Kent ahead at Missy. Came under heavy shell fire and moved back to Les Carrières. Moved forward 1.45 am (15th) to banks of the Aisne. Came under shell fire again and dug in. Casualties – 53 killed or wounded. Further bombardment (16th) and Battalion moved back into La Corbinne Wood. Draft of 9 officers arrived. Relieved 2nd Duke of Wellington's in trenches near Missy (24th). Further drafts had brought strength up to 21 officers, 780 other ranks.

OCTOBER

Relieved by 1st Essex during night (1st/2nd) and to billets near Vassemy. Marched via Villers Cotterêts to Fresnoy (6th). To Verberie (7th) and entrained for Abbeville. Arrived 9 am (8th) and to billets at Drulat. Later to Gueschart. Marched during night (9th) to Haravesnes. To Villièvres (10th) then in buses to Valhuon. Moved later to Annequin and in reserve during attack on Vermelles (12th). Moved back to Le Hamel (14th). Casualties – 18. Relieved 2nd Royal Irish Rifles in trenches in front of Lannoy (18th), then at 6.30 am took part in the attack on Château Wood. Dug in 350 yards from edge of wood and held position under severe shell, machine gun and rifle fire. Casualties – 17 killed, 82 wounded. Relieved by 2nd Royal Irish Rifles (20th) and to Bois-du-Biez. To Festubert (21st), then in afternoon to positions south-west of Neuve Chapelle. Relieved 1st Duke of Cornwall's Light Infantry in trenches at Richebourg l' Avoue (22nd). Enemy attacks repulsed (24th and 25th). Lieutenant-Colonel Bond records that the Battalion's trenches were badly damaged by shell fire. Three men were buried alive. Total casualties – 17 killed, 25 wounded. Second-Lieutenant R.N. Carswell killed (26th). This officer had only arrived from England the previous day. Further attacks (27th, 28th, 29th). Lieutenant-Colonel Bond notes that all companies suffered severely; "A" Company coming in for the worst of the shelling. Relieved by 2/39th Garhwal Rifles (30th) and to Le Touret. Later to Merville. Total casualties since taking over line estimated at 300. Moved to Neuve Eglise (31st) then in buses to Messines. Took part in assault on enemy trenches east of the village. Attack held up by machine guns from western end and Battalion forced to dig in under heavy fire. Casualties – 155 including Captain J.E. Simpson killed.

NOVEMBER
Position held but overwhelming numbers forced withdrawal to north side of the Wulverghem-Messines road (1st). Later relieved by 18th Hussars and to billets at Neuve Eglise. Lieutenant-Colonel Bond notes that the strength on the Battalion now only included one of the original officers, Second-Lieutenant Slingsby. None of the sergeants or corporals had survived. Relieved French troops in trenches south of Douve during night (11th). Relieved during night (12th) then moved via Ypres to trenches on the Menin road. To Hooge Wood (14th) and took part in attack on the Harenthage Château stables. Captain A.B. Smythe and Second-Lieutenant L.E.P. Grubb killed. Heavy shelling caused several men to be buried alive (18th). Captain J. Pyman killed. Later relieved by 1st Northumberland Fusiliers from front line at Herenthage Château and to billets at Locre. Took over trenches east of Wulverghem (28th), Battalion's right on the Douve.

DECEMBER
Relieved and to billets at St. Jans Cappel. Battalion later took over trenches east of Lindenhoek on Hill 75 and upon relief moved to Dranoutre. Further tours in the front line were carried out, the Battalion spending Christmas Day at St. Jans Cappel and located at Neuve Eglise at the end of the year.

KING'S (SHROPSHIRE LIGHT INFANTRY)

"Aisne, 1914" "Armentières, 1914"

1ST BATTALION

AUGUST
Tipperary, Ireland. Part of 16th Brigade, 6th Division. To Queenstown (14th). Left for England and arrived Cambridge (19th).

SEPTEMBER
To Southampton (8th). Sailed for France and landed St. Nazaire (10th). Officers – Lieutenant-Colonel C.P. Higginson (Commanding Officer), Major E.B. Luard (Second in Command), Captain H.A.R. Hoffmeister (Adjutant), Lieutenants R.A. Eakin (Machine Gun Officer), T.D. Perkin (Transport Officer), J.W. Smith (Quartermaster), Captain R.G.H. Tate (RAMC, Medical Officer); "A" Company: Major R. Masefield, Captain C.H. Cautley, Lieutenant J.A.S. Mitchell, Second-Lieutenants C.E. Parker, A.C.P. Biddle- Cope; "B" Company: Captains E.R.M. English, B.E. Murray, Lieutenants W. Grischotti, A.W. Herdman, Second-Lieutenant F.C. Verner; "C" Company: Major W.J. Rowan- Robinson, Captain P.R.C. Groves, Lieutenant G.P.C. Jenings, Second-Lieutenants E.A. Freeman, R. Bryans; "D" Company: Major W.A. Payn, Captain P.C. Huth, DSO, Lieutenants F.H.R. Maunsell, A.P. Williams-Freeman, Second-Lieutenant J.A.M. Charles. Total other ranks – 969. Entrained for Montcerf (11th). Arrived (12th) and moved during night to Crécy. To Jouarres (13th), Rocourt (15th), Buzancy (16th), Mont Nôtre Dame (19th), Courcelles (20th). Moved forward during night (21st) and relieved 1st Wiltshire in front line trenches north-east of Vailly. Lieutenant Mitchell mortally wounded (25th).

OCTOBER
Relieved (1st) and then to positions west of Vailly. Casualties since going into line – 1 officer, 2 other ranks killed, 1 officer, 7 other ranks wounded. Relieved by French troops (12th) and to Fismes. Entrained for Cassel (13th). Moved forward to Sailly (17th) then Bois Grenier. Dug in at Le Quesne Farm (20th). Relieved 2nd York and Lancaster and 1 company of 1st Leicestershire in front line (21st). Came under heavy shelling. Lieutenant Eakin mortally wounded. Enemy attacked in large numbers throughout day (23rd). All attempts to enter Battalion's trenches repulsed.

Records note much hand-to-hand fighting and high casualties among the enemy. some 200 dead being counted in front of 16th Brigade's line. Lieutenant-Colonel Higginson and 4 other officers wounded, Second-Lieutenant Charles mortally wounded. Another attack (24th). Major Masefield killed. Enemy now holding positions within 50 yards of Battalion's line. Enemy broke through (25th) and Battalion withdrew to Bois Grenier during night. Lieutenant Herdman and Second-Lieutenant Verner killed. Total casualties since going into line – 3 officers, 81 other ranks killed, 8 officers, 133 other ranks wounded, 11 missing. Machine Gun Section remained in line and is noted in 2nd York and Lancaster's records as being heavily engaged throughout (26th) at the Rue du Bois level crossing.

NOVEMBER

Relieved 2nd Durham Light Infantry in trenches at Rue du Bois (1st). Lieutenant Jenings killed. Relieved (14th) and to billets at Les Quatre Chemins. Relieved 1st Buffs in front line near Grande Flamengerie Farm (24th). Casualties for November – 12 killed, 34 wounded.

DECEMBER

Relieved by 1st Buffs (9th) and to billets at Rue Delpierre. Relieved 2nd York and Lancaster in front line (17th). Relieved and to Rue des Lettres (23rd). Relieved 1st Buffs in front line (26th). Casualties for December – 5 killed, 9 wounded.

2ND BATTALION

AUGUST

Secunderabad, India.

OCTOBER

To Bombay and embarked SS *Neuralia* for England (13th).

NOVEMBER

Arrived Plymouth and then by train to Morne Hill Camp, Winchester. Joined 80th Brigade, 27th Division. Colours placed in Winchester Cathedral for safe keeping.

DECEMBER

To Southampton (20th) and embarked SS *Maidan* for France. Officers – Lieutenant- Colonel R.J. Bridgford, DSO (Commanding Officer), Captains F.J. Leach (Adjutant), E. Lewis (Quartermaster), Lieutenants W.E. Shaw

(Transport Officer), D. Bell (RAMC, Medical Officer), Second-Lieutenant G.D. Farrer (Machine Gun Officer); "A" Company: Captain C.E. Atchison, Lieutenant J.S. Skinner, Second-Lieutenant A. Davies; "B" Company: Brevet-Major C.A.V. Wilkinson, Lieutenants L.J.B. Lloyd, C.Holman, Second- Lieutenants R.J.H. Green, F.H.Harris; "C" Company: Captains C.W. Battye, DSO, C.F.B. Winterscale, Second-Lieutenants H. Beacall, G.C. Bannister, T.Lloyd, A.J.Talbot; "D" Company: Captains H.G. Bryant, DSO, C.M. Vassar-Smith, J.C. Plowman, Second-Lieutenants E.V.T.A. Spink, V.H. Crane. Disembarked Havre (21st). Entrained for Aire (23rd) and from there marched to billets at Blaringhem.

DUKE OF CAMBRIDGE'S OWN (MIDDLESEX REGIMENT)

"Mons" "Le Cateau" "Retreat from Mons" "Marne, 1914" "Aisne, 1914" "La Bassée, 1914" "Messines, 1914" "Armentières, 1914"

1ST BATTALION

AUGUST

Woolwich. Landed at Havre (11th and 12th) and began Line of Communications duties. Entrained for Valenciennes (22nd). Arrived (23rd) and joined 19th Brigade. Marched forward via Quievrechain to St. Aybert then took up positions along the Mons-Condé Canal. Enemy attacked just after 5 pm, but driven back. Battalion withdrew after midnight via Elouges to Jenlain. Casualties – 1 officer wounded, 4 other ranks killed, 12 wounded. Moved back via Haussy and Solesmes to Le Cateau (25th). War Diary records Germans entering Le Cateau (26th) – Battalion keeping them back until all clear, then withdrawing to wood north of Reumont. Later during morning, dug defensive line north of Les Essarts Farm. Withdrew in afternoon back to Reumont then to bivouacs south of Estrées. Casualties – 2 officers wounded, 2 other ranks killed, 36 wounded, 74 missing. Continued retreat (27th) via St. Quentin and Ham to Ollezy, via Cugny, Noyon and Pont l'Evêque to Pontoise (28th), to Attichy (30th), via the Forest of Compiègne to St. Sauveur (31st).

SEPTEMBER

To Saintines (1st). "D" Company moved to Néry and attacked enemy battery east of the village, capturing 8 guns. Battalion continued retreat to Fresnoy and claims to have captured the first enemy guns of the Great War. Marched via Othis and Dammartin to Longperrier (2nd), through Lagny to Chanteloup (3rd), via Ferrières and Chevry to Grisy (5th). Began advance (6th), marching via Ferrières to Villeneuve St. Denis. Moved through Roman Villers and Villers-Dainville to La Haute Maison (7th). Came under shell fire while approaching Signy-Signets (8th) – 3 killed, 30 wounded then took up positions for night on high ground overlooking the Marne. Relieved by 1st Scottish Rifles (9th) and then to Les Corbiers. Crossed the Marne at La Ferté-sous-Jouarre (10th) then to high ground north of Marcy Farm. Later to Certigny. Marched via Coulombs to Marizy-Ste.-Geneviève (11th), via Chouy to Buzancy (12th), to positions just north-east of Septmonts

(13th), positions south of Venizel (14th). Crossed the Aisne (16th) and moved forward to bivouacs 1,000 yards north of bridge. Moved back to Septemonts (20th).

OCTOBER
Moved to bivouacs in woods west of St. Remy (5th). Marched via Villers-Cotterêts to Vez (6th) then to bivouacs in woods outside St. Sauveur (7th). Arrived Estrée-St. Denis (9th) and entrained (10th) for St. Omer. Marched via Arcques to Renescure (11th), via Wallon Capel and Borre to Pradelles (12th). Two companies took up positions at Rouge Croix and Strazeele. To Bailleul (14th), Steenwerck (15th), Vlamertinghe (16th), Estaires (19th). Dug in along the Fromelles-Pont Pierre road (20th). Moved to positions around Bas Maisnil (21st). Later Headquarters, "B" and "D" Companies moved forward in support of 2nd Argyll and Sutherland Highlanders at Le Maisnil. Lieutenant-Colonel B.E. Ward mortally wounded. Withdrew during evening back to Bas Maisnil. Casualties – 101 killed, wounded, missing. Held line of trenches in front of La Boutillerie under heavy shell fire and infantry attacks. Casualties (23rd-29th) – 12 killed, 62 wounded. Enemy broke through between "C" and "D" Companies (30th). "B" Company made successful counter-attack and cleared enemy from captured trenches. Everard Wyrall in *The Die-Hards in the Great War* records that every man, including servants, pioneers and cooks, took part in the attack – "every German who had penetrated the line was killed – 37 being accounted for in this way – or captured." He also notes that "B" Company had almost ceased to exist. Casualties – 16 killed, 29 wounded

NOVEMBER
Captain A.F. Skaife killed by sniper (1st). War Diary records (3rd) – "Battalion very weak" and (8th) – that "D" and "C" Companies suffered a "fearful shelling" – 2 officers wounded, 11 other ranks killed, 38 wounded. Captain G.R.K. Evatt killed by sniper (14th). Relieved. Casualties (3rd-14th) – 1 officer killed, 2 wounded, 72 other ranks killed, 70 wounded. To Houplines sector (17th). Relieved 2nd Royal Welsh Fusiliers in firing line (25th).

DECEMBER
Remained in Houplines sector. Lieutenant S.C. Bosanquet mortally wounded by sniper (17th). Relieved and to Armentières (20th).

2ND BATTALION

AUGUST
Malta.

SEPTEMBER
Sailed for England. Arrived Southampton and to Hursley Park near Winchester. Joined 23rd Brigade, 8th Division.

NOVEMBER
Embarked Southampton for France (5th). Arrived Havre (6th). Landed (7th) and to No.5 Rest Camp some 5 miles outside of town. Entrained for Merville (8th). To Steenwerck (12th) and came under orders of Cavalry Corps. To Neuve Eglise (14th). Relieved 2nd West Yorkshire in front line (15th). "C" Company on right of line attacked by enemy at 6 pm and 9 pm (16th). War Diary records casualties (the first for the battalion) as – 1 killed, 1 wounded, 15 missing. Relieved (17th) and rejoined 8th Division at Estaires. Little is recorded in the War Diary concerning the battalion's tours of duty in the trenches for the remainder of the year – casualties 2 officers (Captain A.C. Wordsworth and Lieutenant C.M. Harvey) killed, 24 other ranks killed, 36 wounded.

DECEMBER
Carried out further tours in trenches throughout month. In reserve billets at La Flinque (31st).

4TH BATTALION

AUGUST
Devonport. Part of 8th Brigade, 3rd Division. Entrained for Southampton (13th) and embarked SS *Mombasa* for France. Arrived Boulogne (14th) and to rest camp. Entrained for Aulnoye (16th). Arrived and marched to billets at Taisnières. To Monceau (20th), via Maubeuge to Bettignies (21st). moved forward towards Mons (22nd) and established line along the Mons-Condé Canal – "D" Company on right around station at Obourg, "B" Company covering Lock No.5 to Nimy on the left. "C" Company held reserve positions along the Obourg-Mons road and "A" were placed south of the railway line between Obourg and Nimy. Battalion claims first shot of the Great War fired by a British infantry regiment – "D" Company firing on Uhlan patrol. Enemy began to shell positions between 8- 9 am (23rd). Infantry came forward just after and records note how the Battalion's

machine guns and rifles cut through the advancing Germans. Battalion forced to withdraw on Mons during afternoon then via Hyon to Nouvelles. Casualties – Major W.H. Abell, Captains J.E. Knowles, K.J. Roy, Lieutenants J.R.M. Wilkinson and K.P. Henstock killed, 9 officers wounded, 453 other ranks killed, wounded or missing. Moved back via Quevy and Bavai to Amfroipret (24th), through Wargnies and Le Quesnoy, Beaudignies, Solesmes and Caudry to Audencourt (25th). Machine guns opened fire on enemy attempting to cross the Cambrai road (26th). withdrew about 5 pm to Vermand. Continued retreat (27th) via Ham to Genvry, to Cuts (29th), Courtieux (30th), Vaumoise (31st).

SEPTEMBER
To Fresnoy (1st), via Chèvreville, Bregy, Forfry and Gesvres to Monthyon (2nd), via Meaux and Nanteuil to Vaucourtois (3rd), Retal (4th). Began advance to the Aisne (6th), marching via Chârtres and Crevecoeur to Hautefeuille. To Chauffry (7th), via St. Denis, Rebais and Gibraltar to Orly (8th), via Nanteuil to Crouttes (9th), Chezy (10th), via Dammard and Neuilly to Oulchy-la-Ville (11th), Braisne (12th), Chassemy (13th). Crossed the Aisne at Vailly then to St. Pierre. Took part in attack on the Jouy Ridge (14th). Moving forward, the Battalion came under heavy fire, Everard Wyrall recording in *The Die-Hards in the Great War* that – "it was almost impossible to gain ground against an enemy cleverly and strongly entrenched." Battalion withdrew to bivouacs just north of Vailly. To Bois Marin (15th) and took up positions covering the Condé bridge. Moved forward (20th) and relieved 1st Northumberland Fusiliers in trenches north of Vailly. Relieved by 1st Northumberland Fusiliers (26th) and to Courcelles.

OCTOBER
To Oulchy-le-Château (1st), Silly-la-Poterie (2nd), Crépy-en-Valois (3rd). Entrained at Pont-Ste. Maxence for Abbeville, arriving 7 am (6th) and marching to billets at Hautvillers. Marched via the Forest of Crécy, Dompierre and Raye to Hesdin (9th). Travelled in buses to Rermes-en-Artois (10th). Marched to Mont Bernanchon (11th), Vieille Chapelle (12th). Came into action east of the village about 11 am. Lieutenant S.H. Coles and 2 other ranks killed, 4 wounded. Battalion withdrew to Vieille Chapelle. Took part in attack on Croix Barbée (13th). War Diary records that the enemy were pushed through Croix Barbée and Battalion entrenched for the night in rear of the village. Casualties – Captains G.R. Bentley, C.F. Tulloh, Second-Lieutenant G.T.H. Morse killed, Captain W.J. Corcoran mortally wounded, 10 other ranks killed, 2 officers and 35 other ranks

wounded. In action again (14th) – Lieutenant H.A. Tagg, Second-Lieutenant M.A.P. Shawyer and 6 other ranks killed, 2 officers, 38 other ranks wounded. Moved into Croix Barbée (15th) – Lieutenant C.D. Sneath and 6 other ranks killed, 1 officer, 20 other ranks wounded. To Aubers (17th), Le Plouich (18th), Le Riez (19th). Came under shell fire (20th) – Second-Lieutenant R. Sayers and 13 other ranks killed, 2 officers, 45 other ranks wounded. Relieved (22nd) and via Rue d'Enfer to billets near Fauquissart. Took part in successful attack to regain lost trenches at Fauquissart (24th). Casualties – 1 officer and 8 other ranks killed, 9 wounded. Relieved by 2nd Royal Scots (31st) and moved back into support trenches at Bacquerot Farm. Casualties (25th-31st) – 6 killed, 49 wounded, 7 missing.

NOVEMBER
To Le Touret (7th), Zelobes (8th). Two companies to Croix Barbée, 2 companies to Le Touret (9th). Battalion relieved Indian troops in front line at Pont Logy (14th). Heavily shelled (10th-17th) – 10 killed, 17 wounded. Relieved and to La Couture. To Bailleul (15th), via Neuve Eglise to Wulverghem (16th). Relieved 2nd Scottish Rifles in firing line south- west of Messines (17th). Relieved and to Westoutre (24th). To Locre (30th).

DECEMBER
Relieved 1st Gordon Highlanders in trenches east of Kemmel (3rd). Relieved later. Moved forward to Kemmel trenches (14th) and took up reserve positions during 1st Gordon Highlanders attack on Maedelstraede Farm. Later relieved 1st Gordon Highlanders in firing line. Heavily shelled (15th) – 6 killed, 11 wounded, 1 missing. Relieved during night and to Locre. Relieved 1st Wiltshire in firing line (18th). Second-Lieutenant H.D. Hilton killed (19th). To front line (27th). Second-Lieutenant G.W. Hughes killed (31st).

KING`S ROYAL RIFLE CORPS

"Mons" "Retreat from Mons" "Marne, 1914"
"Aisne, 1914" "Ypres, 1914" "Langemarck, 1914"
"Gheluvelt" "Nonne Bosschen" "Givenchy, 1914"

1ST BATTALION

AUGUST
Salamanca Barracks, Aldershot. Part of 6th Brigade, 2nd Division. Entrained at Farnborough (12th). Arrived Southampton and sailed for France. Arrived off Havre during night. Sailed up the Seine early morning (13th) and to rest camp near the racecource at Rouen. Entrained (14th). Travelled via Amiens, Arras, Cambrai to Vaux Audigny. Arrived 1 pm. and to billets at Hannappes. To Landrecies (21st), Hargnies (22nd). Advanced to Givry near Mons (23rd) and entrenched north of the village during afternoon. Came under shell and rifle fire. Began retreat (24th), marching via Treaux and Malplaquet to Bavai then through Aymeric, Pont-sur-Sambe to Maroilles (25th). In support of 1st Royal Berkshire during action at bridge on the Sambre west of village during night. Continued retreat to Venerolles (26th), Mont d`Ourigny (27th), via La Fere to Amigny (28th). "C" Company took up positions around bridge at Condren. "B" company relieved "C" Company during morning. Marched to Coucy-le-Châteaux (30th), via Soissons to St. Bandry (31st).

SEPTEMBER
To Forêt Domeniche de Retz (1st) and took up covering line on northern edge. Came under heavy shell fire. Moved back through wood during evening. Casualties – Lieutenant P.G. Chadworth-Musters and 12 other ranks wounded. Marched via Betz to La Cong, Farm near Trilbardou (2nd), via Meaux, Trilport, Montceaux and Pierre Levée to Bilbarteaux Farm (3rd), to Voisins (4th), via Lumigny to Chaumes (5th). Began advance (6th), marching to Château-de-la-Fontelle then St. Siméon (7th). War Diary noted reinforcement of 2 officers and 100 other ranks arrived. Strength now 1,130. Moved forward via Rebais, La Bone and La Trétoire to La Noue (8th). Crossed the Marne at Charly (9th) then to Coupru. Moved via Marigny to Hautesvesnes (10th). Enemy engaged on Vierley-Chezy road. War Diary records that the Germans surrendered after 1½ hours fighting having lost some 80 killed and wounded. 450 prisoners taken. A report of the action published in *The King`s Royal Rifle Corps Chronicle*

records that the Battalion's strength was 1,150 and that for the enemy, a German rearguard, about 1,200 with a battery of field guns. Casualties – 10 other ranks killed, Lieutenants R.H. Woods, A.L. Bonham-Carter, Second-Lieutenants H.W. Butler, R.A. Banon and 60 other ranks wounded. Bivouacked at Chevillon. Marched to Wallée (11th), Mont Hussard (12th), Duisel (13th), Verneuil (14th). Battalion divided and advanced either side of 1st Royal Berkshire. "B" and "C" Companies to the right came under attack. War Diary records that the attack came from infantry to the front and machine guns on the flank and situated in a wood about 700 yards north of Tilleul – "They put up a very good fight and killed a large number of the enemy" before retiring to Tilleul. During the night the companies advanced to de Courelan then Malval but at midnight withdrew back to Verneuil. On the left, "A" and "D" Companies contacted 1st Irish Guards. War Diary records that this was by a road running north from Soupir, the men after some skirmishing driving the enemy through a wood and inflicting high casualties. The companies dug in on edge of wood under shell fire from the heights near Braye. Captains A.F.C. Machlaclan, DSO, G. Makins, MVO and Second-Lieutenant H.C. Lloyd wounded. "B" and "C" Companies joined "A" and "D" Companies in trenches near Soupir (16th). Lieutenant J.S. Alston wounded (19th). Lieutenant F.W. Cavendish- Bentinck wounded and Battalion relieved (20th). "A" and "D" Companies to Verneuil, "B" and "C" to Moussy. Casualties (14th-20th) – 27 killed, 5 officers and 136 other ranks wounded, 8 missing. Moved to Oeuilly (21st), Bourg (25th). Relieved 1st Cameron Highlanders in tenches near Beaulne (26th). Enemy attack repulsed (27th). Lieutenant- Colonel E. Northey (Commanding Officer) wounded. Lieutenant A.H. Brocklehurst wounded (28th). War Diary records trenches and "C" Company in the valley north of Beaulne heavily shelled (29th). Casualties – 3 killed 11 wounded.

OCTOBER

Relieved and to support trenches (1st). Relieved 2nd South Staffordshire at Rifleman's Point (4th). Lieutenant C.G.E. Clowes wounded (8th). Relieved by French troops (13th) and to Bourg. Lieutenant A. Harman wounded (14th). Marched to Fismes and entrained (15th) for Strazeele. Moved forward and took over billets in Ypres (20th). Moved to support positions about 1 mile north-east of Wieltje on the Passchendaele road (21st). Withdrew to St. Jean during evening. Marched via Potijze and Zillebeke to Klein Zillebeke (22nd) and stood by in readiness to support 3rd Cavalry Division. Returned to St. Jean 3 am (23rd) then later in morning to support positions about 1 mile south-east of Pilckem. Moved back to billets at Pilckem (24th) then via Potijze and Frezenberg to support billets in

Zonnebeke sector during afternoon. To Polygon Wood during afternoon (25th). Advanced early morning (26th) – "D" Company followed by "C" and with "A" and "B" in support. Details from the diary of Lieutenant-Colonel Northey appear in *The King`s`s Royal Rifle Corps Chronicle* and these recall that "D" Company came under very heavy enfilade fire from their left shortly after clearing the edge of the wood. The attack was held up, the Battalion holding its positions until relieved by 1st Irish Guards about 5 am (27th). Casualties – Second-Lieutenant W.G. Cronk (3rd Buffs, attached) and 13 other ranks killed, Lieutenant E.G.W. Bourke, Second-Lieutenant K.H.W. Ward and 34 other ranks wounded. Withdrew to a farm in valley south of Zonnebeke. Advanced again about 9 am – "A" Company followed by "B" Company. Lieutenant-Colonel Northey records that the Battalion having crossed the Passchendaele-Becelaere road came under terrific shell and rifle fire. Casualties – Captain W. Wells (3rd Buffs attached), Lieutenant H.H. Prince Maurice VD of Battenberg, and 24 other ranks killed, Captains A.L.Y. Willis, W.W. Llewellyn (3rd Somerset L.I. attached), Second-Lieutenants T.N. Hone, H. Sweeting and 130 other ranks wounded, 19 missing. Dug-in about 800 yards east of the road and held positions under heavy shell fire. Second-Lieutenant E.R. Waring killed (28th). Enemy attack beaten off by "D" Company (30th). Casualties – Second-Lieutenant J. Casey killed by shell, 4 other ranks killed, Second-Lieutenant R.H. Slater and 10 other ranks wounded. Another attack (31st) – Captain B. Seymour and 10 other ranks wounded. Relieved by French troops during night and moved back to former positions in the valley south of Zonnebeke.

NOVEMBER
Moved into Divisional Reserve north-west corner of Polygon Wood (1st) Later to Hooge Château in support of 1st Division then moved forward to trenches at Herenthage Château. "B", "C" and "D" Companies in firing line, "A" in reserve. Enemy attacked (2nd) and line driven back about 300 yards. "A" Company loosing 3 killed, Second-Lieutenant C. Collins and 9 other ranks wounded. Remainder recorded as 9 officers – Captains W.P. Lynes, H.E. Ward (3rd Buffs attached), Lieutenants A.M. Wakefield-Saunders, G.V.H. Gough, Second-Lieutenants C.H. Reynard, C.F. Schoon, R. Richards, S. Lucas, T. Wader and 437 other ranks missing. Headquarters and "A" Company in close support of 1st Royal Berkshire in wood west of Gheluvelt (3rd). Line held under heavy shelling and 2 infantry attacks (4th). Relieved 6 pm and to north-west corner of Polygon Wood. Moved to positions south of Zonnebeke (6th). "A" Company moved forward in support of 2nd Connaught Rangers (7th). Forward trenches held.

Lieutenant-Colonel Northey records (10th) that he attended a Court of Enquiry regarding the missing companies. Five men shot through the head by snipers (14th). Two heavy howitzer shells burst in trench (15th) killing 2 and wounding 9. Lieutenant-Colonel Northey notes in his diary that 6 shell splinters came through the roof of his dugout. One piece missing his head by a foot, another hitting Second-Lieutenant Birkett's coat while a third passed through a book that was being read. Relieved during night and to Railway Wood. Moved to billets in Ypres 8.45 pm (16th). To Caestre (18th). Casualties for the period 23rd August to 18th November are recorded in *The King's Royal Rifle Corps Chronicle* as follows – Officers: 5 killed, 23 wounded, 9 missing, 1 accidently shot; Other ranks: 90 killed, 417 wounded, 490 missing, 2 accidently shot.

DECEMBER
Moved in buses (23rd) via Hazebrouck and St. Venant to Béthune then marched to Cuinchy and relieved Connaught Rangers in trenches running from the Béthune-La Bassée road to the La Bassée Canal. Relieved by 1st King's Liverpool (25th) and moved back into Brigade Reserve. Marched via Beuvry and Le Quesnoy to Le Hamel (26th) and billets near Les Lobes (29th).

2ND BATTALION

AUGUST
Blackdown. Part of 2nd Brigade, 1st Division. To Frimley Green and entrained for Southampton (12th). Embarked SS *Galeka* and sailed 5 pm for France. Arrived Havre early morning (13th) and to No.2 Rest Camp just north of Le Hanail on the Octeville road. Entrained at Havre (15th) and travelled via Rouen, Amiens and Busigny to Le Nouvion. Arrived around 10 pm and moved into billets close to station. Set up outposts – "A" Company at Malemperch,, "B" Company Fontaine-des-Pauvres, "C" Company Beaucamp and "D" Company with Headquarters just south of Beaucamp. To Le Nouvion (21st) and from there marched to Etroeungt. Marched via Avesnes to St. Rèmy-mal-Bâti (22nd) then in afternoon via Maubeuge to Villers-sire-Nicole. To Rouveroy (23rd) and in evening to Givry. Later moved to reinforce troops of 6th Brigade at Harmignies, taking up entrenched positions on eastern side of village. Returned to Givry (24th) then via Bettignies to Feignies. "A" and "B" Companies took up positions on north side of village during morning (25th) then Battalion marched via Hautmont and Monceau to Marbaix. Moved through Favril to Oisy (26th). The men's packs and 12 or so men that were unable to march were left at

Marbaix. It was later learnt that the Germans had entered the village shortly after the Battalion's departure and a British Staff Officer had ordered the packs burnt. Two men managed to escape, but the others wee taken prisoner. Marched via Wassigny (27th) then in afternoon to billets in farms at northern end of Noyalles. To Origny (28th) and dug in on eastern side of the Oise. Came under shell fire and withdrew to Lucy. Later marched via La Fère to Fressancourt. Marched via Gobain and Prémontré to Anizy-le-Château (30th). Battalion records note that some of the men bathed at the canal bridge just west of the village. Via Soisson to Verse Feuille Fe (31st).

SEPTEMBER
Moved through the Forest of Villers Cotterêts via Villers Cotterêts (1st) and entrenched on southern edge. Later marched through night via La Ferté Milon and Fulâmes to Neufchelles. Entrenched at Le Plessis Placy during morning (2nd) then in afternoon to Vareddes. Marched via Germigny, St. Jean, La Ferté sous Jouarre, and Jouarre to Romeny (3rd), via Bois de Jouarre to Aulnoy (4th), Coulommiers, Touquin and Ormeaux to Bernay (5th), Grand Bréaux, Courpalay, Bois de Blandureau to Vaulnoy (6th), Amillis, Choisy, La Ferté Gaucher to Jouy-sur-Morin (7th), Launoy Brulé, Sablonnières, Hondevillers to Flagny (8th), Nogent-I' Artaud (9th). Crossed the Marne during evening and bivouacked on high ground just south of La Croisette. Advanced via Lucy to Courchamps (10th). Later engaged enemy near Priez – Second-Lieutenant E.V. Tindall mortally wounded, 4 other ranks wounded. Advanced into Rassy during evening. Marched via Cuinct and Batilly to Rocourt (11th), Fère-en-Rardenenois to Pars (12th). Moved forward (13th) and entrenched just south of the Ferme-de-Pincon between Vauxcéré and Longueval. Later advanced to positions just north of Bourg – "C" and "D" Companies on high ground, "A" and "B" Companies on the Vendresse road in support. Moved into billets at Moulins during evening. "C" Company remaining on outpost duty. Advanced (less "C" Company) to attack enemy positions on high ground above Troyon (14th). Moved forward about 3 am and halted in Troyon. "D" Company went forward up main road and came under fire from about 50 yards. Advanced again and fired on from 3 sides after about 100 yards. "A" and "B" Companies came forward in support, "C" joining later. Battalion dug in on line astride the sunken section of the road and continued fighting up the slope towards the Chemin des Dames throughout the day. Relieved by 1st Loyal North Lancashire and 1st Northamptonshire about 9 pm and withdrew to reserve line just north of Troyon. Casualties – 9 officers killed or missing, 7 wounded, 306 other ranks killed, wounded or missing. *The King's Royal Rifle Corps Chronicle* records the plight of some 15 wounded

that came in during the night. All had been shot in the legs and had crawled through fields under fire in pouring rain. It was reported that those that could walk were taken prisoner. One German officer in particular was noted as showing kindness to the wounded. Two killed, 29 wounded from shrapnel fire (16th). "C" and "D" Companies sent forward (17th) to help 1st Northamptonshire regain part of their line recently lost to the enemy. Line retaken and pushed forward 200 to 300 yards north of the Chemin des Dames just east of Cerny. "A" and "B" Companies came up as support later. *The Chronicle* records that about 4.30 pm "C" Company was approached by a party of Germans. Led by 2 officers, the men had their hands in the air and rifles slung over their shoulders. Lieutenant Dimmer, accompanied by Captain J.A. Savage of 1st Northamptonshire, went forward to accept a surrender, but were fired on. Captain Savage being killed. Shortly after, some 300 to 400 of the enemy were seen coming forward in a similar manner towards the Northamptonshire`s trench to the left. Upon reaching the Chemin des Dames, the men again lowered their hands and opened fire. However, Lieutenant R.T.H. Purcell, who had suspected treachery and had ordered his machine guns to be trained on the advancing group, quickly opened fire. The Germans immediately fled but, *The Chronicle* records – "very few if any of them escaped." Later "B" Company advanced towards La Bovell Farm, but were later ordered to retire. Relieved at midnight (19th) and moved through night to Pargnan. Visited by Field- Marshal Sir John French and Prince Arthur of Connaught (22nd). Moved forward to ridge just north of Mouling in support of French troops (23rd), returning to Pargnan same evening. Returned to front line north of Troyon (25th). Brigadier-General Sir Archibald Home (11th Hussars) recalls seeing the "60th" moving along the road in his book *The Diary of a World War 1 Cavalry Officer* – ". . . they look well but it is curious how all infantry walk with a sort of slouch after a lot of hardship." *The Chronicle* records that trenches were held under constant shell fire. The Battalion being relieved usually about every 4 days.

OCTOBER

Relieved by French troops early morning (16th) and marched to Vauxcèr. Moved in afternoon to Fismes and entrained. Arrived Cassel (18th) and via Poperinghe marched to Elverdinghe (20th). To Ypres (21st) and in evening to Boesinghe. Went forward to Pilckem (22nd) and during night took up positions near Het Sas. In action (23rd) – "C" and "D" Companies taking German tenches near Bixchoote on the roads running from the village to Langemarck and Pilckem. Casualties – 36 killed, approx. 60 wounded. Relieved during night (24th) and to bivouacs near Pilckem. Later to Ypres.

Moved forward into Corps Reserve about Hellfire Corner (26th). Advanced into Polygon Wood and on (29th) moved to Herenthage Château in preparation for attack. Moved forward with 1st Loyal North Lancashire during afternoon. Battalion's right on the Ypres-Menin road. Came under heavy shell fire and attack held up just east of Gheluvelt. Dug in during night south and south-east of village. Line held under heavy shell fire throughout (30th). Enemy attacked in large numbers (31st). *The Chronicle* records that "A" and "B" Companies were almost surrounded – ". . . there was severe hand-to-hand fighting all the time." Losses were heavy and Battalion withdrew to high ground east of Herenthage Château. No casualties figures are provided, but Battalion's fighting strength now 9 officers and approx. 300 other ranks.

NOVEMBER

Relieved by 1st Royal Berkshire (1st) and withdrew to Sanctuary Wood. Captain C.F. Hawley arrived with draft of 200 men. Moved forward (2nd) and took part in counter-attack near Herenthage Château. Trenches held by 1st King's Royal Rifle Corps had been overrun. "A" and "B" Companies succeeded in pushing enemy back and occupied line just east of Veldhoek. Captain Hawley killed. Attacked again just before dusk. *The Chronicle* records that a small number of men entered the enemy's line, but most lost their way in the dark. Losses were impossible to ascertain. Line held at night at edge of Herenthage Château grounds and Ypres-Menin road. Positions held under heavy shell fire throughout day. (3rd). Relieved by 10th Hussars (4th) and withdrew to Bellewarde Wood. Ordered forward for attack (5th). Advanced via Zillebeke then came under rifle fire from short range at Zwarteleeu. *The Chronicle* records that the enemy were calling out orders in English and French which led to confusion. Fell back to Hill 60. Attached to 4th (Guards) Brigade and moved forward to reserve trenches in Shrewsbury Forest (6th). Took over front line (10th). Position recorded as being a line of rifle pits and just 150 yards from the enemy. Came under attack (12th), but enemy driven back with heavy losses. During the action Lieutenant Dimmer manned one of his machine guns and was personally responsible for many of the enemy's casualties. Wounded 5 times the officer remained at his post until his Vickers was destroyed. Having made his way back to Headquarters he eventually collapsed through pain and exhaustion but recovered later. He recalled – "My face is spattered with pieces of my gun and pieces of shell, and I have a bullet in my face and four small holes in my right shoulder. It made rather a mess of me at first, but now that I am washed and my wounds dressed, I look quite all right." Lieutenant Dimmer was subsequently awarded the Victoria Cross. Relieved during night (16th) and to Westoutre. To Strazeel (21st) and rejoined 2nd Brigade at Hazebrouck (22nd).

DECEMBER

Moved in buses to Zelobes (20th). Marched to Le Coutre then into close support at Rue de Bois north of Givenchy. "C" and "D" Companies moved forward to front line (22nd), remainder to billets in Rue d`Epinette. Relieved (23rd) and to Essar. To Cambrin (26th) and relieved 1st King`s Liverpool in trenches running from the Béthune-La Bassée road to the La Bassée Canal. *The Chronicle* records that the trenches were – "barely bullet-proof" and that the Battalion was much troubled by enemy sniping. A draft of men from Rhodesia and other oversea dominions had recently arrived and a number of these were chosen for duty as snipers.

3RD BATTALION

AUGUST
Meerut, India.

OCTOBER
Located – Headquarters, "B" and "C" Companies at Meerut; "A" Company, Bareilly with a detachment at Chakrata; "D" Company, Delhi. Entrained at Meerut (10th). Arrived Bombay (13th) and embarked SS *Ionian*. Sailed for England (16th).

NOVEMBER
Arrived Plymouth (15th) and then to Morn Hill Camp near Winchester. Joined 80th Brigade, 27th Division.

DECEMBER
To Southampton (20th) and sailed SS *City of Edinburgh* for France. Landed Havre (21st). Officers – Lieutenant-Colonel C. Gosling (Commanding Officer), Major W.J. Long (Second in Command), Lieutenants J.F. Franks (Adjutant), J.F. Pearse (Transport Officer), A.D. Ponsonby (Machine Gun Officer), A.C. Watkins (Quartermaster); "A" Company: Captain G.M. Atkinson, Lieutenants C.W. Fladgate, C.G.E. Clowes, Second- Lieutenants R.P.G. Ireland, Hon. F.S. French; "B" Company: Captain W.S.W. Parker-Jarvis, Lieutenants J.V.E. Lees, N.C.H. Macdonald-Moreton, Second-Lieutenants H.A.C. Williams, F.C. Cull; "C" Company: Major W.F.G. Wyndham, MVO, Captain Sir R.A.H. Beaumont, Bart, Lieutenant A.H. Brocklehurst, Second-Lieutenants G. Walmesley, R. Fitton, P.K. FitzGerald; "D" Company: Captains F.V. Yeats-Brown, J.B. Brady, Second- Lieutenants Le G.G.W. Haton, D.C. O`Rorke, H.J. Johnson. Entrained for Aire, arriving (23rd) and marching to billets at Blaringhem.

4TH BATTALION

AUGUST
Gharial, India.

OCTOBER
Moved during night (6th) and arrived West Ridge, Rawal Pindi (7th) having halted for 2 hours at Tret and 8 hours at Baracao. Entrained for Bombay (9th) and embarked SS *Ionian*. Sailed for England (16th).

NOVEMBER
Arrived Plymouth (15th) and then to Morn Hill Camp near Winchester (18th). Joined 80th Brigade, 27th Division.

DECEMBER
Embarked Southampton (20th). Landed Havre (21st). Entrained for Aire, arriving (23rd), and from there marched to billets at Blaringhem.

DUKE OF EDINBURGH'S
(WILTSHIRE REGIMENT)

"Mons" "Le Cateau" "Retreat from Mons" "Marne, 1914" "Aisne, 1914" "La Bassée, 1914" "Messines, 1914" "Armentières, 1914" "Ypres, 1914" "Langemarck, 1914" "Nonne Bosschen"

1ST BATTALION

AUGUST

Tidworth. Part of 7th Brigade, 3rd Division. Entrained for Southampton (13th) and embarked SS *South Western* and SS *Princess Ena*. Sailed for France. Arrived Rouen (14th) and to camp at Mont St. Aignan. To Rouen (16th) and entrained for Aulnoye. Marched to Marbaix (17th), Feignies (21st), Ciply (22nd). "C" Company detached and to Harmignies on outpost duty. Later sent to Nouvelles to guard artillery, returning to Harmignies same day. Remaining 3 companies entrenched north of Ciply facing Mons. Position heavily shelled (23rd). Captain W.R.A. Dawes and 3 other ranks killed, 1 officer and 20 other ranks wounded (24th). Battalion later withdrew to St. Waast, then (25th) marched via Gommegnies to Solesmes. Engaged advancing enemy then fell back to Caudry. War Diary records (26th) that Battalion held the eastern side of Caudry and was heavily shelled the whole morning before being attacked by the enemy. Fell back later to Beaurevoir. Casualties recorded as between 80 – 100. Retired via Hargicourt and Vermand to Ham (27th). To Tarlefesse (28th). Took up defensive positions in Bois d'Autrecourt (29th). Retired via Varesnes to Vic-sur-Aisne (30th), Coyolles (31st).

SEPTEMBER

Retreated via Levignen to Villers-St. Genest (1st), to Marcilly (2nd), via Pringy and Meaux to Sancy (3rd). Marched through night (4th/5th) to Châtres. Advanced through the Forest of Crécy to Hautefeuille (6th) then via Faremoutiers to high ground near Le Charnois. Moved back to Faremoutiers (7th) then advanced to Coulommiers. Marched via Rebais to Bussieres (8th), via Nanteuil, Crouttes and Bezu to Montreuil (9th), via Neuilly and Chézy to positions west of Dammard (10th). Moved forward through Dammard to Grand-Rozoy (11th), Cerseuil (12th), Braine (13th), via Brenelle to high ground east of Chassemy (14th). Crossed the Aisne later and in action north-east of Vailly. Entrenched defensive line and held under heavy shell fire. Enemy attacked in large numbers (20th). War Diary records that the Battalion's right was seriously threatened – enemy getting to within 50 yards – "during this time a lot of close fighting took place." Enemy eventually driven back. Captain H.C. Reynolds killed, Second-Lieutenant H.W. Roseveare mortally wounded, 1 other officer wounded, approximately 80 other ranks killed, wounded or missing. Relieved by 1st Norfolk and 1st King's Shropshire Light Infantry (22nd) and via Vailly to billets at Braine. Casualties (14th-22nd) estimated as 160 all ranks. Casualties since arriving in France given by War Diary as – 3 officers killed, 9 wounded, 37 other ranks killed, 200 wounded, 125 missing. Also notes (24th) that the Battalion was now resting for first time since 21st August. Moved forward and entrenched position at Brenelle (25th) returning to Braine same day. Began work entrenching on the Braine-Dhuizel road. Relieved 2nd Royal Irish Rifles at Chassemy (28th) – 3 companies covering bridge at Condé.

OCTOBER
Relieved by 3rd Worcestershire (1st) and via Augy to Grand-Rozoy. To Noroy (2nd), Vaumoise (3rd), Saintines (4th). Entrained near Le Meux (5th). Arrived Abbeville (6th). Marched to La Triqurie Château (7th) – 2 companies providing outpost line east and west of Chancy. To Regnauville (9th) then in afternoon to Hesdin. Moved in lorries to Pernes. Marched via Floringhem, Allouagne and Gonneham to Hinges (11th). Moved forward (12th) and in action at Lacoutre. Casualties – 9 killed, 18 wounded. Advanced (16th) via Richebourg St. Vaast and Neuve Chapelle and relieved 2nd South Lancashire at Bois de Biez. Moved forward (17th) and engaged enemy at Ligny-le-Grand. Dug in east of village during night. Casualties – 8 wounded. Attempted to get forward (18th). War Diary records that the enemy appeared to be strongly reinforced – about 200-300 yards gained – heavy firing continued till 10.30 pm. Second-Lieutenant R.F. McLean Gee mortally wounded, 3 other ranks killed, 21 wounded. Casualties (19th) – 12 killed, 21 wounded. Enemy attacked (22nd) and "D" Company surrounded. Later withdrew to positions near Halpegarbe. Took part in fighting at Neuve Chapelle (23rd-27th). Withdrew (28th) via Pont Logy to Richebourg St. Vaast. Casualties – Captains M.L. Formby and F.W. Stoddart killed, 5 officers wounded, 7 missing, 45 other ranks killed, 150 wounded, 350 missing. War Diary notes that these figures are – "very approximate." Moved forward again in support of 2nd Cavalry Brigade during evening, returning to Richebourg St. Vaast (29th). Heavily shelled during afternoon and moved back to Lacouture. Marched via Lestrem and Estaires to Doulieu (30th), to Merris then Nord-Helf (31st).

NOVEMBER
Marched via Bailleul to Locre (1st). Moved to Dickebusch (5th) then via Ypres to Brigade Reserve positions at Hooge. Two companies moved into firing line (7th) and were relieved (9th). Battalion to firing line (11th). War Diary records that the enemy brought up a gun to within 100 yards. Relieved (13th). To firing line (15th). Enemy attacked during morning (17th) – "D" Company's trenches overrun. Regained later with a bayonet charge. Major T. Roche killed by shell, Second-Lieutenant C. Chandler killed by sniper. Other casualties during day – 11 other ranks killed, 15 wounded. Relieved by French troops during night (20th) and marched via Ypres and Vlamertinghe to Westoutre. To Scherpenberg (27th). Moved forward to Kemmel sector (30th).

DECEMBER
Relieved by 2nd Royal Scots (3rd) and to Westoutre. To Locre (6th), Brigade Reserve at Kemmel (8th). Relieved 1st Lincolnshire in firing line (9th). War Diary records 1 man killed by accident. Relieved by 1/10th King's Liverpool (12th) and to Locre. Relieved 1/10th King's Liverpool (15th). Enemy trenches bombarded by French howitzers (17th). War Diary notes – "good shooting." Relieved by 4th Middlesex (18th) and to Locre. Relieved 1st Northumberland Fusiliers in firing line (24th). War Diary records – "practically no shelling on either side" (25th). Some sniping – 2 killed, 1 wounded. Casualties (26th) – 2 killed, 1 wounded. Relieved by 4th Middlesex (27th) and to Westoutre. to Locre (31st).

2ND BATTALION

AUGUST
Gibraltar. Embarked SS *Edinburgh Castle* (31st) and sailed for England. Officers – Lieutenant-Colonel J.F. Forbes (Commanding Officer); Majors J.R. Wyndham (Second in Command), C.A. Law; Captains A.W. Timmis, E.L.W. Henslow, H.F. Coddington, C.G.M. Carter, C.H.E. Moore, G. Le Huquet, R.P. Culver (Adjutant), K. Comyn (Medical Officer); Lieutenants R. Smith, A.S. Hooper, J.M. Ponsford, A.H. Bleckley, D.A. Ansted, E. Spencer, G. Macnamara, J. McL. Down, S. Hewitt (Quartermaster); Second- Lieutenants F.L.D. Shelford, O.J. Calley, M.R. Fowle, R.P. Rogers.

SEPTEMBER
Arrived Southampton (3rd) and to Lyndhurst Camp. Joined 21st Brigade, 7th Division.

OCTOBER

To Southampton and embarked SS *Turcoman* and SS *Cestrain.* Captain
A.C. Magoe and Second-Lieutenants C.H.R. Barnes, G.P. Oldfield, E.L.
Betts, F. Rylans, W.P. Campbell, E.H.A.H. Burges had joined the
Battalion. Total strength – 1,100 all ranks. Sailed (5th) and later docked at
Dover due to warning of German submarines in area. Sailed (6th). Arrived
Zeebrugge (7th) and then by train to Bruges. Arrived and to billets at
Assbrouck. Marched via Bruges to Clemskerke (8th). To Ostend (9th), by
train to Roulers (13th), Kaiserine Barracks, Ypres (14th). Moved forward
(15th) and entrenched across Menin road. Advanced to Hooge (16th) and
to positions north-west of Reutel (17th). Battalion's right lay on Reutel-
Becelaere road. Enemy advanced to within 400 yards during night. Captain
Magor killed. Moved to Terhan (18th). Covered retreat of 22nd Brigade
(19th) then back to Reutel. Advanced once again on Terhan (20th), but
again fell back to Reutel. Lieutenant Spencer killed. Repulsed several enemy
attacks over next 4 days. Lieutenant H.S. Grimston killed (21st). Major
W.S. Shepherd, MC notes in his history of the Battalion how many of the
rifles became unusable – "continuous shooting from sunrise to sunset had
told on them." Heavy shelling caused great damage to trenches. Many men
being buried alive. Captain C.G.M. Carter and Second-Lieutenant
E.H.A.H. Burges killed (23rd). Second- Lieutenants Fowle and Campbell
killed by shell (24th). Relieved and to Kruiskalsijde. Battalion's strength had
been reduced to 450. Major Shepherd records that there were now just 2
officers – Lieutenant Hewitt, the Quartermaster, and Sergeant Major
Waylen. The latter had recently been promoted in the field and was now in
command. Shell fire continued to cause casualties reducing strength to 250.

NOVEMBER

Moved forward to front line, returning later to reserve positions. Moved to
White Château (4th) and via Ypres to Locre (6th). Draft of 96 men arrived
under Lieutenant P.S.L. Beaver who took command. Moved to Bailieul and
billets at The Graperies in Rue de la Gare. To Ploegsteert in support of 4th
Division (8th). Returned to Bailieul (12th). Major Shepherd records that he
was one of 4 men sent to the Battalion from 1/28th London Regiment
(Artists Rifles) to take on the duties of officers. Drawn from the ranks, the
new Second-Lieutenants were dressed and equipped as privates for quite
sometime. To Sailly-sur- la-Lys (14th). Began tours in line Fleurbaix sector
(17th). Draft arrived – Captain E.L. Makin took command. Relieved by 2nd
Royal Scots Fusiliers (20th). Relieved 2nd Royal Scots Fusiliers (23rd),
relieved by 2nd Royal Scots Fusiliers (26th), relieved 2nd Royal Scots
Fusiliers (29th).

DECEMBER

Relieved by 2nd Royal Scots Fusiliers (2nd), relieved 2nd Royal Scots Fusiliers (5th), relieved by 2nd Royal Scots Fusiliers (8th), relieved 2nd Royal Scots Fusiliers (11th). To Pont de Nieppe (13th), Bac St. Maur (17th). Moved forward to Fleurbaix (18th) and held in support during 22nd Brigade's attack on Rouges Bancs. Drafts arrived, strength now 17 officers, 780 other ranks. Relieved 2nd Royal Scots Fusiliers in front line (24th). During the day the Germans put up a tree decorated with candles which, Major Shepherd records, provided target practice for some of the Wiltshires. Relieved by 2nd Royal Scots Fusiliers (27th), relieved 2nd Royal Scots Fusiliers (30th).

MANCHESTER REGIMENT

"Mons" "Le Cateau" "Retreat from Mons" "Marne, 1914" "Aisne, 1914" "La Bassée,1914" "Armentières, 1914" "Givenchy, 1914"

1ST BATTALION

AUGUST

India – Headquarters, "B", "D" and "E" Companies at Dalhouse, "G" and "H" Companies at Amritsar, "A", "C" and "F" Companies at Jullundur. Part of Jullundur Brigade, 3rd (Lahore) Division. Battalion concentrated at Jullundur (13th). Entrained for Karachi (17th), arriving (20th). Embarked SS *Edavana* (27th) and sailed (29th). Officers – Major H.W.E. Hitchins, Captains F.C.S. Dunlop, H. Fisher, DSO, E.N. Buchan, DSO, J.R. Heelis (Adjutant), C.D.K. Seaver (RAMC, Medical Officer), Lieutenants R.G. Browne, P.Z. Paulson, S.S. Norman, R.F. Lynch, P. O`Brien (Quartermaster), Second- Lieutenants R.H.R. Parminter, C.H. Masse, S.D. Connell, G.S. Henderson.

SEPTEMBER

Arrived Suez (13th) and by Train to Cairo. Lieutenant-Colonel E.P. Strickland and Lieutenant R.I.M. Davidson joined. Entrained for Alexandria (18th) and embarked SS *Edavana*. Sailed for France (19th), arriving Marseilles (26th) and to camp at Borély. Five officers joined from England. Entrained for Orleans (30th) then marched to Camp Cercottes.

OCTOBER

Arrived Estaires (23rd) then to Picantin. To Gorre (26th) then relieved 1st Bedfordshire in trenches east of Festubert. Relieved by 1st Devonshire (28th) and to Estaires. Casualties (26th-28th) – 7 killed, 13 wounded. Relieved 15th Sikhs and 34th Pioneers in trenches near Rue Tilleloy (30th).

NOVEMBER

Lieutenant-Colonel Strickland and 2 other officers wounded (1st). Captain Dunlop killed by sniper (8th). Relieved (16th) and to Le Couture. To trenches around La Quinque Rue (22nd). Lieutenant Davidson mortally wounded by sniper (23rd). Second-Lieutenant Connell killed during attack on enemy`s trenches during night (27th).

DECEMBER

Relieved (3rd) and to Le Couture. Returned to firing line (10th). Captain Fisher killed (15th). Relieved and to Béthune. Crossed the La Bassée Canal at Pont Fixe (20th) and took part in attack on trenches east of Givenchy. Advancing 3 pm, the Battalion engaged the enemy in hand-to-hand fighting at Givenchy and held the village throughout night. Attacked again 6.30 am (21st), but soon came under heavy machine gun and rifle fire. Enemy counter-attacked 11 am and forced Battalion to fall back through Givenchy, where more close quarter fighting took place, to Pont Fixe. Casualties – Captain L. Creagh, Lieutenant Norman and 64 other ranks killed, 3 officers, 123 other ranks wounded, 46 missing.

2ND BATTALION

AUGUST

Curragh, Ireland. Part of 14th Brigade, 5th Division. To Dublin (13th). Embarked SS *Buteshire* (14th) and sailed for France. Arrived Landed Havre (16th). Officers – Lieutenant-Colonel H.L. James (Commanding Officer), Major R.S. Weston (Second in Command), Captains C.F.H. Trueman, H.C. Theobald, DSO, F.S. Nisbet (Adjutant), G.P. Wymer, H. Knox, A.G. Foord, C. Morley, M.C. Fowke, Lieutenants W.G. Mansergh, A.F. Thomas, J.H.L. Reade, N.W. Humphrys, J.S. Harper (Machine Gun Officer), E.R. Vanderspar, V.A. Albrecht, A.G.M. Hardingham, A.J. Scully, R. Brodribb, W.L. Connery (Quartermaster), Second-Lieutenants R.F.G. Burrows, J.H.M. Smith, A.G.B. Chittenden, W.E. Butler, R.T. Miller. Entrained for Le Cateau (17th). Arrived midday (18th) and marched to billets at Landrecies. To Bavai (21st). Advanced to Hainin (22nd) and took up support positions along the Mons-Condé Canal. Enemy attacked (23rd). Covered withdrawal of forward troops, then fell back to Dour. Casualties – 12 killed or wounded. Dug defensive positions near Wasmes (24th). Came under heavy shell fire then ordered to retire via Dous to line near Houdain. Withdrew to Bavai (25th) then via Montay to bivouacs in a field, north-west of Le Cateau at junction of the Cambrai and Bavai roads. Enemy attacked (26th) and Battalion moved to the rear of 2nd Suffolk on right of Reumont-Montay road in support. Ordered to withdraw during afternoon and fell back to Maretz. Casualties – Captains Nisbet and Truman, Lieutenants Brodribb and Mansergh killed, Captain Fowke mortally wounded, 9 other officers wounded, 339 other ranks killed, wounded or missing. Continued retreat to St. Quentin (27th), Pontoise (28th), Carlepont (29th), Bitry (30th).

SEPTEMBER
Continued retreat via Crépy-en-Valois, Sablières and Nanteuil, crossing the Marne at Esby and arriving Boulers (3rd). To Tournan (5th). Began advance to the Aisne (6th), marching via Favières, Le Pilonnerie, the Forêt de Crécy to Château St. Avoe. To Coulommiers (7th), via Pontmoulin to Rougeville (8th). Moved through Saacy (9th) then came under shell fire at Le Limon. Later took part in attack on the Pisseloup Ridge. Casualties – Second-Lieutenants Smith, Chittenden and 8 other ranks killed; 10 officers, 37 other ranks wounded. Moved forward to Chezt-sur-Ourcq (10th), Billy-sur-Ourcq (11th), Chacrise (12th). Crossed the Aisne (13th) and took part in attack on Ste. Marguerite. Village cleared then moved forward to positions west side of Chivres wood. Relieved by 1st Duke of Cornwall's Light Infantry (20th) and moved back to Ste. Marguerite. To Jury (24th).

OCTOBER
To Nanteuil (1st), Longpont (3rd), Fresnoy-la-Rivière (4th), Bethancourt (5th). Entrained at Longueil for Abbeville (6th) then to billets at Fallières. Travelled in buses to Dieval (9th). Moved forward to Hinges (11th) and advanced (12th) to line Rue des Chavattes – Rue l' Epinette. Took part in attack on Richebourg l'Avoué (13th). Colonel H.C. Wylly, CB records in his war history of the Manchester Regiment that the Battalion dug in for the night at the western end of the village. The advance having been slow with every yard of ground, hamlet and house being fought for. Enemy's line noted as being 200-250 yards to the front. Casualties – 10 killed, 3 officers. 40 other ranks wounded. Moved forward (19th) to Les Trois Maisons and held line during enemy attack. Colonel Wylly notes gallant bayonet attacks led by Captain A.G. Tillard and Second-Lieutenant G. Dixon. Forced to withdraw to support trenches near Lorgies at dusk (20th). Casualties (18th-20th) – Captain Tillard, Second-Lieutenant Dixon and 11 other ranks killed; Second-Lieutenant R.F. Walker mortally wounded, 2 officers, 127 other ranks wounded, 70 other ranks missing. Relieved by 1st East Surrey (21st) but soon back in firing line to support 13th Brigade. Casualties – 1 killed, 3 wounded. Relieved again at midnight and then to new line running from crossroads 1 mile east of Festubert. Occupied line to the right of 1st Battalion, Manchester Regiment. Enemy attacked (29th). Centre of Battalion's line taken but retaken during afternoon by Second-Lieutenant J. Leach and Sergeant J. Hogan who were subsequently awarded the Victoria Cross. Later moved to Rue l'Epinette. Casualties (21st-29th) – Captain W.G. King-Peirce, Lieutenant J.H.L. Reade, Second-Lieutenant C.L. Bently and 48 other ranks killed, 2 officers, 48 other ranks wounded, 28 missing.

NOVEMBER

To Le Touret, then Lestrem (1st), Baillieul (2nd). Took over front line Laventie sector, along Rue Tilleloy near Fauquissart (7th). Relieved (11th) and via Estaires moved to Meteren (15th). Moved via Bailleul, Dranoutre and Lindenhoek to trenches facing Messines Ridge (16th). Relieved by 2nd Duke of Wellington`s in trenches at Wulverghem (27th), north side of Messines road, and to St. Jans Cappel. Later to Dranoutre. Casualties for November – Lieutenants J.C. Caulfeild, R. Horridge and 8 other ranks killed, 41 wounded.

DECEMBER

Relieved 2nd Duke of Wellington`s (5th). Carried out further tours in front line resting at Neuve Eglise, St. Jans Cappel and Dranoutre. Relieved by 1st Duke of Cornwall's Light Infantry (29th).

PRINCE OF WALES'S
(NORTH STAFFORDSHIRE REGIMENT)

"Aisne, 1914" "Armentières, 1914"

1ST BATTALION

AUGUST

Buttevant, Ireland. Part of 17th Brigade, 6th Division. To Cork (14th) and embarked for England. Arrived Cambridge (17th) and to camp on Midsummer Common. Moved to Warren Hill, Newmarket (31st).

SEPTEMBER

To Southampton (8th) and embarked SS *Lake Michigan* for France. Officers – Lieutenant-Colonel V.W. de Falbe, DSO (Commanding Officer), Majors L.J. Wyatt (Second in Command), G.E. Leman ("B" Company), Captains R.J. Armes ("A" Company), G. Hume-Kelly ("D" Company), A.S. Conway ("C" Company), E.B. Reid, J. Ridgeway, C.H. Lyon, Lieutenants P. Lyon (Machine Gun Officer), C. Fraser (Adjutant), A.C.F. Royle, H.C. Bridges, A.P.A. Hooper, R.F. Morgan, J.W.L.S. Hobart, C.F. Gordon, E.W. Anderson (Transport Officer), A.C. Adamson, P.G. Harris, C. Langridge (Quartermaster), Second-Lieutenants A.R.A. Leggett, V.V. Page, G.A.B. Chester, W.E. Hill. Arrived off St. Nazaire during night (10th). disembarked (12th) and moved by train to Coulommiers. Arrived (14th) and to billets at St. Cyr. Began march to the Aisne (15th). Arrived Dhuizel area (19th). Moved forward during night (21st) to positions outside Soupir. Relieved 2nd South Staffordshire in front line (22nd). Regimental records tell how Lieutenant Gordon crossed into enemy lines (21st) in order to gain information. He was fired on during his return and lay out in No Man's Land until dark (22nd). He then returned to the British line, now held by 1st North Staffordshire, whistling the Regimental March as a signal to the sentries.

OCTOBER

Relieved and to billets at Ouelly (1st). Casualties since going into line – Lieutenant Royle killed, 19 other ranks killed or wounded. To Dhuizel (6th). Began march to Compiègne (7th) and entrained for St. Omer (10th). Arrived (11th) and marched to Arques. One officer noted seeing French Cuirassiers at Arques, their steel helmets shrouded in khaki covers but the long horsehair plumes still being worn. Moved in buses to Hazebrouck

(12th). Advanced on Strazeele (13th). "D" Company going forward to Merris, "C" Company to Nord Helf, both under heavy fire. Orders received to attack the Bailleul Ridge. Moved forward 1.30 pm, Battalion's right on railway line running out of Hazebrouck, left on road just north of Merris. "C" and "D" Companies leading, "A" and "B" in support. Outtersteene captured about 5 pm and outposts set up by "C" and "D" Companies. Casualties – Second-Lieutenant Chester and 13 other ranks killed, 3 officers, 37 other ranks wounded. Moved forward (14th). Advance temporally held up by fire from Noute Boon. bivouacked for night about 3 miles west of Steenwerck. Reached Steenwerck during morning (15th). Later moved forward and set up outpost line. Battalion records note an encounter with a French patrol. Lost in the dark, the men opened fire on "D" Company and wounded 1 man. A French soldier was killed before firing ceased. Crossed the Lys (16th) and held positions at Bac St. Maur. Took up outpost line in front of Rue du Bois (17th). Moved to reserve positions at la Chapelle d' Armentières (18th) then during evening to Wex-Marquart. "D" Company to firing line. Enemy broke through 2nd Leinster's line (20th) and Battalion moved forward for counter-attack. The gallantry of Second-Lieutenant Leggett is noted, this officer holding out with a party of Leinsters at Premesques until after dark. Captain Reid killed. "D" Company became isolated after being attacked from both right and left. Captain Hume-Kelly killed. Records note that the Battalion – "held on with grim determination", eventually forcing the enemy's withdrawal. The "fine leadership" of Company Quartermaster Sergeant Gould is also noted along with the work of Private Blundred. The latter fetching up ammunition throughout the fighting and subsequently awarded the Russian Order of St. George. "D" Company returned to Battalion after dark. Withdrew to line astride the Armentières-Lille road at dawn (21st). Enemy attacked 3rd Rifle Brigade on Battalion's left at 10.30 pm. "B" Company assisted in regaining line. During the action a German officer was killed and his sword taken as a trophy. The weapon was later placed in the 1st Battalion's Officers' Mess along with an account of how it was taken – "This sword belonged to an Officer of a Saxon Regiment, who was killed on the 21st October, 1914, in front of la Chapelle d' Armentières, north of the Armentières-Lille road. The trenches on our left had been lost, and, during the night our line was heavily attacked, and a considerable number of Germans worked round our flanks attempted to surround the left sentry group of the outpost line. This was held by a section of "B" Company. The men fought magnificently, and drove the enemy off, killing 14 of them, and the Saxon Officer who led the charge on the trench was bayoneted in the throat by No. 6920, Private Nuttall, but at the same time he cut down Private Nuttall with his sword.

This is a very fine example of the excellent state of the discipline in the Regiment, and the determination of all ranks to hold their positions at all costs." Relieved (23rd) and to billets in Fleurbaix. Casualties since (20th) – 2 officers, 12 other ranks killed, 1 officer, 68 other ranks wounded. To Neuve Chapelle area (25th) and attached to 18th Brigade. Returned to Fleurbaix (26th). Relieved 1st East Yorkshire in trenches at Rue du Bois (28th). An amusing story appears in the Battalion's records. A large number of German dead had built up in front of the Battalion's line and Colonel de Falbe put in a request for rope and grappling hooks so that they could be hauled in. Replying to Brigade, Ordnance asked what length of rope was required. Brigade knowing nothing of Colonel de Falbe's request, thought the whole thing was a joke and immediately circulated the following to all battalions – "Report at once by telegram what length of rope is required for the purpose of hauling in dead bodies of the enemy. Brigade offers prize of one bottle of Black and White to Battalion which furnishes the correct answer." Second-Lieutenant L.H. Hughes who had only joined the Battalion 2 days previous, killed (29th). Second- Lieutenant Leggett killed (30th).

NOVEMBER
Enemy attack repulsed (2nd). Trenches held under heavy shell fire. Relieved (17th) and to billets at Bac St. Maur. Rejoined 17th Brigade. Casualties since 28th October – 2 officers and 28 other ranks killed, 2 officers, 147 other ranks wounded. Message received from Brigadier-General W.N. Congreve, VC – Commanding Officer 18th Brigade to CO 17th Brigade, Brigadier-General W.R.B. Dorn – "Your North Staffordshire Regiment has done excellently in every way and I am sorry to lose them. They were always cheery and made light of everything." Moved to billets at the Lunatic Asylum, Armentières (19th). Relieved 2nd Leinster in front line trenches north-east of Armentières – Parenchies railway to L'Epinette (23rd). Relieved by 2nd Leinster (29th).

DECEMBER
Took over trenches in Rue du Bois sector (11th). Battalion records note that these were known as "The Death Trap" or "Dead Man's Alley." During the "Christmas Truce" contact was made with a German soldier who before the war worked as a waiter in Brighton. Uhlan officers, transferred to the infantry, posed for photographs with British officers. The Germans, it was noted, were – "magnificently polished and clean, which unfortunately, the British officers were not." On the second day, a German officer asked to see a British officer. The CO of "C" Company went out and was informed that

hostilities would recommence at mid-day – ". . . and might the men be warned to keep down please." The German officer was thanked for his courtesy. He saluted, bowed, then said – "We are Saxons; you are Anglo Saxons; word of a gentleman is for us as for you." The enemy holding the line opposite the North Staffordshire had been ordered to open fire by their commanders. However, just before mid-day a tin was thrown into "A" Companies line containing the message – "We shoot to the air." Relieved by 2nd Leinster (31st) and to billets at la Chapelle d` Armentières.

YORK AND LANCASTER REGIMENT

"Aisne, 1914" "Armentières, 1914"

2ND BATTALION

AUGUST
Limerick, Ireland. Part of 16th Brigade, 6th Division. Embarked at Cork and Queenstown for Holyhead (14th) then by train to Cambridge. Moved into camp on Coldham Common. To Grantchester Common (27th).

SEPTEMBER
Moved by train to Southampton (7th) and embarked SS *Minneapolis*. Sailed for France (8th). Officers – Lieutenant-Colonel E.C. Cobbold (Commanding Officer), Majors W.F. Clemson (Second in Command), F.E.B. Isherwood, G.E. Bayley, E.C. Robertson, Captains A.V. Jarrett, V.A. Gillam, F.K. Hardy, M.K. Sandys, D.T. Welsh, W.B. Purdon (RAMC, Medical Officer), Lieutenants C.B.A. Jackson, H.P. Philby, H.A.W. Cole-Hamilton, H.F.A. Gordon (Adjutant), N.E.H.. Sim, C.B. Boucher, W.H. Cullen, F.N. Houston, C.R. Ripley, R.P. Wood, R.B. Cowley, E.C. McGuire (Quartermaster), Second-Lieutenants F.L. Norris, J.H.M. Edye, J. Horlington. Arrived St. Nazaire (9th) and to camp at Grande Marais. Moved by train to Mortcerf (11th). Began move to the Aisne (13th) marching via Crécy, Jouarres, Citrey, Château Thierry, Buzancy, Ambrief and Mont Notre Dame. Arrived Courcelles (20th) and during night took over front line trenches from 1st Lincolnshire and 1st Royal Scots Fusiliers north-east of Vailly. "A" Company came under heavy shrapnel fire- 3 killed, 12 wounded. War Diary (30th) records the first use of periscopes – "The use of small mirrors on the end of a stick was found very useful for observing the enemy without being seen." Total casualties for September – 6 killed, 30 wounded, 3 missing.

OCTOBER
Relieved by French troops (12th). Entrained for Cassel (13th). Took over billets in the Rue de Bois (17th). Took part in attack on Radinghem (18th) – moved forward to Le Touquet and with 1st Buffs advanced on village. War Diary records that the battalions were divided by the Bois Grenier-Radinghem road. Village taken, but further advance on to the Château-de-Flanders held up by heavy shell fire around the Radinghem-Fromelles road. One company, however, went forward, and according to

the records of 1st Buffs played an important role in the fighting around the Château. Withdrew from positions on the Château road 10.30 pm (19th) and to billets at Bois Grenier. Casualties – 13 killed, 95 wounded, 27 missing. Reinforced 1st Buffs in front line (21st), moving back to Le Touquet same day. Moved into front line trenches and came under strong attack (23rd). Enemy entered line held by "C" Company. Colonel H.C. Wylly, CB in his history of the York and Lancaster Regiment notes how the Germans were ejected by bayonet charges led by Lieutenants Ripley and Houston. The former officer being killed. "A" and "B" Companies forced to fall back, but line held by Sergeant Tough and 8 men. Captain Sandys killed (25th). Relieved by 3rd Rifle Brigade during evening (25th) and to billets at Fleurbaix. Later moved back into front line.

NOVEMBER
Relieved and to billets at Fleurbaix (14th). Casualties since 23rd October – 2 officers and 33 other ranks killed, 5 officers, 98 other ranks wounded, 7 men missing. Carried out further tours of duty in front line.

DECEMBER
Relieved in front line by 1st King's Shropshire Light Infantry (17th). Took over trenches in front of Armentières end of month.

DURHAM LIGHT INFANTRY
"Aisne, 1914" "Armentières, 1914"

2ND BATTALION

AUGUST
Lichfield. Part of 18th Brigade, 6th Division. War Diary (4th) records that when mobilization was ordered the "Precautionary Period" detachments under Major D`A.W. Mander were in their allotted places i.e. Headquarter Detachment at South Shields – Major Mander, Captain H.V. Hare, Second-Lieutenant V.A.C. Yate and 400 men (137 provided by 1st West Yorkshire). There were also sub-detachments at Hepburn Dock (Captain E.W. Birt and 21 men); the oil depot, South Shields (Lieutenant H.J. Taylor and 25 men); Frenchman`s Battery, South Shields (Lieutenant L.G. Norton and 25 men) and Palmer`s Dock, Jarrow (Lieutenant W.A. Grey-Wilson and 20 men). On the night of (4th), immediately after declaration of war, Major Mander, assisted by Captain Hare, Lieutenant Yate and 30 men, seized a German merchant ship on the Tyne. Detachments returned to Lichfield (6th). Moved to Dunfermline (8th) and went into camp at Transy (11th). To Cambridge (13th) and camp on Jesus Common.

SEPTEMBER
To Newmarket (7th) and entrained for Southampton. Arrived (8th) and embarked SS *City of Benares* and SS *Bellerophon*. Sailed for France. Landed St. Nazaire (9th) and then by train (11th) to Coulommiers. Arrived and to billets at St. Germain. Marched to Château Thierry (15th), Tigny (16th), Chacrise (17th) and via Braine and Dhuizel to Bourg (18th). Took over trenches north of Troyon (19th). Enemy broke through on right (20th) and forced withdrawal. Casualties – Major Mander, Captain Hare, Second-Lieutenant C.M. Stanuell and 36 other ranks killed; Major A.K. Robb, Second-Lieutenant R. Marshall mortally wounded, 5 officers, 92 other ranks wounded. Relieved by 1st West Yorkshire in front line (24th) and to Pargnan (25th). Moved to positions north of Bourg (26th) then at dusk took over support trenches north of Vendresse.

OCTOBER
Relieved (1st) and during evening to Vauxtin. Took over reserve trenches in La Corbinne Wood near Ciry (2nd). Relieved by 2nd Lancashire Fusiliers 2 am (7th) and to St. Remy, then in evening to Largny. To St. Sauveur (8th),

Le Meux (9th) and entrained for Arcques. Marched to Wardrecques (11th) then by lorries to Hazebrouck (12th). War Diary records casualties since 21st September as – 3 killed, 36 wounded. To Vieux Berquin (13th) then took part in successful attack near Bleu. Casualties – Lieutenant W.E. Parke, Second- Lieutenant H.H. Storey and 11 other ranks killed, 1 officer, 60 other ranks wounded. Moved forward to La Verrier (14th) and billeted on the Rue du Leet. To Silly (15th) and set up outposts south of the town. To Bois Grenier (17th). Took part in attack on Ennetières (18th). Moving forward at 3.45 pm. War Diary records operation as – "successful." Casualties – 4 other ranks killed, 2 officers, 74 other ranks wounded, 29 missing. Relieved by 2nd Sherwood Foresters in positions east and south of the village during night and moved back to Brigade Reserve at Fetus. "C" Company remained forward in local reserve at La Vallee. Battalion moved to La Vallee during morning (20th) then "B" and "D" Companies sent forward to support 1st East Yorkshire in action on the Paradis Ridge. "A" Company moved into line at Paradis. "D" Company also went forward and assisted 1st West Yorkshire near Ennetières. Casualties – Major E.A.C. Blake and 4 other ranks killed, Lieutenant L.G. Norton mortally wounded, 2 officers, 46 other ranks wounded, 177 missing. Battalion assembled at Fetus then to Bois Grenier (21st). Later look over line at Rue du Bois. War Diary records that enemy shelling was almost continuous by day and night and sniping caused some casualties and inconvenience. Lieutenant E. Swetenham and Second-Lieutenant H.R. Vaughan (Connaught Rangers attached) killed (26th). The latter had recently been promoted from the ranks of 2nd Durham Light Infantry. Lieutenant Swetenham had joined the Battalion only the day before. Enemy attacked about 6 am (28th) and broke through. War Diary records that many of the rifles jammed due to mud and dirt. Position later retaken with help from 1st East Yorkshire. Relieved by 1st King`s Shropshire Light Infantry during night (31st) and to L`Arme. Casualties since going into line (21st) – 2 officers, 15 other ranks killed; 3 officers, 40 other ranks wounded; 7 missing.

NOVEMBER

To la Chapelle d` Armentières (3rd), Rue Deletre (4th). Relieved 1st King`s Shropshire Light Infantry in trenches at Rue de Bois (14th). Relieved and to L`Armee (27th). Casualties – 14 killed, 39 wounded. War Diary records that most of these were caused by enemy snipers. The German line was just 25 yards away in places. Relieved 1st West Yorkshire in trenches south-east of la Chapelle d` Armentières during night (30th). War Diary records section of line as extending from the Lille-Boulogne roads, about 400 yards north-west of Wez Marquar, to Rue du Bois.

DECEMBER
Relieved by 1/16th London and to billets at L'Armée. Casualties – 2 killed. To Pont de Nieppe (18th). Moved forward to Le Bizet (20th) but returned to Pont-de-Nieppe same day. To Armentières (23rd) and relieved 2nd Royal Welsh Fusiliers in trenches near Frélinghien (26th). Battalion's left on the Lys. Casualties (26th-31st) – 1 killed, 5 wounded.

HIGHLAND LIGHT INFANTRY

"Mons" "Retreat from Mons" "Marne, 1914" "Aisne, 1914" "Ypres, 1914" "Langemarck, 1914" "Gheluvelt" "Nonne Bosschen" "Givenchy, 1914"

1ST BATTALION

AUGUST
Salon and Ambala, India. Part of Sirhind Brigade, Lahore Division. Concentrated at Ambala (14th). Entrained for Bombay (17th). Embarked SS *Sumatra* (20th). War Diary records that the Battalion moved out of docks (23rd). However, the *Sumatra's* crew had deserted, the ship being worked by men of the Battalion. New crew arrived (24th).

SEPTEMBER
Arrived Suez (9th) and to Kasr-el-Nil Barracks, Cairo. Moved to camp at Heliopolis (26th). Headquarters with half of Battalion to Port Said (29th). Battalion's duties included guarding of the water works, oil tanks and the railway bridge at Roswara.

NOVEMBER
Headquarters detachment embarked SS *Sardinia* (20th) and sailed to Alexandria. Rest of Battalion joined (21st) and sailed for France (23rd). Arrived Marseilles (31st).

DECEMBER
Entrained for Orleans (1st). War Diary records moving to Railhead (5th), arriving (6th) and remaining in train for night. Detrained (7th) and marched 10 miles to billets at Vieille Chapelle. Began move forward to trenches around Festubert (11th). "A" Company came under attack (14th) – the enemy bombing their way down some 20 yards of trench near Picket House. Lost positions later reoccupied by party led by Lieutenant R.C. Guthrie-Smith. Attempt to regain positions lost by 1st Ghurkha Rifles failed (15th). Casualties- 2 officers, 7 other ranks wounded. "B" and "C" Companies took part in attack on German trenches near Givenchy (19th) – first wave moving forward at 5.34 am and gaining objective. War Diary records that gains were gallantly held throughout rest of day, but withdrawal was forced later. A "violent explosion" is recorded 9.30 am (20th) followed by a heavy bombardment of trenches. Most of which were blown in. The enemy

followed up with a bayonet charge – "only a small portion of the front line escaped." Relieved (22nd) and to Gorre. Casualties (19th-20th) – Major T.F. Murray, Captains L.G. Pringle, B.H. Baird, W.H.V. Cameron, Lieutenants C.M. Pitts-Tucker, H.R.G. Kerr, C.H. Anderson and R.C. Guthrie-Smith killed or subsequently died of wounds. Casualties amoung the other ranks are recorded in the War Diary as 54 killed, 63 wounded, 266 missing. Moved to Vendin (23rd), Auchel (24th).

2ND BATTALION

AUGUST
Maida Barracks, Aldershot. Part of 5th Brigade, 2nd Division. To Southampton (13th). Embarked SS *Lake Michigan* and sailed for France. Arrived Boulogne (14th) and to rest camp. Entrained for Wassigny (15th). Arrived (16th) and marched to billets at Le Petit Verly. To La Groise (21st), Pont-sur-Sambre (22nd), via Malplaquet to Genly (23rd). Moved to Paturages at midnight. "A", "B" and "C" Companies entrenched positions covering the town at daybreak (24th). Came under heavy shell fire – 14 wounded. Received orders to retire 9 a.m. and fell back to Bavai. Moved to defensive line covering the canal near Pont-sur-Sambe (25th), retiring again at 4 pm to bivouacs at Noyelles. To Barzy (26th), via Nouvion and Guise to St. Quentin (27th), Servais (28th), bivouacs just north of Soissons (30th), Laversine (31st).

SEPTEMBER
Marched via Villers-Cotterêts to Cuvergnon (1st), via Vincy to Chauconin (2nd), Petit Courais via Meaux (3rd), to Giremoutiers (4th), Marles (5th). Began advance to the Aisne (6th), marching to Paradis then La Trétoire (7th). Advanced in support of 4th (Guards) Brigade (8th), War Diary recording that the Petit Morin was crossed without opposition then – "advance stopped by our artillery shelling us." Bivouacked for night at Basseville. Moved forward to Tour (9th) then crossed the Marne to Domptin. To Monnes (10th), Beugneux (11th). Crossed the Vesle near Courcelles (12th) then to Vieil-Arcy. Crossed the Aisne (13th) and took up outpost positions near Verneuil. Took part in fighting at the Tilleul Spur (14th). War Diary records reaching the Chemin des Dames at 12 midnight – "no British troops on right or left, so retired to Verneuil." During day, the War Diary notes, Lieutenant Sir A.C. Gibson-Craig with part of "D" Company charged the enemy. This officer and Second-Lieutenant R.C.F. Powell being both killed. Private G. Wilson gained the Victoria Cross. Moved forward to firing line at Beaulne (15th). Relieved (17th) and to

Verneuil. Back to firing line (18th). Enemy attack repulsed (20th). War Diary records that 2 platoons of "B" Company made a gallant, but unsuccessful, counter-attack. Casualties – Lieutenant J.F.O`Connell (Medical Officer), Second-Lieutenants J.A.H. Fergusson, C.L. Mackenzie, E.R.H.K. MacDonald killed, 2 other officers wounded, 20 other ranks killed, 70 wounded, 25 missing. Relieved by 1st Black Watch (21st) and to Dhuizel. To Courtonne (30th).

OCTOBER
Moved to trenches north of Soupir (1st). Relieved by 48th French Regiment (13th) and to Vauxcéré. Entrained at Fismes (14th). Arrived Hazebrouck (16th) and marched to billets at Morbecque. To Godewaersvelde (17th), Poperinghe (19th). Moved forward (20th) and entrenched position covering the Steenstraate Bridge over the Yser Canal. Moved to positions near St. Julien (21st) and attacked north-east. Advanced to within a mile of Poelcappelle, then caught by heavy fire was forced to dig in along the St. Julian- Poelcappelle road. Casualties – 2 officers wounded, 14 other ranks killed, 80 wounded, 8 missing. German attack repulsed (22nd). Relieved by 125th French Regiment (23rd) and to positions by the railway halt at Hell Fire Corner. Took part in attack on Polygon Wood (24th). Enemy cleared after severe hand-to-hand fighting, then took up line on eastern edge of wood. Relieved (26th) and to bivouacs at north-east corner of Polygon Wood. Took over trenches north of Molenaareshoek from 1st King`s Liverpool (27th).

NOVEMBER
Relieved by French troops (1st) and to reserve bivouacs. Took over trenches east of the Becelaere-Passchendaele road (2nd). Enemy attacked (7th) and occupied part of trench held by "B" Company. War Diary records that the assault took place about 4.40 am and there was hand-to-hand fighting. Lieutenant W.L. Brodie – behaved with great promptitude and pluck – he bayoneted 4 Germans himself, shot 4 or 5 more and mounted a machine gun on a traverse which he fired down the trench. Some 80 of the enemy were killed or wounded and 54 prisoners were taken. Lieutenant Brodie subsequently received the Victoria Cross. Relieved (9th) and to reserve bivouacs. Moved to north-east corner of Polygon Wood (11th). Second-Lieutenant J.W. Mears killed, this officer having been commissioned only the previous day. In support during attack on Nonne Bosschen Wood. War Diary records that "C" Company – "did some excellent practice on Germans crossing open space between woods." Heavy bombardment of trenches (13th) – Captain R.G.I. Chichester, Lieutenant C.L. Cornish and

Second-Lieutenant G.P. Hall killed, 9 other ranks killed, 23 wounded, 2 missing. Shelled again (14th) – Lieutenant A.J. Dickson killed, 17 other ranks killed, 31 wounded, 5 missing. Relieved at night and to bivouacs at Outpost Farm. Moved into trenches north of the Ypres-Menin road (15th). Relieved by French troops (16th) and to Ypres. Casualties since 1st November totalled 346 killed, wounded or missing. Marched via Locre to Bailleul (18th). War Diary notes the arrival of 1/9th Battalion at Bailleul – "Turned out to cheer them." To Kemmel (25th) and relieved 1st South Wales Borderers in firing line. War Diary notes a "difficult" line with much sniping at night and heavy fire from the right. Relieved by 1st Northumberland Fusiliers (27th) and to Bailleul.

DECEMBER
War Diary records (4th) the presentation of the Victoria Cross by HM the King to Private G. Wilson at St. Omer. Moved in buses to Locon (23rd). War Diary records the meeting of 1st Battalion, Highland Light Infantry during journey. This was the first time since 1874 that both battalions had been together. Took over trenches near Richebourg St. Vaast (27th). Relieved by 2nd Oxfordshire and Buckinghamshire Light Infantry (31st) and to Richebourg St. Vaast.

1/9TH (GLASGOW HIGHLAND) BATTALION (TERRITORIAL FORCE)

AUGUST
Glasgow. Part of Highland Brigade, Lowland Division. Moved to Dunfermline.

NOVEMBER
Entrained for Southampton (2nd). War Diary records that 320 men from the Reserve Battalion (2/9th) at Glasgow were to replace those under 19 years of age or unable to volunteer for overseas service. Arrived 11 am and to rest camp. Embarked SS *Novia* (4th) and sailed for France. New rifles and ammunition issued same day. Arrived Havre (5th) and to No.2 Rest Camp. Strength recorded as 30 officers, 1,008 other ranks. Entrained (6th). Arrived St. Omer (7th) and marched to billets at Wardrecques. War Diary records that no time was lost in "commencing" the training of the 320 men from Reserve Battalion. It was noted that these were – "big and well made, as well as being of an exceedingly good class." To Hazebrouck (23rd), Bailleul (24th). Attached to 5th Brigade, 2nd Division. To Kemmel (25th). "A" Company and half of "B" moved into firing line which is recorded as

being too shallow in places and without communication trenches. War diary also notes that no attempt was made to deepen the trench, as the bottom was full of French dead. The bodies having been covered over with a few inches of earth. Troops in firing line relieved by 1/10th King's Liverpool (27th).

DECEMBER
Moved in buses to Locon (23rd). To Richebourg St. Vaast (27th) and relieved 2nd Oxfordshire and Buckinghamshire Light Infantry in firing line (29th).

SEAFORTH HIGHLANDERS (ROSS-SHIRE BUFFS, THE DUKE OF ALBANY'S)

"Le Cateau" "Retreat from Mons" "Marne, 1914" "Aisne, 1914" "La Bassée, 1914" "Armentières, 1914" "Festubert, 1914" "Givenchy, 1914"

1ST BATTALION

AUGUST
Agra, India. Part of Dehra Dun Brigade, Meerut Division.

SEPTEMBER
Entrained for Bombay (4th). Arrived (6th) and embarked HMT *Devanha*. Arrived Karachi Docks (8th). Anchored outside harbour (16th), sailing (21st).

OCTOBER
Arrived Suez (2nd). Sailed again (3rd), arriving Port Said (4th). Sailed for France (6th). Arrived Marseilles (12th). War Diary records Battalion's strength as 24 officers, 885 other ranks and being issued at the docks with Mark IV Short Lee Enfield rifles. Marched to camp at La Valentine (13th). Entrained for Orleans (17th) and Merville (26th). Marched to Vieille Chapelle (28th), Richebourg St. Vaast (29th). Heavily shelled about 4 pm. Later moved to trenches along the Estaires-La Bassée road near Pont Logy. War Diary records (31st) that wounded were collected from the battlefield, the men having been out in No Man's Land for several days and mostly from 1st Royal West Kent and 47th Sikhs.

NOVEMBER
War Diary records that trenches were held under constant sniping and shell fire. Lieutenant P.W.A.D. Mackenzie accidently shot (2nd) – revolver discharged owing to fall from bicycle. "D" Company came under attack (4th), casualties – 68 killed or wounded. War Diary records that the wounded had to be carried over a mile back to the Regimental Aid Post. Heavily shelled (7th) – one shell, War Diary records, made a hole 14 feet by 8 feet and a number of men were buried alive. Also noted is the accuracy of the enemy's snipers who were operating at close range from the outskirts of Neuve Chapelle. Enemy attack repulsed. War Diary records that "D" Company was relieved from positions on Battalion's right due to casualties –

Captain R.S. Wilson and 17 other ranks killed, 1 officer, 63 other ranks wounded. Battalion relieved by 2nd Royal Scots (12th) and to billets at La Couture. Total casualties since going into line – 45 killed, 191 wounded, 1 missing. To Le Hamel (17th). Relieved 2nd Leicestershire and 2nd Black Watch in trenches north of La Quinque Rue near Festubert (17th). War Diary notes (20th) that enemy snipers were operating from just 150 yards in places. Also, various types of grenades were tried out – with poor results. Relieved (22nd) – Headquarters with "A" and "B" Companies to billets at junction of Rue de L'Epinette and Rue du Bois, "C" and "D" Companies to crossroads north of Rue des Berceaux. Casualties (17th to 22nd) – 2 killed, 5 wounded. Headquarters, "A" and "B" Companies in support of attack (23rd). "C" and "D" Companies to Richebourg St. Vaast (24th), Battalion to billets at Le Touret (27th).

DECEMBER
Continued tours in Festubert sector throughout month.

2ND BATTALION

AUGUST
Shorncliffe. Part of 10th Brigade, 4th Division. To York by train (8th), Darlington (9th), York (11th). Marched to Strensall (14th), York (16th). By train to Harrow (18th) then marched to camp at Harroweald. Entrained for Southampton (22nd). Embarked SS *Lake Michigan* and sailed for France. Landed Boulogne (23rd) and to rest camp. Arrived Le Cateau by train (24th) and marched to Beaumont. Moved forward via Viesly to position just south-west of St. Python (25th). Later dug defensive positions north of Viesly. Line running from Fontaine to the Quiévy road. Came under shrapnel fire during afternoon – 1 killed, 4 wounded. Retired about 8 pm via Viesly, Bethencourt and Beauvois to Haucourt. Took up position near St. Aubert Farm during morning (26th) and covered withdrawal of 12th Brigade. Ordered to retire about 6 pm and fell back to Hurlevent Farm. Casualties – 1 officer, 20 other ranks wounded. Marched via Malincourt, Villers-Outréaux, Gouy, Vendhuille, Ronssoy, Templeux-le-Guérard and Roisel to Hancourt (27th). Moved later to Voyennes. To Bussy (28th), Beaurains (29th), via Carlepont, Tracy-le-Mont and Berneuil to Genancourt (30th), Verberie (31st).

SEPTEMBER
Marched via St. Vaast to Baron (1st), via Montagny and Eve to Dammartin (2nd), via St. Mard, Claye, Souilly, Annett and Lagny to Bois de Chigny

(3rd), to Magny-le-Hongre (4th), via Serris, Ferrières and Pontcarre to Chevry (5th). War Diary records march since 8 pm, 25th August as 155 miles. Began advance to the Aisne (6th), marching back through Serris then via Bailly to positions near Tigeaux. Marched via Maisoncelles to Giremoutiers (7th), via La Malmaison to L'Hotel-des-Bois (8th), via Jouarre to Grand Mt. Menard (9th). Crossed the Marne (10th) then via Dhuisy to Coulombs. To Hervilliers (11th) then via Montigny, St. Quentin, Passy and Chouy to Villers-le-Petit. To Septmonts (12th) and took up positions on high ground overlooking Billy-sur-Aisne. Moved through Billy and La Tuilerie (13th). Crossed the Aisne at Venizel and advanced (14th) to La Montagne Farm north of Bucy-le-Long. Came under fire (14th). Commanding Officer, Lieutenant-Colonel Sir E.R. Bradford (Bart), Captain W.E. Murray (Gordon Highlanders attached) and Second-Lieutenant A.J.N. Williamson killed. Other casualties (14th-30th) – 14 killed, 81 wounded.

OCTOBER
Relieved by French troops (6th) and marched via Venizel, Septmonts and Vilemontoire to Hartennes. To Rozet St. Albin (7th), via Villers-Cotterêts to Coyolles (8th), via Crépy to Rully (9th), via Raray to Villenueve (10th). Entrained at Pont-Ste. Maxence (11th). Arrived Arques and marched to St. Omer. War Diary notes bombing by enemy aircraft – some civilians killed. Moved by lorries to Caestre (12th). Marched via Flêtre (13th) and engaged during attack on Meteren. War Diary records that "A" Company got into the enemy's firing line – the position being – "carried at the point of the bayonet." Gains consolidated and held. Casualties – 4 officers wounded, 18 other ranks killed, 66 wounded, 1 missing. Moved forward into Meteren (14th), Bailleul (15th). Moved into billets about 2 miles east of Bailleul on the Nieppe road (16th). Marched via Rabot, Le Veau and Erquinghem to Armentières (17th). To Houplines Station (18th) and later took part in fighting near Le Ruage and Frélinghien. Casualties – 1 killed, 6 wounded. In reserve line south of Frélinghien (19th). "C" Company attacked and occupied several houses held by enemy snipers. Casualties – 1 officer wounded, 4 other ranks killed, 6 wounded. "B" Company attacked enemy's positions (20th). Forward trench taken along with several houses and a brewery. Casualties – Captain D.G. Methven killed leading the charge, Second-Lieutenant J.F. Glass mortally wounded, 1 officer wounded, 3 other ranks killed, 17 wounded. War Diary gives German casualties as 30 killed and 50 prisoners. Gains held under constant fire. Major C.I. Stockwell mortally wounded (21st), 6 killed, 17 wounded at the brewery (23rd-24th). War Diary records (26th) that large shells – 3 to 3 foot-6 inches long, approx-

imately 11 inches at the base, were being used by the Germans. The first did not explode while a second demolished a house. Enemy later attacked and reoccupied the brewery and several other buildings. Casualties – 23 killed, 37 wounded, 3 missing.

NOVEMBER

"D" Company attached to 11th Brigade (2nd) and sent into trenches near St. Yves. Relieved (6th) and moved back into billets near Ploegsteert. Came into action on eastern side of Ploegsteert Wood near the Le Gheer cross-roads (7th). Captain K. Forbes- Robertson and 7 other ranks killed, 1 officer, 33 other ranks wounded, 6 missing. Relieved after dark (8th) and back to Ploegsteert. Rejoined Battalion during night (11th/12th). Battalion relieved (17th) and to billets at Pont-de-Nieppe. To Armentières (18th), Brigade Reserve south of Ploegsteert Wood (19th). Relieved 2nd Royal Irish Fusiliers in trenches near the Douve south of Messines (21st). Relieved by 1st Royal Irish Fusiliers (25th) and to billets in Armentières and Pont-de-Nieppe. To Brigade Reserve (27th), relieving 1st Royal Irish Fusiliers in firing line (29th). Second-Lieutenant M.A. Hepburn killed by sniper (30th).

DECEMBER

Relieved by 1st Royal Irish Fusiliers (3rd) and to Pont-de-Nieppe. To Brigade Reserve (5th), relieving 1st Royal Irish Fusiliers in firing line (7th). Relieved by 1st Royal Irish Fusiliers (11th) and to La Crèche. To Brigade Reserve (13th), relieving 1st Royal Irish Fusiliers (15th). Relieved by 1st Royal Irish Fusiliers (19th) and to billets in Romarin and La Crèche. To Brigade Reserve (21st), relieving 1st Royal Irish Fusiliers (23rd). War Diary records no firing (25th) and able to walk about in the open. One man wounded (26th). Relieved by 1st Royal Irish Fusiliers (27th) and to La Crèche. To Brigade Reserve (29th), relieving 1st Royal Irish Fusiliers (31st).

1/4TH (ROSS HIGHLAND) BATTALION (TERRITORIAL FORCE)

AUGUST

Headquarters and "B" Company at Dingwall. Remaining companies (7) at Tain, Munlochy, Gairloch, Ullapool, Invergordon, Alness and Maryburgh. Part of Seaforth and Cameron Brigade, Highland Division. Commanding Officer – Lieutenant-Colonel D.J. Mason MacFarlane, T.D. Mobilized (4th). To Nigg (5th) digging entrenchments. Returned to Dingwall (8th). To Inverness (10th), Bedford (15th). Battalion headquarters at the Grammar School.

NOVEMBER
Left Highland Division and to Southampton (5th). Sailed SS *City of Dunkirk* for France arriving Havre (6th). Wounded from the 1/14th London Regiment (London Scottish) noted in ambulance train at docks. Marched to Bléville rest camp. Entrained for St. Omer (8th) and from there marched to billets at Ecques. To Arques (22nd). Battalion historian Lieutenant-Colonel M.M. Haldane records that the move was as result of a direct request by the Commanding Officer and due to the unfriendly nature of the people of Ecques. Reorganized into 4 companies. While at Ecques and Arques the battalion was subject to an epidemic of scarlet fever. This, Colonel Haldane notes, keeping the battalion from moving to the front and denying the men a bar to their "1914 Star."

DECEMBER
To Lambres (16th), via Lillers and Chocques to Labeuvrière (17th), Vieille Chapelle via Locon (18th). Large numbers of wounded noted during march. Among them what was left of a battalion of the Royal Irish Rifles led by its one remaining officer. Attached to Dehra Dun Brigade, Meerut Division. To reserve trenches (20th) on the Rue des Chavattes between Richebourg St. Vaast-Hulloch Road and the River Loisne. Half battalion in trenches, half resting at Lacouture. To Vieille Chapelle (21st), Rue des Chavattes and trenches at Chocolat Menier Corner (22nd). Relieved (23rd). Later half battalion took over trenches in front of Richebourg l'Avou, in support of 6th Jats. Colonel Haldane notes that the trenches had been dug by Gurkhas and that the tall Highlanders stood head and shoulders above the parapet. Relieved (24th). To Robecq (25th), Ferfay (26th). Battalion lined streets and cheered when 1st Battalion Seaforth Highlanders marched through Ferfay from front line.

GORDON HIGHLANDERS

**"Mons" "Le Cateau" "Retreat from Mons"
"Marne, 1914" "Aisne, 1914" "La Bassée, 1914"
"Messines, 1914" "Armentières, 1914" "Ypres, 1914"
"Langemarck, 1914" "Gheluvelt" "Nonne Bosschen"**

1ST BATTALION

AUGUST

Plymouth. Part of 8th Brigade, 3rd Division. To Southampton (13th). Embarked SS *Abinsi* and sailed for France. Arrived Boulogne (14th) and to rest camp at St. Martin. Strength – 28 officers, 987 other ranks. Entrained at Boulogne (15th). Left station 3.50 am, arriving Aulnoyn 2.20 pm and marching to Taisnières. Marched via Dompierre to St. Aubin (20th), via Maubeuge to Goegnies (21st). Advanced to Hyon (22nd) and entrenched facing Mons. Moved into line along the Mons-Beaumont road facing St. Symphorien (23rd) and fired on advancing enemy. Lieutenant L. Richmond killed. Fell back during evening to Nouvelles. Withdrew to Quevy (24th) then during night moved via Bavai to Amfroipret. Took up defensive positions west of Audencourt during morning (25th). Later via Viesly and Caudry to Audencourt. Entrenched north of village (26th). Enemy attacked and Battalion ordered to retreat. Withdrew just after midnight via Audencourt and Montigny. Came under fire south-west of Bertry about 2 am (27th) then moved towards Clary. Came under fire again suffering high casualties. Cyril Falls in his history of the Gordon Highlanders records that approximately 500 members of the Battalion were taken prisoner. War Diary records part of Battalion joined Brigade – 5 officers, 215 other ranks then marched through night (27th/28th) to Ham. To Genvry (28th), Cuts (29th), Courtieux (30th), Vaumoise (31st).

SEPTEMBER

To Chevreville (1st). Escorted Divisional Ammunition Column to Bregy (2nd) then via Forfray to Monthyon. Marched via Penchard and Meaux to Boutigny (3rd), through Sancy to La Chapelle (4th) then to Vaucoutois. To Retal (5th). Began advance (6th), marching via Liverdy, Châtres, La Houssaye and Crevecoeur to Hautefeuille. Moved via Faremoutiers and Coulommiers to Les Corvelles (7th), via St. Denis and Rebais (8th) then took part in fighting near Orly. Casualties – 2 killed, 19 wounded, 1 missing. Left Orly and marched via Bussieres and Nanteuil to Crouttes (9th), via

Bezu to Chezy (10th), via Neuilly to Oulchy-la-Ville (11th). Received orders to join General Headquarters as Army Troops and marched to Fere-en-Tarenois. War Diary records that some 700 German prisoners were taken on march. New duties included escorting prisoners to St. Nazaire and searching for isolated groups of Germans. The Commanding Officer of one party of 48 located (13th) recorded as offering to surrender on the condition that his men would not be handed over to the French. Also noted is the return (20th) of the Battalion`s 3rd Draft. The men had been temporarily attacked to 2nd Seaforth and were involved in the fighting at Bucy-le-Long on 14th September. The officer in charge of the detachment – Lieutenant W.E. Murray, had been killed and 18 other ranks were wounded. Relieved from GHQ duties by 2nd Suffolk (30th) and rejoined 8th Brigade at Courcelles.

OCTOBER
Marched via Braine, Cuiry-Housse and Beugneux to Oulchy-le-Château (1st). To Troësnes (2nd), Crépy-en-Valois (3rd), Moru area (4th). Entrained for Abbeville (5th). Arriving (6th) and to billets around Le Titre. Marched via Forêt l`Abbaye, Crécy and Dompierre to Raye (8th). Moved in buses to Pernes (10th) then marched via Avchel, Lozinghem to Le Cornetmalo area (11th). Took part in fighting around Fosse (12th). Enemy counter-attacked during advance (13th). Reached La Bassée-Estaires road (15th). Relieved from forward area (16th). No record of casualties for last few days fighting available. Cyril Falls, in his war history of the Gordon Highlanders however, notes that the figures for 8th Brigade were – 32 officers, 601 other ranks killed, wounded or missing and suggests that the Battalion lost probably about a quarter of that number. Moved forward (20th) to hold Grand Riez. Fell back later to new line around Fauquissart. Enemy attacked (24th) – breaking through Battalion`s line. Cyril Falls records that the assault was with great determination – the Gordons being driven through the orchards of Fauquissart onto the Neuve Chapelle-Armentières road. Part of 4th Middlesex came up later and with 1st Gordons in support managed to regain the lost trenches. Casualties – 7 officers, 197 other ranks.

NOVEMBER
Arrived Croix de Poperinghe (1st) and went into billets. Moved into trenches south of the Ypres-Menin road near Hooge (5th). Enemy attack repulsed (11th). Positions heavily shelled (12th) – Captains K.B. Mackenzie (Seaforth Highlanders attached) and D.C.W. Thomas (Argyll and Sutherland Highlanders attached) killed. Shelled again (13th) and forced to

withdraw. Two companies went forward at dusk and successfully cleared enemy from former trenches. Another attack (14th) – War Diary records that enemy heavily shelled the rear of Battalion's line, thus preventing reinforcements to come forward. The attack was repulsed with heavy loss – 15 killed, 34 wounded. Enemy came forward again (15th) – War Diary noting that some 50-60 Germans were found killed or wounded close to Battalion's front trench. Moved back into reserve trenches (16th). Major A.W. Buckingham killed, Captain M.J. Hamilton mortally wounded during shelling (17th). War Diary records being bombed from the air (18th) – the aeroplanes "passed with impunity up and down our lines all day." Relieved by French troops (20th) then marched via Ypres and Vlamertinghe to Westoutre. Casualties (5th-20th) – 4 officers, 33 other ranks killed, 6 officers, 70 other ranks wounded. Battalion's strength – 10 officers, 430 other ranks. To Locre (26th). Relieved 4th Royal Fusiliers in trenches near Kemmel, on the Kemmel-Wytschaete road (30th).

DECEMBER
Relieved by 4th Middlesex (3rd) and to Locre. To Westoutre (9th). War Diary notes proximity to the border – Headquarters and 3 companies being billeted in houses and farms in France, the other company occupying a farm in Belgium. It is also recorded that recent drafts contained some – "very old soldiers." One man having fought with the 1st Battalion at Tel-el-Kebir in 1882. Some of the men were considered to be unsuitable for a winter campaign, while the younger soldiers appeared to have received hardly any training – service varying from between 3 to 10 weeks only. Second-Lieutenant A. Pirie, recently promoted from the ranks, killed while carrying out reconnaissance of German positions near Maedelstraede Farm. east of Kemmel (12th). Marched via Locre to Kemmel (13th). Advanced (14th) – "A" and "B" Companies taking up forward trenches in readiness for attack on Maedelstraede Farm. War Diary records that British Artillery opened at 7 am, many shells falling short of the enemy's lines – "owing to the inadequate means of communication this could not be reported." Attacked 7.45 am. Enemy immediately opened up with heavy rifle and machine gun fire, War Diary recording that the attacking companies soon disappeared from view – "it was impossible to tell how they were progressing." Report relieved that men were seen entering German trenches 8 am. All attempts to contact forward troops unsuccessful. Message received 4.15 pm from Lieutenant G.R.V. Hume-Gore of "D" Company to the effect that he was isolated with 40 men in a position some 50 yards from German's front trench. He had no knowledge of leading companies – "B" and "C". The officer also reported that 5 messengers had been sent back by him throughout the day – none

having reached Headquarters. Party under Lieutenant W.H. Paterson (Argyll and Sutherland Highlanders attached) later found to be holding a German advance trench. Battalion later ordered to withdraw to original firing line then after relief by 4th Middlesex moved back to Kemmel. Casualties – Captain C. Boddam-Whetham (Black Watch attached), Lieutenants W.F.R. Dobie, J.J.G. McWilliam killed, 4 officers wounded, 51 other ranks killed, 139 wounded, 63 missing. To Locre (15th), trenches east of Kemmel (18th). Relieved by 1st Royal Scots Fusiliers (21st) and to Westoutre. Relieved 2nd South Lancashire in trenches south-east of Kemmel near Lindenhoek (27th). War Diary records – "worst trenches yet held." Relieved (31st) and to Westoutre.

2ND BATTALION

AUGUST
Cairo, Egypt.

SEPTEMBER
Embarked SS *Assaye* at Alexandria (13th) and sailed for England.

OCTOBER
Arrived Southampton (1st) and to Lyndhurst Camp near Winchester. Joined 20th Brigade, 7th Division. To Southampton (4th) and embarked SS *Lake Michigan* (Headquarters, "A" and "B" Companies), SS *Mineapolis* ("C" and "D" Companies). Officers – Lieutenant- Colonel H.P. Uniace (Commanding Officer), Major C.S.G. Craufurd, DSO (Second in Command), Captain J.R.L. Stansfeld, DSO (Adjutant); Lieutenants J.A.O. Brooke (Assistant Adjutant), Hon. W. Fraser (Machine Gun Officer), J. Mackie (Quartermaster), Second-Lieutenant W.J. Graham (Transport Officer), "A" Company: Captain J.L.G. Burnett, Lieutenants P.M. Mackenzie, H.M. Sprot, Second-Lieutenants J.P. Boyd, T.F. Murdock (Black Watch attached); "B" Company: Captains G.N. McLean, K.H. Bruce, Lieutenant J.M. Hamilton, Second-Lieutenants D.G.F. Macbean, J.F. Webster (Black Watch attached); "C" Company: Captain B.G.R. Gordon, Lieutenants L. Carr, C.H. Latta, A.S.B. Graham, Second-Lieutenant Q.D. Bell; "D" Company: Captain F.R.F. Sworder, Lieutenants J.H. Fraser, C.E. Anderson, Second-Lieutenants T.H.C. Thistle (Black Watch attached), W. Duguid, Hon. S. Fraser. Sailed (5th). Entered Dover Harbour daybreak (6th) then sailed again 6.30 pm. Arrived Zeebrugge during morning (7th) and entrained for Bruges. Moved into billets at St. André along the Dixmude road. Marched to Snaeskerke (8th). To Ostend

(9th) and entrained for Ghent. Arrived about midday and marched to the Champs de Manoeuvre. Later took up positions covering retirement of Belgium troops. Withdrew via Ghent to Somergen (11th) then to Thielt (12th), Roulers (13th). To Ypres (14th) and set up outpost line Kruisstraathoek to Voormezeele. Moved to Zandvoorde area (15th), billets in Zandvoorde (17th). Advance to line America to Kruiseecke (18th). Withdrew to Divisional Reserve at Reutel (19th). Took part in reconnaissance towards Gheluvelt (20th), later moving back to positions around Kruiseecke. War Diary records (21st) that the Battalion was – "much worried" by machine gun fire. Several small attacks were made by the enemy (22nd-24th) all repulsed. Sergeant A.E. Robinson was mortally wounded during the fighting and said before he died how disappointed he was not having being able to kill his 40 Germans before 1st January. All ranks had been asked to do this by the Commanding Officer. Drummer W. Kenny awarded Victoria Cross for gallantry (23rd). Retired to Gheluvelt (27th). Enemy attacked (29th). War Diary records that "C" Company became isolated but managed to hold their line throughout the day – ". . . 240 dead Germans being counted in front of one platoon alone." Battalion later withdrew to Veldhoek. Casualties – 100, including Lieutenants Brooke, Hon. S. Fraser, Latta; Second- Lieutenants A. McBride and G.H. McAulliffe (both formally NCOs with the Battalion and recently commissioned) killed. Lieutenant Brooke was subsequently awarded the Victoria Cross. Took part in attack at Zandvoorde (30th). Advance held up by heavy shell, machine gun and rifle fire from wood 800 yards to Battalion's left front. Retirement ordered about 2.30 pm and Battalion fell back to Bodmin Copse. Further withdrawal ordered (31st) but later took part in counter-attack, driving enemy back through Shrewsbury Forest. The war history of the Northamptonshire Regiment tells how that regiment's 1st Battalion, along with 2nd Royal Sussex and 2nd Gordon Highlanders – ". . . with loud cheers charged them with the bayonet, The issue was not long in doubt. After a few minutes hand-to-hand fighting the enemy broke and fled back to Bodmin Copse." Battalion's casualties included Lieutenants J.H. Fraser, Graham and Second-Lieutenant Webster killed. Both the Commanding Officer and Major Craufurd were wounded, along with 12 other officers.

NOVEMBER

Moved to positions near Zillebeke (1st). Strength – 3 officers, 200 other ranks. Relieved (5th) and to Locre. To Bailleul (6th), Meteren (7th). Moved to Fleurbaix sector (14th), Sailly (15th). Draft arrived (16th). Strength now 4 officers, 500 other ranks. To Rue de Biaches (17th). War Diary records (19th) that white smocks were issued for recognisance in snow. Relieved 2nd Scots Guards in trenches – Rue Petillon (20th). Relieved (24th) and to Rue de Biaches. Relieved 1st Grenadier Guards in front line (26th). War Diary records (28th) the issue of steel loopholes. These had been tested at Brigade Headquarters and were found to be bullet proof at ranges of 50 and 100 yards. Relieved by 1st Grenadier Guards (29th) and to Rue de Quesnes.

DECEMBER
Carried out tours in trenches throughout month. War Diary records very heavy rain and trenches flooded and full of liquid mud. Not a shot was fired by either side during the Christmas period.

1/6TH (BANFF AND DONSIDE) BATTALION (TERRITORIAL FORCE)

AUGUST
Headquarters Keith and companies at Banff, Dufftown, Keith, Buckie, Inverurie, Alford, Bucksburn and Huntly. Part of Gordon Brigade, Highland Division. Commanding Officer – Lieutenant-Colonel C. McLean. Mobilized (4th). The battalion historian – Captain D. Mackenzie, MA, MC notes a – "magnificent response" – one man who was seriously ill and could not report had his place taken in the ranks by an ex member who borrowed his uniform. Assembled at Keith (6th-7th) – men billeted at Headquarters, local schools and private houses. Entrained for Perth (11th) – billeted in schools and a granary. Entrained for Bedford (16th) – billeted in private houses in Beverley Crescent, Bromham Road, Cutliffe Grove, Cutliffe Place, Hurst Grove, Winifred Road and Preston Road. Headquarters at the pavilion of the Girl`s High School.

OCTOBER
Reviewed by HM the King (22nd).

NOVEMBER
Left Division and to Southampton (9th). Sailed SS *Cornishman* for France. Arrived Havre (10th) and to No.1 Rest Camp. Entrained for St. Omer (13th) and to billets at Blendecques. French troops wearing long blue coats with red pantaloons and armed with muskets were noted guarding railway line en route. Lined streets of St. Omer during Lord Robert`s funeral procession (19th).

DECEMBER

To Hazebrouck (4th), Sailly sur la Lys (5th). Attached to 20th Brigade, 7th Division. Began instruction in front line Fleurbaix sector (6th). Captain Mackenzie notes much help from 2nd Gordons. He also mentions "The Guards" (1st Grenadier, 2nd Scots) as being tall men, fire-steps in the line being too low for the Highlanders and requiring the addition of 1 or 2 sand-bags to enable them to see over the parapet. Knee and often waist-deep mud is noted and the fact that the men were still wearing shoes, spats and hose. In close support during 20th Brigade attack edge of Sailly-Fromelles road (18th). Mention of several "spy scares" appears in the battalion's records. One tells of an Englishman who had joined the battalion at Bedford being placed under arrest by another unit. He had lost his way and his captors refused to believe that a man with his name and accent could possibly belong to a Highland regiment. Much is mentioned of the "Christmas Truce" and more information gleaned regarding the occasion. Germans began to sing carols during night (24th), calling out – "no shoot to-night Jock! – sing tonight." Men from both sides moved un-armed into No Man's Land (25th). Colonel McLean arrived accompanied by the Padre, Rev. J. Esslemont Adams, and ordered the men back to their trenches. The Padre at once went out and with German officers arranged truce to allow burial of dead. While he was doing this a hare ran through No Man's Land and was immediately pursued by both Scots and Germans. At about 4 pm a service took place in the middle of the 60 yards that divided the British and German lines. The 23rd Psalm was read in English by the Padre and German by a divinity student serving with the Saxons. Captain Mackenzie notes that the truce did not end after Christmas Day, meetings in No Man's Land were commonplace for some time. Coins, buttons, pipes and food being exchanged. When it was learnt that a number of barbers were serving with the enemy their services were enlisted and several men were shaved. A system was arranged between both sides whereas a few shots would be fired into the air whenever Brigade or Divisional Staff were in the area. As soon as they left the truce was resumed and both sides once again walked freely in No Man's Land. An "embarrassing" incident during a visit by the Brigade Commander is mentioned. Noticing one of the enemy walking peacefully around and in full view, the Brigadier ordered one man to open fire. The rifleman aimed high but the German took no notice. Another shot, this time wide, caused him to look up in surprise. A third and this time more accurate round, ordered by the Brigadier, had the effect of sending the astonished German headlong into a trench. The truce came to an end on 3rd January, 1915.

QUEEN`S OWN CAMERON HIGHLANDERS

**"Retreat from Mons" "Marne, 1914" "Aisne, 1914"
"Ypres, 1914" "Langemarck, 1914" "Gheluvelt"
"Nonne Bosschen" "Givenchy, 1914"**

1ST BATTALION

AUGUST
Edinburgh. Entrained for Southampton. Officers – Lieutenant-Colonel J.D. McLachlan (Commanding Officer), Majors A.D. Nicholson (Second in Command), A.P. Yeadon (Quartermaster), Lieutenants K.F. Meiklejohn (Adjutant), S.G. Traill (Machine Gun Officer), D. Cameron (Transport Officer), J.Crocket (RAMC, Medical Officer); "A" Company: Major Hon. A.H. Maitland, Lieutenants N.C.G. Cameron, R.F.L. Johnstone, R.M.MacDonald, Second-Lieutenant J.W.F. McLachlan; "B" Company: Captains A. Horne, A.G. Cameron, Lieutenant J.S.M. Matheson, Second-Lieutenants R.N. Stewart, I.B. Sprot, W.M. Cameron; "C" Company: Captain D.N.C.C. Miers, Lieutenant A.S. Nicholson, Second-Lieutenants A.H. Mackinnon, J.H. Dickson, A.G.R.J. Smith-Sligo; "D" Company: Captains A.H. Mackintosh, Lord J.T. Stewart-Murray, Second-Lieutenants H.W.L. Cameron, I.S.J. Constable-Maxwell, A.J.G. Murray. Arrived (13th) and embarked SS *Gando* for France. Arrived Havre (14th) and to rest camp at Greville. Battalion to serve as Army Troops and attached – Headquarters, "A" and "B" Companies to General Headquarters, "C" Company to Headquarters 2nd Army and "D" Company to Headquarters 1st Army.

Headquarters, "A" and "B" Companies
Entrained at Havre for Le Cateau (15th) then St. Quentin (25th). To Ham (26th). A German prisoner accompanied the Gordons and, according to *Historical Records of the Queen`s Own Gordon Highlanders* (regimental history), was dressed as a member of the Battalion, so as to save him from the attentions of the crowd. Marched to Noyon (27th). Moved by train to Compiègne (28th), then Dammartin-en-Goele (31st).

"C" Company
Entrained at Havre for Landrecies (16th). To Bavai (21st), Sars-la-Bruyere (22nd). Withdrew via Le Quesnoy to Bavai (24th), Bertry (25th). Marched through night (26th) to St. Quentin then in lorries to Ham. Marched via

Noyon to Cuts (28th), via Attichy, Haute- Fontaine, Crépy-en-Valois, Nanteuil, St. Souplet and Esbly to Crécy (30th).

"D" Company

Entrained at Havre for Wassigny (16th). Marched via Prisches to Marbaix (21st), via Dompierre and Eclaires to Louvroil (22nd), via Maubeuge to Gognies (23rd), to Bavai (24th), Vieux Mesnil (25th) then via the Forest of Mormal to Landrecies. To Hannappes via Etreux (26th), Mont d`Origny via Guise (27th), St. Gobain via Ribemont and La Fére (28th), Vauxbuin via Coucy-le-Château and Terny (30th), Villers Cotterêts (31st).

SEPTEMBER
"C" Company

Arrived Tournan (6th). Marched via Faremoutiers, Coulommiers to Doue (7th). Relieved from duties with 2nd Army Headquarters (10th) and rejoined Battalion at Bruyeres (11th).

"D" Company

To Mareuil (1st), Meaux (2nd), La Fringale (3rd), via Montanglaust and Coulommiers to Faremoutiers (4th), Chaumes (5th). Advanced to Chaubisson Farm (6th), Choisy (7th). Relieved from duties with 1st Army Headquarters (8th) and rejoined Battalion at Sablonnières.

Headquarters, "A" and "B" Companies

To Lagny (1st). Entrained for Melun (2nd). To Guignes (4th), Nesles (5th). Relieved from duties with General Headquarters (except Nos 5 and 7 Platoons of "B" Company) and became part of 1st Brigade, 1st Division. Advanced to Voinsles (6th) and came under shell fire. Moved forward again and bivouacked around Le Plessis. Marched via Amillis, Chevru and Choisy to La Ferté Gaucher (7th). Engaged enemy at Sablonnières (8th) – Lieutenant Johnstone and 3 other ranks killed, 3 wounded. "D" Company rejoined. Moved forward via Hondevillers to Bassevelle. Crossed the Marne at Saulchery (9th) then to La Nouette Farm. Marched via Le Thiolet, Lucy le Bocage, Torcy, Courchamps and Sommelans to Ressons (10th), via La Croix and Nanteuil to Bruyeres (11th). "C" Company rejoined. Marched via Fere-en-Tardenois, Loupeigne and Bruys to Bazoches (12th), via Vauxcéré to Longueval (13th). Crossed the Aisne just west of Villars then via Bourg and Moulins to bivouacs between Moulins and Paissy. Moved forward through Moulins and Vendresse (14th) and took part in attack along the Chivy Valley towards German positions at the Chemin des Dames. Moved back after heavy fighting and entrenched in woods above

Vendresse. Casualties – Major Maitland, Captains Mackintosh, Horne, Lieutenant Nicholson, Second-Lieutenants Murray, H.W.L. Cameron, Mackinnon, Dickson and Smith-Sligo killed, 8 officers wounded. Regimental history gives casualties among other ranks as approximately 151 killed or died of wounds and many more wounded. During the fighting, Lieutenant N.C.G. Cameron was wounded but escaped being taken prisoner by pretending to be dead. The Germans cutting his revolver and field glasses from his body as he lay on the ground. Private Ross Tollerton was awarded the Victoria Cross. The "B" Company detachment arrived from GHQ (16th). Relieved (17th) and into reserve north- west of Vendresse. To Oeuilly (19th), Bourg (20th), support positions at Courtonne (21st). Relieved 1st Black Watch in trenches near Beaulne (24th). Enemy began shelling about 7.15 am (25th). Just behind the firing line were a series of caves used by the Battalion as support and rest areas. Around 7.30 am 2 shells landed at the cave being used by Headquarters, buried alive its occupants – Captains Miers, A.G. Cameron, Lieutenants N.C.G. Cameron, Meiklejohn, Crocket and 24 other ranks killed. Only 4 men survived. Several rescue attempts were made, but shelling prevented the removal of bodies from the cave for many days. Relieved by 1st King's Royal Rifle Corps (26th) and to Bourg. Relieved 1st South Wales Borderers in front line near Vendresse – "The Quarries" (27th). Regimental history gives casualties among other ranks for period (18th-30th) as approximately 41 killed and many more wounded.

OCTOBER
Relieved by French troops (16th) and via Vendresse, Bourg and Longueval to Blanzy-le- Fismes. Casualties (1st-16th) – 14 killed, 20 wounded. Entrained at Fismes (17th) and travelled via Creil, Amiens, Etaples and St. Omer, arriving Hazebrouck (19th). To Poperinghe (20th). Moved forward (21st) via Elverdinghe and Boesinghe to Brigade Reserve positions at Pilckem. Later advanced and took part in the fighting east of Bixschoote. In action throughout day (22nd). Regimental history records some 3 battalions of German infantry attacking trenches held by "B" Company about 4.30 pm. The enemy advanced with Colours flying, a band playing, and the men singing. "B" Company opened fire, but their line was soon overrun, Second-Lieutenant I.B. Sprot being among those killed. Later, Captain J.A. Orr and 3 men were seen charging into the enemy with their bayonets – "The heroic four were completely overwhelmed by the tide of Germans, and were never seen again." During a general advance on the afternoon of (23rd), it was noted, the previous day's fighting was marked by German corpses. The Camerons, tartan being seen here and there among the dead. The War Diary

of 2nd Queens records that the Battalion advanced on the Inn due north of Pilckem on the Bixschoote-Langemarck road and after inflicting heavy casualties on the enemy released some 80 men of 1st Cameron Highlanders that had been taken prisoner. Relieved from firing line (24th) and moved back to support positions. Relieved by French troops (25th) and to billets at Zillebeke. In addition to those already mentioned as killed, 12 other officers were wounded during the fighting at Bixschoote. The Medical Officer, Lieutenant G.H. Chisnall being mortally wounded. Total casualties among other ranks are given as approximately 76 killed, 47 wounded. Moved forward (26th) and at night held reserve positions near Gheluvelt, "B" and "D" Companies along the Gheluvelt-Zandvoorde road. "A" and "C" Companies moved forward (27th) and in support during attack on Kruiseecke. Battalion took over trenches eastern side of Polderhoek Château (28th). Position held under constant shell and sniper fire. Several men buried alive (31st). Approximate casualties among other ranks (26th-31st) – 23 killed, 18 wounded.

NOVEMBER

Moved to positions astride the Reutelbeck (1st). Lieutenant R.M. Macdonald killed, Captain L. Robertson mortally wounded (2nd). Moved to trenches around Verbeek Farm during night. Enemy (The Prussian Guard) attacked (11th) and broke through British line towards Nonne Bosschen. Captain E.J. Brodie killed. Relieved (14th) and to positions on the Ypres-Menin road north of Hooge. Moved to Zillebeke (16th) then via railway line to Vlamertinghe. Later to Westoutre. Marched via Locre, Bailleul, Strazeele and Pradeles to Borre (17th). Regimental history notes that of the original officers that left Edinburgh in August, only Major Yeadon remained. The Battalion now contained just 5 officers (including the Medical Officer) and approximately 240 other ranks. Up until midnight (22nd/23rd) some 51 officers and 1,982 other ranks had embarked for service with the Battalion.

DECEMBER

Several drafts received during month. Left Borre (20th) and marched via Strazeele and Merville to Béthune. Moved forward (21st) via Beuvry and Annequin. Crossed the Aire- La Bassée Canal at Pont Fixe and took part in attack on Givenchy. Relieved from firing line (22nd) and moved back to bivouacs just west of Cuinchy. Casualties – Second- Lieutenants A. Crum-Ewing (Seaforth Highlanders attached) and J.W. Graham (Highland Light Infantry attached) killed, 6 officers wounded. Relieved 1st Black Watch in trenches north of Givenchy (25th). Relieved by 1st Black Watch (28th) and to Béthune. Casualties among other ranks (21st-28th) – approximately 66 killed, 35 wounded.

2ND BATTALION

AUGUST
Ghonpuri Barracks, Poona, India. Detachment sent to guard railway at Kirkee.

SEPTEMBER
Detachment returned. Battalion ordered to stand by for embarkation to England.

OCTOBER
Entrained for Bombay (11th). Embarked HMT *Saturnia* (12th) and sailed for England (15th) calling at Aden (16th).

NOVEMBER
Called at Port Said (1st), Gibraltar (8th). Sailed (12th) and arrived Plymouth (17th). Disembarked and by train to Winchester. Marched to Mourne Hill Camp and joined 81st Brigade, 27th Division.

DECEMBER
Marched to Southampton and embarked HMT *Atlantia* for France (19th). Officers – Major (Brevet Lieutenant-Colonel) J. Campbell, DSO (Commanding Officer), Majors L.O. Graeme, P.T.C. Baird, Captains C.W. Maclean, P.W.N. Fraser, DSO, A.D. Macpherson (Adjutant), D.E.M.M. Crichton, R. Campbell, R.B. Trotter, D. Macdonald (Quartermaster), B. Biggar (RAMC, Medical Officer), Lieutenants A. Macduff, H.C. Methuen, A.Y.G. Thomson, A.A. Fowler, W.D. Nicholson, D.G. Davidson, I.C. Grant, L.F. Hussey-Macpherson, R.A.C. Henderson, Second- Lieutenants J.R.H. Anderson, H.A.H. Dunsmure, Alexander Fraser, D. Grant, J. Murray, T. Walker, J.M`K. Gordon, Andrew Fraser, G.Hunter, Rev. A.S.G. Gilchrist (Chaplain). Arrived Havre (20th) and entrained for Aire-sur-la-Lys. Employed in digging trenches about 2 miles north-east of the town.

ROYAL IRISH RIFLES

**"Mons" "Le Cateau" "Retreat from Mons"
"Marne, 1914" "Aisne, 1914" "La Bassée, 1914"
"Messines, 1914" "Armentières, 1914" "Ypres, 1914"
"Nonne Bosschen"**

1ST BATTALION

AUGUST
Aden. Two companies stationed at Kirkee, India. Detachment on Perim Island. Battalion moved into barracks at Steamer Point as part of the Harbour Defence Force. Duties included escort of captured German ships. Kirkee detachment rejoined (16th).

SEPTEMBER
Relieved by 1st Lancashire Fusiliers. Embarked HT *Dilwara* (27th) and sailed for England (28th). War Diary records that 2 men died on voyage. Both landed at Gibraltar sick.

OCTOBER
Arrived Liverpool (22nd) then by train to camp at Hursley Park, Winchester. Joined 25th Brigade, 8th Division.

NOVEMBER
To Southampton (5th) and embarked SS *Anglo Canadian*. Strength – 31 officers, 1,014 other ranks. Arrived Havre, landing (6th) and to No.1 Rest Camp. Entrained for Strazil (9th). Arrived early morning (11th) then to billets around Vieux Berquin. War Diary records that the local people were very friendly and helpful. The area had been looted by the Germans. Moved forwar to Laventie (14th) and took over trenches ("F" Lines) at Rue Tilleloy (15th). War Diary records the Battalion's "Baptism of Fire" – 1 man killed, 1 mortally wounded while taking over trenches. Also, that the length of line held was so long that messages took 1½ hours to move between Battalion Headquarters and the furthest company. There were just 50 riflemen to 250 yards of trench in some places. Patrols were sent out and these established that the enemy kept very few men in their front line at night. Relieved by 2nd Lincolnshire during morning (22nd) and to billets near Laventie. Casualties since going into line – 10 killed, 29 wounded, 2 missing. Returned to front line (24th). Relieved by 2nd Lincolnshire (27th) and to billets at

Fort D'Esquin. "C" Company remained in reserve at Rue Masselot, "D" in local support to 2nd Lincolnshire. Casualties – 3 killed, 7 wounded. Returned to "F" Lines (30th).

DECEMBER

Relieved by 2nd Lincolshire (3rd) and to Estaires. Casualties – 5 wounded. War Diary notes the reduction in casualties. A number of men from each platoon had been selected to act as "Sharpshooters" and these had played an important role in keeping the activities of the enemy's snipers to a minimum. To front line (6th). Captain B. Allgood killed during relief. Relieved by 2nd Lincolnshire (9th) and to Fort D'Esquin. Casualties – 1 officer and 1 other rank killed, 6 wounded. "A" and "B" Companies remained in local reserve at Rue Masselot and Picatin respectively. Returned to front line (12th). War Diary records (17th) the arrival of a draft comprising 1 officer and 93 other ranks. A number of these men (those from the reserve battalions) had never fired a rifle while others were from the 2nd Battalion of the Regiment and had been wounded at Mons. Fired on opposite trenches (18th) during attack by 23rd Brigade on enemy positions in front of Neuve Chapelle. Relieved by companies of 2nd Lincolnshire and 1/13th London (21st) and to Fort D'Esquin. Casualties – 5 killed, 22 wounded, 1 missing. To front line trenches ("E" Lines) (23rd). Battalion Headquarters on Rue Tilleloy near junction with Rue Masselot. War Diary notes the arrival of 64 men from reserve battalions and records the following reports from company commanders – PHYSIQUE: "Fairly good" GENERAL EFFICIENCY: "Fair" MUSKETRY: "not up to standard" "EQUIPMENT: "Good, same as regular army" DISCIPLINE: "Very poor." Lamps placed on parapets of German lines and singing heard (24th) – "If you are English come out and talk to us – we wont fire" called out from trenches opposite. Parties from both sides eventually met in No Man's Land. Cap and helmet badges exchanged. Message received from Headquarters, 8th Division (25th) urging vigilence as ". . . Germans are not to be trusted." Relieved by 2nd Lincolnshire (26th) and to Laventie. Returned to "E" Lines (29th).

2ND BATTALION

AUGUST

Tidworth. Part of 7th Brigade, 3rd Division. To Southampton (13th) and sailed SS *Ennisfallen* and SS *Sarnia* for France. Arrived Rouen (14th) and to camp at Mont St. Aignan. Entrained at Rouen (16th) for Aulnoye. Marched to Marbaix (17th), St. Hilaire (20th), Feignies (21st), Ciply (22nd), Nouvelles (23rd). Withdrew later via Ciply to Harmignies. Took up defensive positions on high ground – "C" and "D" Companies in firing line, "A" and "B" in reserve on the Givry-Mons road. Enemy engaged – 4 casualties. Withdrew to Nouvelles (24th) then via Maladrie and Bavai to St. Waast. Set up outpost line at La Bois Crette. Retired (24th) via Gommegnies, Le Quesnoy, Romeries and Le Cateau to Maurois. John Lucy was on this march and noted in his book *There`s a Devil in the Drum* how a German aeroplane overtook the battalion from the rear. Several men opened fire and succeeded in bringing the machine down into a field. Sergeant Lucy later heard that the pilot, who was killed, was accompanied by a little boy who also perished. Took part in fighting at Caudry (26th) – 60 other ranks killed, 5 officers, 29 other ranks wounded. Withdrew during evening to Beaurevoir. Continued retreat (27th) via Hargicourt to Vermand. Marched through night to Ham, then (28th) to Tarlefesse. Took up defensive line in Bois d`Autrecourt (29th). Moved via Morlincourt, Varesnes and Pontoise to Vic- sur-Aisne (30th), Coyolles (31st).

SEPTEMBER
Marched via Levignen to Villers-St. Genest (1st), via Bouillancy, Marcilly and Barcy to Pringy (2nd). To La Marche (3rd) then via Penchard, Meaux and Boutigny to Sancy. To Vaucourtois (4th) then marched through night via Crécy, Obelisque and Neufmoutiers to Châtres. Began advance to the Aisne (6th), marching back via Neufmoutiers and Obelisque to Faremoutiers. To Les Petits Aulnois via Coulommiers (7th), via Rebais to Bussieres (8th), via Nanteuil and Crouttes to Bezu (9th), via Chézy to Montmafroy (10th), via Dammard, Neuilly-St. Front and Oulchy-la-Ville to Grand-Rozoy (11th), Cerseuil (12th), Braine (13th). Marched through Brenelle and Chassemy to Bois Morin (14th). Crossed the Aisne and took up positions on high ground at La Fosse Margnet. Came under enemy fire – "A" and "C" Companies advancing but forced to fall back. Second-Lieutenants H.P. Swaine and R.H.C. Magenis killed. John Lucy provides a vivid account of this action. He recalls watching his younger brother Denis, who was also in the Battalion, move forward. His rifle at the high port and looking threatening. John called for him to take care of himself. When John`s section went forward the Germans held their fire for a while then opened up with machine guns, rifles and shells which cut into the advancing line. Possibly half of the men, John thought, fell on to their faces. Catholic soldiers blessed themselves. He also noted low fire which tore through the men's legs – one bullet shattering the sole of his right boot. A sergeant, there were no officers, called for the men to get down. A German machine gun then ripped through the huddled bodies, many men being hit in the head – their faces jerking rapidly forward – "This was a holocaust." "C" Company advanced

again (17th), but driven back by heavy shell fire. Held positions under heavy shell fire and infantry attacks. Relieved by 1st Leicestershire during night (21st/22nd) and moved back via Vailly to Augy. Casualties (14th-22nd) – 2 officers killed, 12 wounded, 270 other ranks killed or wounded. Major C.R. Spedding, DSO posted as missing, but later found to have been killed. Began work on trenches west of Braine (24th). Relieved 2nd South Lancashire at Chassemy (26th) – 3 companies taking over positions covering the bridge at Condé. Relieved by 1st Wiltshire (28th) and to Braine. To Couvrelles (30th).

OCTOBER

To Grand-Rozoy (1st), via St. Remy and Billy-sur-Ourcq to Noroy (2nd), via Troësnes, Le Fert,-Milon and Coyolles to Vaumoise (3rd), via Crépy and Bethisy to Verberie (4th). To Longueil Ste. Marie (5th) and entrained. Arrived Noyelles (6th). Marched via Sailly, Letitre and Hautvillers to Le Plessiel (7th). To Regnauville (9th), then in afternoon to Hesdin. Travelled in lorries to Floringhem and took over outpost line on high ground above Pernes. Relieved by 3rd Worcestershire (10th) and into billets at Pernes. Marched via Floringhem, Auchel, Lozinghem, Allouagne and Gonneham to Hinges (11th). Moved forward (12th) and in action at Lacouture. Captain C.L. Master killed. Advanced to positions around Croix Barbée (13th). Lieutenant A.N. Whitfeld killed (14th). Moved forward under heavy frontal and enfilade fire (15th). War Diary records night position as just south-west of the cross roads at Rouge Croix to parallel roads leading into the Neuve Chapelle-Estaires road. Advanced to Bois de Biez (16th), L'Aventure (17th). War Diary notes that from there Germans could be seen moving towards La Bassée along the road from Fournes. Three companies took part in attack on Herlies, later falling back to positions around Lannoy. Relieved by 2nd King's Own Yorkshire Light Infantry (18th) and to billets at Pont Logy. Moved later to Bois de Biez. To L'Aventure (20th) and relieved 2nd King's Own Yorkshire Light Infantry in trenches near Lannoy. Moved to new positions near Halpegarbe (21st). Fell back later to Neuve Chapelle – 3 companies in trenches, 1 billeted in the school. Enemy attack during night (23rd) repulsed and again (24th). War Diary records that the latter was with heavy casualties to the Germans. Captain T.J. Reynolds and Lieutenant V.T.T. Rea killed, Captain H.A. Kennedy mortally wounded. War Diary notes that the Battalion is now – "practically without officers." Enemy driven out of houses on left of Battalion's line (25th). "A" and "C" Companies relieved (26th) and into billets at Richebourg St. Vaast. Enemy attacked later and entered trenches held by "B" and "D" Companies. War Diary records that no further trace of these companies could be obtained.

"A" and "C" Companies recalled and enemy driven back. Enemy broke through on left flank during morning (27th) – "A" and "C" Companies having suffered severe casualties fell back into Neuve Chapelle. War Diary records that only 2 officers and 48 other ranks succeeded in getting back. Captain H.O. Davis and Lieutenant E.S. Mulcahy-Morgan killed. Battalion relieved and to Richebourg St. Vaast. Strength recorded as under 200. To Lacouture (29th), Doulieu (30th), Merris (31st).

NOVEMBER
To Locre (1st). Marched through Ypres to trenches at Hooge (5th). Strength now 250. Attacked by Prussian Guard (11th). War Diary notes that the enemy were driven back with heavy losses. Battalion casualties – 15 killed, 10 wounded, 19 missing. Moved back later into Brigade Reserve – Hooge sector. Fighting strength now 130. Relieved by 1st Northumberland Fusiliers (19th) and moved back to positions near Divisional Headquarters east of Ypres. Moved to Hooge (20th) then later to Westoutre. Draft of 3 officers, 463 other ranks joined. To Locre (27th). Took over trenches near Kemmel (30th).

DECEMBER
Relieved by 2nd Royal Scots (3rd) and to Westoutre. To Locre (6th), Kemmel trenches (9th). Captain J.P. Whelan killed (11th). To Locre (12th), Kemmel trenches (15th). Captain G.A. Burgoyne recorded (see *The Burgoyne Diaries*) how many wounded from the previous day's fighting were still laying out in front of the Battalion's trenches. It was almost impossible and certain death to attempt to bring any of them in. He saw one man of the 1st Gordon Highlanders in a dugout who had been shot through the foot and gave him a morphia tablet to help with the pain. To Locre (18th), Kemmel trenches (24th), Westoutre (27th), Locre (31st).

PRINCESS VICTORIA`S
(ROYAL IRISH FUSILIERS)

"Le Cateau" "Retreat from Mons" "Marne, 1914" "Aisne, 1914" "Armentières, 1914"

1ST BATTALION

AUGUST

Shorncliffe. Part of 10th Brigade, 4th Division. Entrained for York (8th). To Darlington by train (9th), returning to York (11th). Marched to Strensall (16th). To York (18th) and entrained. Arrived Harrow and marched to camp at Harroweald. To Kenton (22nd) and by train to Southampton. Embarked SS *Lake Michigan* and sailed for France. Arrived Boulogne 11 pm. Disembarked during morning (23rd) and marched to camp at St. Martins. Returned later to Boulogne and entrained. Arrived Le Cateau during afternoon (24th) and marched to Beaumont. Took up positions south of Python (25th). Withdrew later via Viesly to Fontaine-au-Tertre Farm. Moved again after dark via Fontaine-au-Pire to Haucourt. Enemy attacked (26th) and Battalion fell back – part to Hurlevent Farm, part to Le Catelet. The party at Hurlevent Farm, led by the Commanding Officer Lieutenant-Colonel D.W. Churcher, marched via Malincourt and Aubencheul-aux-Bois to Le Catelet. The detachment there had already left and both columns met up at Roisel. Battalion then moved on to Hancourt then continued retreat through night (27th/28th) to Voyennes. Moved later to Bussy. Arrived Beaurains (29th). War Diary notes a dog-fight between British and German aircraft, the latter being driven back to its lines. Marched via Noyon, Sempigny, Carlepont, Tracy-le-Val, Tracy-le-Mont and Berneuil to Genancourt (30th). To St. Sauveur (31st) then after dark to Verberie.

SEPTEMBER

To Néry then Baron (1st), Dammartin-en-Goële (2nd), via St. Mard, Juilly, Claye, Souilly and Thorigny to bivouacs east of Bois-du-Chigny (3rd), via Serris to Magny-le-Hongre (4th), Serris, Jossigny, Ferrières and Pontcarre to Chevry (5th). Began advance to the Aisne, marching via Serris to positions west of Crécy (6th), high ground north of Ferrolles (7th) then via Maisoncelles to Giremoutiers. To Les Poupelans (9th), La Ferté (10th). "A" Company detached as escort to Headquarters, 3rd Army Corps. Crossed the Marne then via Dhuisy and Coulombs to Hervillers. To

Villers-le-Petit (11th), Septmonts (12th), via Billy-sur-Aisne to La Tuilerie (13th). Crossed the Aisne at Venizel (14th) and to Bucy-le-Long. Held trenches near Ste. Marguerite under constant shell fire. Five killed, 24 wounded (17th). War Diary notes the day as the "most trying experience" since the fighting at Haucourt. The men were "steady under fire." Moved position forward north of village. "A" Company rejoined (18th).

OCTOBER

Relieved (6th) and via Venizel, Billy-sur-Aisne, Septmonts and Rozieres to Hartennes. To Rozet St. Albin (7th), Vauciennes (8th), via Crépy to Rully (9th), Verberie (10th). Entrained at Longeuil for St. Omer (11th). War Diary records German aeroplane dropping 2 bombs (12th). Moved later in lorries to Hazebrouck area, then marched (13th) via Hazewinde, St. Sylvestre and Caestre to Flêtre. Took part in attack on Meteren. Billeted for night near La Bersace Farm. Moved forward into Meteren (14th), Bailleul (15th). Bivouacked east of La Crèche (16th). Advanced via Erquinghem (17th). War Diary records that the people of Armentières welcomed the troops with gifts of bread, coffee and chocolates. Ground north-east of Houplines made good, "B" and "C" Companies fighting all day. Captain M.B.C. Carbery killed near Le Ruage. "C" and "D" Companies in action at Le Ruage (19th). Battalion relieved after dark and to Houplines. Took part fighting at Frélinghien (20th). Withdrew later to trenches around Houplines. Positions held under heavy shell fire and infantry attacks.

NOVEMBER

War Diary records (1st) that good news was received from the Eastern Theatre (Russian successes in Poland presumably). This having – "a good effect on all ranks." "A" Company sent up to Ploegsteert Wood sector and attached to 11th Brigade (2nd). War Diary records (9th) receiving news that "A" Company – "had done very well." "A" Company rejoined (14th). Relieved (17th) and to billets south of Ploegsteert. Relieved 2nd Royal Scots in trenches south of Messines (18th). Lieutenant C.R. Crymble killed (20th). Relieved by 2nd Seaforth (21st) and to Pont-de-Nieppe. To Armentières (22nd). Relieved 2nd Seaforth (25th). Relieved by 2nd Seaforth during night (29th) and to billets in Nieppe.

DECEMBER

Relieved 2nd Seaforth (3rd). Relieved by 2nd Seaforth and to La Crèche (7th). Relieved 2nd Seaforth (11th). Relieved by 2nd Seaforth and to La Crèche (15th). Relieved 2nd Seaforth (19th). Relieved by 2nd Seaforth and to La Crèche (23rd). Relieved 2nd Seaforth (27th). Relieved by 2nd Seaforth (31st).

2ND BATTALION

AUGUST
Quetta, India.

OCTOBER
Embarked during month for England.

NOVEMBER
Arrived England (20th) and to camp at Winchester. Joined 82nd Brigade, 27th Division.

DECEMBER
To Southampton and embarked for France. Arrived Havre (19th) and from there entrained for Arques.

CONNAUGHT RANGERS

"Mons" "Retreat from Mons" "Marne, 1914"
"Aisne, 1914" "Messines, 1914" "Armentières, 1914"
"Ypres, 1914" "Langemarck, 1914" "Gheluvelt"
"Nonne Bosschen" "Festubert, 1914"
"Givenchy, 1914"

1ST BATTALION

AUGUST
Ferozepore, India. Part of Ferozepore Brigade, Lahore Division. Entrained for Karachi (17th). Arrived (19th). Embarked SS *Edavana* (27th) and sailed (29th).

SEPTEMBER
Arrived Aden (6th), sailed again (7th), arriving Suez (13th). Disembarked (14th) then by train to Cairo. To Alexandria (18th) and embarked SS *Edavana* again. Sailed for France (19th). War Diary records the death of Private P. Stapleton who was buried at sea. Arrived Marseilles (26th) and to camp at Borély. Strength – 22 officers, 877 other ranks. Entrained (30th).

OCTOBER
Arrived Des Aubreis (3rd) and marched to Camp Cercotes. Entrained (17th), arriving Wizernes (19th). To Wallon-Cappel (21st). Moved in buses to Wulverghem (22nd) and relieved 2nd Essex in trenches east of Messines (23rd). Advanced to attack Gapaard 4.20 pm (26th). War Diary records that contact could not be made with troops to the left and right. Message received 6.59 pm that attack had in fact been cancelled as these battalions had not arrived. "C" Company took 3 trenches, but without support was forced to retire. Battalion withdrew to Wulverghem 10 pm. Casualties – 1 killed, 15 wounded, 1 missing. Took over trenches near Messines (27th). Relieved (29th) and marched via Wulverghem and Neuve Eglise to Estaires. To Rue de Bacquerot (30th).

NOVEMBER
Relieved 1st Royal Scots Fusiliers in reserve trenches(1st). Moved forward to reinforce 2nd Gurkhas (2nd) – Lieutenant G.D. Abbott killed. Took part in attack to regain lost trenches (5th). War Diary records that 2 platoons of "A" Company drove the enemy from advanced trench. Later – "the fire

of "A" Company practically ceased owing to the bolts of their rifles jamming." Casualties – Captain C.E. Hack, Lieutenants G. de M. Armstrong-Lushington-Tullock, F.R. George and J.R. Ovens killed, 4 other ranks killed, 30 wounded, 2 missing. "A" and "C" Companies to billets at Rue de Bacquerot, returning to firing line (8th). Three killed, 11 wounded during relief. War Diary records that rifle grenades were issued to "A" Company (9th) and were – "used with great success." Enemy attack on "A" Company (13th) repulsed. Same company heavily shelled (14th) – 2 men buried. Relieved (15th-16th) and to billets at La Gorgue. Moved to Zelobes (17th), via Gorre to Festubert sector (23rd). "A", "B" and "C" Companies took part in attack. Casualties – 2 officers wounded, 6 other ranks killed, 53 wounded, 54 missing. Battalion withdrew at midnight, marched to Le Plantin. and took over trenches from 2nd Black Watch.

DECEMBER
Relieved and to Gorre (2nd). Strength 9 officers, 343 other ranks. To Le Touret (3rd). Draft of 4 officers, 130 other ranks arrived (4th). Amalgamated with 2nd Battalion, Connaught Rangers. Combined strength now 19 officers, 913 other ranks. Moved to Gorre (12th), Béthune (14th). Moved forward to Givenchy (16th), moving back via Annequin to Béthune same day. To Cuinchy (17th) and relieved 1st Manchester in trenches south of the La Bassée Canal. Second-Lieutenant A. Montgomery killed by sniper (22nd) Relieved later by 1st King`s Royal Rifle Corps and to Béthune. To La Beuvrière (23rd). Strength recorded (31st) as 19 officers, 769 other ranks.

2ND BATTALION

AUGUST
Barrosa Barracks, Aldershot. Part of 5th Brigade, 2nd Division. Entrained for Southampton (13th) and embarked SS *Herschell* and sailed for France. Officers – Lieutenant-Colonel A.W. Abercrombie (Commanding Officer), Major W.S. Sarsfield (Second in Command), Captain E. Yeldham (Adjutant), Lieutenants C.F. Dryden (Quartermaster and Transport Officer), W.G.S. Barker (Machine Gun Officer), C.F. Blacker (Divisional Cyslists Officer); "A" Company: Captains L.W.P. de Hochepied Larpent, E.G. Hamilton, Lieutenant W.P. Lambert, Second-Lieutenants R.A. de Stacpoole, R.L. Spreckley, L.N. Aveling; "B" Company: Major H.M. Hutchinson, DSO, Lieutenants R.M.H. Henderson, F.D. Foott, Second-Lieutenants G.R.C. Brook, G. Allen; "C" Company: Major W.N.S. Alexander, Captain W.W. Roche, Lieutenants R.I. Thomas, G.E. de

Stacpoole, Second-Lieutenant V.A. Lentaigne; "D" Company: Captains G.J. O'Sullivan, F.W.M. Leader, Lieutenant J. Fraser, Second-Lieutenants R.B. Benison (Signals Officer), C.A.C. Turner, J.L. Hardy, H.M. Swifte. Arrived Boulogne (14th) and to rest camp. Entrained for Busigny (16th) then marched to Mennevret. To La Croise (21st), Pont-sur-Sambre (22nd), via Malplaquet and Genly to Bougnies (23rd). Later dug in at cross-roads 2 miles to the north. Captain wrote that the Battalion was in support and could see shells bursting ahead and German infantry attacking British trenches. Captain Blacker mortally wounded. Withdrawal ordered and fell back via Quévy-le-Petit, Blaregnies, Malplaquet and La Longueville, arriving Pont-sur-Sambre (25th). Later moved to Laval, then during night to Noyelles. Moved back to Laval (26th) then continued retreat via Taisnières. Engaged enemy at Le Grande Fayt – Captain Leader killed, Lieutenant-Colonel Abercrombie and Lieutenant Baker mortally wounded and taken prisoner, Captain Roche, Lieutenants Hardy and Turner taken prisoner. Some 280 other ranks are recorded as missing. Survivours reached Mont d'Origny (27th) then Battalion continued retreat via Ribemont, Hanregicourt and Le Fère to Servais (28th), Coucy-le-Château to Ternay (30th). Crossed the Aisne at Pommiers (31st) then to Cutry.

SEPTEMBER
To Antilly (1st), Chauconin (2nd), Petit Couroix (3rd), bivouacks near the village of Paris (4th), Marles (5th). Began advance to the Aisne (6th), moving first to positions near Champlet, then Pézarches. To Rebaix (7th) and engaged in fighting north of Pézarches (8th). Advanced to La Tretoire and rook part in attack on Orly. To Pavant (9th), crossed the Marne at Charly, then to Domptin. To Monnes (10th), Beugneux (11th), Vieil D' Arcy (12th). Crossed the Aisne at Pont D' Arcy (13th) then moved forward to Soupir. Took up positions at La Cour de Soupir Farm (14th). Enemy attacked during morning, but driven back with assistance from 2 companies of 2nd Coldstream. Approximately 250 German prisoners taken. Relieved and moved back to Soupir. Casualties – Lieutenants Fraser, Thomas, Second-Lieutenant Spreckley killed, 5 officers wounded, 250 other ranks killed, wounded or missing. To Verneuil (15th), positions on high ground near Tillend (16th). Moved back to support line (17th). Shelled throughout day (18th) then moved back to positions on main road north of Verneuil. Major Sarsfield mortally wounded, 4 other ranks killed. Advanced to firing line (19th). Enemy attack repulsed (20th) – Lieutenants G.R. Fenton, Henderson, Second-Lieutenants Benison, de Stacpoole killed, 35 other ranks killed or wounded. Withdrew into reserve then via bivouacks east of Verneuil to Dhuizel (21st).

OCTOBER

To Soupir (2nd), Bourg (6th), Vauxcéré (13th), Fismes (14th) and entrained for Hazebrouck. Arrived (16th) and to billets at Morbeque. To Godewaersvelde (17th), Poperinghe (19th), bivouacks near Boesinghe (20th). "C" and "D" Companies moved forward and took part in Battle of Langemarck (21st) – 4 killed, 30 wounded. Held positions – 3 killed, 5 wounded (22nd). Heavilly shelled and infantry attack repulsed (23rd) – 9 killed, 2 wounded. "C" and "D" Companies relieved and joined "A" and "B" companies at St. Julien. Battalion then moved to Halte. Advanced along Menin road (24th) and into reserve line at Veldhoek. Relieved 2nd Oxfordshire and Buckinghamshire Light Infantry in Polygon Wood (25th), "B" and "C" Companies moved forweard to Molenaaresthoek trenches (28th) – Captain F.H. Jackson and 10 other ranks killed, 1 officer, 16 other ranks wounded. Part of "C" Company attacked enemy's trenches (31st) – 1 officer taken prisoner, 6 other ranks killed, 30 wounded, 30 missing.

NOVEMBER

"A" and "D" Companies repulsed attack (1st) – 10 killed, 35 wounded. Held line against several attacks and heavy shelling (2nd) – Lieutenants C.J.O'C Mallins and A.T.C. Wickham killed. Relieved by 2nd Highland Light Infantry and to reserve line. Moved back to firing line (3rd). Enemy came forward after dark (5th) – "B" Company driving them back. Second-Lieutenant A. Winspear and 4 other ranks killed, 3 officers and 30 other ranks wounded. Two attacks repulsed (8th). Relieved by 2nd Worcestershire and to positions north-west corner of Polygon Wood. In action (10th) – driving enemy back into Nonne Bosschen Wood. Casualties – 15 killed, 50 wounded. Moved into Brigade Reserve behind Polygon Wood (12th) then to Bellewaarde Farm (16th). To Bailleul (20th), Hazebrouck (24th). Moved via Merville, Lacon and Béthune to Gorre (26th). Battalion transferred to Ferozepore Brigade, Lahore Division.

DECEMBER

Amalgamated with 1st Battalion, Connaught Rangers at Le Touret (5th).

Princess Louise's (Argyll and Sutherland Highlanders)

"Mons" "Le Cateau" "Retreat from Mons" "Marne, 1914" "Aisne, 1914" "La Bassée, 1914" "Messines, 1914" "Armentières, 1914"

1st Battalion

AUGUST
Dinapore, India.

OCTOBER
Entrained for Bombay (10th and 11th). Arrived (14th) and embarked HMT *Saturnia*. Sailed (15th) calling at Aden (16th).

NOVEMBER
Called at Port Said (1st), Gibraltar (8th). Sailed (12th) and arrived Plymouth (17th). Brigadier R.C.B. Anderson, DSO, MC, recalls in his history of the Battalion that it was very cold at Plymouth and the men were still in their light-weight foreign service khaki drill uniforms. Disembarked (19th) and by train to Winchester. Marched to Mourne Hill Camp and joined 81st Brigade, 27th Division.

DECEMBER
To Southampton (19th) and embarked HMT *Novian*. Officers – Lieutenant-Colonel H.L. Henderson (Commanding Officer), Major R.C. Gore (Second in Command), Lieutenants C.H. Patten (Machine Gun Officer), J. Heatly (Quartermaster), G.P. Selby (RAMC, Medical Officer), Second-Lieutenant A.J.G. Murray-Graham (Transport Officer); "A" Company: Captain D.M. Porteous, Lieutenant C.B Purvis, Second-Lieutenants H.R.H. Greenfield, R. Gibb, E.J. McCutcheon; "B" Company: Captain G.A. McL. Sceales, Lieutenant J.H. Young (Acting Adjutant), Second-Lieutenants M.C.C. Clarke, J. Neill, S.G. Rome, I.F.C. Bolton; "C" Company: Captain A.R.G. Wilson, Second-Lieutenants A.McD. Ritchie, W.M.P. Kincaid-Lennox, J. Forbes-Leith; "D" Company: Captain N.D.K. MacEwen, Lieutenant R. Stirling, Second-Lieutenants J.C. Steel, J.L. Rowan-Thompson, E.M. MacDonald. Landed Havre (20th) and to St. Adresse Rest Camp. Entrained for Aire-sur-la-Lys (21st) and marched to billets at La Poudriere. Lieutenant A.R. Boyle (Adjutant) joined from

England (24th). Began work on trenches east of Boeseguem (27th) and south of Pecqueur (29th). War Diary records that ground was very difficult to dig, so built upwards. Parties to front line Messines sector for instruction with 2nd Duke of Wellington's Regiment (30th).

2ND BATTALION

AUGUST

Fort George. Took over 91German, Austrian and Dutch prisoners of war from fishing fleet recently sunk in the North Sea. War Diary records that the men were – "all very cheery" and confined to the moat by day and in casements by night. Left for Southampton in 4 trains (9th). First train with Lieutenant-Colonel H.P. Moulton-Barrett (Commanding Officer), Lieutenants H.J.D. Clark (Adjutant), T.H. Clayton (Quartermaster) the Transport Officer and 50 Headquarters personnel arrived on time at 12.30 pm (10th). Second train containing "A" Company (Captain A.B. Thorburn) and "B" Company (Captain H.H.G. Hyslop); 3rd train – "C" Company (Major A.H. Maclean) and "D" Company (Captain J.A. Fraser and 4th train – Major K.F.C. Marshall (Second in Command), Machine Gun Officer and 50 Headquarters personnel all delayed and held up outside Southampton Docks. War Diary records that the transport horses would not pull in "the new" harness and caused great delay. "A" and "B" Companies embarked SS *Seahound* and sailed for Boulogne. First train party and "C" Company embarked SS *Bertha* but departure delayed and men remained on board overnight. "D" Company and 4th train party marched to camp about 3 miles outside of Southampton. "A" and "B" Companies arrived Boulogne 9 am (11th) and moved into the old barracks. SS *Bertha* arrived and men joined "A" and "B" Companies. Headquarters billeted in the Hotel Bristol. Battalion now on Line of Communications duties. "B" Company moved to billets in a girls'school (13th). "D" Company and remainder of Headquarters arrived on SS *Empress of India* (14th) and moved into billets in another school. Three platoons of "A" Company under Lieutenants W.M. Burt-Marshall, R.M.G. Aytoun and Second-Lieutenant P. Anderson sent to unload trains at railhead (15th). War Diary records concert given (18th) in which members of the Paris and Brussels Opera Houses – "sang with great beauty." The carrying of the late General J. Grierson's body from a train and onto a ship was attended by all officers and "C" Company (19th). Eight men from the Battalion carried the coffin and the Pipers played *The Flowers of the Forest*. Moved by train to Valenciennes (22nd). Took over billets in a school where, War Diary records, the 3 platoons of "A" Company were already located. Battalion now part of 19th Brigade. Marched to

Onnaing (23rd) then in afternoon to Quievrechain and billets in an iron foundry. Later, "C" Company advanced to Quiévrain and took up positions on railway crossing north of village. "D" Company moved forward to Hensies in support of front line. Detachment under Second- Lieutenant C.L. Campbell sent to positions on railway line at St. Homme (24th). Battalion moved to Baisieux then at 9 am retired to Rombies and dug defensive positions. Moved again in afternoon to Jenlain then later relieved 4th Hussars in trenches on high ground south west of Eth. "A" and "D" Companies in front line, "B" and "C" in support. Received orders to hold line at all costs. War Diary records no supplies received and men without food. St. Homme detachment rejoined having been attacked by the enemy in large numbers. Eventually retired via Elouges having had 2 men killed and 13 wounded. Withdrew to Jenlain, then on to Haussy (25th). War Diary records that the transport horses were exhausted and much of the officers' kit had to be discarded during march. Horses still would not pull so traces were cut and wagon set on fire. Took up position on ridge north west of village. Continued withdrawal in afternoon via Solesmes to Le Cateau. "A" Company remained in town, remainder to billets in factory close to railway station. Moved out of Le Cateau 5.30 am (26th). Turned off St. Quentin road to positions on southern edge of wood north of Reumont. Ordered 9 am to take up positions on slopes south west of St. Quentin road and overlooking Le Cateau. Came under heavy shell fire. War Diary records that "B" Company suffered as much from reverse and enfilade fire as it did from frontal fire. "A" Company on left flank moved forward over ridge and were met with heavy rifle and machine gun fire from short range. Several attacks led against the enemy all brought severe casualties. Three platoons sent forward to assist 2nd Suffolk at crossroads south-west of Pont des Quatre Vaux. Enemy attacked in force at 2.30 pm from front and right flank. The Germans, Lieutenant-Colonel C.C.R. Murphy records in his history of the Suffolk Regiment, shouting to the Suffolks and Highlanders to cease fire and surrender. In the Middlesex Regiment war history, Everard Wyrall notes that before being overwhelmed the men from both regiments – "had taken heavy toll of the enemy." He also records that 2 of the Highlanders in particular accounted for man after man, each counting his score aloud as though in a shooting competition. Withdrawal ordered. War Diary records that party led into attack by Major Maclean about 1.30 pm was not seen again and all officers are missing. The Battalion was now divided up into 3 main parties until 5th September and thanks to a detailed War Diary we can trace the movements of each. Lieutenant-Colonel Mounton-Barrett withdrew to high ground north west of Honnechy then moving to the south followed the railway line into Busigny. He later took his party on to Beaurevoir and at

12.15 am (27th) marched to Hargicourt. At Hargicourt the Commanding Officer went to Noyon and the party now under Major Marshal continued march via Vermand to Ham. Marched to Genvry (29th) and travelled by train to Compiègne. Moved to Courtieux (30th) and Crépy-en-Valois (31st). Another party under Captain Hyslop withdrew via Reumont and then along the Roman Road marched to Estrees. Later, at 11 pm, continued on to St. Quentin. Captain Hyslop then took his men to St. Quentin station and at 10 am (27th) moved by train to Noyon. At Noyon some of the party took over billets in the Cavalry barracks, but some 150 men were ordered to remain on the train. Lieutenant-Colonel Mounton-Barrett arrived at Noyon from Hargicourt and set up Battalion Headquarters. Headquarters moved to Pontoise (28th), Laigle (29th), Couloisy (30th) and via Verberie to billets near Salines (31st). A third party under Lieutenant J.C. Aitkin withdrew (26th) to a field just north of Estrees then (27th) marched via St. Quentin to Ham. The party moved on to Noyon (28th) but being unable to find the Battalion entrained for Compiègne. Entrained for Rouen (30th) then to Le Mans. Arrived (31st) and marched to camp at Caserme Chaney. Party now under the command of Lieutenant J.C.R. Rose. The men left on the train at Noyon moved with Captain W.A. Henderson to Ribecourt (28th) and joined Major Marshal at Genvry (29th).

SEPTEMBER

War Diary records (1st) 3 Uhlans arriving at Salines, firing down the street and hitting Second-Lieutenant J.L. Fetherstonehaugh's horse. Also no rations, but 1st Scottish Rifles shared theirs. Moved out during morning to Néry. War Diary records that village had been heavily shelled – "L" Battery, Royal Horse Artillery having suffered heavily, attached to Cavalry Brigade, withdrew 8 am to Fresnoy. Took up outpost positions during evening on ridge covering Baron. Marched into Baron 5 am (2nd). Later in morning to Eve then via Dammartin to Longperrier. To Dammartin (3rd) and with 19th Brigade attached to 4th Division. Later marched to bivouacs east of Lagny. Marched via La Ferrière to bivouacs in orchard east of Grisy. Major Marshall's party left Crépy-en-Valois (2nd) and marched to Nanteuil. To Montyon (3rd), Jossigny (4th). Rejoined Headquarters at Grisy (5th). Lieutenant Rose entrained for Grisy (4th). Arrived 4 pm (5th) and rejoined Battalion. Headquarters, "A" and "B" Companies to Ozoir La Ferrière (6th) then via Villeneuve St. Denis, Montrarbin and Sancy to La Haute Maison. "C" and "D" Companies went to Brie-comte-Robert (6th) and rejoined rest of Battalion at La Haute Maison (7th). Advanced to high ground south of La Ferté-sous-Jouarre (8th). "B" and "C" Companies later went forward to south bank of the Marne and came under heavy rifle and machine gun fire from the northern bank. Fell back to Signy-Signets 10 am (9th) then 7 pm to Jouarre. Advanced into La Ferté (10th). Crossed the Marne then via Marcy to Certigny. Moved via Passy to Marizy Ste. Geneviève (11th), Buzancy (12th), Septmonts (13th), Venizel (14th). Bivouacked at Soissons-Venizel crossroads just south of village. Moved through village (15th) and dug in near pontoon bridge crossing the Aisne. Crossed river (16th) and relieved 1st Royal Warwickshire in positions south of Bucy-le-Long. Began work clearing village and burying the dead. Came under shell fire 11 am and moved to bivouacs in orchard at east end of village. Moved back to Venzel (21st) then on to Septmonts. Began work digging trenches at Acy (22nd).

OCTOBER

To St. Remy (5th), Vez (6th), Bethisy St. Pierre (7th), Pont-Ste. Maxence (8th), Estrées- St. Denis (9th). Entrained for St. Omer. To Renescure (11th). "B" Company took over defensive positions on Hazebrouk road just east of village. With 19th Brigade attached to 6th Division (12th) and marched via La Kreule to Eeecke. Moved via Caestre to Rouge Croix (13th). Advanced in support of attack via Bailleul and Steenwerck (14th). Later to bivouacs west of Mont Lille. Marched via Bailleul to Steenwerk (15th), Neuve Eglise, Kemmel and La Clytte to Vlamertinghe (16th), La Clytte, Kemmel, Neuve Eglise, Steenwerk, Estaires to Laventie (19th), Fromelles (20th) and via Pont de Pierre to Le Maisnil (21st). Entrenched in and around village. Came under shell fire and attack from the south east during morning and from the east at 2 pm. Second-Lieutenant A.H. Blacklock killed. "C" Company enfiladed by rifle and machine gun fire 4.30 pm. War Diary records 4 officers wounded – "casualties very heavy." Withdrawal ordered and fell back to positions 500 yards north west of Le Maisnil 5.30 pm. Later moved to La Boutillerie. War Diary records many wounded had to be left behind during retreat. Five officers and over 200 other ranks missing. Dug defensive positions and lines held against numerous attacks. "A" Company to Le Touquet (23rd).

NOVEMBER

To Erquinghem (1st). "A" Company arrived from Le Touquet 11 pm. To Pont-de-Nieppe (2nd). Began entrenching near windmill west end of village (3rd). To Ploegsteert (7th) and bivouacked in fields at west end of village. Moved forward during afternoon via Le Bizet to support positions at Touquet. Returned to Ploegsteert 7 pm. Relieved 3rd Worcestershire in front line eastern side Ploegsteert Wood (8th). Took part in attack on enemy trenches (9th). Moving forward 11.30 pm between eastern edge of wood and the St. Yves-Le Gheer road. Withdrew to support trenches in wood 4.30 am (10th). Casualties- 3 officers missing, 1 wounded, 10 other ranks killed, 71 wounded, 45 missing. War Diary records that these casualties were from an attacking force of about 330. "B" Company later moved up to front line. "D" Company relieved "B" and half of "A" Company to line near St. Yves (11th). "D" Company rejoined Battalion (12th). Relieved and to billets at Rue Bataille (13th). Took over trenches near Pont Ballot road, Houplines sector (17th). Lieutenant G.S. Hutchison arrived with a draft of 150 (21st) and he noted in his autobiography *Footslogger* that the Houplines position was just a single trench, ankle or knee-deep in mud and slime. There was no fire step and the enemy were 200 yards away. Lieutenant Hutchison (later Lieutenant-Colonel) also records that a sleeping area for the officers was dug out of – "a kind of mausoleum." It was a large comfortable room furnished with doors carpet and furniture taken from local houses. There was even a window with lace curtains that looked across to Battalion Headquarters. Several officers are mentioned by name, one being J.A. Liddell who would later win the Victoria Cross with the Royal Flying Corps. Company of 1/5th Scottish Rifles attached for instruction (28th).

DECEMBER
War Diary records (2nd) presentation by HM The King of Distinguished Conduct Medal to Sergeant R. Roase at Croix Dubac. Also shelling (6th) causing no casualties among Battalion but 5 civilians killed. "A" Company came under attack (9th). Enemy advancing to within 150 yards before being driven back. Relieved by 1/5th Scottish Rifles (11th) and to billets in the Lunatic Asylum, Armentières. War Diary records heavy shelling (14th). More than 700 shells fired over billets, but about half failed to explode. Further shelling during morning (20th). Cookhouse hit and "B" Company's barracks. Casualties – 1 man wounded. Moved to front line Houplines sector 4.15 pm. Germans requested permission to bury their dead (25th). War Diary records that this was granted and that the men were from the 133rd and 134th Regiments. Lieutenant Hutchison records a cease fire, men chatting with the Germans who gave cigars and cap badges. Relieved and to Armentières (26th).

1/7TH BATTALION (TERRITORIAL FORCE)

AUGUST
Headquarters in Stirling; "A" Company – Stirling; "B" Company – Stenhousemuir; "C" Company – Falkirk; "D" Company – Lennoxton; "E" Company – Alloa; "F" Company – Alva; "G" Company – Kinross; "H"

Company – Alloa. Part of Argyll and Sutherland Infantry Brigade, Highland Division. Moved to Bedford.

DECEMBER

Removed from Highland Division and to Southampton (14th). Sailed SS *Oxonian*. Returned to docks due to fire in cargo hold. Sailed SS *Tintoretto* (15th). Landed Havre 9 am (16th).

PRINCE OF WALES` LEINSTER REGIMENT (ROYAL CANADIANS)

"Aisne, 1914" "Armentières, 1914"

1ST BATTALION

AUGUST
Fyzabad, India.

SEPTEMBER
Received orders to embark for UK (27th).

OCTOBER
Entrained for Bombay (11th) and embarked SS *Caledonia* (16th). Called at Aden.

NOVEMBER
Arrived Gibraltar (8th). Here, Lieutenant-Colonel Frederick Ernest Whitton in his history of the Leinster Regiment, records that newspapers carried names of casualties among the 2nd Battalion (already in Europe). Arrived Plymouth (16th) and from there to camp at Morne Hill, Winchester. Joined 82nd Brigade, 27th Division.

DECEMBER
To Southampton (19th) and embarked SS *Lake Michigan* for France. Arrived Havre (20th) and from then entrained for Arques near St. Omer. Marched to billets at Wardrecques.

2ND BATTALION

AUGUST
Cork, Ireland. Part of 17th Brigade, 6th Division. Embarked SS *Graphic* (17th) and sailed for Holyhead. Landed and entrained for Cambridge. Arrived 8.30 am (18th) and moved into camp on Midsummer Common. Moved to camp at Newmarket (31st). Captain (later Lieutenant-Colonel) F.E. Whitton, CMG served with the Battalion and notes in his war history of the Regiment the hospitality shown to 2nd Leinster by Clare College. The officers later presenting them a silver statuette as a token of gratitude. He also records the concern shown at Newmarket regarding the racehorse

training area. Strict orders being issued to all battalions of the 6th Division not to undertake any manoeuvres or marching on the Newmarket "Gallops."

SEPTEMBER

Entrained for Southampton (7th). Arrived (8th) and embarked SS *Lake Michigan*. Lieutenant-Colonel Whitton describes the *Michigan*, normally used to convey emigrants from Europe to the United States, as a "terrible ship" and a "big iron box." Sailed for France. Arrived off St. Nazaire (10th). Landed (12th) and entrained. Travelled via Tours, Vendôme and Paris, arriving Coulommiers (14th) and marching to billets at St. Ouen. The Germans had been in St. Ouen only days before and evidence of their occupation – items of clothing and equipment, half-eaten meals, was in every house. Advanced (15th), crossing the Marne near Charly, marching through Château Thierry to Bézu where the men were billeted in the church. Continued march towards the Aisne (16th). Lieutenant- Colonel Whitton notes lorry loads of wounded, the first seen by the Battalion, passing near Oulchy-le-Château. Passed though Hartennes and bivouacked for night at Villemoutoire. To Villeblain via Taux (17th). An incident took place at Villeblain in one of the houses. The lady owner kindly allotting rooms to each of several officers. "But where will you be sleeping Madam?" enquired one. Turning and pointing to the Company Commander's servant the lady replied – *"Avec lui."* To Courcelles (19th). Passed through Dhuizel (20th) and bivouacked on road about 1 mile north of village. Moved back into Dhuizel (21st). Later advanced via Soupir and during night relieved 2nd Oxfordshire and Buckinghamshire Light Infantry in front line trenches. War Diary records large numbers of dead all around. Trenches were just in front of a large farm called La Cour-de-Soupir and occupied by 2 companies at a time. Support companies were to the rear of the farm and situated in 2 large caves.

OCTOBER

Relieved by 2nd Oxfordshire and Buckinghamshire Light Infantry (1st) and to billets at Dhuizel. Casualties since going into line recorded as about 40. Civilian spy discovered in one of the houses in Dhuizel. Moved to Muret (6th), Dampleux (7th), Orrouy (8th). Entrained at Le Meux (9th) and travelled via Abbeville, Etaples, Boulogne and Calais to St. Omer. Arrived (11th) and marched to billets at Blandecques. Later moved to Arcques. Moved in buses to Hazebrouck (12th). Advanced through Strazeele (13th) and in reserve during 17th Brigade's attack on the Bailleul Ridge. Later advanced to forward positions. concentrated at Merris (14th) and advanced towards Steenwerck. Passed through town during morning (15th) and set up outpost line. Later in evening went forward via Croix-du- Bac. Crossed the Lys at Bac St. Maur and went into billets. To la Chapelle d` Armentières (17th). Took part in attack on Premesques (18th). Went forward 7.30 am, Battalion`s right on the Lille-Boulogne road, "C" and "D" Companies in front, "A" and "B" in support. Lieutenant-Colonel Whitton notes early casualties among the officers – Captain W.G. Montgomerie, Lieutenants C.E. Gaitskell and A. Lecky all being mortally wounded. "D" Company entered objective by 10 am. Casualties – 102 killed or wounded. Dug in and consolidated gains (19th). Heavy shelling and sniping causing some 12 casualties. "D" Company in front of Premesques came under heavy shell fire 8 am (20th) and soon forced to withdraw. Enemy then attacked and entered Premesques. "C" Company overrun and fell back. "B" Company also lost heavily. Captain H.T. Maffett was killed while writing a message to Lieutenant L.D. Daly. Lieutenant E.J. Cormac-Walshe mortally wounded. Lieutenant-Colonel Whitton records the words of a German officer who wrote in his diary – "Not far from our dugout is a captured trench. An English officer, apparently forty to forty-five years of age, lies there in the midst of his men. From his papers I learn that his name is Captain H.T. Maffett of the 2nd Leinsters. Near the dead man I found a message form with this message on it – 'To Lieutenant Daly. My position lies 600 paces north west of Point 42 of Batterie Senarmont, near the edge of the Lille plateau. I cannot advance owing to heavy machine gun fire from enemy trench which is situated in the immediate vicinity of Batterie Senarmont. Please request the artillery to cover it. There is no intention to advance and it is possible that I shall be ordered to retire from this line. Maintain a good firing position, dig in . . .' Here the report breaks off in the middle of a sentence." The German officer goes on to say how he had kept the message and – "Perhaps I shall have an opportunity after the war to forward the last words written by a fallen English comrade to his relations." "A" Company occupied edge of wood facing Premesques and latter held out at Mont-de-Premesques farm. When forced to retire, the survivors carried with them both British and German wounded. Then enemy, it was noted, held their fire when they saw what was happening. Battalion assembled at Wes Macquart during early hours of (21st) and later moved back to a new line about one mile south-west of la Chapelle d` Armentières. Enemy attacks beaten off (22nd). Another attack repulsed (23rd). Relieved during night and to billets at Croix Blanche. Lieutenant-Colonel Whitton records total casualties since (18th) as 434, some 155 of these being killed. He also provides a detailed list of officer casualties – Headquarters: nil; "A" Company: nil; "B" Company: Captains H.T. Maffett, W.G. Montgomerie,

Lieutenant E. Cormac-Walshe killed, Second- Lieutenant W.D. Budgen severely wounded; "C" Company: Captains F.E. Whitton, G.M. Orpen-Palmer severely wounded, Lieutenants A. Lecky, C.E. Gaitskell killed, Lieutenant R.D. O'Conor captured; "D" Company: Lieutenants C.S. Hamilton, A.W. Barton captured.

NOVEMBER

Moved forward via Fleurbaix and Erquinghem to Armentières (12th). Battalion inspected by Lord Roberts on the Rue de la Lys during march. Relieved 2nd Essex in front line trenches south-east of Armentières (13th). Relieved by 1st West Yorkshire (17th) and moved back to Armentières and billets at the Lunatic Asylum. Relieved 1st Royal Warwickshire in trenches north-east of Armentières-Parenchies railway to L'Epinette (18th). Relieved by 1st North Staffordshire (23rd). Relieved 1st North Staffordshire (29th).

DECEMBER

During the "Christmas Truce" a number of Germans were met in No Man's Land that had worked in London before the war. One at Selfridges, another in the music halls. Relieved by 1st West Yorkshire (26th) and to la Chapelle d'Armentières. Relieved 1st North Staffordshire in trenches Rue du Bois sector (31st).

ROYAL MUNSTER FUSILIERS

"Retreat from Mons" "Marne, 1914" "Aisne, 1914" "Ypres, 1914" "Langemarck, 1914" "Gheluvelt" "Nonne Bosschen" "Givenchy, 1914"

2ND BATTALION

AUGUST

Malplaquet Barracks, Aldershot. Part of 1st (Guards) Brigade, 1st Division. Entrained at Farnborough for Southampton and sailed SS *Dunvegan Castle* (13th). Strength – 27 officers, 971 other ranks. Lieutenant-Colonel J.K. O'Meagher in command. Landed Havre (14th). Entrained for Le Nouvion. Arrived (16th) and marched to billets at Boué. Moved forward (21st) and in reserve during fighting at Mons (24th). Commenced retreat. "B" and "D" Companies holding defensive position covering roads to Catillon and La Groise at crossroads 1 mile north of Fresmy (26th). "A" and "C" Companies in front of Fresmy. Part of "A" Company later moving to line south-east of Bergues. Captain S. McCance in his history of the Royal Munster Fusiliers records how "D" Company was divided by a road. Any contact between the two detachments being dangerous as the enemy were firing down the road. When dinners were given out, the meals being prepared on one side of the road, cooks had to sprint from one side to the other carrying the hot food. Enemy attacked and took Bergues about 10.30 am. "A" Company detachment withdrawing to the Sambre Canal then to Oisy. Records show that an order to – "Retire at once" issued to 1st (Guards) Brigade around Fresmy was not received by 2nd Royal Munster. Enemy attacked and overran Fresmy, "C" Company counter attacking later and regaining village. The enemy, Captain McCance records being – "driven back in disorder." Records also note the use by the Germans of cattle. The animals being driven before them in order to cover an attack. Enemy attacked again in large numbers during afternoon and battalion fell back through Fesmy. At 5.30 pm the battalion was located at a crossroads just east of Oisy. "B" Company, however, were missing and the retreat was held up. The company turned up about 6.30 pm, the delay, Captain McCance notes proving – "fatal to the Battalion." Acting as rearguard, the Battalion withdrew through Oisy – "C" Company holding enemy's advance back from the outskirts of the village. Approaching Etreux, the enemy crossed the road ahead and the Battalion became cut off. Numerous courageous attempts to enter village took place during the day (27th). During the evening some 240 men and just 4 unwounded officers were led into an orchard by Lieutenant E.W. Gower. Here the party were soon surrounded and ammunition spent, were overpowered. The *Official History of the Great War* notes that the Battalion had been fighting for almost 12 hours and against overwhelming odds. The enemy's force consisting of some 6 battalions of the 73rd and 77th Reserve Infantry Regiments along with 3 from the 15th Regiment. Captain McCance records the recognition by the Germans of the Munster's bravery. The heroic stand of the Battalion at Etreux, he notes, had enabled the bulk of the retreating British army to get some 12 hours ahead of the enemy. Germans gave permission to bury the dead (28th). In 1921 the orchard at Etreux was purchased by Captain H. Walter Styles, MP, the brother of Lieutenant F.E. Styles of the 2nd Royal Munster Fusiliers. Two crosses were erected, one bearing the names of the officers killed – Major P.A. Charrier, Captains G.N. Simms, MVO, P.G. Barrett, Lieutenants F.E. Styles, C.F.T. Chute, C.F. Phayre, C.E.V. Awdry, Second-Lieutenants J.C.B. Crozier and P.H. Sullivan, the other noting that some 118 other ranks of the Battalion are buried there. A wall was built around the orchard and iron gates leading to the Etreux-Landrecies road put up. A Regimental Memorial was also erected in the orchard at Etreux. This commemorated the action of 27th August along with the fact that 73 officers, 5 warrant officers, 96 non-commissioned officers and 775 fusiliers of the 2nd Battalion gave their lives throughout the Great War. Survivors of the Battalion assembled at Jonqueuse and at St. Gobain (29th) – 5 officers and 196 other ranks answered the roll call.

SEPTEMBER
Battalion split up into detachments and transferred to Army Headquarters (4th). Now to serve as Army Troops with I and II Corps.

OCTOBER
Lieutenant-Colonel A.M. Bent assumed command (4th). Moved to Ypres sector at end of month.

NOVEMBER
Battalion re-formed and joined 3rd Brigade, 1st Division (9th) and sent into line at Bellewaarde Farm. Lieutenant-Colonel H.S. Jervis, MC in his book *The 2nd Munsters in France* records the adverse circumstances that the Battalion had to return to front line positions. There had been no training as a battalion carried out and officers and men were unknown to each other. The Battalion having, as it was, split up for more than 2 months. Went forward via Zillebeke (10th) and relieved 1st Grenadier Guards in

woods near Klein Zillebeke. Captain McCance records that there were no trenches in the wood. Each man having to dig his own shelter. Position lay some 200 yards from the eastern edge of the wood, the ground being covered with unburied dead from recent fighting. Enemy attacked 3 am (11th). During the intense bombardment, Lieutenant-Colonel Jervis notes, the fillings in more than one officer's teeth were shaken loose. He also records that the German advance could be heard long before it could be seen – *Die Wacht am Rhein* being sung by the oncoming infantry. Wave after wave repelled – "A" Company on the left, "B" in the centre, "D" on the right. The men firing in small groups of 2 or 3. Mud put many of the rifles out of action. Enemy eventually withdrew leaving No Man's Land covered with their dead and wounded. Line held against further attacks (12th) – a detachment of "A" Company under Second-Lieutenant H. Lake recorded as holding the enemy off for 16 hours. Movement in the wood, it was recorded – "meant certain death." Food and ammunition being thrown from shelter to shelter. Enemy broke through on left (13th). Counter-attack by 40 men of "C" Company under Captain H.C.H. O'Brien later regained captured trenches. Enemy came forward as if to surrender (14th), but having got to within a few yards of the Munster's line opened fire. Relieved by 1st Grenadier Guards 3.15 am (15th) and withdrew to Brigade Reserve. Later occupied bivouacs near Hooge and Vlamertinghe then to Bailleul.

DECEMBER

Marched to Merville (20th) then via Béthune (21st) to Festubert. "C" and "D" Companies moving forward to occupy dugouts in front between Festubert and Givenchy. Battalion went forward 7 am (22nd) and commenced attack. Advancing some 500 yards ahead of troops on either flank, came under heavy fire from direction of Givenchy Ridge. Captain McCance records that – "men and officers were falling fast, in ten minutes eleven officers and over two hundred men were hit." Order received to retire into reserve line 10.30 pm. Casualties – Majors E.P. Thompson, F.I. Day, Captains H.C.H. O'Brien, F.W. Durand, O. Pemberton, Lieutenants J.F. O'Brien and R.A. Young killed, Captain R.E.M. Pakenham mortally wounded, 2 other officers wounded, over 200 other ranks killed or wounded. Captain McCance records that Captain O'Brien was killed attempting to cover a wounded man in a shell hole. The officer having been first wounded himself. Many of the men had been drowned after falling into shell-holes filled with water. He also notes the dreadful wound of Lieutenant-Colonel A.M. Bent, the CO having had his side opened by a shell and his intestines completely exposed. Laying out in the open for some

16 hours, the Colonel contracted frostbite and double pneumonia, but miraculously survived. Relieved 1st South Wales Borderers in front line (24th). Relieved by 1st South Wales Borderers (26th). Relieved 1st South Wales Borderers (28th).

ROYAL DUBLIN FUSILIERS

"Le Cateau" "Retreat from Mons" "Marne, 1914"
"Aisne, 1914" "Armentières, 1914"

2ND BATTALION

AUGUST

Gravesend. Part of 10th Brigade, 4th Division. Entrained for York (8th). Arrived and to camp at Knavesmire Racecourse. Entrained for Harrow (18th) and then to Southampton (22nd). Sailed SS *Caledonia* – strength: 22 officers – Lieutenant-Colonel A.E. Mainwaring (Commanding Officer), Major H.M. Shewan, DSO, Captains G.S. Higginson, N.P. Clarke, R.L.H. Conlan, S.G. de C. Wheeler, W.H. Supple, A.S. Trigona, R.M.Watson (Adjutant), J. Burke (Quartermaster), P.C.T. Davey (RAMC, Medical Officer), Lieutenants J.E. Vernon, J.F.K. Dobbs, T.J. Leahy, C.H. L'E. West, W.H. Braddell, Second-Lieutenants J. MacN. Dickie, F.C.S. Macky, B. Maguire, J.C.M. Dunlop, R.A.J. Goff, W.M. Robinson and 1,023 other ranks. Arrived Boulogne and to camp on high ground above town. Entrained for Le Cateau (23rd). Arrived (24th) and marched along Cambrai road to bivouacs just south of Beaumont and Inchy. Moved north via Viesly to St. Python during morning (25th). Later to positions near Fontaine-au-Tetre Farm. Came under shell fire for first time. Enemy cavalry fired on – two men brought down. Colonel H.C. Wylly, CB in his history of 2nd Royal Dublin Fusiliers (*Crown and Company*) notes that these were the first shots fired by the Battalion in the war and were by men forming a piquet under Captain Supple. Later withdrew via Viesly, Bethencourt, Beauvois, Fontaine-au-Pire and Ligny to Haucourt. Took up position on right of 1st Warwickshire around the Cattenières- Caullery bridal-path during morning (26th). Later, "A" and "D" Companies under Major Shewan occupied defensive line east of the village. Enemy artillery began firing on Haucourt 2 pm – "B" and "C" Companies coming under severe shrapnel fire. When the German attack began later in the afternoon the troops around Haucourt began to retire. The withdrawal being confused and with units being separated into small, and mixed, detachments. Synonymous with the retreat is the subsequent attempted surrender at St. Quintin by Lieutenant-Colonel Mainwaring (with Lieutenant-Colonel J.F. Elkington of the 1st Warwickshire), Colonel Mainwaring having withdrawn from Haucourt via Caullery and Malincourt with some 40 or so of his battalion. Details of this controversial affair are now clearly set out in Peter T. Scott's book *"Dishonoured."* Major Shewan's detachment (about 400 men) withdrew and marched through the night to Ligny-en-Cambresis then continued retreat towards Clary. Approaching the village, the party came under fire from troops up ahead. Colonel Wylly records that this was from the direction of Montigny and that Captain Trigona who was leading the Dublins thought the firing may be coming from British troops. The officer signalled that his men were Royal Dublin Fusiliers, the reply coming back almost immediately – "Dublin Fusiliers, right, come on." German uniforms were spotted, however, and the Dublins immediately began to fall back on Ligny. Colonel Wylly notes that this move was in a series of rushes, each one seeing higher and higher casualties. Second-Lieutenant Dunlop was killed, 6 other officers were captured, 4 of them also being wounded. Some 44 other ranks had been killed or mortally wounded. Many had been taken prisoner. Party now comprised Captains Clarke and Trigona and just 30 men. The survivors assembled and eventually found their way via Abbeville to Boulogne and then England. "B" and "C" Companies held their positions at Haucourt under shell fire throughout the day, withdrew later to Le Catelet then (27th) marched to Roisel. Here the Dublins were temporally formed into a composite battalion with 1st Royal Warwickshire. Retreated later through Tertry, Monchy-Lagache, Guizancourt, Croix and Matigny, arriving Voyennes 4 am (28th). Continued march 9 am via Offoy to Bussy. Took up defensive positions behind Beaurains (29th) then marched via Carlepont, Champ-du-Merlier, Tracy le Mont, Bascule and Berneuil-sur-Aisne to Genancourt. To Verberie (31st).

SEPTEMBER

To Néry (1st). Held line until afternoon then withdrew via Rully to Baron. To Dammartin- en-Goële (2nd), via St. Mard, Juilly, Nantouillet, St. Mesmes, Messy, Claye, Souilly, Annet and Thorigny to Lagny (3rd), Magny-le-Hongre (4th), via Jossigny, Ferrières, the Forest of Armainvillers to Chevry (5th). Parties of men separated from their battalions during the fighting at Haucourt rejoined. The Warwickshire and Dublins being formed into separate units. Began advance towards the Aisne (6th). Arrived on high ground south of La Ferté (8th) then to Grande Mont Menard (9th). Crossed the Marne near Le Saussoy (10th) then to Coulombs. To Villers-le-Petit (11th), Septmonts (12th). Crossed the Aisne at Venizel (13th) then to Bucy-le-Long. Bivouacked around La Montagne Farm and carried out tours in forward trenches. Second-Lieutenant Maguire killed (14th). Parties of reinforcements arrived, including men that had escaped to England after the retreat from Haucourt on 26th August.

OCTOBER
Relieved by French troops (6th) and moved via Venizel, Hartennes, Rozet
St. Albin and Coyelles to Rully. Entrained at Pontpoint for Wizernes (11th)
then travelled in buses to Caestre (12th). Took part in attack on enemy's
line near Fontaine Houck (13th). To Meteren (14th), Bailleul (15th),
Houpelines (17th).

NOVEMBER
Moved to Ploegsteert sector (17th) and relieved 1st Rifle Brigade in trenches
at St. Yves (19th). Relieved by 1st Royal Warwickshire (22nd) then to
Nieppe. Casualties – 11 killed, 17 wounded. Returned to firing line (26th),
relieving 1st Royal Warwickshire.

DECEMBER
Carried out tours in firing line throughout month. Casualties – 2 officers
wounded, 16 other ranks killed, 35 wounded, 1 missing.

RIFLE BRIGADE (THE PRINCE CONSORT'S OWN)

"Le Cateau" "Retreat from Mons" "Marne, 1914" "Aisne, 1914" "Armentières, 1914"

1ST BATTALION

AUGUST

Colchester. Part of 11th Brigade, 4th Division. Moved to Harrow (18th) and encamped on Harrow School playing fields . Entrained for Southampton (22nd) and embarked SS *Cestrian*. Arrived Havre, disembarked during early hours (23rd) and marched to No.3 Rest Camp. A war record of the Battalion compiled by Captain R.O. Bridgeman from War Diaries and information provided by officers and others, appears in *The Rifle Brigade Chronicle for 1916* and the following officers are listed as those who embarked – Lieutenant-Colonel H.M. Biddulph (Commanding Officer), Major S.H. Rickman (Second in Command), Captains G.W. Liddell (Adjutant) D. Ovey (Brigade Machine Gun Officer), Lieutenant J. Micklem (Machine Gun Officer), Second-Lieutenant G.W. Barclay (Transport Officer), Hon. Lieutenant G. Mitchell (Quartermaster); "A" Company: Captains F.H. Nugent, R.P.A. de Moleyns, H.L. Riley, Second-Lieutenant R.D. Baird; "B" Company: Captain Hon. F.R.D. Prittie, O. Sutton-Nelthorpe, Second-Lieutenant O.B. Graham; "C" Company: Major G.N. Salmon, Captain G.J. Brownlow, Lieutenants E.S.B. Williams, W. Bowle-Evans, G.V. Campbell; "I" Company: Captains G.E.W. Lane, Hon. R.G.G. Morgan-Grenville, Master of Kinross, Lieutenants J.T. Coryton, E.W.S. Foljambe, Second-Lieutenant G.T. Cartland (Orderly Officer to Brigadier). Entrained (24th) and travelled via Rouen and Amiens to Le Cateau. Detrained 5.30 am (25th) and marched to Briastre. Entrenched line running from the Briastre-Solesmes road to almost Fontaine-au- Tartre. Began withdrawal 8.20 pm, marching through Beauvois to bivouacs just north-west of Fontaine-au-Pire. Arrived 2 am (26th) and "C" Company took up outpost positions at Cattenières. Enemy cavalry patrols engaged and driven off. Came under shell fire and German infantry seen advancing. Withdrew via Haucourt to ridge between Fontaine-au- Pire and Ligny and took up defensive positions in a sunken road. Position held under heavy fire. Major Rickman mortally wounded during afternoon. Enemy came to within 100 yards, their fire coming from the front, left flank and rear and causing high casualties. Withdrew to Ligny and assembled in the church. A report written by an officer of "A" Company notes that the retreating companies were unable to move the wounded from the sunken road. Captain Bridgeman records the casualties as follows – Major Rickman and 6 men killed, Captain Lane, Lieutenant Foljambe and 345 other ranks were missing, almost all believed wounded and taken prisoner, Captains de Moleyns, Liddell, Morgan-Grenville, Lieutenant Coryton and 15 other ranks were wounded and reached Ligny church. By 6 pm. Captain Bridgeman also notes that the 11th Brigade was clear of Ligny, and – "the great retreat had commenced." Battalion now became split up, the larger party moving with Lieutenant-Colonel Biddulph via Caullery to covering positions near Selvigny. The Colonel then moved on via Malincourt, Le Catelet, Vendhuile, Templeux and arrived at Hesbecourt about 10 am (27th). Moved later via Hervilly, Haucourt and Tertry. Captains Nugent, Prittie and Brownlow with some 100 men marched with other units of 11th Brigade to Montigny, continuing at 2 am (27th) via Beaurevoir, Nauroy, Bellicourt, Villeret, Le Verguier and joining Lieutenant-Colonel Biddulph during the night at Tertry. Captain Bridgeman notes that neither party knew of the other's existence since leaving Ligny. Marched to billets at Voyennes (28th) then during evening via Hambleux to Libermont. Here, Captain Bridgeman records, some of the men were placed on gun-carriages and taken to Muirancourt, others were moved in lorries to Noyon. The Noyon detachment moved to Sempigny (29th) then during evening to Les Cloyes. Muirancourt party joined 1 am (30th) having marched via Noyon. Began march to Fontenoy 3 am, then during night to Saintines.

SEPTEMBER
Took up positions in reserve just south of St. Sauveur 3 am (1st). Later fell back via Néry and north of Fresnoy to Rozières. Began march in direction of Droiselles 3.30 pm (2nd), but after travelling just over a mile, ordered back to Rozières then to Eve. Marched through night via Lagny to Château-de-Fontenelle near Chanteloup. Continued 4.30 pm (4th) to Coupvrai then via Magny and Ozoir-la-Ferrière to Château-de-Chauvennerie (5th). Set up outposts along railway line to level crossing at Ozoir-la-Ferrière. Captain Bridgeman notes miles travelled during retreat as 156. Began advance to the Aisne, marching via Jossigny to Villeneuve-le-Comte (6th), Maisoncelles (7th), via Signy-Signets to Ventemi Château (8th), via St. Martin to Château-de-Tartarel (9th). "C" Company then moved out to Reuil. Remainder later moved via Le Tillet, crossed the Marne at Chamigny then on to Chamigny. "C" Company rejoined during night, Captain Bridgeman recording that they had caused 30 casualties to the enemy throughout the day. To Radémont (10th) and set up outposts on ridge north-east of

Ocquerre. To Montemafroy (11th) and via Villers-Helon and Rapérie (12th). Crossed the Aisne at Vemzel during morning (13th). An officer of "A" Company records that the bridge had been destroyed by the enemy and the men had to cross one at a time via a single girder. Advanced to Ste. Marguerite and dug in. "A" and "B" Companies in forward positions on ridge to the north of the village. Their line running west, then north to the Le Moncel ravine. "A" Company in wood on the Maubeuge road came under shell-fire from guns at close range. Captain Bridgeman records that "C" and "I" Companies relieved "A" and "B" during the day and thinking they were Germans were shelled by our own artillery. Casualties throughout day – 13 officers wounded, 4 other ranks killed, 33 wounded, 6 missing. Line held and consolidated (14th-18th). Casualties – Lieutenant-Colonel Biddulph and Captain Brownlow wounded, 17 other ranks killed, 58 wounded, 3 missing. Relieved by 1st East Lancashire (19th) and moved back into reserve positions on the spur north-west of Bucy-le-Long. Returned to front line (22nd), relieving 1st East Lancashire. War Diary records that the front was now covered with spiked sticks and barbed wire entanglements. Trenches were comfortable and efficient.

OCTOBER
Relieved (7th) and marched via Vemzel and Rozières to billets at Raperie. Marched during night via La Plessier and Hulen to Billy-sur-Ourcq, then at 5 pm (8th) via Villers-Cotterêts to Largny. Moved to Béthisy St. Pierre (9th), Estrées St. Denis (10th). Entrained for St. Omer (11th). Arrived 4.30 pm (12th) and marched to Blendecques. Moved in buses to Hondeghem (14th) and later marched via Caestre to Flêtre. To Berthen (15th) then via Meteren to billets east of Bailleul. Set up outpost line on the Steenwerk-Neuve Eglise road. Assembled at cross roads near Rabot (16th) and at 8. pm advanced for attack on the bridge at Erquinghem. Battalion with 1st Somerset Light Infantry reached the crossroads near Les-Trois-Tilleuls then attack cancelled and ordered to La Crèche. To positions on the Steenwerk-Le Veau road (17th). Moved to Nieppe (18th) then to billets at the Lunatic Asylum in Armentières. Later moved to positions on the outskirts of town. Moved during morning (19th) to reserve positions along the railway line east of Armentières. Later to Houplines and relieved 2nd Seaforth Highlanders in trenches about Le Ruage. "I" Company took over trench just south of Frélinghien (20th). "B" and "C" Companies relieved (21st) and to the Lunatic Asylum billets in Armentières then (22nd) to Le Bizet. "A" and "I" Companies relieved by 1st Royal Irish Fusiliers same day and sent via Houplines to Ploegsteert. Later joined "B" and "C" Companies at Le Bizet. Moved at 6.30 pm to take over trenches running from Frélinghien to the

crossroads on the Le Gheer road. Captain Bridgeman records sniping from houses in Le Touquet, the enemy often just 20 yards from buildings occupied by the Battalion. Enemy attack driven off (29th). Another repulsed (30th) – Captain O.C.S. Gilliat killed. Captain Bridgeman records that in 1 hour, 35 minutes some 195 heavy shells had fallen near the machine guns resulting in just 1 man being wounded. He also notes that since arriving in France the Battalion had marched 330 miles.

NOVEMBER

Enemy attempted to sap below wire defences (8th). Captain Bridgeman records that heavy losses were inflicted upon them, about 100 dead being noted. Relieved by 1st King's Own (10th) and to billets at Le Bizet. Two companies remaining in support at Le Touquet. Casualties since 22nd October – 55 killed, 91 wounded. Relieved 2nd Royal Inniskilling Fusiliers in reserve trenches in Ploegsteert Wood (11th) then 1st Somerset Light Infantry in front line at St. Yves (12th). Captain G.P.R. Toynbee killed (15th). Relieved by 2nd Royal Dublin Fusiliers (19th) and to Ploegsteert. Took over trenches on eastern side of Ploegsteert Wood (20th). Captain Bridgeman records that 3 companies held the front line and support trenches while 1 company, with Battalion Headquarters, occupied Report Centre on the Messines road and 800 yards from Ploegsteert and later Rifle House in Ploegsteert.

DECEMBER

Took part in attack with 1st Somerset Light Infantry and 1st Hampshire on German positions eastern side of Ploegsteert Wood (19th). Captain Bridgeman prepared a report on the attack for the *Rifle Brigade Chronicle for 1916*, however this, he notes, was deleted by the Censor. Captain Reginald Berkeley, MC, in his war history of the Rifle Brigade, records that the Battalion's 1st objective was the enemy's position known as German House. "I" Company led the assault, while "B" Company held the front line and "C" the support line at Hunter Avenue. Captain Morgan-Grenville at the head of the leading platoons is noted as being killed almost immediately. German House taken and 2nd objective – Second House, reached. Supporting troops could not get through due to bombardment by our own artillery and withdrawal ordered. German House occupied. Casualties – Captains Prittie, Morgan-Grenville, Second-Lieutenant A.S.L. Daniell killed, 3 other officers wounded, 23 other ranks killed, 42 wounded. Company of 1/5th London attached. Captain Bridgeman notes that this enabled each company to have alternately 4 days in the trenches and 4 days in billets – first at Ploegsteert, then Nieppe. One day was spent in support between each change. A document dated 20th December, 1914 and proposing a formal armistice on 31st December was handed to a stretcher-bearer while collecting identity discs in No Man's Land. Captain Bridgeman records that the Battalion replied pointing out that they were not empowered to make arrangements of this kind. The enemy did come out into No Man's Land (25th) and with British troops collected the dead. Captain Bridgeman records Battalion's casualties for 1914 as – 7 officers killed, 15 wounded, 2 taken prisoner, 144 other ranks killed, 318 wounded, 350 missing. Six officers and 441 other ranks had gone sick. Battalion awards included – Distinguished Service Orders to Major G.N. Salmon, Captains G.W. Liddel and H.L. Riley; the Croix de Chevalier, Légion d'Honneur to Captain Hon. F.R.D. Prittie and the Médaille Militaire to Sergeant W. Walker. Seven men received the Distinguished Conduct Medal.

2ND BATTALION

AUGUST
Kuldana, India.

SEPTEMBER
To Bombay and embarked SS *Somali* (18th). Left Bombay for England (20th).

OCTOBER
Arrived Liverpool (22nd) and entrained for Winchester. Arrived (23rd) and to camp at Hursley Park. Joined 25th Brigade, 8th Division.

NOVEMBER
To Southampton and embarked SS *Victorian* (5th). Commanding Officer – Lieutenant- Colonel R.B. Stephens. Sailed 2 am (6th). Arrived Havre (7th) and marched to No.1 Rest Camp. Entrained at Gare Maritime, Havre for Strazeele (10th). Arrived 6 am (11th) and marched to billets at Vieux Berquin. Captain Ralph Verney of 2nd Rifle Brigade wrote in his book *The Joyous Patriot* that near Vieux Berquin he saw 5 motor ambulances flying American flags. Paid for by Mrs Vanderbilt, the vehicles were maned by American medical students who were studying in Paris when war broke out. Moved forward to La Flinque (1 mile south of Laventie) in brigade reserve (14th). War Diary records half of "C" Company sent into support trench, 300 yards to the rear of front line but withdrawn (15th). "B" Company took over trenches behind Chapigny and "D" Company to support line (16th). War Diary notes death of Acting-Corporal Green – the battalion's first

casualty. Ralph Verney records that the death was caused from bullets coming through the loopholes in the trenches. Relieved 2nd Lincolnshire in front line (17th). Trenches ran about 100 yards – 150 yards east of the Rue Tilleloy. Battalion's right just east of Chapigny, and its left in front of Fauquissart, 200 yards north of the Fauquissart-Trivelet road. Distance of enemy line, between 250-450 yards away. Civilians noted not only in forward area, but in front line positions. Commanding Officer made request to Divisional Headquarters for gendarmes to distinguish between local inhabitants and possible spies. Relieved by 2nd Royal Berkshire (21st) and to billets near Laventie. Much is noted in the battalion's records regarding conditions in the trenches – some 44 men being sent to a field ambulance suffering with frostbite in the feet (22nd). Trenches were full of freezing mud and water, a hard 17° frost being recorded for 2 nights. The men's wet boots were frozen to their feet. Continued tours of duty in same front line throughout winter – casualties between 6 and 12 per period. Rest billets – Laventie, Fort d'Esquin, Picantin and once at Estaires. Field behind headquarters at Fauquissart taken over as battalion cemetery. Sheepskin coats issued (24th) and white sheets for patrol work in the snow. Party from "B" Company engaged enemy about 1200 yards out into No Man's Land (27th). Lieutenant E. Durham killed. Major G.M.N. Harman, DSO killed by shell in billets (28th). Captain H. Whitaker killed in No Man's Land (30th).

DECEMBER

Heavy rain noted (7th-9th) and trenches had to be abandoned due to mud. Breastworks behind line occupied and ruined houses in Fauquissart. Major C.V.N. Percival killed (14th). Line extended about 800 yards (15th) and 1 company withdrawn to Brigade Reserve at La Flinque. Order received to be ready to "demonstrate" in front of line (18th) and latter to "harass" the enemy. This operation in support of 23rd Brigade's attack north of Neuve Chapelle on right. Advanced and occupied German saps and forward trenches 4.20 pm. Enemy's fire drawn till 2 am (19th). Records note that mud made rifles impossible to fire. Relieved by 2nd Royal Berkshire (23rd) after 11 days in front line. Princess Mary's Christmas presents received by every man at Laventie (25th). Returned to trenches (26th). An informal truce is noted and no firing on either side until artillery bombardment (British) at 11.40 pm. Battalion records note – "a state of quite" on (27th). The enemy made no effort to take cover and did not interfere with the digging of communication trenches from British line to their own advance positions. Work stopped by British artillery fire. Enemy began sniping (28th) and orders received from Division to allow no truce, either formal or informal. Casualties for 1914 – 4 officers killed and 3 wounded. Among the other ranks, 15 were killed (another 3 died of wounds), 23 wounded and 224 sick.

3RD BATTALION

AUGUST

Cork, Ireland. Part of 17th Brigade, 6th Division. Embarked SS *Patriotic* (17th) and sailed for Holyhead. Disembarked 6 pm (18th) and entrained for Cambridge. Lieutenant W.La T. "Billy" Congreve (later Brevet-Major, VC, DSO, MC and killed on the Somme in July, 1916) was a member of the Battalion and recalls in his diary (see *Armageddon Road – A VC's Diary 1914-1916*, edited by Terry Norman) how during the journey to Cambridge he sent a telegram to his sister informing her that he would be passing through Stafford at 11.30. She was on the platform and he managed to throw a weighted letter almost at her feet as the train passed through the station at about 70 miles an hour. Arrived 4 pm (19th) and went into camp on Midsummer Common. Moved to Newmarket (31st).

SEPTEMBER

Entrained at Newmarket for Southampton (7th). Embarked SS *Lake Michigan* for France (8th). Officers – Lieutenant-Colonel R. Alexander (Commanding Officer), Major C.H.C. Lord Henniker (Second in Command), Captain Hon. C.H. Meysey-Thompson (Adjutant), Lieutenants M. Godolphin Osborne (Machine Gun Officer), E.R. Kewley (Transport Officer), L. Eastmead (Quartermaster), Captain R.E. Porter (RAMC, Medical Officer); "A" Company: Captain H.F. Somerville, Lieutenants C.T.E. Swan, H.S.C. Peyton, D.E. Prideaux-Brune, Second-Lieutenant T.O. Jameson; "B" Company: Captains Hon. E.A.C. Weld-Forester, N.J.B. Leslie, P.A. Kennedy, Lieutenant M. Alexander, Second- Lieutenant M.T. Boscawen; "C" Company: Major A.D. Boden, Lieutenants M.K. Mackenzie (KRRC attached), D.B. Landale, Second-Lieutenant G.W. Sherston; "D" Company: Captain A.K. Hargreaves, Lieutenant W. La T. Congreve, Second-Lieutenants A.E.P. Ellis, J.H. Smith. Arrived off St. Nazaire (10th). Landed (12th) and entrained 6.30 am (13th) for Coulommiers. Arrived early morning (14th) and marched to billets at St. Ouen. Marched via Nanteuil-sur-Marne and Romeny to Azy (15th), Château Thierry to Visigneux (16th), Taux to Villeblain (17th). Moved to Paars (19th) and bivouacs just south of Dhuizel (20th). Moved into Dhuizel (21st) and in afternoon went forward and relieved 1st Royal Berkshire in trenches 2 miles north of Soupir. Casualties (22nd-23rd) – 7 other ranks killed, 1 officer, 21 other ranks wounded, 1 man missing. "A" and "D" Companies relieved during night (23rd). "C" Company and part of "D" Company attacked enemy line 4.15 am (25th). Came under heavy machine gun fire and only small parties reached the German parapet. Casualties – 3 other ranks killed, 1 officer, 26 other ranks wounded, Major Boden, Lieutenant Mackenzie and 23 men missing.

OCTOBER
Relieved by 2nd South Staffordshire (1st) and to billets at Bourg. Casualties since 26th September – 5 killed, 20 wounded. To Maast (6th), Dampleux (7th), Gilocourt (8th), Compiègne (9th). Entrained for St. Omer (10th). Detrained at Blendecques (11th). Marched to Arques during afternoon and then moved in lorries to Hazebrouck (12th). Moved forward (13th) and took part in action around Strazeele. War Diary records Battalion Headquarters established about 2.30 pm – all four companies engaged along the Bailleul Ridge. Casualties – 3 officers, including Colonel Alexander, wounded, 11 other ranks killed, 65 wounded. Dug line from mill north-east of Merris to edge of Outtersteene during morning (14th). Later marched to Noote Boom and took up positions along road running eastern side of Blanche Maison. Moved to Steenwercke (15th) then at 7.15 pm to bivouacs near Croix du Bac. To billets on Rue Bataille (16th). Moved forward to la Chapelle d' Armentières (17th). Took part in attack on Pèrenchies (18th). Leading troops held up, "A", "D" and part of "C" Companies held up halting south of Le Fresnelle. Captain Leslie killed, 2 other officers wounded, 13 other ranks killed, 51 wounded, 2 missing. Held positions (19th-20th). Battalion records note German reinforcements coming up via an armoured train. Casualties – 12 killed, 31 wounded, 1 missing. Withdrew to new line near Porte Egal Farm (21st). Enemy attack repulsed (22nd). Large numbers of German dead noted in No Man's Land. Another attack (23rd) caused high casualties, particularly among "C" Company – Lieutenant D.B. Landale killed, 17 other ranks killed, 43 wounded. Relieved by 2nd Essex (24th) and to billets at Fleurbaix. Later, during evening, marched to Bois Grenier. Attached to 18th Brigade. Moved into line east of La Guernerie (25th) then in evening to Flamangerie Farm. Relieved 2nd York and Lancaster in front line. Medical Officer, Captain Porter killed (26th).

NOVEMBER
Rejoined 17th Brigade and took over trenches near la Chapelle d' Armentières from 1st Royal Fusiliers (21st). Relieved by 1st Royal Fusiliers (28th) and to billets at la Chapelle d' Armentières.

DECEMBER

Relieved 1st Royal Fusiliers in front line (5th). The Battalion's 1914 war records appear in *The Rifle Brigade Chronicle For 1916* and these mention that during the "Christmas Truce" a German juggler entertained both sides in the middle of No Man's Land. Three men are noted as missing as a result of – "an informal visit to the German trenches." Lieutenant-Colonel Alexander recovered from wounds received on 13th October but was again wounded after his return to the Battalion on 22nd November. He subsequently died (29th). Total casualties for 1914 are given as 2 officers killed, 1 died of wounds, 11 wounded, 104 other ranks were killed, 19 died of their wounds and 365 were wounded. Some 35 men were missing and 240 went sick.

4TH BATTALION

AUGUST
Dagshai, India.

OCTOBER
Left Bombay for UK.

NOVEMBER
Arrived Devonport (19th) and to Magdalen Hill Camp, Winchester. Joined 80th Brigade, 27th Division.

DECEMBER
To Southampton (20th) and embarked SS *Austerlind* for France. Strength – 27 officers, 921 other ranks. Sailed (21st) and arrived Havre during early hours of (22nd). Entrained (23rd) for Arques and from there marched to billets at Blaringhem near St. Omer. Began work (27th) on reserve trench system around Blaringhem and Steenbecque.

HONOURABLE ARTILLERY COMPANY (TERRITORIAL FORCE)

1/1ST BATTALION

AUGUST

Armoury House, Finsbury, London. Began duties guarding railways and waterworks in London.

SEPTEMBER

Inspected by HM The King (12th). Officers present – Lieutenant-Colonel E. Treffry (Commanding Officer), Major H.T. Hanson (Second in Command), Captain M.G. Douglas (Adjutant), Lieutenants G.H. Mayhew (Quartermaster), T. Carnwath (Medical Officer); No.1 Company: Major P.C. Cooper, Captain C.F. Nesham, Second-Lieutenants E.L. Dobson, S.H. Byron, W.A. Blake, M.N. Schiff; No.2 Company: Captains C.A.J. Whyte, E. Garnsey, Second-Lieutenants D.G. Collins, F.A. Garrett, T.C. Bower, C.F. Osmond (Transport Officer); No.3 Company: Captains A.L. Ward, W.S. Newton, Second- Lieutenants H.W. Perkins, J.G. Gibson, C.W. Holliday (Machine Gun Officer), F.M. Merson; No.4 Company: Captains R.C. Cole, E.A. Lankester, Second-Lieutenants J. Goddard, G.F.T. Murnane, W.C. Hayden, C. Tatham. Later entrained at St. Pancras for Purfleet Rifle Range Station, Essex. Arrived and to camp at Belhus Park, Aveley. Received orders (16th) for 29 officers and 800 men to proceed overseas (18th). Major G. Goold Walker, DSO in his war history of the Regiment, records that at this time the Battalion had no equipment, rifles or ammunition. The transport comprised vehicles provided by civilian firms – Pickfords and Frederick Gorringe, a milk cart and a water tank on wheels owned by one of the London Borough Councils and used for watering the streets. Equipment and rifles eventually arrived and issued out during night (17th/18th). Entrained at Purfleet for Southampton (18th). Arrived and embarked SS *Westmeath* for France. Arrived St. Nazaire (20th) and allotted Line of Communications duties. No.3 Company to Nantes (22nd), Headquarters, Nos.1 and 2 Companies to Le Mans (23rd). Part of No.2 to Havre same day.

OCTOBER

Rest of No.2 Company to Havre (2nd). While at Le Mans, No.1 Company provided a Guard at the Maroc railway sidings. Major Goold Walker notes that civilian labourers were employed, these, he records, were "scallywags, who caused endless trouble, being usually drunk and always undisciplined." No.3 Company to Le Mans (25th). No.4 Company also to Le Mans (27th). Part of No.1 Company to Abbeville same day. Lance Corporal C. Smart died of injuries received after a horse fell on him. G.S. Wagons, Ammunition and water carts arrived to replace transport vehicles previously mentioned. Entrained for St. Omer (31st). Began work digging trenches around Blendecques.

NOVEMBER

As the Battalion was soon to go into the line, Colonel Treffry pointed out to the Commander-in-Chief's Military Secretary that many of his men had not had opportunity to fire their new rifles. Major Goold Walker records (4th) that arrangements were then made for the Battalion to use a local 200-yard range. Received orders to move forward and travelled in London buses to Bailleul (5th). To Estaires (7th), Les Lobes (9th) and attached to 8th Brigade, 3rd Division. Began work digging trenches around Rouge Croix and Croix Barbé. Came under shell fire for the first time (13th). One man killed, 8 wounded (14th). Moved to Bailleul (16th), Neuve Eglise (21st). One man, who's diary was published in Percy Herd's book *The Fighting Territorials,* recalls talking to some refugees who were being paid 4 francs a day for digging British trenches. They told how the Germans had demanded 12,000 francs, or they would destroy their house. Although the money was paid, the occupiers were turned out in the middle of the night and the building looted and shelled. Began instruction in firing line opposite Messines. To billets at Westoutre (27th). Later to Shepenberg.

DECEMBER

Inspected by HM The King and HRH The Prince of Wales (3rd). Later moved forward – 2 companies attached to 2nd Royal Scots in trenches north of Kemmel, Headquarters and 2 companies in support at Shrapnel Farm near Kemmel Château. Relieved and to Westoutre (6th). Relieved 1st Royal Scots Fusiliers in trenches in front of Spanbrock Moelen (9th). Now attached to 7th Brigade, 3rd Division. Relieved by 1st Royal Scots Fusiliers (12th) and to billets at Locre. Returned to same trenches (15th). Relieved by 2nd Suffolk (27th).

MONMOUTHSHIRE REGIMENT (TERRITORIAL FORCE)

1/2ND BATTALION

AUGUST
Headquarters, "A" ,"B", "C" Companies – Pontypool, "D" Company – Abercarn, "E" Company – Blaenavon, "F" Company – Llanhilleth, "G" Company – Coleford, "H" Company – Crumlin. Part of Welsh Border Brigade, Welsh Division. Moved to war stations at Pembroke Dock (6th). To Oswestry (10th), Northampton (20th). Changed to 4-company system.

NOVEMBER
Left Welsh Division and to Southampton. Embarked SS *Manchester Importer* and to France (5th). Strength – 30 officers, 984 other ranks. Arrived Havre (6th). Entrained for St. Omer (8th) and from there marched to billets at Wizernes. Moved forward (18th), marching via Hazebrouck and Le Bizet to Bailleul. Came under orders of 12th Brigade, 4th Division. "C" and "D" Companies to trenches Le Touquet sector (21st). Came under instruction of 2nd Lancashire Fusiliers and 2nd Essex. First casualty (22nd) – Private W. Crowley killed by sniper. "A" and "B" Companies to trenches for instruction.

DECEMBER
Training completed and relieved 2nd Essex (2nd). Continued tours in same trenches for remainder of month resting at Le Bizet and Nieppe. Corporal A.E. Pinchin and Private E. Jones awarded Distinguished Conduct Medal. In his history of the battalion, Captain G.A. Brett, DSO., MC recalls the Christmas Truce. "A page of the *Pontypool Free Press* was tied to a rifle and waved as a flag of truce." The enemy, some 50 yards off, came forward and souvenirs were exchanged. Later in the day a man of "D" Company was shot and killed. Detachment of 2 NCOs and 12 men under Captain A.H. Edwards formed for mining operations.

LONDON REGIMENT (TERRITORIAL FORCE)

"Messines, 1914" "Ypres, 1914" "Gheluvelt" "Nonne Bosschen" "Givenchy, 1914"

1/5TH (CITY OF LONDON) BATTALION (LONDON RIFLE BRIGADE)

AUGUST

Headquarters – 130 Bunhill Row, Finsbury. Part of 2nd London Brigade, 1st London Division. To annual camp at Eastbourne (2nd). Ordered to return to London within hours of arrival. To Wimbledon (20th), Hersham (21st), Bisley (22nd).

SEPTEMBER

To East Horsley (8th), Reigate (9th), East Grinstead (10th), Crowborough (16th).

NOVEMBER

To Southampton (4th) and embarked SS *Chyebassa* for France. Officers – Lieutenant- Colonel W.D. Earl Cairns (Commanding Officer), Lieutenant-Colonel C.G.R. Matthey (Second in Command), Major A.D. Ducant (RAMC, Medical Officer), Captains A.C. Oppenheim (King's Royal Rifle Corps, Adjutant), A.L. Lintott (Machine Gun Officer), Lieutenants P.A. Slessor (Intelligence Officer), J.R.S. Petersen (Quartermaster), Second-Lieutenant C.W. Trevelyan (Transport Officer); "A" Company: Captain R.H. Hussey, Lieutenants G.H. Morrison, G.H. Cholmeley; "D" Company: Major N.C. King, Lieutenant J.G. Robinson; "E" Company: Captain C.H.F. Thompson, Lieutenant H.B. Price, Second- Lieutenant H.G. Vincent; "G" Company: Captain (Hon. Major) C.D. Burnell, Lieutenants E.L. Large, A.G. Kirby; "H" Company: Captain H.D. F. MacGeagh, Second-Lieutenants G.H.G.M. Cartwright, K. Forbes; "O" Company: Captain M.H. Soames, Second- Lieutenants W.L. Willett, G.C. Kitching; "P" Company: Captain J.R. Somers-Smith, Second-Lieutenants H.L. Johnston, G.E. S. Fursdon; "Q" Company: Captain A.S. Bates, Lieutenant R.E. Otter. Arrived Havre (5th) and to No.1 Rest Camp. Here the officers learnt that it was the practice on the Western Front for them to dress similarly to the men. Swords and Sam Browne belts being placed into store. Entrained for St. Omer (6th). Arrived (7th) and to billets in French Army barracks. Henry Williamson was a member of the London Rifle

Brigade and recalled in his book *The Wet Flanders Plain* seeing soldiers at St. Omer station. They were relaxed, he noted, and wore often buttonless tunics – "they were Mons heroes!" Excited and eager to learn of conditions at the front, the men of the LRB would quieten as their questions were answered. The charge of the London Scottish at Messines was mentioned and – "we were even more silent." Marched to Wisques (8th) and billeted in Benedictine convent (later used as GHQ Machine Gun School). To Hazebrouck (16th), Bailleul (17th), Romarin (19th). Attached to 11th Brigade, 4th Division. Half companies attached to regular battalions (20th) and began instruction in front line trenches Ploegsteert Wood sector. First casualty (21st) – Rifleman J.L. Dunnett killed by shell. To Ploegsteert (22nd). Eight company organization changed to 4 (24th). Continued tours in trenches. Also dug defence line in Ploegsteert Wood called "Bunhill Row."

DECEMBER
Men had first baths since leaving England at Armentières (1st). In reserve at Ploegsteert Wood during brigade attack (19th) – 2 companies at Bunhill Row, 2 in support behind. Moved up into Hunter Avenue during evening. War Diary of 1st Rifle Brigade records that 1 company of the London Rifle Brigade was attached in the forward area. Rifle Brigade positions then on eastern side of Ploegsteert Wood. German trenches decorated with fairy lights (24th). Casualties for December – 11 killed, 26 wounded.

1/9TH (COUNTY OF LONDON) BATTALION (QUEEN VICTORIA`S RIFLES)

AUGUST
Headquarters 56 Davies Street, London W1. Part of 3rd London Brigade, 1st London Division. Set out for annual camp at Lulworth (2nd) but train turned back to London at Wimborne. To Richmond (21st), Englefield Green, Egham (22nd), Bullswater Common Camp, Pirbright (24th). Here the men were invited to volunteer for foreign service, each being asked individually by his company commander.

SEPTEMBER
To Bramley (8th), Horsham (9th), Haywards Heath (10th). Battalion passed by HM The King at Cuckfield Cross during march. To St. John`s Hill Camp, Crowborough (12th)

OCTOBER
Began guard duty on railway line between Farnborough and Eastleigh.
Ordered overseas. Left 1st London Division and to Winchester (29th),
Southampton (30th).

NOVEMBER
Sailed for France on SS *Oxonian* (4th). Officers – Lieutenant-Colonel R.B.
Shipley, TD (Commanding Officer), Major V.W.F. Dickins, VD (Second
in Command), Captain G. Culme-Seymour (King's Royal Rifle Corps,
Adjutant), Major T. O'Shea (Quartermaster), Captain F.W. Roe (RAMC,
Medical Officer), Lieutenant F.B.A. Fargus (Machine Gun Officer),
Second-Lieutenant H. Shepherd (Transport Officer); "A" Company: Major
T.P. Lees, Captain R.G. Warren, Second-Lieutenants G. Fazakerley-
Webster, J. Nichols, K.W. Johnson, J.B. Hunter; "B" Company: Captains
S.V. Shea, R.W. Cox, Lieutenants J.C. Andrews, E.W. Hamilton, Second-
Lieutenants G.H. Woolley, P.S. Houghton; "C" Company: Captains H.
Flemming, H.E.L. Cox, Second-Lieutenants E.P. Cawston, W.H. Carter,
R.B. Murray; "D" Company: Captains S.J.M. Sampson, R.H. Lindsey-
Renton, D.W. Bolton, Second-Lieutenants A.L. Cowtan, C.F. Griffith,
D.L. Summerhays. Arrived Havre (5th) and to No.1 Rest Camp. Entrained
for St. Omer (6th). Arrived (7th) and to billets at Arques. Lined streets at
St. Omer and buglers sounded *Last Post* during Memorial Service for Field-
Marshal Lord Roberts (17th). To Hazebrouck (19th). German aircraft
bombed town while marching out. To Bailleul (20th). Bombed again (21st)
– 3 wounded killed in hospital. To Neuve Eglise (27th) and attached to 13th
Brigade, 5th Division. Began tours of duty by companies in trenches at
Wulverghem (29th). Position running off Wulverghem-Messines road. In
his book *From Ypres To Cambrai* Frank Hawkins, a rifleman with 1/9th
London, refers to the smell of the area – mildew, rotting vegetation and
decomposing corpses of men and animals being a "permanent fixture" in
the front line.

DECEMBER
In a letter sent by Captain Culme-Seymour (1st) reference is made to an
officer (Second- Lieutenant G.H. Woolley) taking up a shell that had landed
unexploded in the trench and throwing it out. G.H. Woolley would later, in
April, 1915, be awarded the Victoria Cross for gallantry at Hill 60. Records
also note the – "good shooting" of the men and coolness throughout their
baptism of fire. Telegram received (2nd) by Commanding Officer from 2nd
King's Own Yorkshire Light Infantry – "I think the attention of the
Divisional and Corps Commanders should be drawn to the steadiness

shown by the 9th Rifles yesterday under peculiarly trying conditions for a first experience of the trenches." A number of letters from members of 1/9th London were sent to newspapers at home and published . . . "The country around is a terrible scene of desolation and the wanton destruction is terrible to witness . . . where we are taking possession the people are reappearing and living in the ruins of their former homes" *(Daily Telegraph);* "We have been right up in the firing line for three days – only 400 yards from the German trenches. We lost 1 killed and 2 wounded. The poor chap who was killed fell into my arms shot through the head. The `Jack Johnsons` are awful, but I saw the quality of the British Artillery the other afternoon, and the Germans got hell." *(Daily Express);* "In our part of the trench our chaps placed their hats on a sort of ledge at the back of us. A sniper spotted them and apparently thought they were fellows watching the effect of our shells on the German trenches. He started potting at those hats and made some very good shots" *(Evening News).* To divisional reserve at Dranoutre (11th). Took over front line trenches at Lindenhoek (16th). According to Frank Hawkings his position was a stream with one bank converted into a parapet and the Germans some 40 yards away. Records also note the area as being covered with French dead. Relieved (20th) and to billets in Lindenhoek. To trenches north of the Wulverghem-Messines road (22nd). Relieved by 1st Devonshire and to Lindenhoek (23rd). Marched via Dranoutre and Bailleul to St. Jans Cappel (23rd). One member of the battalion in a letter talks of conditions in the trenches and comments that if ever he heard anyone refer to a Territorial as a Saturday afternoon soldier – "there will be trouble." For the Christmas period parcels were given out (25th), a football match played between "A" and "C" Companies and Princess Mary`s gift boxes distributed (26th). Sheepskin coats (referred to as "Teddy Bear Coats" in one diary) issued (27th). To Neuve Eglise (29th), trenches near Wulverghem (31st).

1/12TH (COUNTY OF LONDON) BATTALION (THE RANGERS)

AUGUST

Headquarters – Chenies Street, Bedford Square. Part of 3rd London Brigade, 1st London Division. Left Waterloo in 2 trains for annual camp at Wool, Dorsetshire (2nd). One train stopped at Southampton West, the other at Winchester and battalion ordered back to Waterloo. Mobilized (4th). To Richmond (14th), Stains (15th), Bullswater Common Camp near Pirbright (17th).

SEPTEMBER

To Bramley (1st), Horsham (2nd), Haywards Heath (3rd), Crowborough (5th).

OCTOBER

Began duty guarding London and South Western main line railway between Waterloo and North Camp (11th). Lance-Corporal Trant of "F" Company killed by train.

DECEMBER

Relieved from railway duty (11th) and assembled in Roehampton House and Dover House, Roehampton. Resumed training at Richmond Park. Left 1st London Division and entrained at Barnes for Southampton (23rd). Sailed for France (24th). Arrived Havre and to camp outside of town (25th). Entrained for St. Omer (29th) (Rifleman A. Allison killed in accident) and from there marched to billets at Blendecques.

1/13TH (COUNTY OF LONDON) (KENSINGTON)

AUGUST

Headquarters – 4 Iverna Gardens, Kensington. Part of 4th London Brigade, 2nd London Division. Entrained at Addison Road for annual camp at Salisbury Plain (2nd). Ordered back to Headquarters same night. Mobilized (5th). Men billeted at Headquarters, Kensington Town Hall and local schools. Colours handed over for safe-keeping at Town Hall. Marched along Edgware Road to Canons Park (16th). To Abbots Langley (17th).

NOVEMBER

To Watford (3rd) and entrained 11 am for Southampton. Sailed SS *Matheran.* (4th). Landed Havre and to No.1 Rest Camp. Entrained for St. Omer (5th). Senior officers – Lieutenant-Colonel F.G. Lewis (Commanding Officer), Majors H.J. Stafford, TD, H. Campbell, Captains H.L. Cabuche ("A" Company), C.C. Dickens ("B" Company), H.W. Barnett ("C" Company), A. Prismall ("D" Company), E.L. Parnell ("E" Company), A.H. Herne ("F" Company), E.G. Kimber ("G" Company), J.E.L. Higgins ("H" Company). Total strength – 29 officers, 835 other ranks. Arrived 8.30 pm (6th). Half of Battalion billeted in town barracks, half to Blendecques. Moved forward (12th), bivouacking at Boeseghem that night. Battalion historians – Sergeants O.F. Bailey and H.M. Hollier recall being overtaken by a staff car while on march. The vehicle contained Field-Marshal Lord Roberts who having alighted saluted the Battalion as it marched past. To Vieux Berquin (13th). Reorganized into 4 companies. To Estaires (14th) and billeted in cotton mill on river bank. Attached to 25th Brigade, 8th Division. "A" and "B" Companies took over 600 yards of front line from 2nd Royal Berkshire in Picantin area (18th). Regimental historians record Battalion's baptism of fire while marching to line along Rue Tilleloy. Machine gun bullets overhead and shells landing in fields at side of road. Trenches are noted as being full of mud, about 6 foot deep,3 to 4 foot wide and some 300 yards from the enemy. The was no shelter and the men had to dig into side of trench for cover. It was intensely cold. First casualties (19th) – Privates Webster and Mooring wounded. Private H.J. Perry killed (20th). "C" and "D" Companies relieved "A" and "B" in front line (21st). Continued 3-day tours in trenches resting at Estaires.

DECEMBER
While "A" and "B" Companies were in line (24th), Germans began calling out "English soldiers, English soldiers, Happy Christmas. Where are your Christmas trees?" Battalion historians record (25th) hesitancy at first when enemy called out – "come over and talk." Seeing battalion on right move out into No Man's Land, however, the men began to approach the German wire. It was noted that apart from the officers, all the Germans appeared to be elderly men. At the same time, the enemy were also surprised to see how young the soldiers facing them were. Officers instructed the men that food, tobacco and cigarettes could be given as gifts, but no buttons or badges. Truce continued with no shots being fired for 4 days. Casualties recorded up to (25th) as 15 killed, 29 wounded. There had also been large numbers evacuated to hospital suffering from exposure. Rest area moved from Estaires to Laventie (26th). Billets in old racing stables.

1/14TH (COUNTY OF LONDON) BATTALION (LONDON SCOTTISH)

AUGUST
Headquarters – 59 Buckingham Gate, Westminster. Part of 4th London Brigade, 2nd London Division. Entrained at Paddington for annual camp on Salisbury Plain (2nd). Arrived Ludgershall Camp and ordered back to London same night. Mobilization began (5th). Caxton Hall taken over to accommodate extra recruits. To Canon's Park (16th), Abbots Langley (17th).

SEPTEMBER
Left 2nd London Division. Marched to Watford (15th) and entrained for Southampton. Sailed for France. Officers – Lieutenant-Colonel G.A.

Malcolm (Commanding Officer), Majors B.C. Green (Second in Command), J.H. Torrance, Captain C.H. Campbell (Cameron Highlanders, Adjutant), Lieutenant J. Paterson (Scout Officer), Second-Lieutenant R.G. Ker-Gulland (Machine Gun Officer), Lieutenant F. Downie (Transport Officer), Captain W.E. Webb (Quartermaster), Captain A. MacNab (RAMC, Medical Officer), Rev. J.M. Vallance (Chaplain); "A" Company: Captain A. MacDonald, Second- Lieutenants E.M. Stirling, F.C. Walker; "B" Company: Captain H.S. Cartwright, Lieutenants H.E. Stebbing, C. Cornock Taylor; "C" Company: Captain I.M. Henderson, Lieutenant H.A.H. Newington, Second-Lieutenant G.H.G. Williamson; "D" Company: Lieutenant A. Blaikie, Second-Lieutenant D.L. Grant; "E" Company: Captain F.H. Lindsay, Second-Lieutenant A.G. Duncan; "F" Company: Lieutenants R.Dunsmore, T.H.K. Allsop, Second-Lieutenants L.S. Lindsey Renton, H.C. Palmer; "G" Company: Captain E.G. Monro, Second-Lieutenant J.C.L. Farquharson; "H" Company: Captain G.C.K. Clowes, Second-Lieutenant W.H. Anderson. Arrived Havre (16th) and ordered to GHQ Troops at Villeneuve St. Georges. Companies scattered for various duties. Right half-battalion to Le Mans but later rejoined Headquarters. Employed on unloading stores and ammunition at railway station, also removal of wounded from trains. One company provided guard at Sir John French's Headquarters at La Fère-en-Tardenois. Two companies sent to Orleans for work on railway and construction of camp for Indian troops. Detachment acted at military police in Paris.

OCTOBER
One company to St. Omer and another to Abbeville during first week. Battalion ordered to concentrate at St. Omer (25th). Boarded London buses (29th) and travelled throughout night to Ypres. Rested in Cloth Hall. Marched through Menin Gate (30th) and halted at the White Château (Sir Douglas Haig's Headquarters) 9 am. Received orders to move forward and marched towards Hooge. In his history of the London Scottish in the Great War, Lieutenant-Colonel J.H. Lindsay, DSO recalls Lieutenant-Colonel Malcolm's concern regarding transport. The Scottish had none. It was explained by a Staff Officer that the battalion was to have that belonging to 1st Coldstream Guards. The Colonel wondered how they could spare it, the officer replied that the Coldstream had been almost destroyed, and that their transport was just about all that was left. Took up reserve position in Sanctuary Wood. Later moved to Hooge. Ordered back to Ypres 5 pm. At the Cloth Hall embussed for St. Eloi. Marched to positions south-east of St. Eloi in support of Cavalry Corps (31st). Ordered to Wytschaete 8 am and from there took the Wulverghem road. Left road and to positions at L'Enfer

Wood. Advanced up slopes of Messines Ridge to firing line just east of Messines-Wytschaete road. Heavy casualties among leading companies at crest of ridge. Enemy attacked about 9 pm and were driven back by rifle fire and a series of charges. The rifles in use had been issued at Abbots Langley and were the Mark 1 pattern converted to take Mark VII ammunition. Battalion records show that not a man had opportunity to fire the new weapons. It would soon be discovered that the magazines had springs too weak and that front stop clips were the wrong shape for Mark VII rounds. The rifles could only be used as single-loaders. However, Lieutenant-Colonel Lindsay notes that – "steady shooting beat off the attack." A second attack also repulsed – "remembered it was Hallowe'en . . . saw a party of men in kilts in our rear. Did not know if they were our men or Germans. They got within a dozen yards, when we saw they wore spiked helmets, and shot them. Were attacked in both front and rear", wrote one man present. A third attack forced the Scottish back – "they advanced in quarter column with a brass band at their head, playing the Austrian National Anthem." Another eyewitness mentions seeing the Medical Officer, Captain A. MacNab, bayoneted and killed whilst attending to the wounded. Forward trenches almost surrounded. Reserve line at Enfer charged the enemy. Lieutenant-Colonel Lindsay records – "a prolonged and confused struggle . . . there was hard fighting, bayonets were crossed, fire was exchanged at close quarters . . .officers, sergeants and men had to act on their own initiative."

NOVEMBER
Withdrawal ordered towards Wulverghem (1st). Paul Maze, a liaison officer with the 2nd Cavalry Division, saw the Battalion after the fighting at Messines and recalls in his book *A Frenchman in Khaki* – "His kilt in rags, looking utterly exhausted, a sergeant of the London Scottish was forming up his men who stood like sailors being photographed on a shore within sight of their wreck." Dug in on Wulverghem Ridge. Came under heavy shell fire all day. Later to Kemmel and then bivouacs at La Clytte. Casualties at Messines – 394 all ranks. Telegrams of congratulation received by Commanding Officer – "I wish you and your splendid Regiment to accept my warmest congratulations and thanks for the fine work you did yesterday at Messines. You have given a glorious lead and example to all Territorial troops who are going to fight in France." (Field-Marshal Sir John French) – "I venture to ask you to convey to your Regiment my deepest gratitude and admiration for the work they performed on October 31 and through the following night. No troops in the world could have carried out their orders better, and while deploring the losses you have incurred, I unhesitatingly

affirm that the Allied Armies in France owe to the London Scottish a place of high honour amongst their heroes." (Brigadier-General C.E. Bingham, 4th Cavalry Brigade). To billets near Bailleul (3rd). Some men issued with new rifles. Ordered to Ypres front (4th) and by nightfall at Bellewaarde Farm. To Shrewsbury Forest (5th) and attached to 4th Guards Brigade. Relieved 2nd Oxfordshire and Buckinghamshire Light Infantry in front line (9th). Position recorded as just a line of shallow rifle pits. Just 1 man every 6 yards and no reserve. There had been fighting in the area and men that had not been re-armed at Bailleul took up abandoned German rifles. Lieutenant Ker-Gulland killed by sniper (11th). "H" Company on battalion's right almost overrun during enemy attack which was repulsed by charge led by Colonel Malcolm. Relieved by 4th Dragoon Guards (13th) and retired to wood near Gheluvelt in close support of 1st Guards Brigade. Relieved (15th) and to Pradelles.

DECEMBER
Left Pradelles with 1st Guards Brigade (20th) and marched via Strazeele and Merville to Béthune. To Cuinchy (21st) – 23 casualties from shell fire during march. Took up reserve positions at night and later moved into line – Givenchy sector.

1/16TH (COUNTY OF LONDON) BATTALION (QUEEN'S WESTMINSTER RIFLES)

AUGUST
Headquarters – 58 Buckingham Gate. Part of 4th London Brigade, 2nd London Division. Entrained at Paddington for annual camp at Perham Down, Salisbury Plain (2nd). Ordered to return to Headquarters same night. Mobilized and men billeted at the Endowed Schools. Assembled in Hyde Park (14th) and marched via Edgware Road to Edgware. To Leverstock Green area near Hemel Hempstead (15th). Leslie Walkinton joined the Battalion at Leverstock Green and recalls in his book *Twice in a Lifetime* that he was billeted in a barn opposite a pub called *The Leather Bottle*.

NOVEMBER
Left 4th London Division and entrained at Watford for Southampton (1st). Sailed SS *Maidan* and arrived Havre (2nd). Landed (3rd) and to rest camp outside of town. Strength – 892 all ranks. Officers – Lieutenant-Colonel R. Shoolbred, TD, DL, JP (Commanding Officer), Majors J.W. Cohen, TD (Second in Command), N.B. Tyrwhitt, TD, Captain H.J. Flower (King's

Royal Rifle Corps, Adjutant), Lieutenants J.H. Kelly (Quartermaster), H. Murray (RAMC, Medical Officer), Second-Lieutenants J.B. Baber (Machine Gun Officer), S.G.L. Bradley, DCM (Transport Officer); "A" Company: Captain S. Low, Lieutenants S.R. Savill, J.A. Green; "B" Company: Captain E.G.H. Cox, Second- Lieutenants R.S. Dickinson, F. Barwell; "C" Company: Captain J.Q. Henriques, Second- Lieutenants W.M. Henderson-Scott, M.E. Trollope; "D" Company: Captain J.B. Whitehouse, Lieutenant F.G. Swainson; "E" Company: Captain M.M. Shattock, Lieutenants C de B. James, S.L. Townsend-Green; "F" Company: Captain H.R. Townsend-Green, Lieutenant P.E. Harding, Second-Lieutenant S.G.L. Bradley, DCM; "G" Company: Captain G.H. Lambert, Lieutenant E.G.S. Waley; "H Company: Captain O.P.L. Hoskyns, Lieutenant P.M. Glasier, Second-Lieutenant H.M. Masson. In his history of the battalion, Captain (later Major) Henriques records how the news of the London Scottish (1/14th London Regiment) at Messines – "stirred everyone with pride." Entrained for St. Omer (4th). German prisoners noted being marched to prison camp. Arrived (6th) and to billets in French Army barracks. Captain Henriques notes the presence also of what remained of the 2nd Royal Irish Regiment. (This battalion had suffered over 500 casualties at Le Pilly on 20th October). Dug reserve line of trenches on high ground some 6 miles to the east of St. Omer (7th). Two companies fired their new rifles for the first time on 250- metre range (9th). Lord French visited battalion and noted in his book *1914* that – "the Queen's Westminsters were so good that they were able to be sent to the front immediately." Marched to Hazebrouck (10th). Captain Henriques noted French cavalry marching through town, apparently just out of battle. Dress-uniforms with plumed helmets and metal breast-plates still being worn. Both men and horses looked exhausted. To Bailleul (11th) and billeted in convent school. Reorganized on 4-company basis. Flashes of guns in action at Ypres seen and firing of heavy guns heard constantly. To Erquinghem (12th) and joined 18th Brigade, 6th Division. Inspected by Field-Marshal Earl Roberts in afternoon. (Lord Roberts died on 14th). Local inhabitants spoke of severe treatment by Germans. No.1 Company acted as support to 16th Brigade at Calvert Farm just south of Bois Grenier during night (16th/17th). To billets at Gris Pot (17th). No.2 Company in support of 16th Brigade during night. Part of company dug communication trench from Calvert Farm to La Flamanderie Farm. Individual companies began training in front line (18th) – trenches facing La Houssoie and south of Rue du Bois. Bolts of new rifles jammed. There was a shortage of rifle oil and bacon fat was used as a substitute. One company to Desplanque Farm in brigade reserve (24th). Several letters sent by French soldiers to their home addresses were received

– "I am glad to hear that our English friends are occupying my house, and beg you to consider it as your home." Another asked for news of his wife and parents and also – "What do you think of the wine in the cellar? You would oblige me very much in leaving one or two bottles, so that I may be able to shake my glass to the victory of great England and sweet France when I return."

DECEMBER

War Diary (5th) notes the removal of the wooden holes in parapet which were found to have provided the Germans with – "a beautiful target from the front, and act as a funnel caching bullets and directing them down into the trench." Relieved by 1st West Yorkshire and to billets at L`Armée at 5 pm. Casualties – 3 killed, 10 wounded. Battalion took over front line opposite Wez Macquart from 2nd Durham Light Infantry (9th). Positions just east of Rue du Bois to the Lille-Boulogne road. War Diary records wet and muddy conditions – 18 inches of water and 6 inches of mud. Parapets constantly falling in – men employed day and night digging out. Relieved by 1st Royal Fusiliers (18th) and to la Chapelle d` Armentières. For next 4 nights 1 company in brigade reserve lines at Desplanque Farm. Returned to trenches (23rd), relieving 1st Royal Fusiliers. Water now waist deep in places. During night (24th) German line lit up and men began to sing carols. Applause from British trenches. Truce arranged (25th) – gifts exchanged in No Man`s Land. One German officer (107th Regiment) was from Catford in London. His men, he said, believed they were just outside Paris and that German troops were occupying London. Relieved by 1st Royal Fusiliers 4 am (26th) and to Houplines. Billeted in factories. Casualties since 24th November – 6 killed, 31 wounded.

1/28TH (COUNTY OF LONDON) BATTALION (ARTISTS RIFLES)

AUGUST

Headquarters – Duke`s Road, St. Pancras. Army Troops attached to 2nd London Division. Commanding Officer – Lieutenant-Colonel H.A.R. May, VD. To annual camp at Perham Down (2nd). Ordered back to London same night. Mobilized (4th). Extra premises for recruiting taken over at Manchester Street and Lancing Street Schools (5th). Commenced special duties in London which included the guarding of German prisoners at Olympia. Later took over Lord`s Cricket ground.

SEPTEMBER
Moved to Tower of London and began public duties.

OCTOBER
Joined 2nd London Division for training in Bricket Wood area near Watford
(17th). Left division (26th) and to Southampton. Embarked SS *Australind*
and sailed for France (27th). Arrived Boulogne (28th) and entrained for St.
Omer. Occupied French Army barracks, moving to billets at Helfaut (29th).

NOVEMBER
To Bailleul (5th). Lieutenant-Colonel May sent for by Lord French (12th)
and asked if he could select personnel from his battalion to replace officer
casualties in units of the 7th Division. The men were to be "rapidly" trained
from privates and not taken from existing officers. Some 52 men were immediately chosen and special permission given for the issue of rank insignia.
There would be no new uniforms available and stars were worn attached to
the shoulder straps of the men's other ranks service dress. Another 62 men
selected and trained by (22nd). The battalion had now become an Officer
Training unit and would provide a steady flow of men to units of the British
Expeditionary Force. Also supplied and trained some 100 men as machine
gun instructors by end of December.

HERTFORDSHIRE REGIMENT (TERRITORIAL FORCE)

"Ypres, 1914" "Nonne Bosschen"

1/1ST BATTALION

AUGUST
Headquarters in Hertford; "A" Company – Hertford with drill stations at Watton, Hatfield and Berkhamsted; "B" Company – St. Albans with drill stations at London Colney and Harpenden; "C" Company – Bishop's Stortford with drill stations at Sawbridgeworth, Braughing, Widford, Ware and Wadesmill; "D" Company – Watford with a drill station at Chorley Wood; "E" Company – Royston with drill stations at Letchworth, Baldock and Ashwell; "F" Company – Hemel Hempstead with drill stations at Great Berkhamsted, Ashridge, Tring and Ivinghoe; "G" Company – Hitchin with drill stations at Welwyn, Stevenage and Whitwell; "H" Company – Waltham Cross with drill stations at Wormley, Cheshunt and Hoddesdon. Part of the East Midland Infantry Brigade, East Anglian Division. Moved to Romford, Essex then later to Bury St. Edmunds, Suffolk.

NOVEMBER
To Southampton (5th) and sailed for France. Arrived Havre (6th) then by train to St. Omer, arriving (9th). Moved forward to Ypres sector and began instruction in front line (11th). Relieved 2nd Oxfordshire and Buckinghamshire Light Infantry in trenches between Polygon Wood and Nonne Bosschen Wood during evening (14th). Relieved by 2nd Coldstream in trenches at Klein Zillebeke (19th) and marched via Ypres to Meteren. Attached to 4th (Guards) Brigade, 2nd Division.

DECEMBER
Left Meteren for Béthune with 4th (Guards) Brigade (22nd). Rudyard Kipling refers to Battalion as "The Herts Guards." Relieved Indian troops in trenches near Le Touret (24th).

REGIMENTAL INDEX

Argyll and Sutherland Highlanders 309

Artists Rifles 349

Bedfordshire Regiment 90

Black Watch 200

Border Regiment 174

Buffs, East Kent Regiment 37

Cameron Highlanders 292

Cameronians (Scottish Rifles) 134

Cheshire Regiment 117

Coldstream Guards 7

Connaught Rangers 305

Devonshire Regiment 71

Dorsetshire Regiment 191

Duke of Cornwall's Light Infantry 167

Duke of Wellington's Regiment 171

Durham Light Infantry 272

East Kent Regiment 37

East Lancashire Regiment 156

East Surrey Regiment 160

East Yorkshire Regiment 87

Essex Regiment 214

Gloucestershire Regiment 142

Gordon Highlanders 285

Grenadier Guards 1

Hampshire Regiment 182

Hertfordshire Regiment 351

Highland Light Infantry 275

Honourable Artillery Company 336

Irish Guards 20

King's Liverpool Regiment 60

King's Own Royal Lancaster Regiment 39

King's Own Scottish Borderers 131

King's Own Yorkshire Light Infantry 237

King's Royal Rifle Corps 248

King's Shropshire Light Infantry 240

Lancashire Fusiliers 107

Leicestershire Regiment 97

Leinster Regiment 316

Lincolnshire Regiment 66

Liverpool Regiment 60

Liverpool Scottish 62

London Regiment 339

London Rifle Brigade 339

London Scottish 344

Loyal North Lancashire Regiment 221

Manchester Regiment 262

Middlesex Regiment 243

Monmouthshire Regiment 338

Norfolk Regiment 64

North Lancashire Regiment 221

North Staffordshire Regiment 266

Northamptonshire Regiment 224

Northumberland Fusiliers 43

Nottinghamshire and Derbyshire Regiment 217

Oxfordshire and Buckinghamshire Light Infantry 207

Queen Victoria's Rifles 340

Queen's Own Royal West Kent Regiment 233

Queen's Royal West Surrey Regiment 30

Queen's Westminster Rifles 347

Rifle Brigade 327

Royal Berkshire Regiment 229

Royal Dublin Fusiliers 324
Royal Fusiliers 54
Royal Highlanders 200
Royal Inniskilling Fusiliers 139
Royal Irish Fusiliers 302
Royal Irish Regiment 101
Royal Irish Rifles 297
Royal Lancaster Regiment 39
Royal Munster Fusiliers 320
Royal Scots 24
Royal Scots Fusiliers 111
Royal Sussex Regiment 179
Royal Warwickshire Regiment 49
Royal Welch Fusiliers 121
Royal West Kent Regiment 233
Royal West Surrey Regiment 30

Scots Guards 15
Scottish Rifles 134
Seaforth Highlanders 280
Sherwood Foresters 217
Somerset Light Infantry 81
South Lancashire Regiment 194
South Staffordshire Regiment 187
South Wales Borderers 128
Suffolk Regiment 76
Welsh Regiment 197
West Yorkshire Regiment 84
Wiltshire Regiment 257
Worcestershire Regiment 147
York and Lancaster Regiment 270
Yorkshire Regiment 104